Noble Poverty

Noble Poverty

A Teacher's Life in Silicon Valley

Jim Kohl

Writers Club Press
San Jose New York Lincoln Shanghai

Noble Poverty
A Teacher's Life in Silicon Valley

Writers Club Press
an imprint of iUniverse.com, Inc.

For information address:
iUniverse.com, Inc.
5220 S 16th, Ste. 200
Lincoln, NE 68512
www.iuniverse.com

ISBN: 0-595-16791-8

Printed in the United States of America

I dedicate this book to my wife, Kristin, with love.

ACKNOWLEDGEMENTS

I would like to recognize the following people for their help with this
work:
My parents for being my first readers, my sister, Diane for being my first
editor, Bob Drews for his excellent editing, support, and kind words,
Rick, Dolores, David, Pam and the rest of the LeyVa Middle School faculty, Abovehealth Corporation and Pete for taking a chance on a school
teacher with limited technology skills, Art Rodriguez for his inspiration
and advice, my wife Kristin for belief, support, patience and love, my
kids for the same, all the kids that ever sat in Room 5 and gave me their
attention, even if I didn't portray you in this book, you are still as
important to me now as ever—look me up when you have graduated
college and are looking for a job, and thanks to you, Elizabeth, wherever
you are, and to you, the reader, I offer my most humble thanks.

INTRODUCTION

I used to be Mr. Kohl. That is, I had 150 students rely on me and that name became a persona for the character that I had created when I stood in front of a classroom to teach, to watch over kids' safety on the yard, and to console them or scold them as necessary. It's the character I played when I watched them come into my room in September as eager and scared 7th graders. That character watched them mature and heard their voices change. That character gave advice and listened in an attempt to make their lives a better place to live. That character tried to make them better writers and thinkers, and tried to help them see the beauty and benefit of each. That character held many hands and escorted sometimes-reluctant graduates to the door on the last day of school. I used to be Mr. Kohl, but he's gone now.

"Teachers are born, not made," people say. The career holds a Romantic, innate quality that appeals to many of its practitioners. We love it when people say things like, "That's a noble profession you've chosen," or "Man, that must take some patience-you must be a saint." We like to hear that many people in society feel that we are unappreciated and underpaid because in a bizarre way, that feels like we are appreciated.

Teachers like to help. Any teacher will tell you about the amazing sense of elation when a child looks to you and finally understands something for the first time, or the joy of just seeing the kids walk into your room in the morning. There are people in the profession who do not feel these things and never have, but they are not teachers. They have the job title because someone tried to make them teachers, or they were born teachers and have since mutated, but you have to feel those things and want to give and never receive to truly be a teacher. Those qualities cannot be purchased from a university catalog, and that's why teachers can't be made.

When I was a kid going through the public schools and hating every minute of it, I knew I was a teacher. Truthfully, I didn't know, but I should have known. I can remember evaluating my teachers' lesson plans and the way things were presented with judgments about whether or not the material was presented well. I can remember thinking in 7th grade English that the teacher did everything wrong. We were given books to read and we were told what they meant and why they were important. Parts of *Beowulf* were presented in this manner.

I figured out that I would like reading a book more if I knew something about the author. The book didn't materialize out of thin air, so knowing something of the mind that created it would be a great thing. In *Beowulf*, the author is unknown, but there is a fascinating story concerning the only written copy of it that survived medieval times. Some guy rescued the sole manuscript from a burning castle and threw it out a window, and that is the only reason we have that story today. Too bad I had to wait until college to hear this story. Maybe if I had been told this story in middle school, my life hating, 7th grade-self would've put the angst on hold long enough to give a damn for a second. As I sat in those public school classrooms, it turns out I was writing my own lesson plans that profited from the mistakes and victories of my own teachers.

I knew that many of my teachers were boring and that I could do it so that it would not be. I knew I could do it better, and this confidence (which approached conceit) drove me through all the classes and red tape necessary to legally stand in front of a group of kids and do what I was born to.

Having been born a teacher, the questions begging to be answered are: Why am I no longer Mr. Kohl? How could I be a born teacher and no longer have the job? How could I walk away from the career and the kids that I loved so completely? Why would I re-invent myself after almost 5 passionate years and switch gears to be a technical writer-possibly the polar opposite of my previous life's ambition? These legitimate but complicated questions deserve full examination and answers, and that is why I sit here two days after the end of my teaching career to write this book.

Follow me through this adventure. Meet the kids from LeyVa Middle School. Watch my Romantic dream of purity fall into the hands of everyone else. Sit back while my life unravels. Be there when I make the hardest decision of my life and watch me make the impossible happen. Right now you can still call me Mr. Kohl, but when it's over, you can call me Jim.

CHAPTER I

I turned in the Blue Book to the instructor, nodded to him in silence and never looked back. The halls of San Jose State University knew my look; they had been watching it for around a century on millions of students. I took in the scenes as I walked down the hall to the stairs. Flyers, so many you never really noticed any of them, hung on bulletin boards like multi-colored butterflies with pins stuck through their torsos. The office doors with opaque windows and names both familiar and forgotten in white letters on black plaques. The brown elevator that I never used because it looked like it was probably powered by some guy pulling on a rope. The staircase with the scratched up railing where countless students ran their hands as they walked to or from class. The Smothers Brothers were the most famous dropouts that San Jose State had ever had. I wondered if they used this railing. I pushed open the awkward double doors and stepped into the crisp December air. I had finished.

The most peculiar thing about college graduation is the solitude of it. In high school and junior high, there are hundreds of kids all wearing the cap and gowns together. They had all been counting the days until graduation like pennies in a piggy bank. Then the day comes and they all say goodbye to a portion of their life. Some cry, and some don't until later, and some never do. College has a huge ceremony, but when the last final exam is over and so is your college career, a lot of times the only one you have to share it with is you. I had finished.

I walked the grounds of campus towards the Student Union to grab a cup of celebratory coffee. Other people rushed past me with coats pulled close and notes in hand, staring at them anxiously in the final seconds before the test. I had finished.

I walked 200 steps and saw no one that I knew that I could share this victory with, but that was the nature of San Jose State. I walked along and saw the library where I should've and could've studied harder. It was busy this time of year. The electronic door hardly had a chance to close before someone else would approach and swoosh it open again. You couldn't see in through the black windows, but that was just as well. Who cared? I had finished.

I could see my breath that day. I was near the Roost, the campus coffeehouse where I had once seen Wavy Gravy eat his morning blueberry muffin, when I saw Monica. She was so cute that I had never spoken to her until now, two years after we met. "How's it goin'?" I asked. She was engaged, and that meant I could be her friend without the fear of romantic rejection.

"Hey… What's up?" she smiled.

"Nothing. Uh…I'm finished."

"Finished? You mean all your tests? Man, I've got one today in a few minutes and two more tomorrow, but then I'm done." She wasn't with me on this.

"No, I mean, this is it man!! I'm graduating!"

"Oh my god!! Congratulations! How come you didn't tell anyone?" I didn't tell anyone anything in those days. I didn't think they'd care, and I didn't want my suspicions to be proven. "Oh my god we need to celebrate!"

"I'm getting some coffee right now. They have music at the bottom floor of the Student Union where they've set up a temporary coffeehouse sort of thing." I had seen this really cool girl named Janice A play guitar and sing. I had been with bands, but I really wanted to do the folk singer thing and I wanted to watch other people do it every chance I got.

"Well, what are you doing later, cause, you know, I've got this test right now?"

"Oh…uhm… whatever, give me a call later." She didn't, but neither did I.

"Okay…Well, Merry Christmas if I don't see you, and remember, my wedding is in June."

"Oh I'm there for sure, man." I was.

"See ya."

"Yeah. Good luck on your tests!"

I thought back to my last day of elementary school. It was a big deal because we were the last graduating 6th grade class. They were changing junior highs (grades 7, 8 and 9) into middle schools (grades 6, 7 and 8). We would be the first 7th grade group to not be the babies of the school. We were also the last 6th grade class to graduate from my elementary school since it was closing. We couldn't wait for that summer bell to ring, and we couldn't wait to be older. The bell rang, we all screamed, I ran outside and broke a pencil in two and threw it up in the air. School was out. I had finished.

I shook the memory from my head and bustled into the Student Union cafeteria with the rest of the masses. Books were open on every table, and every table was taken. That was fine with me because I wasn't staying here. I was heading downstairs to the coffeehouse to hear some classic-rock-guitar songs good enough to make you cry.

The union halls were jammed with stands where you could buy handcrafted Christmas presents if you had money. The air smelled of cinnamon. It was a Noel indoor Grateful Dead parking lot. I headed downstairs with just enough money for an eggnog latte.

White Christmas lights framed the temporary espresso bar. The stage occupied the wall area opposite the bar. The goateed man behind the bar nodded to verify that it was my turn.

"Eggnog latte, please."

"Three ninety-five." He started up the reverse vacuum song of every espresso machine you've ever heard. He slid the foamy masterpiece to me and handed me a nickel which I clinked into his tip jar. One other guy was hanging out down here. I guessed he had finished too, and I wondered if he was as finished as I was. Since I didn't talk to people, I don't know to this day.

Some girl played "Oh, Come all Ye Faithful" on the clarinet. This was all wrong. Where was my Janice A and her classic rock? Where were my last cool moments at San Jose State? Where was anybody to talk about the last four years of my life with? That other dude was dating the clarinet player, and I was just down here because I was a loner. I had finished, but now what? I had an English degree, and now what? What do you do with an English degree?

My ex-girlfriend's father's face came to mind. He was an old Asian man like Fu Man Chu without the name-inspired mustache. They had been celebrating his wife's birthday when they got to discussing where greeting cards come from.

"Who writes this stuff?" asked my ex's brother, Jason.

"I don't know," said Lily.

"I know who writes 'em!" said her father like it was the most exciting thought he'd ever had in his long life. "English majors! You can write these cards someday, Jim!"

They all thought that was about the funniest thing in the known world. I didn't want to write cheesy greeting cards. I laughed along wishing they'd find a new joke besides me. I took myself way too seriously in those days. I thought I was an artist. I thought I had integrity. I was no one's greeting card writer, right? God, I hoped not.

Sitting in the basement of the Student Union listening to "Oh Little Town of Bethlehem" sipping on a cold eggnog latte, I hated that memory more than usual. My face reddened as if the guy sitting there eyeing his girlfriend as she lipped her clarinet could see my festering memory like a TV show. I got up and threw away a quarter cup of that coffee. I could hear the clarinet version of "Joy to the World" become fainter as I climbed the stairs toward the studying masses. I saw the main exit and turned to it. I pushed into the cold air and breathed it out just to see the steam. The cold forced my hands deep into my denim jacket pockets.

"What am I going to do, be a freelance grammar checker?" I said to no one.

There was a stick in my pocket with my hand. I pulled it out. It was an old, yellow pencil with a nub of an eraser left. I stared at it a minute. I snapped it in half and tossed it toward the ground. I heard the weak wooden cripple of its pieces bouncing. I had finished. Now what?

CHAPTER II

I had had jobs all through college and high school, and I had worked a variety of retail jobs before I finally left retail forever (hopefully) for other things. The second to last job I had as a college student was as a phone canvasser for an organization called Campaign California. They were an activist group that raised money in support of environmental legislation. We were neo-hippie eco-warriors battling the powers that be.

Nightly, I would sit at a boxed-in workstation with a phone and call people all over the state to inform them about environmental legislation that was going through the California State Congress. The phone call always started with information about the legislation followed by a sense of urgency for the issue, and the finale was the request for money. You would start off by asking for a "dollar a day for the year—just 365 dollars. Could you do that?" Usually, you would end up with a promise for $20, but what you wanted was an amount above $50 and a credit card number. Credit cards pledges could be deposited that night. Promised checks rarely arrived. At the end of the month, if we did well, we would have a pizza party and an awards banquet.

I trained people at this job. I was pretty good at raising funds, and I apologize to you now if I ever interrupted your dinner. One of the bosses, Jane, told me that I was a born teacher.

"You're so easy to understand! I have been out and didn't know about this issue at all until you explained it to me. I felt completely comfortable asking you questions because you come off as patient enough to listen to them and answer them without making me feel dumb."

She couldn't have paid me a higher compliment. It was important to me for people to know that I wasn't the stereotypical woman-dominating, homophobic, racist white male. She was a 40-year-old lesbian with some real men issues. I raised my hand to high-five her once, a common practice in the office, and she flinched and drew back. A compliment from her meant that maybe I was okay.

Aside from my selfish drive to be politically correct, this moment marked an epiphany for me. Like many of my epiphany moments, it really was a mix of, "Ah-HA!" and "No shit!" with the latter being the dominant ingredient. It was surprising to me to be described as a good teacher, and yet I felt like I had known it all along. A seed planted in me started to germinate. Maybe I could be a teacher someday. Maybe I could stand in front of a classroom and lead a discussion or help people understand new things.

One night at work, Leslie, the boss, announced that our doors would be closing. "Our work, and the need for it is over," she said to us, the Birkenstock-wearing conglomerate. We sat around a large rectangular table and she stood and addressed us from the head of it. "Our lobbyists will be leaving Sacramento, and we will be closing down. Silicon Valley Toxics Coalition will continue to work in the field (door to door) and on the phones to monitor local companies, but the statewide fight…" She went on, and no one could believe that our work could be over. How could environmental work ever be finished? Isn't it always going to be important to protect the Earth?

"Our final issue," Leslie went on, "is to inform the voters of California who the best environmental candidates are on a national level and on a local level. We will be raising money to compile a list of these candidates in all of the voting districts in the state." This was the election that first brought us President Clinton.

How could this be? The election was one month away. If there was no list of environmental candidates by now, there wouldn't be in time for the election. It would be a huge task and getting the information to the people would require millions of dollars in postage alone. Two weeks before the election, I asked Leslie where the list was. "We're still drafting it." She assured me. I started getting the feeling that this list was a lie. If this issue was a lie, then…It was too horrible for my mind, filled with idealism, to handle.

My friend, Dave, had turned me on to this job in the first place. One night we were all partying at his place. "You know," I said standing in the room with all my co-workers lounged on the floor, "I think this whole final issue thing is a load. I think all the issues were a load, as a matter of fact. I think we were just raising money for pizza parties and beer."

My statement was unpopular, and I knew it would be. I had been taken in by a con as far as I was concerned, and cons needed to be exposed. I had dialed phones nightly and believed with each dollar I raised that the organization was pure and good. Now, it seemed that there was no way that it was, and I was angry. I was angry with myself for believing there was sincerity in this world. I was angry at the world for being itself. I went off on a tirade about how we were all well paid liars that hid behind phones and environmental issues to steal from the rich and give to ourselves. I had a knack for messing up parties.

"Screw you, Jim!!" Dave finally yelled. Dave rarely yelled because he was a neo-hippie type now. His former "surfer-dude" image had moved south with our friend Bill. "This place was a good place! It gave me something to believe in for a while, and even if the whole thing turned out to be a lie, at least it was a lie I could believe in for a while."

"Why do you need something to believe in? You sound like a Christian fanatic!" Dave hated religions and religious people because they were "weak minded."

"At least we had something to be anchored to. So it's all crap!! Who cares!! At least we had the illusion, and that's all there really is anyway. You're not gonna find purity in this world, so you better just believe something is pure." I really pissed Dave off this time. His face raged red behind his beard, and he almost stood up.

"There is something real!! I'm gonna find it too! But I'm not gonna find it with a bunch of liberal posers pretending that they don't care about money, when every phone call they make is about money."

I left.

The bottom line was that I needed a new job because I couldn't be without one. I found one, ironically, doing phone-marketing research for Intel, one of the enemies of the environmental movement. The environmentalists told me that they were not careful when they dumped the solvents used in the production of their computer chips. It was close to a high tech job, and I'd never had anything quite like it.

I walked into Campaign California about eight days before they were shutting their doors. "Jane," I said, "This is it for me. I have a new job, and I'm starting tomorrow."

"You should really finish out this issue. Tell your new job to wait."

"They need me to start tomorrow." This was true.

"You shouldn't burn your bridges…" Jane said this the way you would speak a warning with her voice rising in pitch and then fading in volume.

"It's only a bridge if there is something on both sides. This is more like a cliff." It was one of those rare moments when you think of the perfect comeback and are able to use it on the spot.

College would be over in a month, and while I was just a temporary employee, my new boss let me stay on until school was over. Sandy, my boss, would invent things for me to do just so that I could have a job to finish school with. Mainly, I would call computer retailers and wholesalers and ask them if they needed any more marketing materials to push the new slogan "Intel Inside." The 486 was the best chip out there at the time, and the Pentium was just on the drawing board. When all the phone calls had been made, she had me calling information operators nationwide to try to locate numbers that had come up disconnected. I never thanked her enough for keeping me on.

"What are you going to do after college?" asked Sandy one day.

"Geez, I'm not sure, maybe…teach?"

"Do you like teaching?"

"I think I would. I coached a swim team and taught swim lessons. I think I would like it." I had no idea. My future was so uncertain that I didn't even like to think about it.

"I think you would make a great teacher!" She was always really supportive, and this was the second boss that told me that I would make a good teacher.

"Thanks!" I loved to be told that, yet I still couldn't figure out what I should pursue after college. Sometimes, you don't see the wall that you're continually slamming into.

On a daily basis, I kept showing up to that office job and making phone calls in the name of technology. It was about a week away from my last final when I got a haircut. Sandy noticed immediately.

"Hey!" she said excitedly, "Jim got himself an interview haircut! Looking good!"

"Yep. Thanks." I didn't know what else to say. I had no interviews coming up. It was nice to pretend I did, but I had no direction and no clue. What the hell was I going to do, anyway?

Chapter III

My sister, Diane, graduated from private high school at the same time I finished college. We shared a graduation party at my parents' house.

On the day of the party, the house was filled with friends of my parents and sister. A few of my friends were there. I don't really have that many friends, but the ones I have are true and close.

Parties in my honor used to embarrass me, so I was very glad to share the spotlight with Diane. Everyone was toasting us and clinking half-full glasses, so they could empty them to fill them again.

"Hey, Jim," said Ted, a friend of my parents, "I got just one word for ya…Plastics!" He let out the greatest laugh I had ever heard. There was an old movie called *The Graduate* starring a young Dustin Hoffman in which Hoffman had just graduated from college and some guy at his party tells him to invest in plastics. I got the allusion, and laughed along with him, wondering if I was going to have to sleep with his wife. The allusion also reminded me that even though we were celebrating some sort of accomplishment that I had achieved, I, like Hoffman's character, had no direction.

"Hi Jim! How're you doing?" Jan was the most positive friend my parents had. She could find the bright side of a black hole in the deepest corner of outer space. "Congratulations!!" She handed me a gift. They were all so nice to me, and I had no idea what I was going to do. I didn't deserve kindness. "You must feel great! Isn't it awesome to have it all behind you!"

"Yeah!" It was, truly, but what about in front of me? I'd like to have something in front of me besides visions of nothing. Diane, at least, had college ahead of her. I had to be an adult now. Right after this party and the rest of the pomp and circumstance, I was expected to begin contributing to society. Did anyone need some grammar checked? "Thanks!" I said, motioning to the gift.

"Oh you're very welcome! Wow, so an English degree! Do you want to teach?" Jan had been a teacher for many years. She had been a substitute teacher in my fourth-grade class and had since taken a full-time position with fourth graders.

"I don't know..." I shrugged and sipped a beer.

"We could really use you in the profession. Believe me, I can tell you'd be great at it! I tell you, the way I've seen you affect the lives of the kids on our swim team so positively...you have the gift!"

"Thanks." Maybe I could teach.

Somehow Jan and I separated, and I stood with only a beer to talk to. I don't know how to butterfly around a room and talk to everyone. I'm the type that stays in one place and waits for butterflies.

I saw my friends, Kristin and John, come in. Kristin and I had met in a swim class that we both took to fulfill the PE requirement at San Jose State. We had become friends, and I thought I felt something for her, so I asked her out. That's when I found out about John.

John worked as an electrician and initially was a bit angry that I was in the picture. He mentioned to her that he was going to use his knowledge of electricity to blow my house up. When it was clear to him that I only asked his girlfriend out because she had never mentioned him, I was okay in his book.

"Congratulations!" Kristin purred as she hugged me.

"Congratulations, man," John said as we shook hands.

"So...What are you going to do now?" Kristin asked me.

I shrugged and let my eyes wander the room.

"You know, most college graduates don't ever work in the area of their major."

"Really?" I would be glad to at least think that I was going to work.

"Yeah. As a matter of fact, I'll bet you a lunch that you're not working in your major within six months from now even."

"That's cool, dude, I'll take that bet." I called everybody dude back then.

"Hey, the other thing we were wondering is," she paused and flipped her jet-black hair, "Well, John and I are thinking of getting a place, and we were wondering if you wanted to go in with us."

"When?" You may be noticing about now that John doesn't talk. The whole time I knew these two, he only spoke around her to echo her thoughts and opinions. He also spent many hours out of the house shooting darts in a bar. I was there many of those hours, and eventually was to blame for those hours because she didn't want to think that her relationship had a problem. John taught me how to play darts; I'm sure he's still shooting darts somewhere today-with or without her.

"Oh, not until after the holidays for sure. We're thinking of looking in Los Gatos or Cupertino." No wonder they needed a third, those were two of the most expensive housing places around.

"Well, you know, I don't have a job, and I don't know if I'm gonna find one, and…" You're a complete psycho and moving in with you will spell the end of our friendship! I didn't know this yet of course, and I ended up moving in with them.

"That's cool, you know, no pressure. If you find a job and it works out, that would be awesome." She smiled. "You'll find a job."

"I hope so. Then you'll owe me lunch."

The end of a party fascinates. People begin dribbling out of the house randomly until there are a few hangers on. You walk each to the door and tell them it was great to have seen them and, in this case, thank them again for the gift. When one person leaves, it begins a bit of an avalanche of people that "had better go." This leaves a few people, normally the closest friends of the host who begin to offer to help clean up. Eventually, everyone is gone and the quiet in the house is initially overwhelming. Random cups, plates smeared with icing and balled up napkins remain to prove you celebrated. A pile of gifts stared at me demanding thank you notes be written, and of course, I never did, so if you were there, please consider this book your thank you note.

The gifts I received that day were fitting a young career man. I had a brand new briefcase, a small black pouch that contained office supplies, a new calculator and some coffee cups. What more could you need for that first day at the office? An office to go to, perhaps, but you can't wrap that up and give it to someone-at least no one at this party could do that for me-especially since I had no career path. I carried the pile of gifts back to the bedroom where I spent adolescence and wondered if I would indeed ever have a need for something like a briefcase.

CHAPTER IV

"What you need to do," my mom told me the next morning in the living room over coffee, "is get a resume together and look through the newspaper to try to find something that you want to do. Then you have to send your resume out all over the place and see if it leads to anything. Look for anything having to do with writing or anything else that you may want to do."

"Yeah, that sounds pretty good. What sort of stuff should I put on a resume? I mean, I haven't really done anything except retail and those phone jobs." I rested one leg over the arm of the white living room chair.

"You coached the swim team." I nodded, and she continued. "You'd have to ask your father about setting up the resume and what it should look like."

Because I had no idea what I should do, I was reluctant to even get started. I was disillusioned when there was just not a clear path cut for me in the career search jungle. I had an English degree, and I loved it, but you needed a machete to make your own path and find a job. Why didn't I like computers?

I also believed that I was too good for a cubicle-type job. I was never going to sell out and be a business drone. I was an artist, and I didn't need money to have satisfaction in life. I didn't want to network and exchange business cards and meet each new person with the unspoken, "I wonder how I can improve my own status by knowing this person." I was not going to be part of the dog eat dog world, the rat race or the corporate scum circle. I wasn't going to "do lunch." Those people could never have a good life because, by definition, they were bad people. They were the enemies of the arts, the killers of creativity and the captors of the human soul.

The front door clicked and opened as my dad returned from his morning workout. He took his black workout bag back to his room, got a cup of coffee and sat down in his normal morning chair, diagonal across the living room from me.

"How was your workout, dear?" my mom asked.

"Pretty good."

"That's cool." I still say this when I just need to say something. I needed to open the subject of resume building, but I didn't want to, and I didn't know how to. "Hey, dad, uh…later do you think you could show me how to put a resume together?"

"What kind of job are you thinking of getting?"

"I have no idea."

"Well, you really need to decide on the sort of job you'd like to have first. That way, you can tailor your resume for the sort of work that you're hoping to get …" I started to zone out. How could it be that I had to decide on a job type before I even wrote up a resume? "…develop a generic resume for any sort of job, you should first list education…" I heard enough to know that I was overwhelmed. I decided just to sit down at the computer, make a resume and show it to him to see if he had any suggestions.

"Well, I'll just make one and see what you think."

"Sure, I'll look it over when you have something.

I sat down at the computer and created the worst resume you can imagine. It had my name, phone number, address, the fact that I had a BA in English and the dates that I worked at my phone jobs and my retail jobs. Many of these dates were approximate, which still bothers me to this day. I should be more organized and know exactly the dates I've worked each job. That was the extent of my resume—who I was, where I was and sort of when I worked and where.

"This is pretty good." My dad said. He and my mom have always been the best supporters you could want, but I knew he was stretching the truth. This resume stunk. It only took me 20 minutes to make the whole thing-including a bathroom break. "You may want to add some of the specific skills you've picked up along the way."

"Like what?"

"Well, you've done customer service, albeit not very well." He and I both knew that retail was not my strong point. I would have been good at it if it weren't for the customers. "You've used cash registers, you've had that…phone experience. You know a little about word processing. Just list anything you can think of."

I added those things to the resume and hit the newspaper. Those were the days before the Internet when you had to look through newspapers and use fax machines to job-hunt. You could also mail resumes, but the turn around time was very slow. I didn't have easy access to a fax and relied on the postal service to apply for jobs.

New jobs came out in the paper on Sunday and Wednesday. Those were the best searching days because they were filled with what I considered to be up-to-the-minute leads. "Hey, mom," I said one Wednesday from behind the newspaper, "a real estate company called Alain Pinel is hiring someone to write the ads for house listings that they have. I could probably do that, huh?"

"You sure could, does it say what it pays?"

"No."

"Well, send them your resume and see what happens. It can't hurt, Jim"

"Yeah." I sent it.

A few days later I was still waiting to hear from them and a few other jobs I had applied for. My mom suggested that I take a resume over to IBM. "They're always looking for people, and they would be a really great company to get in with."

"Okay." I had to look like I was trying to avoid the shame and failure that comes with not trying. I had no interest in the sort of people that I figured probably worked at IBM-corporate scums, guys in ties whose only sincerity is their insincerity. "I'll go drop off a resume tomorrow."

In December, San Jose, California, fills with rain. It's windy, and the rain comes in from all directions followed closely by the leaves from the trees. We don't have a lot of weather changes, but we sure have some rain. It was just such a rainy day that I promised myself in front of my mom that I would drop my resume off at IBM. If I didn't go, it would seem like I was not trying.

I'm a firm believer in first impressions, so I figured I should wear a suit to drop off my resume just in case I ended up talking to someone. I printed up a resume, stepped into the only suit that I owned and dodged the rain in front of my house the best I could while trying to preserve the ink on my resume from the nuttiest rain of the year. I ran down my driveway with no umbrella (I keep it in my car in case it rains) with rain trying it's hardest to soak the resume and me. All I had to ensure the quality of my resume was a manila folder and my well-dressed arm. I threw myself into the driver's seat of my gray Honda CRX and slammed the door.

I couldn't believe my luck. I hadn't seen rain like this since the flood of 1986. The wind rocked my miniature car and threatened to push it right over. I started the car and headed for the IBM building on Bailey Road.

To get to Bailey Road, you need to head south from the Almaden area of San Jose to McKee Road. The road is an open country one with plenty of room for wind and rain to sprint before slamming themselves against your car. If you've never seen a Honda CRX, they were little two seaters that had the weight of a large dog. Many times that morning I was nearly blown into what would have been oncoming traffic if even one other soul had been foolish enough to venture out that morning. I had to look like I was trying.

The climax of the drive is a curvy but short road that leads over a hill. On the other side of the hill, Bailey Road straightens out as far as you can see, and IBM is on your left. My size-impaired car tried to grab the slippery curves of the hill while I wondered if looking like you're trying is really worth all this. If you die because your CRX has been blown into nearby Callero Reservoir, does the fact that you were trying to get a job at a place you had no interest in working make you some sort of martyr, or are you just an idiot?

Right about halfway over the hill, my windows started fogging up. I've never had a car where the window de-fogger worked properly. I turned it on, and within seconds, visibility was down to nothing. I rolled down the window just to see my way over the hill. Now my hair was wet and windblown, and I couldn't wait to turn in this resume so I could say that I did.

I turned into the IBM parking lot and searched for a spot. I found one near the left side of the building. Now, I had to find a way into the building. There was a door facing where I had parked. I could see it from my rearview mirror. I just needed to get from my car to the door without rain smearing my resume like a crying woman's mascara. I ran to the door, and amazingly, it was unlocked.

This was not the main lobby, and I had a feeling this door was left unlocked by mistake. Normal visitors to the building never come in through that door, but we're talking about me here. There were hallways leading every which way like a hospital. I saw no one. Oddly, no one saw me either; I thought a place like this would have tighter security. I wandered around a little and finally ran into a man.

"Um…did you need something?" he asked, recognizing that I didn't belong there.

"Yeah, I'm here to drop off my resume." I handed him the wet manila folder.

"Okay, well, I'll make sure it gets to the right people."

"Thanks." That was it. At the time, I didn't know of the tenacious nagging necessary to get an interview and a job. I walked back into the rain and drove home.

For my efforts, a couple days later, I got a letter telling me that IBM had received my resume and that although there was not currently a match for my skills, my resume would remain on file for a year and be reviewed against future openings. You've probably had a pile of those in your life too. I was encouraged, since I thought they meant it. At least I was trying.

Not long after that, Alain Pinel, the real estate agency I had applied to, called and asked me to interview. My interview was on a Thursday, so I had a couple days to get a haircut and press the rain stains out of the suit.

"Where is this place?" asked my mom, making conversation.

"It's halfway between Los Gatos and Saratoga."

"That's a nice area."

I should've had a clue then. This place was a real estate office, so I thought I was going into a place like Century 21 in one of those strip mall offices. You should always look into a prospective employer before the interview. That's why the Internet is such a good thing.

I woke up on Thursday morning to the sound of driving wind and pouring rain. I couldn't believe it! Was it impossible to put this suit on and not have a downpour? I owned no overcoat to protect my suit from the rain; I had just graduated from college! It never even occurred to me that there was such a thing as an overcoat until just now as I write this at age 30.

I showered, suited up, printed a resume and shoved it into manila folder part 2.

This place differed from IBM in that I found the correct entrance for a visitor. It had tall brown doors with decorative glass and polished handles. When I walked in, there was a receptionist behind an elevated gray marble desk. "May I help you?" she greeted.

"I'm Jim Kohl. I have an interview at 10 o'clock."

"With?"

"I'm not sure-it was a woman." Note to self-to avoid feeling stupid, always have the name of the interviewer.

"Well, have a seat, and I'll find out who you're supposed to be with. Could I get you a drink? Coffee, tea, water, soda…"

"No thanks, I'm okay."

"Are you sure?"

"Yes, thank you."

She walked away. This place was more lavish than any I had ever been. There was a huge conference room to my right that had glass walls. In the conference room was a heavy looking long table. It was straight out of a movie about millionaires. The dark wood had elaborate carvings up and down each leg. Black cushy chairs on wheels surrounded the table, and they were tall enough for you to rest your head against when you sat. The whole collection sat on two-inch thick lush green carpet. The place reeked of cash. I hated it. It was exactly what I pictured when I heard the word corporate scum. They would all stab me if it helped them get ahead. I was an artist. These people were art killers. I wouldn't write a word for these people.

A well-dressed woman approached me and introduced herself as Rachel. She ushered me into the glass conference room, and I sat in one of those chairs.

I don't remember the dialogue of the interview, but I remember the odd feeling of trying to convince the interviewer that I was interested in a job that I would rather die than accept. The whole time, I sat there wondering if she could see the tie-dyed T-shirt through this suit. I answered all her questions to the best of my ability. I hated her. She was a sellout.

Finally, we shook hands and I left. Along with the feelings of corporate disgust, I had another feeling surfacing. This was the real world, and I didn't fit in.

CHAPTER V

A week went by, and I hadn't heard a thing from Alain Pinel. Each time the phone rang, my hopes raised, only to be shot down as the voice on the line was a friend of mine or asked for someone else. I desperately wanted them to call and say something, but they didn't. I took it as rejection and allowed myself to become depressed over it.

The craziest thing about all of this was that deep inside, I knew that I didn't want that corporate scum job anyway but at least I would be done looking if I got hired. I didn't know what I wanted to do and that feeling was evolving into not caring what I ended up doing as long as it wasn't retail. The phone rang again.

"Hey dude." It was Kristin.

"Hey."

"How's it going?"

Well, let's see…I can't get a job, I don't want a job, and I need a job. "Fine. How about you?"

"Have you thought more about moving out?"

"I'd like to. It's weird being back here, I mean, there are no problems, but…" I did feel like a loser moving back with my parents after having had my own place.

"Well John and I think we have found a place, but we want you to look at it too in case you can move in."

"Where is it?"

"Los Gatos right near the Campbell border. It's a 3 bedroom, 2 bath."

"What's the rent?"

"You'd be paying $300 a month, and we'd each be paying $350 a month because we would have the master bedroom."

"I don't know, man, I don't have a job right now…"

"We wouldn't be moving in until January 15th. That gives you about a month to find something." When I look back, it's clear that they could not have afforded the place without me. They probably didn't even have the deposit without me. At the time, it seemed like a good idea. I checked the place out, and I liked it. Now I just needed a job.

Christmas approached as quickly as it does once you're not six anymore. I felt pretty sunk career wise because I didn't think companies hired near the holidays.

About six days before Christmas, my mom told me she'd been talking to her friend Gayle. I had coached Gayle's kids on the swim team, and I had taught her son beginning guitar. Gayle worked at a place called the Children's Discovery Museum, and there was an opening for a writer to work on their monthly newsletter. "Awesome!" I said.

This was great! It was a museum, so it wasn't corporate. Kids were involved, and I liked working with and around them. I loved writing, so this could be my big chance to have a really fun non-corporate job. It felt like a sure thing because I would be going in with Gayle as a reference. I sent the resume and got the interview.

It was a bright, crisp winter afternoon as I drove downtown in my suit. My freshly printed resume was in manila folder part 3, and I knew this was going to be great! How could they not want me? I was an English major, and this was a writing job. I was young and ambitious and straight out of college. I had the recommendation of a founding employee of the museum. I suddenly cared and wanted a job, and I knew what I wanted to do. I was going to write for the museum.

Right where Highway 87 skims the border of Downtown San Jose stands the Children's Discovery Museum. It has a unique geometric shape and a purple paint job. The inside is filled with all sorts of things for kids to play with and on. They have real-life cars, ambulances and a fire engine that were donated by local organizations. The kids can dress up in the fireman's clothes and go crazy all over the truck if they want to. There are stations that teach kids how to cook. There are aquariums. You can watch bees make honey. You can play with light. The kids don't even know they're learning anything, which is the best sort of learning. I couldn't wait to be part of it.

I parked my car and carried my manila folder to the back entrance that Mary, who would be interviewing me, told me about. A security guard in a navy blue uniform greeted me with a nod. "Can I help you?"

"Yes, I'm Jim Kohl, and I'm here for a 2:30 interview with Mary."

"Just a second." He made a phone call. His station was at the bottom of a modest stairway. It thrilled me not to see any pretentious marble counter where the receptionist is high enough to look down on everyone that walks through the door. This is what I want. "Okay, go on up. Mary will meet you at the top."

"Thanks." This was it! The steps I climbed symbolized my climb to success. I could start writing here and eventually move up and write for a newspaper or a national magazine or publish a novel or a book of poetry. I couldn't wait to get to the top of the stairs and start the conversation with Mary that equaled the beginning of a professional life as a writer.

How would I write the newsletter? I hope they would allow me the freedom to be myself on the paper. I need to let the personality show in my words. My readers need to feel that there is a real person creating for them and not just a bunch of words splattered onto the page. I was at the top of the stairs now, and I opened the door.

"James Kohl?"

"Yes."

"I'm Mary, we'll sit down over here. Could I get you anything to drink?" Mary was about 43 and dressed simply and professionally. Graying hair framed her face and she wore glasses.

"No thank you, I'm fine." They always offer, but I never take it. I held manila folder part 3 in my hand and sat with it in my lap. She had the copy of the resume that I sent to her, so there was no need to dig mine out.

"First let me tell you a little about the museum. We work in conjunction with the City of San Jose and anyone else who will help us out with sponsorship in order to bring a hands-on learning environment to our patrons. We were founded about six years ago, and we've been growing ever since. Have you ever been in the museum?"

"No, but I've heard a lot about it from Gayle and her son, and it sounds awesome." I'm not sure if you should say 'awesome' in an interview, but if it's in your personality to do so, they're going to find out sooner or later. Still, I flinched on the inside as the word came out of my mouth. I'm trying for a job as a writer, and the best word I can summon is 'awesome!'

"On your way out, I'll let you walk through so you can see what we have so far. The museum is in a constant state of 'so far.' It will always be a work in progress. What attracted you to this position?"

"Gayle approached me about it originally, and I like the fact that kids are involved. I have coached swim teams, as it says on there." I motioned to my resume on her desk. She nodded. "Also, being an English major, the writing of the newsletter sounds great to me. That's something that I'd really like to do."

"Have you done any writing?"

"I've always written for fun, and of course, in college I wrote a ton." I looked forward to that accidental rhyme fading into the past.

"The position that we need to fill is really a receptionist sort of position. Writing the newsletter would only be one aspect of the job. On a normal workday, you would spend a lot of time answering phones and directing calls. Have you ever used a switchboard?"

"No, but I have phone experience as a telemarketer."

"With a college degree, you're a bit overqualified for this job, that's why I really wanted to know why this job appealed to you." Mary set her gold-rimmed glasses on the desk between my resume and a coffee cup.

"It seems like a good job, and I'm truly interested in the newsletter aspect." Who was I kidding? Probably no one-she was looking for a secretary. I thought of moving to Los Gatos and reminded myself that no job is forever. We shook hands and thanked each other. She showed me to the door that opened onto a stairway leading down to the museum and invited me to stay there as long as I wanted. My suit weighed me down as I watched children jumping around on all the cars and screaming at the life-sized skeleton. I convinced myself I was having the best time ever, and then walked to my car after almost five minutes.

Maybe Alain Pinel called, I thought on my way home. Maybe this job wouldn't be so bad. I switched the radio from station to station on my preset buttons. It never ceases to amaze me that all my stations can be playing advertisements at the same time! I tore off my tie and stuck it on the passenger seat.

The light on the answering machine was blinking when I got home, indicating that I had messages. This is it! I played the message.

"Hey Jim this is Kristin, how did the interview go? Did you get the job? Anyways, John and I were wondering if we could meet up tonight to go look at the place again. Gimme a call." I didn't call back. I went to the living room to find the newspaper.

CHAPTER VI

The want ads made looking for a job seem like a full-time job without pay. Even finding the want ads was a task. They were never in the same section of the paper. You had to flip through all the ads for cars, yard sales, scalped tickets, and housing before you got to the employment pages. Your hands would be covered with so much smudgy black ink that everyone thought you had sneaked into the newspaper printing house to volunteer to set the type in order to sneak an early look at the job offerings.

I would circle things that sounded good and either go back and call later, mail a resume or try to figure out where a fax machine was and how to use it. Sometimes, I thought homeless people sleeping under newspapers just ended up trapped under a mountain of the stuff while looking for a job and simply never got out from under it.

The newspaper was in the family room next to the green chair. I started by looking up English, thinking that maybe they would list the jobs by the degree that was required. All I found there was engineering jobs. After days of all the hundreds of engineering jobs being listed and grabbed by others, I wondered if I had majored in the wrong thing.

But then I realized quickly that I couldn't have been an engineer because engineering meant a definite answer for all things. There was no impossible or implausible or supernatural, there was only poor engineering that made the impossible seem possible to the untrained eye and good engineering that made the impossible truly possible. I didn't believe in atoms in high school, and I did not believe that anything in the world could or should be exact, so any sort of science or math was really out for me.

I flipped more through the classifieds to the "W" section. Maybe somebody needs a writer. All the writing jobs were for technical writers. "Technically," I joked to no one in particular, "I know nothing!" I should've taken more computer technology classes, and I should've paid attention in the few that I did take.

Maybe I could get a job at a newspaper! I looked under reporter and journalist. I would occasionally find some listings, but they wanted to see my "clippings"-articles that I had written for other newspapers. I hadn't written a newspaper article since I was in high school when I was in Mrs. O's journalism class. Most of these journalism employers scoffed when I mentioned my high school career and wanted to see something from at least a college newspaper. I actually took a beginning journalism class in college, but it had a really boring instructor, so I left the major. Maybe the next class would have been fun. I'd never know, and my college degree seemed to be more and more useless with every turn of the newspaper's pages.

Flipping back to the "E" section, I noticed some editing jobs. I had often edited friends' papers in college because I thought it was fun. I was the perfect nerd for the job. These jobs all wanted experience and didn't seem to think that mine warranted an interview.

I looked under "Teacher." One place was hiring Montessori teachers, so I gave a call to the number they listed.

"Hi, uh, I'm calling about the teaching job you have listed in the paper?"

"Are you Montessori trained?"

"Probably not, because I don't know what that is."

"Montessori teaching is a method developed by…" Whatever else she said was instantly buried in the "stuff I don't know" file in my brain.

There were also quite a few teaching jobs available in pre-schools, but I had no ECUs (Early Childhood Units) so I wasn't qualified to do this either.

I sunk.

"What's wrong?" asked my mom.

"There's no job that I can get. I'm either too qualified or not qualified."

"The right one will come around." My mom is always an optimist. "What sort of job are you looking for now?"

"Everything! Writing, editing, reporting, teaching…"

"You'd make a good teacher." There it was again, but my mom thinks I'm great at whatever I do.

"You need a teaching credential to do that." I had actually looked into the program about a semester before graduation, but I wanted out of college for a while. I had had my fill of the university system after 4 ½ years.

"Jan says that her district is always looking for substitute teachers, why don't you look into that?" suggested my mom.

"How do you think I would do such thing?"

"I guess just call whatever district you want to work in and ask them how you get signed up. Jan works in Alum Rock, but there are plenty of districts around here." My mom handed me the phone from the couch, and I traded the newspaper for the phone book.

I started by calling San Jose Unified and the disappointment slammed me to the floor. I had to apply and be considered and go through an interview and screening process. I couldn't believe you had to go through all that just to be eaten alive by kids. I remembered how we treated our subs when I was a kid.

"Try another district." They can't all be that way.

"Here's one called Oak Grove." I dialed the number. When they answered I said, "Hi, I'd like to talk to someone about becoming a substitute teacher."

"That's human resources," said the receptionist like she hated direct-ing calls, "Hold please." That could've been me at the Discovery Museum. I winced at the thought.

"Human resources," greeted the voice on the line.

"Hi, I'd like to talk to someone about becoming a substitute teacher."

"Oh, you need Millie. Hold please." How many people did they need to work in a district office? I couldn't believe they had one person in charge of just substitutes!

"This is Millie."

"Hi, Millie, I was told that I need, I mean…I want to become a sub-stitute, and I was wondering how I would do that."

"Okay, do you have a degree?"

"Yes." So far so good.

"Have you passed the CBEST?" The CBEST is a test that prospective teachers have to take.

"Yes." That stupid thing was worth something after all!

"Do you have a teaching credential?"

"No." Oh man! Why do you need one of those to be a sub, a glorified babysitter in most cases? "I didn't know you needed one to be a substi-tute."

"You don't need a full credential, but you need at least what's called an emergency credential."

"How do I get one?"

"You need a statement of need from any district. I can send you one because we need subs right now. You need to take that down to the County Office of Education and apply for an emergency credential. When you've applied, you need to bring all the paperwork over here, and I can sign you up."

So it was that simple! I was going to be a substitute teacher. "Great! Thanks a lot!" I gave her my address so she could send it out to me. I was on my way! I had found a job. Teaching included possibly teaching English, so Kristin owed me a lunch. Cool! Nothing had ever felt so right to me in my life! I was going to teach kids. If I liked it, maybe I could get a real credential and be a real teacher someday!

I had a future-at least for now.

Chapter VII

The next day, the envelope from the Oak Grove District showed up at my house just as it was supposed to. In it was a Statement of Need that said that the district was hiring substitute teachers and that I was welcome to be one. It also had detailed driving directions to the County Office of Education, which, at the time, shared a building with the public television station. I was to take my statement of need to them and present it at the credentials desk. No interview, no garbage, just go and get the job.

I drove down to the County Office with my letter and my checkbook, because it cost $120 to get an emergency credential. I was going to be making $80 a day for subbing, so it would more than pay for itself with two days of work. I drove through downtown San Jose and scoffed as I passed the Children's Discovery Museum. They didn't call me back, and who needed them anyway? I was not selling out, and I was making better money than the museum was offering, and this was going to be the easiest job in the world to get. I pulled into the County Office parking lot excited to know that I would be driving home a substitute teacher on the verge of an exciting career in education.

I found a door and walked in. There were colorful displays made by the children of Santa Clara County. There was a wall for each district. I had graduated from San Jose Unified School District. I found our wall.

Among the artwork, our wall had portraits of all the district's principals. I knew quite a few. Many of them had been vice principals or even teachers when I had been going to school. Maybe I would be on a wall like this some day as a principal. Nah! I didn't want to be away from the kids. I felt it then, and I still feel it a bit today as you read this book.

I left the brown paneled hallway of districts when I found a door that seemed to lead into the main office area. I was disgusted! It was a maze of cubicles much like my worst nightmares about corporate scum life. Everything was a drab gray, and phones rang in every direction. There were numbered signs at the corners of some of the cubicles. A copy machine whirred a hundred copies of some document as if all this conformity had originated in its identity crushing gut. I got someone's attention.

"I'm looking for the credentials desk?" At the interruption I had made, she looked up from the heaviest file cabinet in the world.

"You are in the East Wing and credentials is in the West Wing. You need to go up to cube corner 158," she said, motioning with her hand, "and take a right. Go through the double doors and pass through the hall. Go through the other double doors and that's the West Wing. I'm not sure where it is from there." At least the Cheshire Cat smiled at Alice.

I followed the directions and found myself in an identical cubicle nightmare to the East Wing. The two only differed in name and location, and ironically, the name was the location.

I found another friendly soul to ask for directions. Then another and another because I got lost twice. Finally, I found the desk right by a door that lead to the outside. At least I would be able to find my way out even if it meant walking around the whole outside of the building to get back to the car.

There was no one at the credentials desk when I got there. Within a minute or two, a woman in her mid-40s showed up. She pulled some files from another of the largest file cabinets in the world. She brought them to the desk and had to talk to me now.

"Can I help you?"

"Yeah. I am here to get an emergency credential, so that I can be a substitute teacher." I was still proud. I would downplay the substitute part for my entire stint as a sub, but it was a major move for me, and I felt pride even though this lady would rather drink the ink in the photocopier than help me.

"For which district?"

"Oak Grove sent me my letter of need."

"Statement of need."

"Yeah." I handed it to her.

"Did you take the CBEST?"

"Yeah." That stupid thing turned out to be the most important two hours of my professional life so far!

"Do you have your scores with you?"

No! Oh man! Wait a second. My scores just happened to be on a card I had in my wallet. Hah! "Uh, yeah, I do." I showed it to her. She took it and made a copy. It wouldn't be long now. I could call Kristin and collect my lunch.

"All I need now is a cashier's check for $120 and your fingerprint cards."

"You can't take a regular check?" I asked, motioning with my San Francisco 49er checkbook.

"No. There are banks very nearby where you can get one." She was a robot programmed by thousands of ignorant guys like me throughout the years. She had no emotion in her voice, and my face showed a crushed young man. "Do you have your fingerprint cards?" She knew the answer.

"What are those?" I asked, knowing that I was not leaving there today with a credential of any sort. She reached into a drawer and pulled out two white paper cards with five squares outlined in light blue on each of them. I looked at the grid where my fingerprints would have to be before I was anything besides a college graduate. "Do you guys do this here?" I asked about the fingerprints. I feared the answers, and my fears were confirmed.

"You have to go to DMV." DMV! People took days off from work just to drop money off at the DMV.

"So all I need is a cashier's check for $120 and my fingerprints and then I'm all set?"

"Yes."

I thanked her, but she was already back in the file cabinet.

My car was waiting for a substitute teacher on the verge of an outstanding career in education, but it let me drive it home anyway. So much for the easiest job to get in the world. My in and out career start turned into a scavenger hunt of epic proportions. It was a good two weeks before I could align all the papers just so and get my emergency credential. Even after standing in line for a day at DMV and paying a service charge of $5 on top of the $120 to get a cashier's check at my own bank, I still only was issued a temporary emergency credential pending analysis of my character and fingerprints by Sacramento. The temporary one was a pink piece of paper from the bottom of a triplicate form, but it got me a job and my prize lunch, and I moved to Los Gatos with John and Kristin.

Chapter VIII

In less than a month after graduation, I was a substitute teacher in three districts: Alum Rock, Oak Grove, and Santa Clara Unified. I had no idea until this time that some districts were kindergarten through eighth and that only unified school districts had high schools attached. That was the first fact that came my way in this new life. The next one was that each district wants to see all the paperwork you showed the county office, plus the pink temporary credential, before they would put you on their substitute teacher list.

I drove around from district office to district office carrying a manila envelope (there was too much paper for a folder) filled to the brim with a pile of papers that needed to be presented to work as a sub. I had my pink temporary credential, my CBEST scores, my Social Security card, my driver's license, copies of my fingerprint cards, and copies of transcripts from college. It was quite a stack, and not every district wanted to see the same things, so you had to be prepared.

Your life is unpredictable as a sub. You may or may not be working the next day. You may find out where you are working the day before, or you may find out at 5 a.m. where you need to be in two hours. There were a couple of times when there was no sub for a school, and they didn't call me until 10-a good two hours into the school day. I enjoyed going from school to school and seeing the different activities that teachers came up with. You never knew who or what you'd be facing from day to day, and that was exciting to me.

When I was doing it, you could make up to $400 a week as a substitute. The money seemed a fortune to me.

Each district had its own person calling me in the morning: Millie from Oak Grove, Gladys from Alum Rock and Kathy from Santa Clara. All of them told me I could probably work every day except for Alum Rock. "I may not call you at first," said Gladys when I was showing her my pile of paper, "but just nudge me once in a while and I'll call you in more often." Eventually, I started calling Alum Rock the "Alarm Clock District" because they were always the first ones to call in the morning.

Alum Rock was the lowest socioeconomic district that I subbed in. The schools were poor, and some were a little rundown. Their books were old, and a lot of the windows were boarded. You were paid more money to work in their middle schools than in their elementary schools. After a year, I decided that the extra $20 a day I earned in their middle schools was not worth it. You can only have things thrown at you so often before you get sick of it. The mood of the staff was often depressed in these middle schools.

Oak Grove was wealthier. The schools were newer, the books were newer, and there were computers in the classroom. Overall, I had a good time there and the people were friendly.

Santa Clara had the most money. They had a school called Cabrillo where I learned how to teach middle school. This school had made a deal with Intel, and each room had five computers hooked up to a network with a version of Encarta so kids could research right from their classrooms. Each teacher desk had a computer as well, and all the teachers could e-mail each other. Instead of filling a teacher's box with paper notices that would not be read, the school secretary would e-mail everyone. This was the first place I ever saw e-mail. This was the first school I knew of that was Internet enabled. They were pretty cutting edge for 1993, but that's getting ahead of myself.

One morning in early January, my phone screamed and I jumped at it. The clock said 5, and I knew this was probably my first subbing job. It was Millie, and she had an assignment for me at Herman Middle School for a guy named Jerry McCaffrey. It was a 7th grade GATE (honors)

English class. This was great because I had been a GATE student in English, so the kids would probably be like me. That means that no matter how much they hate being there, I probably could relate to them and get through to them if I had to. It had only been nine years since I was in middle school.

"You got a job?" my mom asked. I wouldn't be moving in with John and Kristin for another two weeks.

"Yeah! It's in Oak Grove. Seventh grade GATE English."

I put on a pair of jeans, a button down shirt, and a tie. I always wore a tie as a sub. I climbed into my CRX with my map of the Oak Grove School District that Millie gave me when I registered with them. Each district gives you one of these maps, so they don't have to give each sub driving directions each morning.

I stopped at the donut shop near my parents' house to get a cup of coffee. The shop was jammed with men and women in business clothes, and I was one of them except I wasn't a corporate scum sellout like they were. The Asian girl behind the counter poured my coffee, and I was out the door like a working man. I was fighting the good fight to make sure kids were educated. I was going to be the best sub ever.

I arrived at Herman 40 minutes before class started and sat in my car looking out the window. Was I ready for this? There were kids with backpacks slung over their shoulders slouching their way to some-where. They were bigger than I pictured. They didn't look the way my friends and I did when we were their age. All the boys had really careful haircuts the way the New Wave kids did in the '80s. I was a Metal Head when I was a kid, so my hair was as long as I could make it. I didn't see anyone that I thought I could relate to. I didn't see anyone I thought I could reach.

"This is what you want, and this is what you are. Go be the teacher that you said you could be when you were 13 and sat in your own dreadful 7th grade English class," I told myself as I opened the car door and stepped into a whole new world that would shape my life for the next six years.

I found the office. I went in and was greeted by the secretary. "Good morning. Can I help you?"

"Yeah, I'm here to sub for Jerry…"

"McCaffrey?"

"Yes." Even if you're not sure who you're coming in for, the school secretary always knows.

"You're Jim Kohl. Have you ever been here before?"

"No, this is my first day subbing." I said, tentatively.

"Well, welcome! Jerry has a great group of kids. He's in room 20, and if you go out this door and make a sharp left, it'll be in the second pod of rooms on your right. Here is his room key and his sub folder. The faculty room is in the building to the right of this one as you face the school. Most of the teachers eat in there. Is there anything else you need?" Her voice bubbled out of her mouth.

"I don't think so, thanks a lot."

"Sure, Jim."

I found the room right where she said it would be, and I turned the key.

"Hey, are you a sub?" some kid yelled.

"Yeah."

"Fresh!" I didn't know what he was talking about.

I entered the room and found the light switch. I had this sub folder in my hand, and I didn't even know what it was. I thumbed through it to find that it had a list of when Mr. McCaffrey's yard duty was and a map of the school and a copy of his schedule. According to the schedule, he had a whole period without kids! It was called a prep period. Teachers only taught five classes and kids had six. Amazing! I never knew this.

I found his lesson plans on his desk. His classes were working on group projects, and I just had to let them work and make sure they were working. I had to take roll at the beginning of all five classes and fill in a bubble next to absent students' names. That was all there was to it.

I saw that there was a white board in the room. I remembered that substitute teachers would usually write their name on the board. That's the thing to do, but no one can ever pronounce my name. I wrote "Mr. Kole," figuring that at least the name would be pronounced correctly.

The door opened and in walked a man with thinning hair and glasses. "Hi, I'm Jerry McCaffrey."

"Jim Kohl." We shook hands. "I'm your sub."

"Great. Well, I'll be on campus for a meeting today, and I just need to pick up some things from the room. My kids are good. He squinted at me through his glasses with his head cocked to the side. "I haven't seen you around."

"This is my first day subbing."

"Okay." Jerry nodded. "Well, let me know if you need anything."

Jan, my mom's friend, had told me to network myself and try to get to know some teachers so that they would want to request me to sub for them. "I think I'm fine. Sort of nervous, I guess."

"You'll be fine-these are good kids." That's what they all say. "I'll see you later." He took his things and left.

The bell rang-the warning bell. My heart pounded. I was going to be fine. The door opened and kids came in. "Are you the sub?" I nodded. Like a bunch of hyper squirrels, they chattered unrecognizable babbles to each other accompanied by hand gestures and facial expressions that made me nervous. They were all very different from me. I was never like them. I was going to die.

The bell rang again. This meant that class was starting, and so was I. They were all talking at their desks. "I need your attention please." They quieted! My God, this was going to work! "My name is Mr…"

"Good morning, students, and these are your announcements." The PA system always has a wonderful way of interrupting. I had just gotten their attention; what if I could never get it back! How long can these announcements be? I actually had them listening. Maybe I could get them to listen again. I couldn't even take roll until they stopped. I learned it right then. The most important thing about teaching is: Plan it, but when it doesn't happen your way, don't be surprised.

Finally the announcements ended. "Okay. I'm Mr. Kohl, and I will be your sub today. Mr. McCaffrey is on campus at a meeting, and he says that you have projects you've been working on concerning the Elizabethan times." Some of them nodded. "You'll have the whole period to continue work on these. It's important that you make progress today because they are due at the end of the period tomorrow. I have to take roll first, so if you could please listen up for your name." They did.

It was amazing! I couldn't believe I was playing this off as if I was a teacher or something! I had the tie on and I was standing in front of the room, but two weeks ago I had no clue what I was even going to do with my life. Now I was a teacher-the guy with all the answers. They listened to me! I was forever, though briefly, a part of their educational history. I needed more. I loved this!

All through the period, they worked on their projects. I walked around the room to see what they were doing and to see if they needed anything. They didn't. I felt like a waiter going from group to group saying, "Is everything all right here?" It went better than I could've imagined, but then period one ended and period two started.

"Are you a sub?" They always ask this. I nodded again. I started into the routine that I used with first period.

"Hi, I'm Mr. Kohl, and I am your sub today. Mr. McCaffrey is on campus at a meeting, but he left us a plan. You're supposed..."

"Are you married?"

"Yes." I lied, "Otherwise I wouldn't be *Mr.* Kohl. Anyway, the projects that you've been working on are due..."

"Why did you spell your name wrong?"

"Huh?'

"Your name, I saw it on the absence list and it wasn't spelled that way. Why did you spell it wrong?" She was in the front row. I didn't know what she was talking about because I had never heard of an absence list.

The absence list is generated daily at a lot of middle schools. It has the name of every student that is marked absent during first period. You're supposed to check the absence list against your own roll, but few teachers that I have known ever really do that. Most of them look for the names of kids that are annoying and hope that the name is there. The absence list also lists the names of absent teachers and their subs. Most students try to get a glimpse of the absence list for the same reason that teachers look at it.

"How do you know that I spelled it wrong? Maybe the school spelled it wrong."

She shook her head in obvious doubt. My suggestion was not even a possibility.

"Well, to be honest with you," in the back of my head I remembered that teachers lied a lot-at least that's what I thought in middle school. I figured I'd give the truth a shot. "A lot of people mispronounce my name because of the 'H.' I figured it would be easier to pronounce if I spelled it 'Kole.'"

From the back of the room some guy said, "It's your name! Make people learn to say it right. Don't give up your name! Geez, man…"

The room agreed that what I had done was stupid and that there was no way in the world they would change their name for anyone. They grumbled and mumbled for a good minute or two about this. I changed the name on the board to the spelling that would've made my ancestors proud.

They settled into their work after I took roll and gave directions. I noticed a guy in the back wearing a Megadeth T-shirt, listening to a Walkman, and I knew I had to do something about this. I dreaded the conversation as I walked over to his group. My friends and I had listened to Megadeth, and I was about to bust the only person in the room that reminded me of me.

"How you doin'?" I asked.

"Fine."

"What are you doing back here?" I figured I would give him the opportunity to explain himself because I was rarely given that opportunity in school.

"Oh, uh, my group is done. I just have to type up part of the project at home tonight on the computer." This seemed reasonable, and the other faces in the group seemed to corroborate this story.

"Okay. Be sure to get it done because it is due tomorrow. All the other groups are getting done, so if you're just not working because I'm a sub, it'll probably hurt your grade." I had to know. "What are you listening to, anyway?" He mentioned some band I'd never heard of and offered me a headphone. It sounded like the old metal stuff I listened to when I was his…never mind.

The day went on with classes that were similar to these. At lunch, I approached and entered the faculty room with an odd feeling of intrusion. Faculty rooms were for teachers only. You dare not set foot in a faculty room as a kid. This feeling was so carved into my brain that I hesitated before going in. I creaked the door open, and the teachers were all sitting around a square table eating from paper bags or white Styrofoam cafeteria plates. They looked like regular people.

The staff was very nice and supportive. "You can send one to me if they give you any trouble." Some woman offered.

"Thanks." I was fine though. They were good kids.

At the final bell of the day, I knew that I wanted to teach. I turned in my key to the office after writing Mr. McCaffrey a note about how the day went, and I knew that I could do this forever.

Chapter IX

Subbing gave me an apartment in Los Gatos. I shared a three-bedroom place with John and Kristin from January until about October. Kristin bought me a lunch at Hobee's to settle our bet. I got to know John and Kristin really well, and then the three of us got to wishing we had never met at all. That, my friends, is a book of its own, and maybe John or Kristin will feel like writing it someday.

I subbed for two years. There were good times and bad times, and some of the bad times were as bad as it gets before the cops come.

I spent two weeks once at Shepherd Middle School in Alum Rock where the principal's office window had been broken the night before I started. I had an eighth grade U.S. History class. Alum Rock middle schools had no teacher prep period, so I taught six classes a day. The lesson plan called for reading *My Brother Sam is Dead* and completing a series of projects and worksheets based on what was read. Easy-I thought.

One period of the day was a sheltered version of history, which means the whole class was made up of non-native English speakers, or ESL kids as they are commonly labeled. I had people in the room who spoke Vietnamese, Spanish, Punjabi, and Laotian. They could barely understand me. I thought they were putting me on until I asked another teacher about it.

"That one period I'm teaching," I mentioned to a woman in the lunch room, "they don't seem to understand a thing I say, and they are a lot less responsive than the other classes."

"Oh, that's the sheltered period. Yeah, they don't understand much English. Just try to get them to do anything."

"Can they read?"

"Some of them might be able to read a little."

The other classes were filled with kids who didn't want to be there, and if they had to be, they definitely didn't want me to be there. They gave me nothing at best and their cruddy attitudes at worst. The first five or six days they would throw things at me and yell things to me and make strange gestures with their hands that I would later learn were gang symbols.

"We godda dodge the Bloods and Crips every day on the way to school, eh," one girl told me.

This was the first place I saw "sagging," which was a gang style of dress for a while. They would wear really baggy pants and have their boxer shorts hanging over the top, blue belts with their first initial in the buckle, and the belt would pass through the buckle and hang lower than their knees. The jackets were blue windbreakers. Most of them had blue hats that they wore sideways. They weren't allowed to carry blue bandanas (which they called rags) because the school decided that was gang-related material. Nearly all of them were in a crew.

Crews were groups of kids that "had each others' backs" in a fight and would jump in to defend each other. They would often start fights too. Crews weren't full blown gangs, but they could evolve into that if they got enough members.

There were crews of every sort. There was one called TBG (True Blue Gangsters) that would be really embarrassed if they knew that I knew what it stood for. No adults were supposed to, but we all did. These guys, like their name implied, wore all blue. They wanted to be in as much trouble as possible and never failed to attempt some sort of disruption so they could get the coveted referral to the office. This was a badge of courage and much more of a status symbol than a passing grade in a class.

There was a crew called Asian Girlz. Guess who was in their crew. I saw this tiny Filipino girl write "Asian Girlz" on her desk, so I asked her, "Why did you write that?"

"Write what?" The whole two weeks I would watch crimes followed seconds later with denial by the perpetrator.

"Asian Girlz." I pointed to it on her desk as I said it.

"What's Asian Girlz, what's Asian Girls?" she said with a crazed look in her eyes. That's when I knew it was her crew. Because having a crew was against the school rules, no one admitted to an adult that there were crews. Doing so would not only get you in trouble, the other members of your crew could be in trouble too, and that would get you jumped unless you could find another crew to get your back, which could get you jumped also. It's all very simple. Getting in trouble was cool unless you got in trouble because someone ratted you. That was also sort of cool because then you could jump them.

There was one kid who was never awake in my class except when he was practicing tagging (making graffiti). I didn't know what he was drawing. I told him he had to work on something else (like the assignment) and he looked at me as if cockroaches were coming out of my mouth and eyes. This kid was the only real gangster in the school, according to one teacher, and he had a hard time staying awake because he was out all night.

One girl came in with a swollen jaw. "What happened?" I asked.

"My dad punched me again." I verified this with the office. CPS (Child Protective Services) had already been called on this incident and the previous incidents. If you can't be safe in your own home, no wonder there are crews. You need to feel safe somewhere.

There was a nerdy little white kid whom no one liked. He got on my nerves the way a mosquito would, but I yelled at him because he was too much for me on top of all this other stuff. My temptation was to slam him into the ground, so I threw him out of class. This made him cool in the other kids' eyes until they remembered that he was a geek.

I had one kid in my class named Oscar, who wore a Philadelphia Eagles jacket every day. His was one of the few non-blue jackets. He saw the pandemonium that was breaking out under my "control." He saw the things being thrown. He heard what they were calling me in Spanish. He saw my looks of shock at their normal life occurrences. He saw my face redden in rage on a once-a-minute basis. He saw me send kids to the office who were all too glad to go. "Hey, you ain't gonna make it, homes." He told me.

"What do you mean?"

"The two weeks, eh. You ain't gonna make it, Meester."

"Yeah, I am."

He walked to the door after class, shaking his head.

He told me the same thing every day, and I told him the same thing. I stuck it out, though, and I think we were both surprised. When it was finally over, he said. "You made it, eh! I never thought you would, but you did it. You need to be tougher, ese." You're probably right, Oscar.

I learned a lot in those two weeks. I learned I needed to develop my classroom control, and I started to define for myself what my classroom control was going to look like. I had let a bunch of kids get the better of me, and now I could recognize that and plan for when it started to happen again. I hated those two weeks when they were happening, but from where I stand now, I realize their necessity in shaping the teacher that I am.

Not the whole subbing experience was as bad as all that. There were many good times and many good kids. I made many great friends at Cabrillo Middle School in Santa Clara. They had some "problem" kids when I was subbing there, but nothing compared to what I saw in Alum Rock, so to me it was easy. I quickly became known as a "good" sub, so many teachers at that school requested me.

This school exposed me to team teaching. In the sixth grade where I was primarily working, one teacher taught English and Social Studies to a group of kids, and another teacher taught the same kids Math and

Exploratory/P.E. Exploratory was like an elective except the student didn't get to choose it. The kids went to someone else for Science, and whatever period your kids had Science was your prep. Whatever teacher you shared kids with was your partner, and the two of you had the same prep. The two of you planned together so that the kids were being taught uniform material across the curriculum. If they were studying Ancient China in Social Studies, they were learning about the Abacus in Math. Their whole day had a similar theme except Science.

I got my first big break at Cabrillo. Mrs. Garcia was leaving the school year early, and the principal asked me to take her place for three months! There is not a better way to learn a job than to do it. I shadowed her for two days, and then I took the reins. I made a lot of mistakes and had some behavior problems, but I was doing better already. It was great to be joining a staff, even temporarily, full of people I knew and liked. The secretary, Stephanie, gave me a coffee cup on my first day.

I walked into room 25 and took a look around. This was the one room in the school with no computers because the students had smashed in the screens when they had a different teacher at the beginning of the year. There was still a Gummi Bear stuck to the center of the clock that had been thrown on that teacher's last week. She was temporarily relaxing in a special hospital. These kids had taken advantage of a truly ill woman.

The next teacher they had, Mrs. Warren, was switched to Science when Ms. Weaver left the profession for the cubicle world in the middle of the year. She was an awesome teacher, and I was disgusted and shocked that she would sell out like that and leave the kids.

Mrs. Garcia came next. She was known for her strict disciplinary teaching approach. The kids began the day with one page of writing. She would give them the topic. They would then read from a Reading Book and answer the questions at the end of the story. They had to copy the question out of the book before answering it. There was no talking, no class discussion, and no variance from the daily routine. There was no slouching in their seats. There were no jackets to be worn in class. The school brought her in because of the many changes in instructors and the fact that kids feared her, which would squash the possibility of any more of the vandalism that these kids caused earlier.

I was not this rigid, and I didn't know that I had the energy to be. The kids didn't like her, so maybe they would listen to me just because I was not her.

"I'm Mr. Kohl, and I'll be your teacher for the rest of the year."

"Sure you will." It was this girl in the front row, and isn't it always, named Tiffany.

"Excuse me?"

Tiffany went on to explain to me that they had had three teachers leave them this year. I was number four. I already knew this of course, and although it's not the best situation to be entering, it beat what I had already seen.

"Why should we believe you when you say you're staying the rest of the year?"

"You don't have to believe me, but on the last day of school, you'll see that it's true."

I was partnered with Karen. I learned a lot from her about listening to kids. We had some kids with real problems. Desiree made bad choice after bad choice concerning boys. Mark had no ambition because no one cared at home. Karen showed me how to listen to them, so that you at least know where to start with them. I watched her do it, but it didn't sink in. I knew it was a good thing, but it took me a few years with my own room to learn it on my own.

"Why do you sub?" some of the faculty would ask me on occasion. I had been working as a sub for them for two years.

"I like it."

"If you like subbing, you'll love teaching full time." I heard this over and over. I bet I could be a teacher.

I got many letters of recommendation from members of Cabrillo's staff, and to this day I consider them all friends, but the one class that really let me know that teaching was what I wanted was Mr. Gregg's sixth grade at Del Robles Elementary School in Oak Grove.

They listened to me and told me I was interesting. They told me I made learning fun. They messed around in class, but they stopped when I asked them to. They didn't ask me "Are you a sub?" They shouted my name when they saw me step out of my car in the morning. I would break other commitments to work in their room. We laughed and learned and had a great time. I still have pictures they drew for me as gifts.

They made me feel like a real teacher. They showed me that I could make a difference with that look they gave me when they understood what I was talking about.

"I never get it when Mr. Gregg talks about it," Nicole said to me one day. "I always get it when you explain." I could do this.

"I know they're getting a teacher when you come, and it makes it a whole lot easier to be out knowing you're coming in," Mr. Gregg told me once. "When I know you're coming in, I know the class won't be a day behind because I can ask you to teach what I would've taught and I know you'll do it." So, maybe I really am a teacher.

I went with them on their sixth grade end of the year field trip-a cookout and swim party in the pouring rain. They all still swam and couldn't believe that I didn't want to.

"C'mon in, Mr. Kohl!"

"No thanks, I'll just sit over here and eat this soggy hot dog. You guys have fun though."

I was there on their last day of sixth grade. They all thanked me and I thanked them. I told them that I was going to go take the classes to be a real teacher because of the fun we had. They all cheered. They were so nice to me. People always talk about teachers making a big difference in a student's life, and we can, but no one ever talks about the difference the students make in our lives.

CHAPTER X

I had announced my intentions to everyone who would listen. One weekend near the beginning of summer, I was at my parents' house. My dad and I were in the garage doing something requiring tools when he turned to me suddenly.

"I just wanted to take you aside and let you know I'm very proud of your decision to become a teacher. We hardly ever have a chance to talk since you moved out, but I've known all along that you would make an excellent teacher. Even back when you were young and in school I could see the qualities in you."

I thought, "How come everyone knew and no one told me!"

"Thanks." I said.

"It's an admirable profession, and I hope you find a lot of joy in doing it. I've always hoped that my children would find joy and a sense of accomplishment in whatever they chose to do for a living."

"I think I will. I really like subbing." My dad designed nuclear missiles for the government. He made tools of destruction and gave me too easy of a life because of the money he made. I had wisdom enough to know that you need to suffer to understand life. Because I never wanted for anything, I was less of a person. This was his fault for choosing the evil path.

"I thought of being a teacher many years ago, but chose against it because they don't pay teachers what they deserve."

"This is what I have to do. Nothing has ever felt this right." There are a lot of people that try to talk you out of things. You have to ignore what people say and follow what you know you want. I was already dodging the main bullet of people talking you out of teaching-the money. Even teachers try to talk you out of doing the job for this reason! I'd made a decision that felt right-a lifetime commitment-and no one was going to make me re-consider.

"I'm not trying to talk you out of this, but you are aware that you'll never be rich. However, you'll always have the satisfaction of knowing that you're doing the most important job in the world."

"That's why I'm doing it. I love the feeling I get when I expose kids to new concepts and ideas, and they get them and make them their own. As far as money goes, I just want to be comfortable. I could do that while teaching, don't you think?" I didn't know. I really wanted to know if he did.

"I'm sure that's possible. You're a born teacher. You'll be a great one. Have you thought about where you'd like to go to get your credential?" Getting a teaching credential is about 30 extra college units. It's the equivalent in units to getting a master's degree.

Half of the units are for student teaching. You are assigned to a Master Teacher, and they watch you teach and give you pointers, and you watch them teach and take techniques that you like from them. It's like the unpaid internship that a doctor would have. The whole program can last as long as two years.

I shrugged because I hadn't thought about it yet. "San Jose State." It was really more of a question than a statement.

"They're supposed to have a good program."

"Their English department was sure good."

"I've hired some very promising young engineers from their Engineering school."

"Yeah?"

"Anyway, I'm proud of you." We shook hands.

"Thanks, Dad."

I applied to return to San Jose State for the fall semester of 1994. I filled out all the applications and sent in all the fees. I even paid for and ordered transcripts from San Jose State just to mail them still sealed to San Jose State.

"Aren't the transcripts kept in the Office of Admission and Records?" I asked the woman on the phone.

"Yes, they are, sir." For God's sake, I'm not a sir! I'm 24!

"Well, then why can't you guys just look at them when you are looking at my application?" It seemed reasonable to me, but nothing reasonable is the foundation of a bureaucracy.

"There is a different committee that stores records. The same committee does not store records and evaluate admission."

"Fine. How do I get the transcripts?" I already knew the answer.

"You need to fill out a Transcript Request Form and pay the $5 processing fee, and we will mail you official transcripts within 5 to 10 working days."

"And then I mail them back to you?"

"Yes, sir."

Am I the only one that thinks that is crazy! This is the same school that mailed me a letter after I graduated telling me to come to the school to pick up my diploma because, due to tight budgets, they could not afford to mail my diploma! With that said, it really wasn't that surprising.

A month later, my mom called me.

"You've got some mail over here from San Jose State. Do you want me to open it?"

"Yeah!" Cool! I was in, or maybe I wasn't. I hate these tense moments. I could hear the paper of the envelope tearing. What if I didn't get in? Then what? I would be a loser substitute with no chance to improve. I would have reached my own lowly potential on the ladder of education. My dream would be over.

"Let's see, blah blah blah…You've been accepted to San Jose State University! Oh, congratulations, Jim"

"Thanks. That's awesome! I'm going to be a teacher." I called everyone and told everyone who cared to hear about it.

I looked in the course catalog from San Jose State to see what I had to do next. I was supposed to go down to the teaching department and register for an interview and a group orientation.

I got in my car that minute. Just in case, I swung by my parents' house to get the letter. I'd been burned by not having the necessary paperwork in my hand before.

When I reached downtown, I circled to the top of the seventh street garage, which was crowded with the cars of summer session students. I got out of my car and stood on the roof of that garage. I could see all the brick dorms, Sweeney Hall, the Event Center and the huge gray Science building where I barely got a "C" in Biology. I was back. I had only been gone for two years, and here I was again, but this time, I had a direction. I was going to be a teacher. Go ahead, ask me what I'm going to do with my life because I have the answer.

I climbed down those steps like a conqueror coming down the mountain. The metal railing felt good in my hands. The paint on it seemed chipped in a perfect tribal design. I could smell the fresh pine tree that crushes the stairwell against the garage. Students walked casually with their backpacks slung across one arm looking for direction in a universe crammed with infinite possibility. "You'll find what you want." I thought, "Even I did."

The Credential Program's main office was in Sweeney Hall at the corner of 7th and San Carlos. There used to be an intersection there, but now the street is closed and the area in front is a grassy walkway. I went in to Sweeney Hall overflowing with the confidence that I had when I went to the County Office of Education to become a sub. That should have been my first clue.

The Credential Program's office, like any office at San Jose State, had a huge line. I stood in this line for about a half-hour and presented my letter victoriously at the window. "I'm here to schedule my orientation meeting and my initial interview."

The clerk was Asian and had an accent. She glanced at my letter, but she didn't really look at me. "What's your Social Security number?"

I gave it to her. She clicked it into her computer, and wrinkled her forehead just above her eyes. The computer beeped. She typed the number in again after checking it on my letter. She bit her lower lip and shook her head. "You're not in our system."

"But the letter says I have been accepted and that my concentration is 'Teaching Credential.'" I showed her where it said that. She took my letter to another woman who was working at a desk far behind the counter. They spoke. The Asian woman came back to me.

"This letter says you're in the university. You have to be accepted in the program before you can schedule orientation."

"You mean I'm in the college, but I'm not in the Credential Program yet?"

She nodded.

"When will I know?"

"Month or two."

"Thanks." I left.

I couldn't believe that it was so easy for an organization like San Jose State to keep people's dreams on hold. There was also the possibility that even though I was accepted to the university, I wouldn't be accepted into the program at all. All I wanted to do was teach, and no one wanted to let me. If I could just get through the craziness invented by God knows who, I knew I could make a big difference in some kids' lives.

It was late July. I wanted to start the program in late August. That was not very much time to get accepted, have an orientation and an interview, and start classes. It turns out my application had missed cutoff for a fall start. The program was impacted (lots of applicants) and mine missed the lucky turn on the lottery. I was being evaluated for a spring start.

I would wait. It was worth the wait. It doesn't matter what sort of bull you throw at me. I'm going to be a teacher and there is nothing anyone can do to stop me.

CHAPTER XI

"I was talking to Jan the other day," my mom said as we sat in the family room of her house. I was in the green chair and she was to my right on the couch. This is where many of our important discussions took place. She pulled me out of some thought with her voice, and I turned my face toward her.

"Yeah?" I figured this must be about teaching because Jan is a teacher.

"Have you ever heard of National University?"

"No."

"Jan said that Kim is going there. She said that the program is faster than State's program." Kim was Jan's daughter. She taught at Shepherd before she got married and whisked off to some tropical country.

"That's cool."

"You know, it would be something to look into. Have you heard from San Jose State yet?"

"No." I had a plan. San Jose State was my plan. I did not feel comfortable altering my plan because that was a sign of someone with no direction. You can't just go off all crazy. You need a plan, and you need to stick to it. I had spent enough time drifting. Such is the wisdom of youth. I dismissed this whole conversation as if it didn't happen. "Yeah…maybe I'll look into them."

Within a week I got my acceptance letter to the Teaching Credential Program at San Jose State. Now I was in. I was admitted to the school and the program within the school. No one could stop me now.

I went back to that same office and successfully scheduled an orientation meeting. "What about the interview?"

"You can't schedule that here," the woman behind the counter told me in the noncommittal voice that San Jose State must teach its clerks.

"Why?" Not that any of this was a surprise, but I wanted to know. "Where do I schedule that?"

"The entrance interview is scheduled at the end of the orientation meeting."

"I'm a cog in their system, so I am going to have to follow their system," I thought. That's okay. I'm going to be a teacher, which will give me the freedom to be who I am. I'll be no one's number anymore. I have dodged the path filled with cubicles and ties and Dilbert jokes.

A week later, I filed into a classroom at San Jose State with all the other future teachers. We were the next group to go fight the battle of ignorance. We would serve our country by providing it with geniuses. There were about 30 of us taking seats in that room. I was in the minority because I'm a man. This was getting better all the time!

The way we all took our desks was like the first day of high school. No one spoke and most people only looked at their desk, hands or a book that they had brought with them. We didn't know what to expect. There was an air of potential and mystery. Together, we were braving step one in a life-long commitment to excellence.

An older man and woman entered the room. "If I can have your attention, we can get started." You have mine.

"This is the first step in your career path." He told us. "You are here because you are pursuing the most important career a person can have: educating our youth. By a show of hands, how many of you are pursuing a multiple subject credential?"

Hands went up.

"I assume the rest of you are pursuing a single subject credential." Some nodded. My hand had not been up, and I had not nodded. I didn't even know the difference! "Here's another decision I'll have to make," I thought. "I can do it."

"I will make general comments about the program and specific comments about the multiple subject program," he continued. He motioned to the woman he had arrived with. "Doris will talk about the single subject program. At the end of both of our presentations, we will schedule your entrance interviews. Questions before I start?" He shot his eyes around the room from behind his thin-rimmed glasses.

He went on about a variety of things concerning the program and what it was like. He told us that the program was 30 units. "Half of it is in the classroom, learning about the theories, history, and techniques regarding teaching. Half of it is student teaching where you will spend a semester teaching two different groups of students. This will be a real hands-on internship. During this time, you will have two different Master Teachers that will guide you along in the pursuit of your credential. This was unpaid, and San Jose State does not allow you to do this under contract. There was no way to get paid while you student teach and also receive a credential from San Jose State. We do not allow it." I didn't know anyone did, so why was this guy harping on this so much?

"The credential classes are held during the morning hours. There are no night classes." This concerned me. I was planning on subbing while I got this credential so I could have real world and classroom world experience simultaneously. Besides, subbing was my job!

I would have to find something else to do. I was paying for most of this credential myself. My parents were helping a little. I didn't know of anything that paid as well as subbing that I could do, so I would probably have to move back home. This was okay because things were bad between me and John and Kristin, so it would give me an excuse to get out of their house.

It was mid-September, and I was going to start the program in February. It would take two years. I could substitute until February and save money, I guess. What job would I have for two years? The man was still talking, but he lost me as I planned my life.

The woman got up, and by now I understood that a multiple subject credential meant that I could teach anything from kindergarten to 8th grade, as long as I taught more than one subject per day. A single subject credential meant that I would be teaching one subject at a high school most likely. I decided right then to get a single subject credential because then I could just teach English. One less major decision lay in front of me.

They ended the meeting by mentioning something they were calling a CLAD credential, which would have to be added to our credentials by law in the future. "This credential will train you to teach kids that do not have English as a primary language. More and more of our children are from Mexico and will need special language help."

I feared this. I had seen bilingual education first hand in some of the schools that I had been subbing in. More often than not, I had seen English-speaking kids on one side of the room and Spanish-speaking kids on the other. They each had the same textbooks printed in the language that they knew. The teacher would present the lesson in Spanish, and the English-speaking kids would do what kids do when the adult in charge is not paying attention to them. The teacher would then present the same lesson in English. It was the Spanish kids' turn to do what kids do when no one is monitoring them.

In my opinion, this was not bilingual education because the kids were not learning the language that they did not know. Writing "Welcome" right above the word "Bienvendios" does not make for bilingual education anymore than eating tacos will teach you about Mexican culture. Essentially, there were two monolingual classes being taught in the same room. By the way, what about all the Vietnamese kids who didn't know English or Spanish?

The CLAD credential meant extra classes and extra time in school before I could begin my career. Oh well, I would worry about that later. The world would probably be destroyed by then anyway.

At the end of his presentation, I signed up for an interview appointment. I was to meet with a woman in two weeks to discuss why I wanted to be a teacher. Finally, something easy! I could tell you all day why I wanted to be a teacher. I loved subbing, and real teaching would be even better. I loved working with kids and helping them reach conclusions and insights. I loved helping students further their own lives by allowing them, under guidance, to become aware of their own potential and its use. Besides all that, I thought it was fun.

I went for my interview appointment in early October. I had started the teaching year at Cassell Elementary School. I had a fourth-grade class, and I had been their teacher since the first day of school. They were horrible, and I was horrible, and I realized that I could be a better teacher with some training, so maybe it wasn't such a bad thing to have to wait a couple of years for my own classroom.

I left work that day and slipped a clean shirt and tie on before I went to San Jose State. It was cloudy. It looked like rain would fall any minute, and the air was thick.

I went to Sweeney Hall and found the room where the interview was going to take place. Someone was in there already. I was 15 minutes early, so I fidgeted about the building until it was my turn to go in.

"Hello, I'm Maria Escobar." She was a short Mexican woman wearing a brown business type suit, nylons, and matching shoes. Her face was in the first stages of wrinkling, and she had a gold crucifix hanging around her neck from a chain. We shook hands.

"I'm Jim Kohl." She showed me to a seat and sat across from me at a table.

"So, Jim, you want to be a teacher?"

I nodded.

"Why?"

I went through my canned response that I listed a couple pages ago.

She nodded along with me. "Tell me about your experiences with children."

I relayed all about the swim team and my two years of substitute teaching experience.

"Do you have any experience with bilingual students?"

"Quite a bit." I was so glad I had subbed in Alum Rock. "I have subbed in many bilingual classrooms over in the Alum Rock District. I feel comfortable working in bilingual classrooms."

"Are you bilingual?"

"No." She made an abrupt humming sound as if I had shocked her with sad news. "But I've worked with many kids that are."

"Yes. Well, what sort of subjects do you like to teach?"

"I'm an English major, and I feel most comfortable working with literature, writing and grammar, but I also feel comfortable teaching levels of math up to Algebra II." I had tutored a lot of math students for extra money now and then.

She paused for a second and closed the notebook she had been scribbling in as I talked. I couldn't figure this woman out. I thought things were going pretty well. Then she said, "How are you going to teach the holidays?"

I wrinkled my forehead. Did she mean Christmas? "I hadn't planned on teaching the holidays. My understanding was that holidays should not be taught because of the separation of church and state."

"What is your opinion of Christopher Columbus?" she asked me next.

For those of you unaware, Christopher Columbus equals Satan on the West Coast. He slaughtered the Native Americans, and he called them "Indians," which they were not, and the name stuck for centuries. The schools no longer have Columbus Day off; we switched that holiday to Martin Luther King Day. In Baltimore in 1994, I was shocked to see that Columbus had a statue in his honor in the middle of the city. Being from California, I would have been less surprised to come across a public execution than anything honoring Columbus. Unfortunately, I did not hate him as much as I politically correctly should have.

"I think he did what everyone was doing at that time." I continued
with my opinion, even though I knew it was wrong, and it was definitely
not what Maria Escobar was looking for. "It was a violent time period.
People were burned at the stake on a regular basis back then. Columbus
was an explorer. They went to foreign lands and claimed them for whatever country sent them there." I could see in her face that I was making
myself very unpopular. I went on anyway, "I don't think it's fair to
impose our opinions about what is acceptable and unacceptable behavior on people that do not live in our day and age. From a historical perspective, he was just doing his job. It only seems barbaric to us because
of our 20th-century perspective."

She stared at me. Unless you are on a date, this is never a good sign,
and even on a date it's only a good sign about 50% of the time. She
exhaled slowly.

"The student population of California is about 43% Hispanic," she
said, finally. "The prediction is that if the population continues to grow
at the same rate that it currently is, that Hispanic students will be the
majority in California before the turn of the century." She said this with
a stern and precise vocal inflection that made me think she was planning on getting all the Hispanics together to beat me up. "How do you,
as a white male, think that you could possibly teach Hispanic students?
How can you think you can relate to them feeling the way you do about
the man that more than likely killed many of their ancestors?"

Why didn't I just say what I knew she probably wanted to hear? "I'm
just gonna teach them English. I won't be teaching my opinions because
I want my students to have their own."

"But you still have those opinions." And I'm still white. Why don't
you just finish your thought!

"Columbus was a long time ago," I said. I stared at the crucifix
around her neck, the symbol of forgiveness to so many Catholics. "Are
you still mad at Pontius Pilate?" I asked her.

She thanked me for coming in.

I had blown this interview. I could pretty much count out a recommendation from Maria Escobar. I could pretty much see my time at State could be a bit uncomfortable with a woman like her in charge. My head spun the way it does when you feel you've been treated unfairly. My face flushed, and my heart was pounding its way out of my chest. "That bitch does not know me!" I told myself. "She does not know the teacher I am, and she probably never will!" I walked faster and faster away from that building with each step. I would hang out with Columbus over her any day of the week. He would probably at least admit the destruction he caused.

I found a payphone, and I dialed my mom's number.

"Hello?" she said.

"Hey, Mom."

"Hi!" My mom has a way of making you feel like your call is the most important one she has ever received in the way her voice shows recognition.

"Hey you know, um, what was the name of that school that Kim went to. American University?"

"National University. Why?"

"Well, my interview went a bit poorly today at State, and I was thinking of checking them out. Where is it again?"

"It's down there on Lawrence. How do you know the interview went poorly?"

"I'll tell you later. I'm gonna drive over and check out this National place right now."

When we hung up, I called National and got directions. It was raining. I drove over there and rode the elevator to their second floor offices.

"Can I help you?" asked a man in a suit.

"I want to get a teaching credential."

"Okay. Gloria will be right with you."

I sat down, and Gloria met me there in about a minute.

"Can I help you?" she asked.

"I want a teaching credential."

"Single or multiple subject?"

"Single."

"You know if you get the multiple, you just have to pass a test to have a single as well. If you decide to take it, and you pass the single subject test, you'll be more marketable because you'll be able to teach kindergarten through 12th grade instead of kindergarten through 8th grade."

This sounded great to me! "Okay. Multiple. Thanks!"

"Sure," said Gloria, "What's your name?"

It was that simple! She put my information in the computer and told me some things about the program. Classes were only at night, so I could work as a sub all day. Courses lasted one month, and at the end of each month you took a final and started a new course at the beginning of the next month. The whole program was over in a year, including student teaching. "Any questions?"

"When do I start?"

"January." I had three months to wait, and I would be finished a whole year faster than I would at State. It was more money, but they didn't care what I thought of Columbus. I was on my way…again.

CHAPTER XII

The History of Teaching in America was the first course that I took toward my credential. I don't remember the man's name that taught us, but it was a fine welcome to the program. He was a kind and supportive man who had been retired from teaching for about 10 years. "I just had my 17th birthday," he told us. "My birthday is February 29." The fact that he had been a teacher added to his credibility for me. I've heard of other programs where the instructors have never taught grade school themselves. With teaching, unless you've been there, you don't know.

The most shocking fact I picked up in this course was that in the old days, teachers were expected to hold a certain level of morality. Like today, the majority of the teachers in the old days were women. It was considered inappropriate for them to date. They had to present a positive role model for the rest of society, and dating was not part of the image acceptable for a school teacher. To do so could result in the termination of their position, but it would also forever damage their reputation and character. They had to dress modestly and conservatively. The more I heard, the more it sounded like a religious order. I was glad it wasn't like that anymore.

I met Amy and Kim in that class. Amy was by far the most stressed-out person I have ever known. She came across as completely having her act together. She was well put together and carefully manufactured. She stressed hard to make sure that no one knew that she was scared to death of practically everything. She had me fooled the whole time.

She once talked about fainting spells she would have in the gym. Her boyfriend was trying to rub a knot out of her shoulder and she collapsed. I don't think she ate enough. She seemed to be carrying a whole lot of baggage, but I knew she could still make a great teacher because she had an obsessive attention to detail that many of my teachers had when I was a kid. She was also very nice.

Kim should have stressed more. She and I became good friends, but at the end of the program, she was the only one I knew who wasn't beating their head against the wall trying to get a job. I never understood that.

These two were close to my age, but there were quite a few people who were a lot older than we who were also just starting the program. These were people who had never had a job because they spent their lives raising kids, or they were people who were changing careers from the dark side of cubicle life to the pure teaching lifestyle. John had sold insurance, Molly had been a housewife, and Mark had been a bartender.

The cool thing about National was that we all went through the classes together. There were only about 28 people at each level of the program at a given time. Therefore, by the time the second class was starting, you already knew all your classmates pretty well. A network of teachers was automatically made for you. We all student taught at the same time. We all searched for jobs at the same time. We all knew what we were all feeling, so we were there to support each other in the grim moments and celebrate together in the shining ones.

There was a How to Teach Reading class, a Psychology class, and two practical application classes. These and the History of Teaching class made up the 15 units of lecture classes, and the semester of student teaching was the other 15 units. Of all of them, the practical application courses were the best, but I took something away from each of them.

I thought Student Psychology was a bit of a time filler. A black hair dyed woman taught this course. She talked too much about how her middle school kids loved her. We started off the month by watching the old two-colored version of *Lord of the Flies*. I'm still not sure what her point was in showing us this because she didn't say before or after to my recollection. I guess it was the whole children unattended would end up out of control theme that she was trying to show us.

I learned a term in this room that followed me through the rest of my career.

"You all have access to schools, right?" she asked us one day. Our responses ranged from nothing to a few nods. It was a late Thursday night, almost 9:30, and we all had worked all day and then rushed to National for this 5:30 to 9:30 class. This was our life every Tuesday and Thursday for five months. "I need you to find and report on an 'At-Risk' student. This should be a real student whom you know or have worked with. Do not use the real name of the student in the report."

"Where am I gonna find one of those?" I whispered to Amy.

She shrugged.

"There is a pretty good definition of an 'At-Risk' student in your text-book." She meant the one I hadn't opened yet on the third week of class. "Basically, an 'At-Risk' student is one who is 'At-Risk' of failing a class, an entire grade, and in the cases of older kids, dropping out of school. Part of what you'll be doing as a teacher is watching for the signs of an 'At-Risk' student and trying to catch her or him and save them before it is too late."

"I'm not gonna do that." I thought to myself. "If they don't want to learn and better themselves, oh well."

I wanted to be a teacher, so I had to do the assignment. I called my mom's friend, Jan, whose fourth-grade class had one kid who I thought fit the mold for 'At-Risk.' I figured I'd ask her. I was supposed to sub for her before the paper was due, and if the kid came to school that day, it would be a good day to watch him and take notes.

"Hi. Jan, it's Jim Kohl. I'm supposed to do a report on an 'At-Risk' kid. Is that a real term, or are they just giving me a new buzz word?"

"I've heard it."

"Cool, well you know that kid Anthony in your class? Do you think he's an 'At-Risk' kid?"

"Absolutely."

"Well, I'm supposed to watch him and decide why he's 'At-Risk' and see what I could do to help the situation so that he's no longer 'At-Risk.'"

Jan chuckled. "I think Anthony is a great choice, Jim. Let me know if you have any questions about him because I've been working really close with his family."

From doing the report on Anthony and listening to the other reports, I learned that kids are "At-Risk" for lots of reasons. Some don't like school. Some have families that would give the average person nightmares. Some eat at the beginning and middle of the month, but then they scrape for food until the check and food stamps come on the first.

I was glad I wasn't going to have too many of these sorts of kids in my career. I was getting a job at Cabrillo in Santa Clara. I had too many connections there not to get in.

At the end of the Psychology class, the hair-dyed woman said, "You're going to take the reading class next month. Remember this: Because of the current trend in teaching reading to kids, if you buy the *Hooked on Phonics* game, you will have a line of parents at the door of your room a mile long desperate for you to help their children."

"That was pretty cryptic," I muttered to no one. No one answered.

The Reading course began on the first Tuesday of the next month. The teacher had brown hair cut short to frame her aging face. It curled up at the bottom in the style of the early '60s, but it had lost the bounce it must have originally had. She was teaching/preaching to us the value of the "Whole Language" method of teaching reading.

"For years," she told us, "kids were taught to read by the drill and kill method called phonics. They learned the sounds of all the letters, and they learned how to 'sound out' words using the sounds of the letters."

Yes. This is how I learned to read. I've always loved reading.

"Kids hated this method."

Huh?!?

"It was boring to them. They lost the continuity of the story. If you have to stop and sound out every word, you don't get to follow the plot. You lose all the richness of literature."

So, then, how are they going to know what the words are?

"Instead of teaching them the sounds of the words and boring them with drill and kill methods," she paused as if in hopes of a reaction. A couple people smiled. "Have you guys heard that? You can't drill information into students' heads. All you will do is kill that information for them forever. Anyway…We don't teach the sounds of words anymore, we teach them sight words. We teach them the whole language rather than separate pieces of it. We save a step this way because the kids don't have to put the words back together. This process of teaching reading is called Whole Language."

I wasn't sure about this from the beginning, and as she continued to drill it into my head for the rest of the month, I doubted it more. She went on.

"Why do you guys read?" She asked us and was given the normal silence that comes with the first day of class. "C'mon, you guys do read right? Otherwise, you never would have made it this far in school."

"For fun," said Mark, the ex-bartender, who was always willing to be the first of us to speak. God bless him for it.

"That's right!" Evidently, this was the only correct answer. "Most adults who read on a regular basis read for fun. So why does reading have to start out as work? Why don't we make it fun from the very beginning? If you read good, quality, rich literature with kids, they will learn to read because they want to, not because they have to. I will show you how to model reading and writing so that your kids get the whole language at once."

It came down to handing all your students the same book. You read out of the book from the front of the room. They follow along in their seats. They are told that every time you say a word, they need to move their eyes to the next word. Once in a while, you stop and ask a kid what the next word is in the story. If they don't know, that means that they need more practice. More practice means more of what I described above.

On a video that we saw in this class, they made it look pretty good by using a book like *Green Eggs and Ham.* It has so many phrases that repeat that it can appear that a non-reader is a reader in this sort of situation. However, they may in fact be good at oral, rote memorization, but it looks like reading.

To teach writing using Whole Language, you write a paragraph sentence by sentence on the overhead projector. You take oral suggestions from the class as to what the next sentence should be. When you get one that makes sense, write it on the overhead projector and have all the kids copy it down. When you do this enough, they will learn to write. Don't be discouraged if some of your kids do not write or read, everyone develops at their own rate.

I listened to this for about three weeks, and I didn't believe a word of it. I figured I must be old fashioned, but what are you supposed to do, memorize the appearance of every word in the English language?

I raised my hand. I never do this because some of my biggest mistakes started out by raising my hand to talk in class.

"I'm not really sure that these techniques are going to work." I said after she called on me. "I don't see how every kid is going to memorize all the words necessary for competent reading by appearance just because I read them a good story. Phonics worked for me…"

"You're not going to make a very good teacher," she said. I looked at her in shock. Had that just come out of her mouth? "You're going to drill and kill reading for your kids if you try to use Pho…"

"How do you know what kind of teacher I'm going to be?!?!" This was the Columbus thing all over again. My face was heating up and reddening. This lady was going to take the pent up feelings I had for the Columbus lady too.

"You didn't let me finish…" She began again.

"Actually, you interrupted me first!" I was yelling.

"Jim...Let it go." Whispered Amy. I shot her a look telling her that I was not about to.

I had everyone's attention now. "I had a simple question, and you cut me off to tell me that I was not going to make a good teacher! I pay too much to this school to be spoken to in that way. I am the customer, and you are going to listen to me!"

"Okay, I'm sorry, I'm listening. What was your question?" She was speaking very softly now. I had been a stone silent student for weeks, and my first words to her were threatening at best.

"I don't wanna ask it now because you probably can't answer it anyway. Just go on with your class." I leaned back in my seat.

The room was silent for about a minute. She just stared at the floor. I did too.

"I think what Jim was trying to say..." This was Mark. He re-stated the question that I was getting to. God bless him again.

I never spoke in class again for the rest of the month, but at least I learned that Whole Language was a phrase to be avoided in my career in education.

The last two classes were technique classes. Both had the same instructor, and the two really blended into one. All the same people were there. These were the last classes before we went out to student teach. This was the last controlled environment we would ever see. We would be shipped off to various stations around the county to fight against ignorance and the dreaded apathy. These kids were raised by MTV, which assaulted them with new visual stimuli every 15 seconds. The challenge was to compete with this short attention span theater.

These technique classes aimed at preparing us for this very challenge. It was taught by a woman in her 40s that reminded me a bit of what Mama Cass would have looked like had she lived. She had brown hair with silver streaks in it. It went past her shoulders and had an out of control quality about it. She looked familiar the way a déjà vu does.

"Madeline Hunter. Know the name. She is the guru of modern teaching. She developed something called the five-step lesson plan." We all wrote it down. She went on and listed the steps necessary for the five-step lesson plan along with a definition of each step. We took careful notes in these steps. We memorized them. We cognitively tattooed them on the most easily accessed portion of our inner minds. We practiced them. We gave presentations in class using them. We were graded by how well we incorporated all the steps. Then, when we went out to student-teach and our eventual careers, we never thought about them again-not even once. The real world doesn't fit in a bag.

Regardless of that, the classes were the best ones in the program. We all taught concept lessons and how-to lessons. I taught how to make a paper airplane, and at the end of the lesson, I had them all throw their airplanes while playing sound effects from the movie *Top Gun*. We also learned how to make origami, bake cookies and, from Mark, the ex-bartender, we learned how to pour a shot of alcohol like professionals. The presentations were a blast, and we all built strong relationships with each other. I still couldn't figure out why this instructor looked so familiar.

The concept lesson was a lot more challenging. Instead of showing the steps to make something happen, we had to introduce and try to convey the essence of an abstract noun. "What is history?" is a topic that could work, but I did "What is punk rock?"

I pretended the class was being taught in the year 2084, and the class was 'The History of Popular Culture in the 1900s.' We were doing our unit on the '70s, and had reached the beginning of punk rock. Using music and video, I showed what it was about. Then I had them take a normal (I use the term loosely because I drew it) human face and turn it into a punk rocker using safety pins and pens and junk to paste on. I had fun, but could I have this much fun with kids and still have them learn something from the California Curriculum Guide?

Who was this teacher anyway? I know I know her!

During this unit we also learned what a rainforest was, what Chinese New Year is, and what an appropriate touch of a child is. John did this last one.

John always smelled like cigarettes, and he looked like a pile of ashes. His skin was browned, and his hair was like dry weeds about to ignite. His clothes seemed to have brown overtones as if everything he owned was coated with nicotine residue.

During his 'Appropriate Touch' lesson, he showed us a bunch of pictures. One of them had a man with his hand on top of a little boy's head. As a class, we were supposed to decide if the touching or action shown in the picture was appropriate or not. We all decided that a man could have his hand on top of a boy's head. Another picture showed a woman giving a baby a bath. We decided that this too is okay. Another picture showed a man giving a little boy a quarter. This was fine too, we said.

"You're wrong on all counts!" John announced to us with the snide tone of cynicism strong in his voice. "The man with his hand on the boy's head could be showing his domination over the boy. The woman giving the baby a bath may be having sexual feelings as she bathes the child. The man giving the boy the quarter could be giving it to him as a bribe to be quiet about what happened between them."

We stared at him. I thought I was a pretty paranoid person until this moment. I then realized that the word for me is cautious. I couldn't help but wonder if this guy suspected everyone of all sorts of things all the time. Why did he trust the cigarette companies?

Who was this teacher, anyway? I got my answer near the end of the course. She told us that she was the principal of a middle school in Alum Rock. She told us that her school had no gang activity. She told us about crews, but made it clear that her campus did not tolerate them. She told us she worked at Shepherd, the same school where I had spent my two Hell weeks as a sub. That's why I recognized her.

From this class, I took the four, wait was it five-well anyway, some number of steps lesson plan. I learned that some teachers are neurotically paranoid, and that some administrators are full of denial. That's every job, though, isn't it?

CHAPTER XIII

The red tape webbed thick across the path of my student teaching. All my friends from my classes got their assignments, and mine had not come through yet. I was allowed to choose the district I wanted to student teach in, so I chose Santa Clara hoping that they would place me with one of my friends at Cabrillo.

It was less than a week before I was supposed to start, and I had been calling National every day believing that if I nagged them enough, they would assign me somewhere. Finally, I got the call that I would be student teaching under a woman named Lynne in her fifth-grade class at a school called Haman. Since there are two assignments involved with student teaching, (you have to teach two different grade levels) it was still possible that I could be at Cabrillo for the second half. My supervisor would be a retired teacher named Dr. Martini.

"What's a supervisor again?" I guess I hadn't been listening at one of the meetings we had had.

"Your supervisor is a National University employee that will evaluate your progress as a teacher by watching you teach a lesson in the class that you're assigned to. He'll be calling you within a week."

I got directions to Haman from the woman on the phone and headed down San Tomas Expressway toward Homestead. I hoped Lynne was cool! School had been in session for a week, so she should still be at the school at 3 p.m. if she was any good at all. Oh man! Please don't stick me with the sort of nightmare woman whom I hated when I was in school. Please let me be able to relate to her on a personal and professional level. I need a friend and advisor, not a boss. As I drove to Haman for the first time that afternoon silently asking for these things, some-one was listening.

I arrived at the school and slanted my car into a parking space. I went to the office first because you're supposed to. All schools want visitors to check in at the office so they know that you are not a psycho before they allow you to be on campus. I guess they figure that psychos won't follow this request, so that way they will instantly know if a psycho is on campus.

The secretary took a few minutes to acknowledge me, but I was used to this by now.

"Can I help you?"

"My name is Jim Kohl, and I am supposed to start student teaching here tomorrow with Lynne." I had written down the name! Look how far I had come!

"Lynne is in room 21." She directed me to the room, and I went to face my future. If only she is sort of young! I can't do it with the old-fashioned ditto maker sort of teacher.

I walked into room 21 and found Lynne. She had thick long curly hair like a black lion's mane.

"Hi," she said to me, holding out the vowel sound longer than you usually do when you don't know someone.

"Hi, are you Lynne?" I couldn't look directly at her. I was looking all around the room shocked at this young Asian face that didn't match the Polish last name she had neatly written in perfect school-girl cursive on the green chalk board. The desks were arranged in groups. There was an Apple computer against the back wall, and an orange couch to the left of the chalkboard next to an overstuffed bookshelf. Lynne's desk was directly across from the front door of the classroom. The classroom also had a back door that was behind her desk.

"Yes." Her voice bubbled across the room and welcomed me in.

"I'm Jim Kohl, and I'm supposed to start student teaching with you tomorrow." What if she hadn't even heard I was coming?

"Oh great! So, you start tomorrow."

I nodded and smiled.

"Great! Well…This is a fifth-grade class. I have 33 kids. They're all very nice. They know you are coming, but we didn't know when."

"I didn't know either, or even where I was going, until about an hour ago."

"Isn't that always the way? Why bother actually telling the student teacher anything!"

"Yeah, I haven't been anxious to get started or anything!" This was going to be fine.

"I thought I would set you up here." She motioned to a student's desk that she had pushed up against the left side of her own. It was facing the front of the room. "Is this going to be okay?"

"Yeah!" I didn't think I'd have a work area at all.

"Tomorrow, I figured you could just come in and observe the day and meet the kids. Next week, you can start teaching things. How long are you supposed to solo teach?"

"A minimum of 10 days, I think."

"Okay. Those will probably be your last two weeks here. There's one thing I want you to be aware of before you start up tomorrow. I have a little girl this year named Liz. She has spinobiphida, which is a form of paralysis-she's in a wheel chair-that also affects her ability to reason. She really belongs in a special day class, but her mom insists on main-streaming her. We have an IEP for her just as if she were in a special ed class, and I will tell you basically how to handle her needs and what to expect from her as we go along."

"I remember hearing the term IEP in one of my classes, but I don't remember what it means."

"Individualized Education Plan."

"She probably thinks I'm an idiot now," I thought, "Why did I ask that?!" We talked more about Liz and about the class in general.

"Well, we're really looking forward to working with you, Jim."

"Me too. What time should I be here tomorrow?"

"I'm supposed to be here at 7:30, but I'm normally in about 7."

"Cool! I'll be here about 7 too."

We said goodbye, and I felt like I was leaving an old friend.

The next morning, I showed up at Haman with my shirt and tie on. On most campuses, you can tell the male student teachers and subs by their ties. The veteran staff hardly ever wears them, and some don't even wear button down shirts.

The schoolyard was quiet. It was a bit overcast for mid-September, and the custodian was the only soul in the play yard. He dragged a bundle of tetherballs behind him like bunch of heavy helium balloons. Their chains clinked as he fastened them each to their steel pole, and they swayed in waiting for the first child of the morning. I walked through the haze to room 21. Lynne was there.

"Hi!" She greeted me just as she did the day before. I felt like the most important person in the world walking into her room. "How do you feel?"

"I'm a little nervous."

"Oh don't worry about it, you'll do fine. You're just watching today." I actually calmed down a little.

"I have morning yard duty this morning out on the playground. You can either come with me, or stay here."

"I'll wait here if that's okay. I'll go out there tomorrow."

"That's fine! Go ahead and get accustomed to the room, and I'll be back in about a half hour with the kids."

So this was it. I took a seat at my desk and pictured what the kids would be like. I assured myself that they were probably nice. Lynne had said they were nice, and there wasn't any of the telltale graffiti that surrounds a school with a hostile environment. Besides, she would be in the room with me, so the chance of them throwing things at me was drastically reduced.

I walked around the room and read the names on the desks to try to get a feel for what the kids were like from them. "Roy, Valerie, Evelyn, Liz, Cody…" This was a pointless exercise, but I found myself doing it nonetheless. This wasn't the first time I'd been in a classroom, what was my problem? Why was I so jumpy? Why couldn't I untie my stomach?

This was the first time I'd been in a classroom where I felt like I had to impress someone. I always felt like I was a good teacher. People always told me I was a good teacher. People told me I would make a good teacher long before I ever dreamed of getting this far. What if I sucked?

Lynne walked her kids in and sat them down with a morning math exercise. "This way, I can take roll." She whispered to me. I nodded. They worked in complete silence for about 10 minutes, and then Lynne went over all the answers to the morning math. After this, she introduced me to the class, and they all stared at me to figure out what I was about just like I had done with their names. They were right though, of course, in whatever their first impression was.

"Mr. Kohl has been waiting in this room for like 50 years while we were all out at recess." Their hands all went up. "Oh that's right, that was an exaggeration wasn't it." This was a game they all played that I didn't know the rules to yet. They were supposed to point out all of her exaggerations by raising their hands.

I sat and watched the whole school day from that desk next to Lynne's. She was really good. She was a hard act to follow. The kids loved her. She could quiet them with a look. Her enthusiasm for them and for the subject matter boiled the room. I don't remember what she taught that day, but I know I learned a lot about teaching. She would be perfect for me.

Lynne slowly gave me control of the room. I started by teaching math to them because it was the easiest to teach. Stay one page ahead of the kids in the book, and you have it. There is no discussion about whether an answer is correct or not. Two plus two is four. In literature, two plus two is four, unless I can show you some good reasons in the text why it's five. New teachers freak out at the possibility that their students might have a better opinion. New teachers, myself included, would rather teach math all day.

Lynne mothered me through my entire time with her. She gave me lessons to teach. She encouraged me on a daily basis. She was always in the room to support me. I felt like we were really working for the same goal. She wasn't an authority figure, she was a mentor.

She let me make mistakes and later we talked about how to avoid those mistakes. Each time I taught a lesson, we would debrief the good and the bad of what had just happened. I learned quickly not to let the board clutter up during a lesson. Erase things that you are not using anymore. The less on the board, the more the kids will understand. Too much on the board is sensory overload for many of them. I also quickly learned that when you teach adjectives, and it's time for them to practice using them, don't let them orally describe each other. They are not as nice as you are, and you are the one to blame for the hurt feelings you caused.

"You guys are all being rude!" I told them after the third person used the adjective stupid to describe one of their classmates. All their hands went up. "Evelyn?" I said, pointing to her.

"That was an exaggeration, Mr. Kohl. Some of us didn't say nothing."

"True." What else could I say? "And it's anything."

"Anything." She repeated.

Later, Lynne and I talked about this. My heart pulsed with failure, how could I be so stupid?

"What would you have changed about that one?" Lynne asked me without even looking at me.

"I should have had them describe something else."

She nodded.

About two weeks into student teaching, Dr. Martini, my supervisor, called me.

"Jim!?" His tone was that of someone I had known for years, but I had never talked to him before in my life. It was the same tone that military recruiters use when they call to talk to high school boys about to graduate.

"Yeah." What's this guy selling?

"This is Dr. Martini. I'm your supervisor for student teaching, and I need to set up an appointment to come out and watch you teach."

"A full day?" I hoped not. I couldn't believe someone would come and watch me for a full day.

"No, no," he was laughing, "I just want to see one lesson. You know, about a half hour."

I made the arrangements to have him come in and watch a math lesson. I had taken over a couple of subjects by this time, but I still felt most comfortable with math because I had been doing it the longest with these kids. He needed me to write up a five- step lesson plan for him. This was so that he could see that I could, and that I knew what it was. "After this time, just give me an informal outline of what you are planning."

He would be coming in the morning. Lynne helped me plan my entire lesson. I couldn't believe the stress I was under. What other job involves someone coming and watching to make sure you are doing it correctly? What is correctly, really?

The ceiling of Lynne's classroom was shaped like a lightening bolt lying on its side. There was a section of the ceiling that was about two feet in measurement that was at a right angle to the floor. This part of the ceiling had windows in it. There were curtains that you could close if you needed to darken the room. At first I thought that was a cool design, but I quickly learned to hate those windows.

The morning Dr. Martini came into Lynne's classroom to watch me teach I could not calm down. My hands shook as I handed him my lesson plan. This had to go well. This was my career on the line. This was to keep me away from a cubicle. This was everything I had been working toward for the past two years. I could blow it all in one minute. At least I was not teaching adjectives.

The bell rang. I was on. Dr. Martini sat in the back of the room and smiled at me when I looked at him. I called for the class's attention. They had just shown up for the morning. I got them going on the morning math problems that I had written on the board in the closest approximation to a teachers printing that I could do. I took roll.

"Mr. Kohl." Said Rachel.

"Just a minute, Rachel." That's all I needed was for some of these kids to get out of control. I had to stop any calling out right now before they continued talking when they shouldn't. I could get kicked out of the program if it seems like I have no control.

"But…Mr. Kohl." I shot her the meanest look I could summon. She looked scared. Good! She didn't want me mad. That's a sign of respect. I noticed her blue eyes were looking up at the windows in the middle of the ceiling. She pointed.

"Mr. Kohl." Now it was Roy!

"Roy, you know you need to work on the warm up problems and not talk, please."

"But." I shot him my look too. His whole table was pointing up.

I looked at the window and wished I could die. There was a porn magazine pressed up against the window opened to a picture that someone must have liked very much. I know only that the woman in the picture was a true redhead, and that the guy in the picture made me feel like half a man. I had a room full of fifth graders. I could picture the lawsuits. I could smell the end of my teaching career. I could already hear the news sound byte: "Do porno mags make good visual aids for grade school kids? Film at 11." Dr. Martini and Lynne could not see these windows from the side of the room they were sitting on.

I reached up in what seemed like slow motion to me. I grabbed the curtain pull string. I walked with my arm stretched up pulling the curtain over the poor redhead and restoring her modesty. I'm sure some of the kids felt like the best moment of their life was over. To Lynne and Dr. Martini, it looked like I was just closing the curtains.

I didn't look at the kids that pointed this out to me for the rest of the lesson. I taught the lesson, but I don't remember any of it. I seemed to be on auto-pilot at this point. It must have gone okay because I wasn't thrown out of the program. I never heard of the kids talking of this again.

"Why did you close the curtains?" Lynne asked when Dr. Martini was gone. I told her. "I'll call the custodian," she said.

CHAPTER XIV

"Lynne, I'm supposed to go to a staff meeting at some point during my time here. When do you guys have them?" I had been there a few weeks and hadn't been to one yet. My question wasn't exactly an innocent one because I had heard Lynne tell another teacher, 'I want to keep Jim away from staff meetings for as long as I can.'

"Oh, we have staff meetings every Wednesday morning from 7:30 until 8. You can come with me to the next one if you want, but just remember that anything you see there is not as important as the kids."

"Okay."

She and I went into the meeting that Wednesday morning. We took a seat around the circle of tables. When the meeting started, they were all speaking vaguely about something that had happened. From what I could gather, the staff was divided right down the middle on some unnamed issue.

"What we need to do, in my opinion," started one woman, "is…" tears swelled in her eyes and rolled out on her cheek, "move on from this and start treating each other good again." Her voice was a whisper by the end of her sentence. I looked around the room. No one was looking at anyone. I had been to staff meetings at Cabrillo and had seen members of that staff bicker, but I had never seen anything like this. They all seemed like such nice people that loved their jobs and their school. They were all so enthusiastic on the yard and with their students, but they all hated at least half the staff. Teaching is a form of theater. The show must go on because if it doesn't, neither does our future.

"Geez, that was pretty heavy Lynne," I said on the way back to our room.

"That's nothing you need to worry about. There are some people that don't agree on one particular issue here on campus, but it's best not to be involved. Wherever you're hired later, there will probably be similar situations. It's not always easy to separate yourself, but remember that you are there for the kids. The rest is crap." Crap was the worst word I ever heard Lynne use while we worked together. This was the only time she said it.

Lynne sheltered me from the politics that were shattering her school while I was learning to teach in it. She never had an unkind word to say about any faculty member, and she had me believing that I was teaching in a utopia the way a mother can make her child feel like the world is one. "It's sort of a trip, Lynne," I told her, "I had no idea things were so chaotic, and here I am getting a credential. You can be successful in the classroom no matter what is going on in the school or district. You just have to do your job and worry about *your* kids."

"Don't ever forget that," she said.

My time with Lynne ended in late November, and I needed to be placed somewhere new. I ended up in the same school with another young teacher named Diane. She taught right across the hall from Lynne. Lynne reminded me that she would be nearby if I ever needed her. I thanked her and walked across the hall to teach a second and third grade combination class.

Diane welcomed me to her room, "Lynne has said some nice things about you!"

"She's very nice." I didn't want to seem stuck up.

Diane set me up with a table to the right of her desk. The room had a couch, bookshelf, and lots of student work on the walls. There were bulletin boards with art projects on them. Fall leaves and turkeys were carefully pasted together and on display on a wire that ran diagonally across the classroom. Their desks were small, and Diane had them arranged in a "U" shape so that there was a wide-open area in the middle of the room that you could use when you taught.

"When the kids come in, I'll start them off, and I was hoping you could teach math at about ten this morning." This sort of threw me back. You mean I'm not going to watch all day?

She showed me the page they had for homework that night. I had a couple hours to prepare. I would be fine. Then I remembered that this was a second and third grade combination class. "Is this math lesson for the second or third graders?"

"Oh, I teach everyone the same concepts, and they all work mainly out of the third-grade book. Occasionally, I'll run off some stuff from the second-grade book if I think it shows the concepts better. Second and third-grade math really isn't that different as far as curriculum."

"What about next year when these second graders have to work out of the third grade book again?"

She put her hand in the air and wrinkled her face. "Do you like coffee?" she asked.

"Yeah." Actually, "like" is too weak of a verb for my relationship with coffee.

"Come with me."

We walked down the hall to Al's room. Al taught special education and did not believe the adage that special education classrooms had to be plain in order to help the kids focus. He had more stuff on the walls than any teacher I have seen to this day. Every spot on the wall was covered with some sort of poster. Every piece of metal was covered with some sort of magnet. The colors in the room were so mismatched and motley that your eyes kept moving. You could never see it all. It looked like a thrift store had exploded all over the walls.

"It keeps their brains up and active, I think," said Al. He was an older man with little hair left and a short Santa Claus beard. He had coffee for us every morning. It was a great way to start out the day. The caramel-chocolate smell of coffee filled the room and made the place feel like the warmest diner there ever was. Different teachers came in and out. I wondered why Lynne never came over here.

Al had an aid with a prosthetic arm named Rachel.

"Rachel, can I go to use the bathroom?" It was a little boy in a green sweat outfit.

"Go ahead. Class hasn't even started yet, but don't play with your wiener." He walked away, and she grumbled to herself, "All these boys want to do is play with their wieners."

"So, your Lynne's boy, huh?" asked Al with more volume than necessary. He always spoke that way.

"Yeah."

"Uh huh." He answered me. "Well, welcome to the other side."

"Thanks." This was obviously the faction that disagreed with Lynne's faction. I didn't even know that Lynne had a faction. I could hear her in my head telling me not to concern myself with this "crap." I'm here for the kids. Besides, if I start a fight with these guys, I'll not only blow the second half of my student teaching; I might not be allowed to have coffee anymore!

The bell rang and told us that we had five minutes until school started. "We better go get them. Thanks for the coffee, Al." Diane said.

"Yeah, thanks, man." I added.

"See you guys later." He said.

Diane's kids lined up right out in front of her door. There was a boys' line and a girls' line. They were all about six inches shorter than the average fifth grader, so I felt like a giant at five feet nine inches. I went to my table near the front of the room, and Diane led them in. They all took their chairs down from on top of their desks. She had them go through a stretching ritual that, I think, was really more cute than useful, but they were used to it and they demanded that it not be skipped the time I tried.

After their stretches, two of them gave each other warm fuzzies that were compliments accompanied by a literal fuzzball that the recipient got to keep on his or her desk until it was time to give warm fuzzies the next school morning.

"What a gimmick! You won't catch me dead doing that!" I thought until I got one from a little girl named Jessica C. one day and my mind changed forever.

Diane introduced me. They all looked at me. Some of them smiled. "He's going to teach you math today." Some of them clapped. Little kids love teachers. What happens to us?

I sat and watched Diane teach for an hour. Recess came and went faster than it did when I was young, and it was math time. I was up. "I'm going down to the office. See ya later." I looked in time to see Diane's back disappear through the door.

"She's not even going to watch me!" I thought, "How is she going to know what I'm like? What if I'm a serial killer or something?" I looked out at the 60 tiny eyes looking at me. "What if one of them is?"

I dove into the lesson. "I need to talk slow." I told myself, "I should make no sudden movements. One of them could flip out at any time." It was math-better still-it was easy math!

After the lesson, I set them to work. The room was grave quiet. I monitored the room and answered the occasional question. They all whispered their questions to me when I got to their desks. "Where's the tens place again?" asked Holly. I pointed.

"What numbers mean round up?" Jonathan asked. I told him.

"What is the name of this place again?" asked Steven.

"School." I'm such a jerk.

"Huh?" He wrinkled his whole face at me. I could see that this kid had made a fortune recently from the tooth fairy. "Oh," he smiled, which I wasn't ready for, "I get it Mithter Kohl! But I mean which place in the numbers."

"Hundreds."

"Thankth."

"Anytime, Steven." That kid's all right.

A few minutes later, I saw Steven tap the girl next to him, Jessica C, on the shoulder. She turned her head to look at him. He said something I couldn't hear. She reached into her desk, pulled out an eraser, and handed it to him. He rubbed it furiously on his paper. He handed it back to her.

Two minutes later, he tapped her again. She turned her head more sharply this time. He said something to her. She rolled her eyes, reached into her desk, yanked out the eraser, and tossed it onto his desk. He picked it up, frowned at it, rubbed it furiously on his paper, and handed it back to her. She left it out this time.

Less than five minutes later, Steven tapped Jessica C. on the shoulder. She turned violently toward him and exhaled loud enough to be heard across the room. He said something to her. She jammed her hand into her desk and pulled out a pair of silver scissors. She grabbed the eraser, cut it in half, and slammed half of it on Steven's desk. He picked it up and held it between his fingers, staring at it suspiciously. He rubbed it furiously on his paper.

"Thankth." He told her.

"What other job includes this show?" I asked myself.

When it was time for the next recess, Diane came back into the room. "How was it?" she asked.

"Very funny-these kids crack me up!"

"They do?"

"Yeah, have you ever just sat and watched Steven? The guy is a show, and he doesn't even know anyone is watching."

"I was down at the office making phone calls."

"That's cool."

"I'm so glad you're here, because I'm getting married this summer and this is giving me a chance to make the phone calls and the arrangements."

"Oh, wow, congratulations." I was glad I had Lynne first. Lynne had mothered me through our time together, and Diane was leaving me on someone's porch in a basket.

CHAPTER XV

After I taught all day, I had to work in order to pay for the right to student teach. Student teaching is considered a class, so even though you are doing the job like a professional, you pay to do it.

I had an after school job at the Kor-Am Learning Center. Yoon ran it, and it was essentially a tutoring service that specialized in Korean American children. The classes were small, and the pay was great.

One of the students I worked with there was Sammy. He was Yoon's son, and he hated school. He was having a hard time learning to read. He was 6, and he was in the first grade. His imagination was wonderful, his energy intense, and he could be the biggest pain in the butt that ever walked the Earth. I was crazy about him.

"So what's going on in your reading class at school, Sammy?"

He stared at me deadpan with his little buzz-cut hair standing black and straight on top of his head. His eyes were just bigger than slits. His lips were shut and motionless. This makes it a little hard to get to know a kid, but at the same time, he was showing me quite a bit about himself. Forget the small talk that I usually start lessons with. I'm getting right down to business with this kid.

"Sammy, I have three books here. I'd like you to read to me whatever you can." One of the books was *One Fish, Two Fish, Red Fish, Blue Fish*, and the other two were harder to read.

He still stared at me.

"Which book do you want to read from?"

No change.

"All right, well, I want you to try this one." I chose the one that was in the middle of the three books level wise. I opened it. Sammy stared at me. He looked down at the book, but then his poker face went back to burning a whole through my entire head. "Look, Sammy, I'm not here to mess around. Read this book to me."

He smiled.

"What?" Maybe he would at least tell me what was funny.

"You're face gets red when you're mad." It was the most matter of fact tone I had ever heard. "And your jacket looks like a space man's." He giggled.

"That's cool." This was a start. "Can you read to me from this book?"

"No."

"Why?"

"It's too hard. I don't know the words to that book."

"Can you sound out the words for me?"

He wrinkled his forehead-the international sign for "What the heck are you talking about?"

"What happens when you guys read at school, Sammy?"

"We don't read. The teacher reads."

"What do you guys do?"

"We look at the book."

"Which book?"

"One like the teacher's except soft." The patience had left his tone, and he looked at me knowing that I was an idiot.

"So you guys all read along…"

"I can't read."

"Yeah, but the teacher tells you to read along, and you just sit there looking at the book?"

"Yes." I thanked him silently for not saying "DUH!" to me. Sammy was in a Whole Language classroom, and it wasn't working for him. He needed phonics. I was never trained in teaching phonics, but I knew them from when I was a kid. I was going to teach this kid phonics even though it had gone out of style. So had a lot of '60s rock, but I listened to it everyday.

I worked with him for a couple of weeks and saw huge improvements in his reading. He was responding to phonics even though he was supposed to be bored by them, according to the latest research.

One day when I came in to work with Sammy, Yoon, who was his mother and my boss, was crying. I asked her what was wrong.

"I just got off the phone with Sammy's teacher." She had a thick Korean accent, so I had to listen to her very carefully and watch her lips while she spoke. She gasped for breath between sobs. Her eyes were red. "She said she thinks Sammy should be tested for special education."

I looked at her. I knew what was coming. I already had seen this enough to anticipate the next question.

"Do you think she is right?" There it was right on schedule.

"I haven't worked a lot with special education kids, but he doesn't strike me as that sort." I gave my honest opinion, but what did I know about this stuff? "I do know that they have to test him before they can determine that. They can't just stick him in a special education class without doing this."

"He gets in so much trouble at school. He's a good boy, isn't he?" She was still crying.

I thought of the little girl that worked with Sammy and me on Saturday. This was the only day that he had to share me. He had tormented her despite what I tried to do to stop him until she cried and refused to work with him anymore. He was a relentless monster sometimes.

Yoon was still crying. There was no way I was going to squeeze more tears out of those eyes. "I don't have a problem with him. It sounds like this teacher is trying to dump off a behavior problem on the special ed department at her school."

"Will you write him a letter that says you don't think he needs to be in special ed?" I was a real teacher to Yoon. I was not a real teacher to the

State of California because I didn't have my credential yet. Any letter I wrote would be laughed off the principal's desk and into the toilet.

"Sure." This would not be the last time that I was comforting an upset parent. I didn't believe he was a candidate for special education, but part of me just wanted her tears to stop.

"You know if he is a special education student," her eyes flooded again, "it's because of me. I made mistakes as a mother." I never considered the reality that Yoon lived under; a special education student would bring shame to her and her family.

"No Yoon, if he's special ed, it's because he is. It's no one's fault-but he's not, anyway." I hoped.

I wrote the letter. I never heard from the school, but I can imagine what they must have thought considering I was a student teacher. The sort of student teacher that probably thought he knew everything. I was the sort of thing they hated more than anything-a young know it all.

I worked with Sammy longer than he really needed me to. I watched him struggle through the sounds in Dr. Seuss books when we first started, and I was there when he could read *Curious George* all by himself and laugh at the funny parts. I taught this kid to read. I made a reader out of him. No matter what else happens to me the rest of my life, I taught a kid to read from scratch. Do it sometime-it feels great!

Sammy's teacher sent a note home to Yoon after I had been working with him for four months. She said that his reading skills were improving and that her class was finally starting to work for him. He was behaving better too. She guessed he just needed more time with the approach she was taking to reading than the others did. Yoon showed me the note and thanked me.

CHAPTER XVI

The time in Diane's room continued much the same as before. By the second week in her room, I was doing the whole day. By the third week, I was planning every lesson for the whole day. She would plan her wedding while I did her job for free. We would go to Al's for coffee. I would go to Lynne when I felt overwhelmed. Dr. Martini would pop in and out to observe me. No more pornographic episodes occurred while he was there. Diane would watch me at least once or twice a day. I was a teacher.

The kids and I got very close very quickly, and I knew it would be hard to leave them when the time came in January. While the school provided me with hours of experience, Steven and Jessica C. provided me with hours of entertainment.

I learned about centers in this room. Centers are a group of activities that each deal with a separate curriculum. You set them up in a specified area of the room. One center may have the students working on a math skill, one has an art project, one has a tape to listen to and read along with etc. They stay in each center for half an hour, and at the end of that time, they move to another center. It's a great way to fill a day. We did it once a week in that class. Whatever center activity they don't finish becomes homework for the night and/or work to do when there is "nothing to do." The teacher just walks around from center to center to make sure the students are focused.

The room hums while they work on centers. They talk, but most of the talk is the sort that accompanies learning. There is no screaming or yelling. If there is, it is quickly found and corrected. Once, above the hum of conversation, I heard the glassy strains of a young girl's singing voice. I followed the sound.

"You are my sunshine, my only sunshine. You make me ha-py…"

Where was it coming from? I had to find it and return the room to the productive hum before things got out of hand.

"When skies are gray. You'll never know dear…"

My head swung from group to group to see if I could put my eye on the young diva.

"How much I love you…"

I couldn't find her.

"Mr. Kohl." The voice was meek and came from my back. "Mr. Kohl…" I turned around. It was Patrick, a shy, round blond boy.

"What is it Patrick?"

"Jessica C. won't stop singing."

"What do you mean she won't stop singing?" What a stupid question that must have seemed! How much clearer could he explain it?

"Please don't take my sunshine a-way. You are my sunshine…"

"She's over there, and she won't stop singing." He pointed to the art center, where, sure enough, I could see Jessica C.'s mouth moving in time to the tune that seemed a permanent part of my thoughts at this point. Patrick followed me back to the art center.

"You make me ha-py, when skies are gray…"

"What are you doing, Jessica?" I asked. My eyebrows were raised because I wasn't sure if I should seem stern or not.

"You'll never know dear…" She looked up at me with her brown eyes and stopped her song for a couple of beats. "I told Patrick, that I was going to sing until he shared his crayons with me." With that her eyes returned to her work, and her heart raised again in her anthem. "How much I love you. Please don't take…"

"Make her stop, Mr. Kohl!" Patrick had his hands slammed on his ears and his face reddened.

No one in teacher school, even in that amazingly helpful Psychology class, ever prepared me for this particular form of protest. She was doing her work. The song was appropriate for the classroom. Just because Patrick didn't delight in her young soprano tones did not mean that she had to stop. It was Center time, so she was not required to be silent.

"…my sunshine a-way. You are my sunshine, my only sunshine…"

"Why don't you just use your own crayons?" I suggested.

"You make me ha-py…" She stopped again and looked up at me in the same way as before. "I need a blue-green crayon. My crayons don't have that color. Patrick has one." She went back to cutting out her art project pieces. "…when skies are gray. You'll ne-ver know…"

"Patrick! Just let her use the crayon before it's too late!" Jonathan had had enough and was jamming his fingers in his ears and squashing up his face in agony.

"Yeah, Patrick," I offered, "why don't you just let her use the crayons?"

"I don't want to," said Patrick.

"Why not?" I couldn't believe this. We complicate our own lives, don't we?

He just shrugged.

"Well," I said after I made one of those split-second decisions that become second nature to teachers, "you don't have to Patrick. They are your crayons. But, Jessica C. is allowed to keep singing if she wants to. There is not really a rule against it because she is not too loud and she is doing her work." I walked away.

"…dear, how much I love you. Please don't take my sunshine a-way."

"Patrick!" Jonathan yelled.

"Not so loud, Jonathan." I corrected without turning my head back to them.

"You are my sunshine, my only sunshine…"

"Here," said Patrick.

"Oh! Thank you Patrick!" chirped Jessica C. and the serenade ended. Peer pressure is often the best teaching method. It taught Patrick to share.

Steven had a problem with tattling. There was no event too small to report for this kid. He told on Patrick for "stealing" his pencil. He told on Anthony for "only pretending to read and not really reading" at the reading center. He told on Anthony again for "calling him the 'A-word'" after he told on Anthony for the reading thing.

"Now Steven," I finally told him after the 20th tale I heard on one Wednesday. "Pretty soon, none of the kids are going to like you if you keep on telling on everyone all the time. The only time you need to tell on someone is if they hurt you on purpose. Do you understand what I mean?"

"Yeth, Mithter Kohl." He looked down at the ground.

This put an end to Steven's tattling for about an hour. I reminded him each time that tattling is not a good idea unless someone hurts you on purpose. Each time he agreed that I was right. I, after all, was "Mithter Kohl." How much more right could you be?

One cool, misty morning, I was standing out on the blacktop of the playground on yard duty. This had become second nature, and I laughed when I thought of my apprehension about yard duty when I had that first day with Lynne. It seemed like a lifetime ago and it had only been a month. I surveyed the yard and saw all the kids playing Chinese jump rope, chasing each other, flipping around on the monkey bars. Some of Lynne's fifth graders would yell, "Hi, Mr. Kohl!" and I would wave back. Christmas was coming, and there was no more exciting time to be with 30 little kids who still knew Santa Claus was real. I should try to sneak down to Al's room…

"Mithter Kohl!! Mithter Kohl!" I didn't even have to look, but I did. There was Steven running up to me with his 49ers jacket and hat. He kept running towards me until he was about an inch and a half away. He looked way up at my face to make sure he had my attention.

"How's it going, Steven?"

"Fine." He panted. "Mithter Kohl…" he let out about 16 little breaths and tried to regain his normal breathing pattern. "Mithter Kohl…"

"Yes."

"Mithter Kohl, Timothy took hith bike, and he…"

"Now, now, Steven." I held up one finger in front of his little brown face. His huge eyes were bulging full of whatever he had to tell me, but I had to stop his tattling. "This sounds like you're going to tell on someone. Did this person hurt you on purpose?" Timothy may have; he was the problem child of the class. You could tell he didn't get enough attention at home by how needy he was. He acted out a lot and got in a lot of fights, especially for a third grader.

"No," Steven moaned. He looked at the ground again. I needed to pick up those crushed spirits in some other way than letting him tattle again. "Thorry, Mithter Kohl."

"That's cool! You made the right decision, and I'm proud of you." He still looked down. "Did you see the 49er game last night?"

"Yeah! Jerry Rithe is the greatest! Steve Young is great too!"

"Young's not as cool as Montana though." This was before Young's Super Bowl, and I wanted to teach the children correctly.

"No one is as cool as Montana." The bell rang, and Steven told me he had to go and ran off. A minute later, I was letting him and the other students into the room. As I took roll, I noticed that Timothy was not there.

"All right," I said, "Let's start your morning stretches." They all got up out of their seats as Diane walked in with a cup of coffee for me. "Okay. Stretch all the way down to the ground." I modeled this behavior for them, and they all followed along. "Now stretch up and see if you can touch that ceiling. All right good job."

The intercom buzzed on the wall. In those days, teachers didn't have phones in the room. There was a phone-shaped object that was used like a phone but sounded more like two tin cans with a wire pulled tight between them. This is how the office contacted a teacher, and for a teacher to contact the office, we had to pick up the intercom and wait while it buzzed dead in our ear. After a minute or two of this, we would send a kid down to the office to ask them to pick up their end. On this morning when our end buzzed, Diane motioned to me that she would pick up the intercom, so I continued with the morning lesson.

"All right, who has a warm fuzzy to give out?" Hands went up. Jessica R. gave one to Tammy who had given one to her the day before. Jonathan gave one to Patrick. Michael gave one to Robert. One of them was missing. "Well, we'll find it later." We lost at least one warm fuzzy a week. "Tomorrow, if you are a boy, I want you to think of a girl that you can give a warm fuzzy to, and if you're a girl, I want you to give it to a boy."

"Mr. Kohl!!" They all said, sure that what I suggested was pure madness.

"If you really have a problem with it, you can come and talk to me later."

Diane walked up to me at the front of the room. "Timothy is missing," she whispered to me.

"Yeah, I know I marked him absent."

"No I mean, he's not here and he's not at home either."

The school called the homes of absent kids to make sure that everything was okay. A kid like Timothy would be one of the first homes called because of his history of getting in trouble. I pictured his picture on flyers all over town. I pictured the Find Timothy headquarters being shown on the 6 o'clock news. Then I remembered. I looked around the room and saw Steven sitting at his desk, rolling a pencil back and forth across the top of it. I walked over there.

"Steven." He looked up at me immediately. "What was that you were starting to tell me about Timothy this morning?" So much for not tattling-go ahead kid, tell me everything you know.

Steven looked at me blank for a second. "Oh yeah! Timothy got on his bike, called the other teacher a 'B-word' and rode away."

"Which way did he go?"

"To his house. I told him 'Where are you going?' and he just kept riding and said nothin'. But he was going home, I think. Yeah. I think he was going home."

"Why did he say that to the other teacher?" In this job you become a master of talking about profanity without using profanity.

"She was mad at his panth."

"What?"

"She said his panth was too loose and he said no. She said yeth. He said no they're not and then the B-word. Then he got on his bike and rode away."

I relayed most of this to Diane, who picked up the intercom and then walked down to the office to tell them what we knew. They called the house. By then, Timothy was there with his big brother who had decided, along with Timothy, that Timothy had had plenty of school for this particular day. "They let that kid get away with murder," said Diane.

"How come you wanted me to tattle on Timothy after all?" asked Steven.

"We thought he might be lost."

"He wasn't lost." His face crumpled in intense cynicism, "He was on his bike."

"I guess you're right, man."

My time as a student teacher was ending. Diane had given me enough feedback toward the end as her wedding fell into place. She made a huge list of all that I had accomplished in her room and all the things that I did well as a teacher. Dr. Martini, Lynne, Diane, and Haman's principal, Dave, wrote me shining letters of recommendation that I would be shoving into envelope after envelope in the coming months.

Diane and I walked across the play yard to the office near the end of my student teaching.

"Where are you planning on applying?" she asked.

"All over the place, but I really like this district because it has always been good to me as a substitute teacher. Plus, I know a lot of people that work in this district, so it feels like home."

"That's cool."

"It'll be nice to have a job. I have that Kor-Am Learning Center thing going on, but it doesn't pay enough to really do anything for me."

"Well, wait till you get your first teaching check and you can't believe how fast the money is gone."

"She's wrong," I told myself. "It's just because she's getting married that she's hurting for money so bad. How can she not be happy with the fact that she has kids like Steven and Jessica C. to hang out with? She probably lost her calling because I'm never going to need more money. I don't even have a girlfriend and I don't see one in my near future. I'll be fine. Money's for scums."

She held the office door for me, and we made some copies.

Two more weeks in Diane's room found me solo teaching and left my head spinning. After that, there were some goodbye parties and well wishes. Each student drew me a picture. Steven brought me a picture he drew of a big brown fish with a red shirt on. "Hey, this is a great picture Steven! What do you call it?" I've found that this is a much better question than "what is it?" because it implies that you do recognize what the attempted image is. It also gives you time to teach that all works of art have names.

"Oh, that ith what Jerry Rithe would look like if he wath a fish." Of course, Steven, what else would it be?

So I left Haman that day. Jessica C. would not let go of my hand until she had to. I had finished the credential program! Now I just needed to take another trip to the county office of education, bring them another cashier's check, and wait for my credential to show up in the mail. While

I waited, I would start applying to districts and hope that Santa Clara hired me. It all sounded so set, but lots of teachers didn't get hired. There were tons of applicants in those days.

CHAPTER XVII

After I left Haman, I went back to subbing. I lucked into a job as a long-term sub at Cabrillo once again. My friend, Tracy, was ending the teaching year early to go on maternity leave. I would have her class from March until June. She had a sixth-grade English and Social Studies class.

"That's great!" said my sister, Diane, who was still in college. "They'll probably just want to keep you around if they have any openings."

"Yeah." I could only dream. Cabrillo was the school I wanted to work for. They had small disagreements among the staff, but at least I already knew the problems that they had. My grandpa used to say that the devil you know is better than the one you don't.

I kept my job at the Kor-Am Learning Center until one day in late February when I showed up for work and the door was locked. I waited around and read a book in my car to see if anyone would show up. I worried that maybe Yoon had had a car accident or something. I called the center from a pay phone in the parking lot. The machine picked up.

"Hi, Yoon, it's me, Jim. I'm here for work, but the door is locked and I don't see any students showing up or anything. Give a me a call later and let me know what's going on."

I never heard from her again.

I applied to the Santa Clara Unified School District exclusively at first so that they could have the first shot at me.

"You're putting all your eggs in one basket," Mom advised.

"They're my favorite, but I'll apply to other people starting in June."

"Okay." My mom's "okay" had a way of hanging in the air like a bad omen.

I worked hard at Cabrillo for the rest of the school year, pretending it was my real job. I took a group of kids on a field trip all by myself, We went roller skating. Well, they did; I went Coke drinking.

June came around and Santa Clara called me in for an interview.

"See!" said Diane when I told her the news, "You're already in one of their schools, so if they have openings, I'm sure they'll pick you up. Don't you think?"

"I hope so."

School had not let out for the year yet, so I had to call for a substitute in order to go to the interview. I decided I would go to work for half the day and have a sub cover the other half. In those days, I taught in jeans and a button down shirt with no tie. I had my suit in my car. I would find a place to change on the way over.

I released the kids to lunch. "I will see you tomorrow. You will have a sub after lunch." They cheered and ran out. One stayed behind. There was always one kid lagging when you really need to get out of the room.

"You're going to leave us?" asked Mayra. She heard me telling one of the other teachers about my interview. Mayra was truly my student because she had never known Tracy; she joined our class after Tracy had left.

"I'm hoping this interview will actually let me stay. You see, I'm temporary. I'm only here because the real teacher left to have a baby."

"To me, you are the real teacher. You're the best teacher I ever had." This always melts me.

"Thanks. I've really liked working with you too." We walked out of the room together and I headed for that gray CRX in the parking lot. My suit was freshly dry cleaned in its plastic bag and lying in that cargo space in the back of that two-seater. My resume sat on the passenger seat in yet another manila folder. This time, my resume had a new look and attitude. Lynne had helped me re-shape the whole thing. It was her creation, and it looked like hers, and it was going to work.

I drove out of the lot and turned on the radio. My palms were starting to slip around the wheel already. I had been waiting and working my entire life for this interview. I turned on the radio, but every song they played bugged me so I turned it back off.

On Homestead, not too far from Haman, there was a Taco Bell. I headed there and changed into my suit and tie in their bathroom. I shoved my casual clothes into a gray duffel bag, and thought about the time I had changed clothes in this very bathroom after a day's work at Haman on the way to a Grateful Dead concert. Now I was dressed to start my professional life.

I pulled into the full lot at Santa Clara's District Office and circled around while the sweat beaded beneath my hairline. I would have to park on the street.

The heat slapped me as I stepped out of my car and headed toward the front door. "So that's it." I thought, "It either has to be pouring rain or a heat record whenever I put this suit on." I had my manila folder and resume under my arm. No one ever asked to see my resume, but at least this way, I feel like I have something to carry in.

I exhaled hard and long. This was it. This is the interview of my life. My guts wrenched and twisted at the notion that if I blew this, my world would end. "I belong in the Santa Clara District." I whispered to myself as I grabbed for the door handle. "I hope." I thought as I entered.

"Are you here for the interview?" asked the receptionist.

"Yes. I'm Jim Kohl."

She had a clipboard very much like one that would be carried by a hostess at a restaurant. She ran her finger down what appeared to be a lengthy list of names. When she flipped the front page over and continued sliding her finger down the list, I knew that the competition for the job would be intense. I remembered Steve, the principal at Cabrillo, telling me that the district hired 60 people the year before, but it looked like there would only be about 10 openings this year. "I don't see your name?"

I felt every capillary in my face rupture. "Uhm…It's K-O-H-L"

"Oh with a 'K'?"

I nodded

"I was looking for a 'C'. Let me check again." I watched her finger trace the names on the pages one more time as my manila folder wrinkled and began to show signs of water damage in my hand.

"James?"

I nodded and breathed.

"Go ahead and follow this hallway around like an 'L'. You'll see a lobby where everyone is waiting. There is coffee, water, and some pastries on a table over there." She looked at her watch. "I'm not sure if there are any pastries left, come to think of it, but you can help yourself to anything you would like."

"Thanks." My folder and I followed the "L" until we found ourselves in a room humming with conversation. There were at least 30 people standing and sitting around the lobby. The ages varied from about 22 to about 42. Everyone had a suit or dress on, and everyone had a manila folder, briefcase, leather folder, or something under their arm. Some people were called in for their interview while the rest of us waited. The crowd never shrunk because new people continually arrived. People who were sitting had been in the lobby for at least 20 minutes. I must have seen about 80 different candidates before I left for home, and this was only one of the days that the district had set aside for first round interviews. Steve said 10 possible positions.

"I'm good enough for this job." I told myself. After all, I had long-term subbed in the district two years in a row. I had student taught in the district. I had a letter of recommendation from two of their current teachers, one current principal, and one retired and well-liked administrator, Dr. Martini. Lynne said I was good. Diane let me take her class so she could plan her wedding. Lynne had helped me prepare for this interview by telling me what they had asked her and coaching me on the sort of answers that they are looking for. I was going to do fine. I looked in my hand and saw a tiny rip in my manila folder.

I finally got a chair and sat across from this blond guy with mousse in his hair and a bright purple suit. I almost questioned whether I really saw him, or if he was just an invention of my nervous mind. His suit reminded me of the Joker from Batman. He talked louder than anyone in the room to just about anyone that he thought might be listening. "Check out my portfolio. I had the kids do this art project where…" He proceeded to show this one woman work samples from kids he had worked with. Each page of sample art in his binder was carefully filed in a plastic covering. As he showed each piece to the woman, he loudly explained what the projects were about and the sort of planning that went into them. Then he got out a separate binder of writing samples from the black leather bag that he kept by his side. Then he got out his videotape of him teaching. "There's only about three lessons on here, but I think that's enough to give them a taste of what I'm about. Do you have your CLAD?" he asked the woman he had been presenting to.

She shook her head. I didn't have it either. Supposedly, it was going to be required for everyone in a couple of years, but you could get away without it for now. I was out of money, so I elected not to get it yet. Besides, I wanted to teach English, so why would I need bilingual specialization?

"I have it," continued Purple Suit to no one's surprise. He reached into the black bag again. "These are some photos of me teaching." I was wondering when he was going to pull out the fireworks display that he undoubtedly had in that bag somewhere. I would never be like this guy and his purple suit. I looked down at my manila folder once again and thought about tossing it in the garbage can. "If this guy is a teacher, then I'm probably trying for the wrong line of work because I'll never be as perfect as he is." Just as I started to feel down, I got called into the next step in the interview process, and I never saw Purple Boy again.

They took a few of us at a time into the next waiting area and gave us a blue questionnaire to fill out. It was a basic job application with questions like my name, address, Social Security Number, whether or not I was ever convicted of a felony. It also asked about my teaching experience. I hadn't heard the Great Grape in the lobby mention any subbing experience, so that was one thing I had. I had two solid years of real classroom time before I even came to this interview. Surely, that would count for something even if I don't have a dog and pony show for each and every concept I ever taught a student.

I filled out the form the best I could. The last question was why I wanted to be a teacher. I wrote, "I want to be a teacher because I feel that children are our most important resource. I want to teach them to think for themselves so that they can become successful and contribute to society. Most of all, I think teaching is fun." I still agree with all of that even as you read this.

They called my name, and I went into the last room of the interview. Two or three people sat at the table with me and asked me about myself and my goals and my experience. One of them took my blue questionnaire and put it in a file with all the application materials that I had sent in a couple of months earlier.

My heart beat very near the back of my throat as we talked. I felt like I stammered my way through the whole interview. I tried to emphasize the fact that I had strong ties in and a strong love for their district. I dropped names like crazy. "My supervisor, Dr. Martini…" I watched a couple of them nod and smile. "I have long-term subbed at Cabrillo the past two years…" They scribbled down some notes. The car wreck in my gut progressed into a train wreck and then a train that had been crashed into by a plane.

"Do you have any questions for us?"

I asked about benefits. They explained them, but I didn't listen because I didn't understand benefits anyway. My parents just always told me to ask about benefits.

The next thing I knew, I was back out in the Santa Clara heat. I clawed my tie off, and tossed it on the passenger seat. I lay my suit jacket in the cargo space of the CRX. I drove home.

They said I would hear from them.

Now, I needed to apply to every district possible.

Chapter XVIII

"How was the interview?" asked my mom as I walked into the house. She was in the kitchen making dinner.

"I don't know." I really didn't. "There was a big crowd of people and I felt pretty nervous the whole time." I tossed my suit jacket on the green family room chair.

"But you know you're a good teacher..." It seemed like there was more to the sentence that was left unsaid. My mouth wrinkled at the thought. That purple suit flashed through my mind like an embarrassing memory. "Should I carry around a videotape?" I wondered.

"I know I'm a good teacher, but how are you supposed to show that to someone that has never seen you teach? How can anyone judge the type of teacher I am from an interview? You can't ask someone a bunch of questions that we all have memorized answers to and see who the real teachers are! Someone could be really great at interviewing and a really lousy teacher and still get the job instead of me."

"How do you know you're not good at interviewing?"

"Because it makes me so sick it's like a mangled car wreck in my gut-the kind of carnage that even a Catholic nun would slow down to look at. I don't even remember what they asked me!" My mom just looked at me. "Some dude had all the things that any student ever turned in to him to show off to people. He had this obnoxious purple suit too."

"Someone is going to know you're great, Jim. Someone is going to see your talent."

"Yeah. I'm going to go change." I hung up the suit and wondered when I would need it again.

113

School ended a couple of weeks after the interview with Santa Clara. I began coaching the swim team again. I also picked up some hours at the neighborhood pool as a lifeguard and swim instructor. My black baseball hat with the Grateful Dead logo on it faded to a dull gray that summer. My body bronzed, and I followed every lead there was toward a teaching job.

"Where are you going to apply?" asked my dad.

"Everywhere except Alum Rock. I had enough of them as a sub." The teachers in that district work hard, but the administration does not support them. The labor battles are always bitter and all over the television news.

"That's good. You're a smart man not to put all your eggs in one basket. When are you supposed to hear from Santa Clara anyway?"

"Anytime. They didn't say." They had so many applicants and so few openings that it didn't matter to them how long they made us wait. "I really want to get in there though."

"I hope you do. But a job is a job. You can always move into Santa Clara later in your career if you want to."

I nodded. "I would have to do it within the first five years, though, so I could carry all those years of experience to the new job." The way teachers get paid is by the years they have taught and the college units they have completed. The pay scale has a vertical column of years taught and a horizontal row of units completed. To find your salary, you go down the scale to the number of years you've been teaching and across the page to the column beneath the number of units you've completed. However, if you teach 10 years and move to a new district, by law they only have to give you five years experience on the pay scale while they enjoy your 10 years of expertise in the classroom.

All this was okay because I wasn't a money grubbing corporate scum. Whatever I made in the top right hand slot of the pay scale, no matter which district I worked in, would be more than I made as a lifeguard.

National University sponsored a teacher job fair at the campus in late June. Representatives from many local districts sat in the same classrooms where we learned how to teach and conducted informal interviews.

"Are you going to go?" asked my mom. She watched me open the letter.

"Yeah. Santa Clara is going to be there, so it would be good to make contact with someone else from the district or to reconnect with some-one I already talked to. The more they see me the better, I think."

"What other districts are going to be there?"

I looked at the list on the letter. "Let's see…Milpitas, Union, Alum Rock-yeah, right-Santa Clara, San Jose Unified, Evergreen, and Los Gatos."

"Oh! Jan says great things about Evergreen. She says they're growing all the time, and she says that all the families moving into those big houses over there on the hill will be sending their kids there. She also says they pay the most to beginning teachers."

"It's not about the money, mom."

"I know." She held up her hand and tilted her head back. "But if you're doing the job anyway, you may as well get paid the most for what you do as possible. Don't you think you're worth a lot of money?"

"That's true." It never occurred to me what I was worth. It didn't matter to me enough to think about it.

I drove down to National that summer afternoon with a manila folder filled with resumes. The sun slammed down from the sky and back up from the blacktop of the parking lot. I parked the CRX and headed into the elevator like I did just over a year earlier in the pouring rain after I stood up for Christopher Columbus. Where was Maria Escobar now? I was about to be a teacher.

Mark, the ex-bartender, stood waiting by the elevator when I walked up.

"How's it going, man?" I asked. We shook hands.

"Hey! How've you been?"

Neither of us had landed a job yet.

"What district are you hoping for?" He asked.

"Santa Clara."

"That's a good district."

I nodded. "What about you?"

"I have some friends in Union that I was sort of hoping to get to work with. I did a lot of subbing over there, and they all want me in. It would be cool to be in a place where you're really wanted."

"Right on!" I said as the elevator presented us to the second floor. "Take it easy man."

"Good luck!"

I figured out which room Santa Clara was in and went right to them. I had never seen the woman they had sent before. They had a line of about 10 people, so I looked for another district while the line worked itself out.

The line for Milpitas was short. I had already requested and received an application from them in the mail. Lynne had worked there before she got married and moved into the Santa Clara District, and she said they were good to her. When I got up to the man in the suit and the thin black hair they had sent, he spoke first. "Do you have a CLAD certificate on your credential?"

"No, I want to teach English." This bilingual thing is nuts!

"Well, we're not talking to anyone without the CLAD. Sorry."

I walked away. I threw away their application when I got home.

I went back and checked the Santa Clara line again. It was still really long. I spoke briefly with San Jose Unified and Union, and I took an application from each of them. The Santa Clara line was still long.

"Hey!" It was Amy from my classes.

"Hey, how's it going?"

"Pretty good. Which districts have you talked with?"

I told her. "I also had an interview with Santa Clara a couple weeks ago. You can't get near those guys today!"

"I know! I interviewed with Campbell."

"How was it?"

"It seemed okay. It's hard to tell."

"I know. There seem to be a lot of us right now. All these districts have the time to choose, and they're all taking their time." She nodded in agreement.

"Have you talked to Evergreen yet?"

"No, but this one teacher I know says they're pretty cool."

"I've heard they pay well."

"That's what this lady said. Do you know where they are?"

"They're up on the next floor," she told me.

"I'm going to go check them out. Take it easy."

"Good luck."

"You too."

The elevator dinged open and I stepped in and pressed the 3 button. As the doors opened, there was a paper sign with Evergreen and Cupertino written on it and arrows pointing in opposite directions. "Here I go," I thought. "At least I can tell my mom I looked into them." I wondered where their district even was.

I walked into the room with Evergreen on the door. There was a stout man with a beard. He wore a green khaki suit and sat at the table on the side of the room directly opposite the door I came in through. He smiled while I walked toward him. "Hi, welcome," he said as he stood to shake my hand. "I'm Charles, and I'm the principal of one of the middle schools in the Evergreen School District."

"I'm Jim Kohl."

"Great, have a seat, Jim."

"Thanks."

"Do you have a copy of your resume handy?"

"Yeah, here you go." I settled right in. I had no stomach storm to speak of. He looked over my resume and read some of its highlights out loud. I sat there nodding.

"Looks like you've done most of your work in Santa Clara. Have you ever worked in our district at all?"

"No. I'm not even sure where it is to be honest with you."

"Oh." He got a map out of one of the application packets he had piled on the table. "We're over on the East Side of San Jose near Eastridge Mall, and we're developing new land out by the country club." He pointed to the area that the district covered on his map.

"Hmm." I said, nodding.

"So what grade level do you see yourself teaching?"

"Fourth and up is my preference, but I'd be willing to go as low as second grade." I thought of Steven and Jessica C.

"Would you want to teach middle school at all?"

"Yeah! I really like middle school. Most of my subbing has been in middle school."

"Great. What subject would you like to teach in middle school?"

"English. As you can see, that was my degree, and I have a supplement to my credential that allows me to teach departmentalized English up to the ninth grade." My actual credential was kindergarten to eighth grade, but since I had a bachelor's in English, I was able to get this extra authorization just by asking for it.

"Okay." He scratched his fingers through his beard, "What would you say makes you different from all the other applicants?"

This threw me. I had to think of something concrete. My initial thought was, "Well, I'm better than they are." You need a concrete example that shows this. "I use a guitar to teach sometimes." I had done this with Diane's class. "I did it with second graders, but I don't know about using that in middle school."

"Oh I think you should. My brother teaches eighth grade, and he uses his guitar all the time. The kids love it. They think he's a rock star or something."

"Oh that's cool."

"Are you bilingual?"

Yeah, I speak punk rock and English. "No." Here it came, I braced myself, and I could feel the car in my gut skidding and careening all over the road.

"Do you have the CLAD credential?"

"No."

"Well, a lot of our district is ESL. We are looking for people with the CLAD."

I stayed calm. "Do you mean that in order to teach English in your district, I need to have this CLAD credential? Because, if that is what you're saying, then I don't think I'm interested in working for you guys. Thanks though." I stood and turned toward the door. I blew this interview. It was Maria Escobar and Christopher Columbus all over again.

"Wait a second, Jim."

I turned back around.

"Take one of our applications just in case. We may be hiring some people without CLAD credentials, but we are trying to get as many certified with the CLAD as we can."

I walked back and took the application packet from him. "That's cool. Thanks." We shook hands, and I walked out of the room wondering why he bothered to chase me down. Why didn't he just let me leave? It occurred to me as I walked through the halls of this job fair and passed by all sorts of women, that in the elementary school system, there are not a lot of men teachers. For the first time in my white boy life, I was the minority that could benefit from Affirmative Action sort of thinking. Had I been another woman without a CLAD, I may not have been so encouraged to apply CLAD-less. It made me sick that such sexism went on, but if it got me a job…

NO! I'm starting to sound like all that I hate! It's wrong to only care about getting hired. He just didn't want me to walk away mad; that's why he chased me. Who cares why, really?

I picked up an application from the Cupertino and Campbell school districts before heading back to the CRX for the afternoon. I had a lot of filling out to do.

CHAPTER XIX

I went home and filled out one application a day for the next week. I tried to apply to at least one district per day, and if I didn't apply, I would at least try to find a new district to call and request an application from. I was amazed at the number of school districts that are clustered all about San Jose. I had never heard of some of them like the Cambrian District.

Every application was a bit different than the one before it. Some wanted an essay explaining why I chose education as a career. Some wanted three letters of recommendation and some wanted two. No one ever asked for more than three, but I had a loaded six gun of these letters if necessary. I had one from Lynne, Diane, Dave, (Haman's Principal), Mr. Gregg, Dr. Martini, and Karen, my supervisor when I coached the swim team. Some districts wanted a photocopy of my license, some wanted a photocopy of my Social Security card, some wanted both, and some didn't want either.

Each day I coached the swim team for a couple of hours in the early morning, filled out some applications when I got home and made a pilgrimage to Kinko's. I had a large manila envelope filled with frequently photocopied documents. These were the originals of my recommendation letters and my resume. My license and Social Security Card were in my wallet just in case.

"Where are you applying today?" My mom would sometimes ask.

I would tell her. "I have to apply or at least get an application every day or I don't feel like I'm trying hard enough. Looking for a job is a full time job."

I ran into Kinko's with my copy card in one hand and my envelope in the other. I kept whatever completed application I was sending out that day on the passenger seat of my car. I would slide my copy card into the machine and see if there was any money left on it. If not, I would slide it into the machine that allowed you to add money to it and hope that the dollar eater would swallow my dollar and not stick it back out at me like a green tongue.

Once the money was on my card, I would run off hot new copies of my letters and resume. I would make copies of my ID cards if necessary. Kinko's and the whirr sound of the copy machine tattooed itself into my memory forever. I can still see the bright light through the crack in the closed copier lid and the perfect likeness of my original sliding into the tray. I can smell the whiteout that the woman at the worktable was using. I knew how to use every copier in the place, and I joked with myself that I should list that fact on my resume.

So it went on a daily basis until I had successfully applied to Milpitas, Cupertino, San Jose Unified, Campbell, Cambrian, Berryessa, Oak Grove, Union, and Los Gatos. I had paperwork flying across the desks of Human Resources Departments in every district within easy driving range, but I wasn't hearing anything back.

"These things take time," my mom told me.

"Why doesn't someone just figure out that I'm a great teacher and offer me a job?"

"These things take time," she repeated.

"But summer is almost over, and I want a job by September!" Actually, June wasn't even over yet, and Jan had told me that teachers often get hired in the final weeks of August when the last-minute retirements are announced. Some old teacher finally decides that one more year is too many, and calls the principal to empty out a room for someone like me. Then, the new teacher crams the room full of newly bought posters and tries to figure out what the heck is going on in that particular grade level. They spend each waking hour decorating the room to produce an environment conducive to the learning process and memorizing curriculum and standards that need to be met. If the teacher breathes, the first day of school crushes down on them and the kids stare up from their desks trying to figure out how much they can get away with and/or come away with. So after a year or two of preparation stuffed into one week, the new teacher gets tossed into the situation to see if anything will happen.

I had to get hired before August. I needed to walk into that room with a good grasp of what needed to be done. "Why don't they call me?!? I spend my life in front of that copy machine running off my life on paper. I'm a freaking expert at Kinko's-I'll tell you that. Those dorks would probably hire me. They've seen my work every morning at 10. They even know I'm reliable! Maybe I should see if one of those Kinko's guys would write me a letter of recommendation! Do you think the districts even read any of that crap that they insist I include?!" I paced the living room as I spoke. My hands clawed out in front of me. "For God's sake! I have the stinking credential now, and I'm still exactly where I was without it! My life is no more certain now than it was a year ago!" My mom just watched me rant.

"Have you applied to Evergreen yet?" She asked.

What did this have to do with the fact that my life was unraveling right here in front of my mom? These were the words of support in this desperate hour?

"No, that's tomorrow. But have you been listening to anything I've been saying?" I looked at her as my body peaked in tenseness. I was an over-wound rubber band.

"I don't know what to tell you, honey."

I just looked at her.

The phone rang.

"There you go." She said as I jumped across the room to grab it.

"Hello?" I said with hope.

"Jim?"

"Yeah." This sounded too informal to be the call I wanted.

"Hey, It's Kim." Kim from the credential program.

"Hey!" Kim was a good friend. She was a bit older at 29, but we had a good time hanging out sometimes.

"Hey, so what's up?"

Well, Kim, the world is falling down and I still don't have a teaching job. "Not much, how's it going with you?"

"Not much. So, hey, God…It's been a while, huh?" I hadn't talked to Kim since before student teaching. I was surprised she even bothered calling me.

"Yeah, it has been." I said. "How did your student teaching go?"

"The second part was okay. The first part was a nightmare! That lady did not like me at all, Jim."

"Really? Are you sure?"

"Yeah. You know, like when you just know that someone doesn't like you? You know, I just think I must have annoyed her or something."

"Did she ever say anything to you?"

"No. Well, kind of…I mean you know I just had this feeling. It's kind of hard to explain."

"Obviously." I thought.

"Do you want to maybe get together later tonight for a beer and talk about stuff?"

"Sure yeah, that sounds great." Maybe this was the phone call I had been waiting for after all. If you can't get the interview call yet, at least you can get the call about beer and friends. Kim gave me directions to her house, and we planned to go out about 8 o' clock. I had a few hours to get ready.

I drove to Kim's and found her apartment complex pretty easily.

"Jim! Hi! You lost weight." I had been running the treadmill literally as well as metaphorically in those days.

"Yeah, thanks. I've been working out for the first time in a few years."

Kim wasn't ready and I watched as she sat on the floor and put on her tennis shoes.

"So, student teaching wasn't so great for you, huh?" I asked.

"Oh my God, let me tell you, Jim, it was hell! This lady told me to read with the kids at a circular table, right?"

"What grade did you have?"

"Second. So anyway, I sat at the little reading table with about four of them and they all took turns reading. When one of them had a hard time, I would try to help them figure out the word." This story continued as she locked the door to her apartment, and we walked down the steps of her complex into the night. "So when we got through the whole book, we stopped reading and I let them go back to their desks. So my master teacher comes back in the room and sees that the kids are at their desks and tells me she wants to see me at recess. Can you believe this?" I shook my head. I opened the car door for Kim. "Thanks. And so, now I feel like I'm in trouble, and I have no idea what I could have possibly done. So, I'm all nervous for recess to come like I'm a kid being sent to the principal or something, you know? I mean, they shouldn't be allowed to make you feel like you're in trouble, should they?"

"No." I agreed as I shook my head again. "Not to interrupt, but I was thinking we could go to Gordon Biersch downtown. Is that cool?"

"Oh, I love that place."

"Cool."

"Anyway, so recess starts and she comes over to me and tells me that I should have made them read through the book more than once if we got through it. So I asked her why. She got really mad, Jim. She's just this old lady all set in her ways and she doesn't even have a reason for the things that she thinks are so important. So I complained to my supervisor, and she said that I have to do what my master teacher says, and that I should apologize to her!"

"Geez!"

"I know, I'm like…" She went on about this some more and the tales twisted more as she went. I was only half listening as I turned into the parking garage on Second Street downtown. I was thinking about Lynne and how lucky I was that I had liked my master teachers. I was also wondering how much Kim liked me. Her blond hair shined against the night sky outside the car window. I hadn't had a girlfriend for about five years.

We walked down to Gordon Biersch, an upper class looking micro-brewery that features fake sounding blues bands and generic jazz. Since they make their own beer, you can sometimes smell fermenting barley as you slide in to the booth with the white tablecloth and unfold your white starched napkin to put it in your lap. The beer is good, but it's a yuppie paradise. I would drink their beer, but I hated each and every one of those sell-outs that cheered on the false blues of three white guys in tuxedos.

"So how was your student teaching, Jim?"

"Oh it was great! My first master teacher really helped me a lot. My second one was getting married, so she left me alone a lot so she could make phone calls to plan her wedding. I was ready for it though, so it was cool." Our beers arrived at the table. We both ordered the Marzen, a dark beer, and when my pint was halfway gone, Kim's blue eyes started to shimmer.

"See," she said, "you're lucky that you had such great master teachers. It's my luck that I ended up with what I ended up with."

We talked about other things as we drank a couple more beers. We remembered John and his paranoia about perverts. We talked about Amy and both wondered what happened to her. We laughed about some of the things that would go on in the classes that we took and that we student taught in.

"Have you had any interviews yet?" I asked.

"No, have you?"

"I had one interview in Santa Clara."

"Really? How was that?"

"It was all right." I told her about the guy in the purple suit and his suitcase containing his life's work.

"You don't have to worry, Jim. You're so smart and funny, they're gonna hire you for sure." Why couldn't Kim be a principal somewhere? I felt my cheeks heat up.

"So, have you sent out any applications at all?"

"No. I don't know. My sister is a teacher too, and I'm probably going to teach a little summer school where she works in August. Maybe they'll have room and just hire me. But I have this job as a waitress in this Mexican restaurant in Los Gatos. It's pretty fun. I'm making enough money there." Kim sipped her beer.

I couldn't believe that anyone would go through a whole year's worth of training and then not use it. It's really two years worth of training, but we all got it finished in a year simply by spending extra money. "You don't think you're going to try to get a teaching job?" I wanted to make sure that I understood this.

"Well…not this year. Maybe next year I'll apply to some places, or…I don't know maybe I'll apply to some places this year. How many places have you applied?"

"I think about seven districts or something like that." They dimmed the lights in the bar and I had that strange feeling that all was fading to black.

"See that is so good, Jim. Someone will hire you for sure. I'm just not sure about me. You're such a good teacher."

"You're a good teacher too." We had seen each other teach plenty of times in the Applications class.

"Really? You think so? Thanks-I don't know."

"What?"

"It just seems like such a lot to do."

Our beers were empty.

"Do you want another one?" Kim asked pointing to my empty glass.

"No I'm gonna mellow out so I can drive eventually." I sort of panicked, "You're not in a hurry to get home are you?"

"No, I'm going to buy another beer. Are you sure you don't want
another one?"

"No thanks, I really need to mellow. Thanks though." She got up and
walked to the bar. The fake blues rolled across the bar like neon smoke.

How can you work so hard for something and then just throw it
away? She's just going to be a waitress the rest of her life? I tapped my
Bloodstone ring against my empty pint glass. I zoned out on Kim's
empty chair and tried to figure this all out. How could you give up a
teaching career for anything?

I sat for about 10 minutes alone at the table thinking back and forth
on all that had happened. The beer had my brain and showed me lots of
fairy tale notions about what this life is. I could see myself teaching. I
was going to get hired, and I was going to make a big difference. I was
on the brink of super stardom. My life would begin its ascent towards a
peak like the cliché blues crescendo that I was hearing in this bar. I
thought of Lynne, but I shook her from my brain because I didn't want
her in my head next to this buzz in case she could psychically tell I had
been drinking and think I was a loser after all. I had her fooled pretty
well. Where was Kim anyway?

I turned and saw her at the bar talking with some dude with gray
hair. She sat next to him and acted as if she came alone. I burned inside.
I heard him say he was 35. He had 10 years on me. "When I'm 35, I'm
not going to be hanging out in bars trying to pick up women, you
loser!" I thought. She spent the next half hour at the bar with this guy.
She never so much as thought of me as I sat alone watching the foam in
my pint slide down the side of the glass and dry up. I couldn't let her
know that I was mad. If I was so funny and smart-smart and funny
enough to get hired-then why wasn't I smart and funny enough to make

Kim want to hang out with me? Girlfriends do this to each other, and it's obvious that Kim considered me one of her girlfriends.

Why did she want to keep waiting on tables? Oh well, tomorrow I can fill out some more applications through my cloudy hangover.

CHAPTER XX

I continued filling out applications and going to Kinko's until I was afraid that the ink on my original letters might fade. June quickly closed in front of me. I counted each day as a missed opportunity as I waited for the phone to ring to tell me that Santa Clara wanted me after all. I walked to my desk in my cluttered bedroom to see which application would use up at least a couple hours of my day. I pulled it out from beneath a crayon drawing that I had been given by one of the swimmers on my swim team.

"Evergreen." I said the name out loud. Their application packet came in an off-white folder with green writing on it boasting the slogan, "Evergreen and Ever-Growing." They had the salary schedule in the folder. The first-year teacher pay was higher than most other districts at the time by about $2, 000 a year. "This doesn't affect me one way or the other," I told myself, but at the same time I had no interest in the Union School District, which started teachers out at about $2,000 less than most districts at the time. Was I starting to sell out? No! You could never do that as long as you had a career in education.

I began going through the process of filling out all the same old forms once again. I had my driver's license number memorized at this point. I could nearly recite my work experience including the dates that I worked at places. At Kinko's, I knew that I needed exactly $1.03 on my copy card to make enough photocopies for the average district. I always had a black pen handy because many of the districts wanted the applications printed in black ink or typed. I finished filling out the Evergreen application and headed to Kinko's again.

"I'm headed out to do my thing," I called to my mom.

"Okay." She shouted back from the laundry room.

When I got back from Kinko's, my mom sat on the couch in the family room with a smile on her face. She looked like she couldn't wait to tell me something.

"Hi." I started. "Well, there goes another one out in the mail."

"Some guy from the Cupertino School District called." She smiled the words right out of her mouth. "His name and number are over there." She motioned to the kitchen table. The world moved slowly around me as I headed for that yellow Post-It note. It had the phone number that, once I called it back, would open my future in front of me like a child's colorful pop-up book.

"Right on!" I said. I grabbed the cordless phone off the counter and dialed the number with all the confidence I could muster. I asked for Human Resources like I had learned to all those years ago.

"Thank you," said the receptionist as she transferred my call. They had hold music! 'They must be a pretty rich district!' I thought.

"Human Resources, can I help you?"

"Yes, I need to speak with Mr. Franklin, please." My voice wavered in excitement.

"Who is calling please?"

"Jim Kohl."

"One moment, please."

The receiver rang in my ear as my heart pounded with joy. This had to be it. I would interview with them and get the job. I would get an apartment over in Cupertino so I wouldn't have a bad commute to work. I would live alone and not have to worry about having psychotic roommates.

"Jeff Franklin, speaking."

The voice startled me. "Uh, Mr. Franklin. My name is Jim Kohl, and I had a message to call you back?" Oh man! I ended a statement like a question-nothing shows a bigger lack of self-confidence.

"Oh, yeah, let me see here." I could hear him rummaging through a pile of papers on his desk. Someone actually got one of those oversized packets I had been sending out! "Okay, here we go…Jim. We would like to bring you in for an interview. You haven't been hired yet, have you?" The heavens opened up and "the light was all shining on me" as the Grateful Dead said!

"Great! And…uh no I haven't been hired yet," I said. I tried not to show too much excitement. I didn't want to sound like a schoolgirl winning a radio contest.

"We're setting them up for next week right now. How is Monday afternoon for you?"

"That'll be fine." If it's a time during my life, it's fine! I can be there at 3 o'clock in the morning if you would like!

"How about 2 o'clock Monday afternoon?"

"That would be great!"

"The interview will be at the Cupertino School District Office. Do you know where that is?"

"Not really." Not at all, I had never been there in my life. He gave me directions and I scribbled them down, eager to get off the phone and scream and yell ecstatically. We finally hung up.

"Hey mom!" I yelled. "I have an interview!"

I took my suit to the dry cleaner so that it would be ready for Monday. I spent the weekend telling everyone willing to listen about this interview. I was most excited about this because they didn't know me at all in Cupertino; I had never worked in that district or had any contact with them at all. That meant that my resume was good enough to catch the eye of someone in a Human Resources department that had never heard of me. I looked good on paper.

Kim called that Saturday night. When I told her about the interview she said, "Oh, hey, that's great. I know they'll hire you Jim, you're such a good teacher."

Yeah, but I'm not as cool as that fossil you were hanging out with at the bar when you left me sitting there. "Thanks." I told her.

Monday rolled around and, and I followed the normal routine of swim practice, application, Kinko's, post office, and back home, hoping that there was a phone message from Santa Clara. They hadn't called again, but at least I had the interview today. "They're gonna miss out on me if they're not careful." I thought. My confidence soared as I got in that suit one more time. It was about 102 degrees that day. I printed up a resume and stuck it in a manila folder.

"Good luck," said my mom as I headed to the CRX that sat like a pressure cooker in front of my parents' house. "If I get this job, I'll start looking for an apartment right away." I thought. I wanted to make a life for myself. I couldn't make a life without a job, so once again, my whole future sat dormant waiting for someone to give me my chance. This was the last step though; once I got my teaching job, it would all be over, and I would never have to wait on someone hiring me again.

I broke into a sweat as soon as I slid into the driver's seat and placed my manila folder in the shotgun seat like I had so many times before. "My next car will have air-conditioning." I vowed. The sweat beaded on my forehead, and I wiped it away as the engine came alive. I rolled down both windows and reached into my pocket for the directions that I had written down while I was on the phone with Mr. Franklin. I went down the street while Bob Dylan sang "When I Paint My Masterpiece," a song about a hopeful future as soon as the impossible is accomplished. It was my personal theme song that summer. I listened to it over and over on the way to the interview.

I found Cupertino's District office right where Mr. Franklin said it would be. I pulled into the lot and headed to the main door. The air-conditioning hugged me as soon as I opened the office door, and I was glad to be 15 minutes early so that I could cool down a bit before the interview.

The office lobby walls were coated in brown panel board. The couch was a dark chocolate color. In the corner of the lobby diagonal from the door I came through was a plexiglass window the receptionist sat behind that gave the room the feel of a doctor's office. I went to the window.

"Can I help you?" She was younger than a normal district receptionist.

"Hi, I'm Jim Kohl and I have a 2 o'clock interview." She checked her book. "Um…It's K-O-H-L." I said, as I saw her finger slide past it on the page of her appointment book.

"Oh! Here you are!" She highlighted my name in yellow. "Go ahead and have a seat, and I'll let them know you're here."

"Thanks." Always be nice to the receptionist. I've heard of times when the receptionist is asked how the potential employee seemed to them.

I went over to the brown couch and sat with my manila folder in my lap. I was the only one in the lobby. On the table next to me were three middle school yearbooks. I figured I would take a peak at the sort of thing I would be in for.

All the kids looked happy. There was not much of the tough guy or hard girl pictures that I had seen so often in other middle school yearbooks. They smiled and beamed off the pages like a new found talent. "I could do this!" I thought. "I could do this very easily." I flipped through the book and saw the same faces at Halloween dressed as vampires in flowing black gowns. I saw a shy boy looking sideways at the camera dancing with a girl who was slightly taller. The two are captured forever at the Holiday Dance. I saw the hearts on the wall and the boys getting taller at the Valentine's Dance. I saw them all playing soccer and running the track. I couldn't remember that many sports available when I was in junior high. I know we had a basketball team, but I…

"James Kohl?" The voice came from the door next to the Plexiglas window. "Yeah." I stood up with my folder under my right arm and headed in.

"I'm Jeff Franklin." We shook hands.

"Jim Kohl. Nice to meet you."

"Come back this way, Jim." I followed him down a winding corridor that lead to a rather large room with a big brown rectangular table in the middle of it. I sat down with Jeff and two other men. "Could we get you some water, Jim."

"No thanks, I'm fine."

"Jim, this is our first round of the interviewing process. We're bringing people in to get acquainted with them, and then we're inviting some people back for the second round. This interview will last about 15 minutes, so don't be discouraged by that because that is the way we have designed the process. Do you have any questions before we get started?"

"No." I sat and wondered if there had ever been a day of chaos in any of their lives.

"Tell us a little about yourself."

I went through it.

"What grades would you most want to teach?"

I told them.

"Is there any grade you would not like to teach?"

I thought for a moment. "Kindergarten."

"Any particular reason?"

"I don't have it in me."

They laughed. "Why do you want to be a teacher?"

I recited.

Before I knew it, the 15 minutes were over. "We'll contact you one way or the other over the next week. If you are chosen for the second round of interviews, we should tell you that those interviews are video-taped and then shown to all the principals. Would you have any objections to being videotaped?"

"No, that would be fine."

"Do you have any final questions for us?"

"No. Thank you, though, for bringing me in."

"No problem. It was a pleasure meeting you."

"You too." We shook hands again.

I was out in the heat tearing my tie off before I really knew I was in there with them. "How could they possibly tell what sort of teacher I am from those questions?" I wondered. How is anyone going to know what sort of teacher anyone is from an interview? I better learn to interview better.

I drove home and followed my normal post-interview ritual. I tossed my tie and jacket over the green living room chair and asked if anyone, like Santa Clara for example, had called. No one had.

"How did this one go?" My mom asked from the couch as she put down the book she was reading.

"It was fast. They said it would be no more than 15 minutes, and they got me out a little quicker, I think. They said I would hear from them one way or another within a week." I sat in the green chair. "Check this out! This was the first round for their interviews, and the second round, if I go," I crossed my fingers, "is videotaped!"

"You're kidding? Why?"

"I don't know. They videotape the whole interview, and then if a principal needs a teacher, they come down to the district office and watch the video to see if they are interested! It's like some sort of video dating service or something!"

"I've never heard of such a thing!" My mom said, smiling.

"I wish I could just get a video of me doing the perfect interview and then just send it to these people when they call." I thought for a second. "If they call."

"Now honey," my mom began, "You've been in for two interviews already and it's not even July yet. Remember that Jan said a lot of districts don't even hire anyone until August."

"I know."

"Someone will hire you."

"I just freak out during these interviews. I feel tense, and I'm not sure if I'm saying the right things because I can hardly remember what was talked about two minutes after it's over. What if I just sit there blabbing like a moron with drool dripping from my lip and I'm not even aware of it?"

"Now, Jim..."

"Well! I mean...I wish I knew something about interviewing."

My mom thought for a couple of seconds, raised her eyebrows and said, "Well, I don't know about these teaching interviews, but when I was interviewing, I used to just tell them I could do anything they asked. Even if they asked me something I had never heard of in my life I would tell them I could do it because I figured I could learn it."

This was lying. I found this fascinating because this woman brought me up with very definite opinions about how lying was not okay. Later on, I asked my dad about interviewing techniques. He gave me very similar advice.

"Isn't that lying dad?"

"It's not lying. It's interviewing." The idea is that if you truly think you could learn to do something, than saying you could do it is not a lie. There's a fine line between being a liar and getting hired, I guess.

I called Lynne, my first master teacher, to ask for some more advice about interviewing. "You need to be positive. You need to make them know you can handle the situation. Try to use anecdotes from your experience to illustrate your answers. Like if they ask about your classroom control, talk about a time when you either lost control and what you would do to get it back, or talk about how you keep the kids under control. Throw around some buzzwords."

"Like what?"

"You know all that stuff about the different modalities of learning? Right now, they all want to hear about how you're going to attempt to address all the different learning modalities."

The modalities refer to how some kids learn better by hearing information, and some kids learn better by reading information. Some kids don't learn it until they write it. With 30-some kids in the room, you have to be sure that you are addressing multiple modalities because the chances that you have a classroom full of kids with the same learning modality are zero.

"When I throw around these buzzwords, I should mean it, right?"

"Well, yeah. But what you need to do is tell them what they want to hear to get you in the door. You're a good teacher, and education needs you. Once you have the job, you can toss out the buzzwords because you will figure out what your kids need. The buzzwords are just for show. Did you ever see me follow a Madeline Hunter five step lesson plan?"

"No." I laughed.

"There you go!" She squeaked. "When they call you back for the second interview, just go in there and show them what you know. Be excited. That's all it takes."

"By the way," I had to know if this seemed weird to her, "This second interview with Cupertino is going to be videotaped!"

"Oh yeah!" She gasped it out. "They're the ones that do that! Well, that's okay. The same strategies will work. Wow. Let me know how that goes."

We hung up. That was the extent of my interview advice: Be loose with the buzzwords and tell them you can do anything while coming off as being happy.

A couple days later the call came through, and I was heading down to the videotaped interview. My usual ritual was followed: dry clean the suit, print up the resume, get the manila folder, find my Dylan tape with "When I Paint My Masterpiece" on it, and expect either stifling heat or a barrage of rain. I took the normal good luck message from my mom and headed out with a distant hope that this may be the interview to end all interviews; this interview may free my potential and let me do what I was born to do-teach.

I turned my CRX into the parking lot at the Cupertino School District Office. I went and spelled my name for the receptionist who asked me to have a seat. I picked up from where I had left off in the middle school yearbooks. My manila folder sat and waited by my side as I pictured my photo in the "K" section of the faculty pictures in the yearbook.

"James Kohl?" It was Mr. Franklin. I put down the yearbook on the brown end table and headed to the door. "Nice to see you again."

"Nice to see you too." We shook hands. 'This has to be it, right?' I thought as I was led down the same curvy hallway as before.

"As you may remember, Jim, this interview will be videotaped. The only reason that we do this is that our principals are often too busy to come and meet the candidates. The video is a way for them to see if you will fit their school without having to ask you to come down and meet them one at a time."

I nodded. "So," I thought, "this is for my convenience."

"Let's go in here." He motioned me into a room with another large deep brown rectangular table. We sat at one corner of it, and the camera stood on a tri-pod diagonally across the table. "We need to sit here so that we are in the picture. Did you want some water or anything?"

"Yes, please." I don't normally take it, but I'm not normally video-taped during an interview either.

"Would you like the camera to see you from a certain angle?"

"Excuse me?"

"Some people have a preference as to whether the camera should shoot them from the right or left. Do you have a preference?"

"No, not really…" He did not appear to be kidding. He left the room for a second and brought me cool water in a clear plastic cup.

"During this interview, you can look at me, or you can look at the camera, or you can look in both places. Don't try to figure out where to look; there is no wrong way. Look wherever feels most natural. This interview will last somewhere between 45 minutes and an hour. Do you have any questions before I turn on the camera?"

"No."

"Okay." He walked to the other side of the room and turned the camera on. I could see the red light near the top of that dark three-legged shape, and it seemed to shine on my forehead like one of those red beams from a sniper's assault rifle. "This is James Kohl, a teaching candidate in our district with a BA in English and a Multiple Subject Teaching Credential from National University."

I smiled into the camera but held back my urge to wave.

"James, I'm going to start out by asking you a series of 'What if' questions. You just answer them the best you can."

"Okay." I noticed a small microphone with a charcoal colored foam cover about six inches away from us on the table. I shot my voice toward this microphone.

"What if you had a student in class that was not doing his work?"

I looked at the camera. I looked back at Mr. Franklin who sat and waited for my response. "I would ask the kid why he is not doing his work and try to convince him that he should." I looked back at the camera, picturing a whole parade of principals nodding at my first response.

"How would you convince him?"

"Well, it would depend on the kid." I need to stay positive! "I would find something the kid was interested in and see if I could gear the concepts of the class towards those interests."

"What if he still didn't do any work?"

I'd kill him. "I'd call his parents and let them know that there is a problem with his grades."

"That would be your second step?"

"Yes."

"Would you call a child's parents for behavior problems in the classroom?"

"No. Behavior in the classroom is my responsibility. The parents would only need to know about academics."

"So you would never call a parent for behavior?"

I felt like I should maybe have counsel present. "I would call home for behavior in extreme cases like a fistfight in the classroom or a weapon." Mr. Franklin had to manually reinsert his eyeballs. Evidently, the Cupertino District does not have these kinds of problems. Stay positive! Tell him you can do anything!! Throw out a buzzword or two. He wasn't asking those sorts of questions, and I can't come off as overly happy when discussing calling a student's parents. If you're calling them, it is usually because of a very non-positive situation.

"What if you have a child in your class with special needs?" He asked.

"What sort of special needs do you mean?" That was good. He now knows that I know that there are many sorts of "special needs" students out there. Plus, I got to use a buzzword.

"Let's say you have a kid in a wheelchair."

"I would make sure that they have a desk near the door. Depending on the degree of the disability, I might accept late writing assignments and give them extra time on tests if their arms were affected as well. I had a girl in a wheelchair…" I told the story of Liz in Lynne's class. She had a seat near the door, a special aid to help her a couple times a day, and adaptive PE, which means that physical activity is modified to the ability of the student.

I was using anecdotes! I was saying that I could do the job, and I was staying positive! The whole time the bright red Cyclops eye of the camera stared me down. The interview continued on. He asked me about many things and I don't remember many of them.

"Name some classroom rules you would have." He said.

"Take your seat before the bell, one person talks at a time, respect others. I would also clarify what respect is, you know, how it means not to steal things or touch anyone or say mean things to one another."

"Would you have these rules posted in the classroom?"

"Of course, yes, they have to know what is expected of them." I thought that was pretty good. My eyes kept darting from the camera to Mr. Franklin and back. I didn't know what to do with them.

"What would your consequences for breaking rules be?"

"In my experience, each school has a discipline plan that I would follow. However, I would initially give a warning, and then detention. If the behavior kept up, I would have to remove the student from the situation by sending him to the office if it was a middle school. I would take away all or part of a recess if it was an elementary school." They don't like to hear that because of the California State law that mandates recess, but every teacher does it.

"How do you want your students to think of you?"

I never thought about that. "I want them to think that I am strict but cool. I make them work, but I am also someone they can trust."

"Strict, but cool huh?"

"Yeah."

I don't think he liked that last answer, but my hour had ended anyway. Mr. Franklin thanked me for coming in and told me they would be in touch. I shook his hand and thanked him too. I walked out to the CRX again. I looked down the street on this summer day and saw the heat waves rising from the blacktop of the road make the world look like it was melting. I tore off my tie, and threw it onto the passenger seat along with my suit jacket and the manila folder that always came with me just so I could have something in my hand. I rolled down both windows, and wiped the sweat from my forehead. I turned on the radio, but the music was too loud. I drove home with not nearly enough breeze flowing from the windows to cool me down. My back stuck to the seat. I was positive, I said I could do it, and I used as many buzzwords as I could. What did they want from me?

Two days later, Santa Clara still had not called. I got a letter from Cupertino telling me that they were not interested. It was July now. I had failed my "screen test." Santa Clara had abandoned me, and the summer was waning.

Chapter XXI

My friend, Mike, always loved guitars and computers. As a kid, I can remember being at his house looking at the newest video games, which, at the time were little blobs and squares that played "football" against each other. When the game was over, he would show me the riffs he had been working out on the guitar. These passions shaped his adult life as well, and right about the time I was searching for my first full-time teaching job, he had landed his first job as a computer MIS guy. His guitar collection had grown, and he had spare computer parts lying around on his floors and overflowing from his cabinets. I visited him for a housewarming party when he had just moved in to an apartment complex in Campbell. We all sat in the dark because Mike had forgotten to tell the power company he was moving in. A battery-powered CD player blared out Black Sabbath, Mike's favorite band.

Sitting in the dark by the light of a single flashlight, I thought how cool it would be to have an apartment like this one. Everything was his, and he didn't need to worry about anyone coming or going. "If I could only get my life going," I thought, "I would like to get a place just like this for myself." I sipped at a room-temperature beer and fantasized about what it would be like to live like an adult. Mike took me aside, planted a hand on my shoulder and screamed to me over the music.

"There's some empty apartments in this complex!! You should look into getting one!!"

"I can't really do that until I get hired somewhere!!" I yelled back. There was nothing that felt worse at the time than not having a job. My life was being delayed by circumstances that were truly beyond my control, yet I had a knack for dealing myself the guilt that a slacker should feel anyway. Mike took me outside to show me the apartment that was vacant right down the hall.

"There it is man-203 B. It could be yours! Think how cool that would be! We'd be neighbors again!"

Mike and I had grown up in the same neighborhood, and we had lived around the corner from one another during the last semester I was in college. The two of us nearly created a beer shortage during that neighborly stint. It would be good to live close to someone I knew so I could cruise over there if I got bored. "Man," I told him, "it would be perfect! I'd totally dig living here."

The thing that made it even worse was that I had enough money to move in and pay the first two months rent. Of course, if I didn't get hired anywhere, then that would be a problem when the rent for the third month was due. That was why I couldn't start my adult life yet. I would live at my parents' house indefinitely with no chance for parole in sight now that Cupertino didn't like me on film and Santa Clara still hadn't called me back.

Mike's housewarming party broke up about 1 in the morning, and I drove back home to my parents' house.

"That's a cool apartment." I said to my friend Martin as we headed through the night.

"It's all right," he said.

"How was Mike's new apartment?" my mom asked the next morning.

"It's a great place! There's an empty one just like it down the hall. I would love to move in over there! Mike's got no electricity, though. He forgot to activate it."

My mom's lips curled into a smile and she huffed out her nose. "Could you even see the place?"

"I got a pretty good idea. We had flashlights and stuff." My tone dropped. "Man, I wish I just knew what was going to happen. If I was hired someplace, I could go and get that apartment down the hall from

Mike's right now. Why do they need to interview me? Why don't they just watch me teach?"

"It's just not the way things are, dear. I don't know what to tell you."

"How come Santa Clara hasn't called me?"

"You could call them, you know."

This had never occurred to me. I could call them? "What would I say to them?"

"Just tell them you interviewed with them and you were just following up to see if they had made any decisions yet. People do it all the time, Jim."

I called Santa Clara later that morning. "We still haven't placed any teachers." Kathy, in human resources, told me. "You can check back in about two weeks if you want."

I headed down to Kinko's right after the call. I wasn't giving up. There were millions of districts nationwide. I didn't necessarily have to stay in San Jose. It would be rough because all of my friends and my immediate family are here, but sometimes you have to go where the jobs are.

If I went someplace else, there might not be such an emphasis on the CLAD credential. There might be another part of the country with less of an ESL population. I had nothing against teaching ESL students, but since I didn't have a CLAD attached to my credential, the State of California didn't think I was qualified to do it. "I guess I should go and apologize to all those ESL kids that I already taught." I thought, "I did them a disservice, just ask our politicians."

Kinko's was empty as usual on that summer day around 12:30. I added a couple of bucks to my copy card, ran off a resume and a letter of recommendation or two, stuffed an envelope and mailed the whole thing off on my way home. I wasn't even paying that much attention to which district it was that I was applying to anymore. I was running out of local districts. Maybe I would start calling some of the districts I had applied to just to be sure they had received my application. While they have me on the phone, they may just want to bring me in for an interview. I could dream.

I opened the classified section of the newspaper when I got home from Kinko's. I went back to it now and then just to see. Most of the teaching jobs they had listed were for daycare assistance. That's not the sort of teacher I was.

The ad hit me like a cannonball. They needed English teachers in Japan. I looked through the whole ad. There was no mention of the CLAD credential! I called the phone number, and when they answered, I said, "I saw your ad in the San Jose Mercury News, and I had a couple of questions about it."

The man on the phone explained to me that they needed teachers to teach Japanese kids how to speak, read and write English. They would give you an apartment in Japan rent-free and pay you too. You would work six days a week. "Japan…" I thought. "It might be a cool experience."

"Would I need a CLAD credential?"

"A what?"

"Like a special teaching credential to teach ESL?"

"You said you had an English degree right?"

"Yeah."

"That's good enough for us." He had never heard of a CLAD credential. The man told me he'd send me some information and forms to fill out.

This conversation was amazing to me! Here in America where the language is predominantly English, I was considered less of a candidate because I didn't have a CLAD credential. In Japan, all they wanted was my expertise in English to teach English. For the next few days, I entertained the idea of leaving the country so I could teach English.

June came and went. July passed too. I was starting to lose hope. Santa Clara still wasn't making any decisions. I kept beating myself up over what I could have done to make my video interview go better.

I also kept thinking about that empty apartment down the hall from Mike's place. In my room, I stared at the unopened packet that came to me from the people that would send me off to teach in Japan. I picked it up, and looked at my name and address written across it in blue ink. I almost opened it, but then I slapped it back down on my desk. I wasn't one for waving white flags-not today anyway. If I could stop myself today, I could let myself decide again tomorrow. The phone rang. I walked to the kitchen and saw my mom getting the phone while I was still in the hallway.

"Hello?" I heard her say. "Just a minute, please." She turned to me when I had reached the living room. "Jim, the phone's for you."

I reached out to get that phone like a slow motion instant replay. "Hello?"

"Hello, Jim?"

"Yeah."

"This is Connie from the Human Resources Department in the Evergreen School District."

"Are you still looking for a teaching job this fall?"

My heart was pounding.

"Well, great! We'd like you to come in for an interview. We'd like you to meet with Rick, the principal of LeyVa Middle School. Do you know where that is?"

"No."

She gave me directions, and I wrote them down on the back of a used envelope. "When is a good time for you to meet with him?"

This minute! "I could come down on Tuesday." That would give me the weekend plus a day to think about it.

"Okay, great!" Her enthusiasm was fantastic, but I was trying to keep it cool. "How about 2:30?"

"That sounds great." I told her, wishing that the clock said Tuesday at 2:29 this very second.

Kim called on Saturday. "Hey, I have another interview," I casually mentioned.

"Really! Wow, Jim, that is great! Someone is gonna hire you! You're such a good teacher." She was great for self-esteem building.

"How about you, Kim? Have you had any interviews?"

"No."

"How about that summer school job? How is that working out?"

"It's okay," she whined.

"Well, does it look like they're gonna want you to come on full time?" She had mentioned that there was a chance of this, I thought. "Your sister works there, right?"

"Well, yeah, but…I don't know, you know. I'm not sure that this is what I want after all. Like with you, you totally want this and you're totally good at it, but I just don't know. With me, it's like, working at the restaurant is paying me really good money, I mean really good! And I'll probably have to give that up if I start teaching."

"That's cool then." I didn't get this at all. How could you work your butt off for something for a whole year and then decide you don't want it? Whatever, she seemed happy with this decision, and it was one less person I had to compete with for a job.

"Hey, do you want to get together for a beer later or something?"

"Yeah, that sounds great."

We headed out to Gordon Biersch that night. I don't know if Kim ever got into teaching. A few years after this, there was a huge demand for teachers because of the law that California passed about class sizes. All grades from kindergarten through third could have no more than 20 students per class, and schools were hiring teachers that had no credentials at all. Maybe she got picked up at that time. I don't know. I lost track of her.

The Sunday before my interview, I drove out to LeyVa just to be sure I could find it. It was a set of brown buildings surrounded by chain link fence, and an older school from the look of it. The neighborhood had some red tagging, and no one was really out on the street. The houses right by the school looked nice enough-some had manicured lawns and some had dead grass with car parts lying around. Some of the houses had bars on the windows. I had seen worse.

Tuesday came, and, as I could have predicted, the day I scheduled the interview was over 100 degrees. The air conditioning in my mom's house clicked on at about 9 in the morning, which always means record-setting heat. By the time I tied my tie, I could feel sweat dripping from the top of my head. I would be a puddle by the time I got to the school.

I walked out to the family room armed with my trusty manila folder. One of these days, I would be walking out of this house with my manila folder for the last time. This could be it.

My mom saw that I was ready to leave and switched off the vacuum. "Where are you going for this interview again?" she asked.

"It's at a school in Evergreen. It has a weird name. The guy I'm meeting with is Rick." I wiped my forehead.

"Jim, why don't you take my car. At least you'll have air conditioning, and you'll be more comfortable when you get there."

"Are you sure that's okay?"

"Good luck!" she said as she handed me the keys.

In those days, my mom was driving a green LHS. It had a CD player and automatic everything. I would not be able to hear my Dylan tape on the way to this interview, but maybe not hearing it would be lucky for a change. I had listened to it on the way to every interview so far, and I hadn't been hired yet.

I pulled onto Monrovia Drive off of King and headed down to the school. The fence that surrounded it was open at the parking lot, and I pulled in and found a visitor spot. The lot was a small one of about 20 spaces. "Where do they all park when school is in session?" I wondered.

There were two patches of grass on either side of the concrete walkway that led to the front door of the office. The office, like the rest of the school, was the color of coffee-stained paper. It had dark brown trim and a sign with gold letters on a purple background that said George LeyVa Middle School. There was an emblem indicating that the school had been awarded The California Distinguished School Award. "Impressive," I thought.

The front door opened. "Did you need something?" asked a petite Mexican woman with light skin and jet black hair.

"Um…" I was totally off guard, "I'm Jim Kohl, and I'm here for an interview with Rick." I looked at my watch. "I'm a little early."

"Oh, okay, come on in." She stuck out her hand, "I'm Lisa, one of the assistant principals. Have a seat, and I'll tell Rick that you're here."

The lights were off in the office, and fans buzzed from every direction. It seemed like all the fans did was move the heat from one place to another and back again. There were glass cases with trophies from various sports. There was a receptionist counter with two desks behind it. The walls had pictures of graduating classes, sports teams, and kids dressed in the costume of their ancestry.

"Hi, Jim?" asked a small man with a beard and glasses. He was wearing shorts and tennis shoes with white socks. I was a bit overdressed. I heard my mom's voice in my head, 'You can't be too dressed up for an interview.'

"Yes." I said, standing up.

"I'm Rick, the principal. I'm waiting for Mike the assistant principal, and you already met Lisa. We have one other assistant principal, but she is not here today. Mike and I do the interviews, and he just stepped out for a second-I'm sorry about that. We'll be with you shortly. Would you like some water?"

"No thank you." I had taken some for that crazy video interview.

"Okay, well, we'll be with you in a moment." He disappeared around the corner. He seemed like a nice enough guy. I was relieved that it wasn't the guy that I had run into at National who told me I would need a CLAD and insisted I take an application anyway. "I wouldn't be here right now if it weren't for him though-he did give me the application." I thought.

"Jim, we're ready for you now." I hopped out of my seat with my manila folder. "This is Mike, our assistant principal." Rick motioned to a tall man with glasses. He had dark brown hair and light skin with a boyish face. I thought he might be a little younger than I was. I shook hands with Mike, who was holding a Taco Bell soda cup. "So that's why I had to wait! Mike had made a run for the border." I said to myself.

We went into a small room that had three smaller offices around it. "This is where we get the best breeze." Mike said. The three of us sat around a glorified card table.

"Do you have a copy of your resume?" Rick asked. I handed it to him. He looked it over and passed it to Mike who put down his Taco Bell cup. I watched the condensation glisten down the cup. The lights were off in this room too, and the only light came from the open door at the opposite side of the room. The room was so small that the door was only about five steps from us-three steps for Mike.

I looked about the room as they looked over my resume. There were more pictures. There was one of what looked like a female Mexican dance troupe and another of a cheerleading squad from the days of feathered hair. The room was so hot, even with the lights off and the fans, that I half expected the pictures to start curdling in their frames.

I could feel sweat all over my body. I wish I had known that the principal would be wearing shorts. I still wouldn't have-you just don't wear shorts to an interview. "Maybe this means that Rick is just a cool, down to earth guy." I thought. I had time to plan my whole career in this place while these two looked over my resume.

Finally, Mike put my resume down and took a sip from his soda.

"Jim, we're just here to talk, so I want you to relax and talk with us about why you like teaching," Rick said, his voice as soothing as a parent's lulling a child out of a nightmare. It wasn't until he said this that I realized that I was leaning slightly forward and every muscle in my body was flexed. "I want you to relax, truly." I felt the air leave my lungs and my body slouch back into the chair I was sitting in. It was a hard plastic chair like you find in most schools, but it suddenly felt like the best couch you could ever sit on. I looked at Rick and Mike, and I no longer saw the challenging "impress me" attitude of an interviewer. Instead, I saw two friends that had the same passion for education that I had. They just wanted to talk about it. So Rick in his shorts, and Mike with his Taco Bell cup, and I in my suit with my manila folder sat for about a half hour and talked about teaching.

Chapter XXII

My suit was hung and I was back in my shorts and T-shirt before I joined my mom, dad, and sister in the family room. The air conditioning helped me think straight again. I flopped down in the empty green chair.

"So how did it go?" my mom asked. She was sitting on the couch with my dad.

"Pretty well, I think. The principal was a really nice guy. He wore shorts! Man, if I had known that…"

"It's still better that you were in a suit." I nodded. I knew it was true, but I was so uncomfortable.

"He gave me his card and asked me to call him if I get offered a job anywhere else. I think that's a good sign." They all looked like they agreed. "He said he'd call me within the next couple of days."

"What would you be teaching there?" Diane asked from the other green chair.

"They have an opening for a seventh-grade English teacher or a sixth-grade self-contained class. That means that I would have the same kids all day long. That could be cool. I told him I would prefer the seventh-grade English, but that I would be willing to do the sixth as well. Do you think that's an okay thing to say in an interview?"

"Sounds reasonable," my dad said.

"It shows you really want to teach and that you feel comfortable teaching nearly anything." Diane added as she grabbed a water bottle and sipped. I watched the air bubbles travel to the end of the bottle.

"The school seems really into standardized test scores." I continued. "They have some sort of writing test and the test where the kids fill in the bubbles, and the principal made it pretty clear that he wanted to do well on these tests. It's his first year as principal, so that might be why." This was the only interview I had that even mentioned standardized test scores.

"What else did you guys talk about? Did he ever talk about you in the position?"

"No. They asked me if I would be willing to coach, so I told them how I coached the swim team. The principal said that they hadn't started digging the pool yet, so would I be willing to coach anything else. I thought of you, mom, because I told him that I could even if I had to learn about the sport from a book. They have a lot of sports there: wrestling, track, basketball, soccer, cross-country, and some others."

"Track!" my dad repeated. "We didn't have track until high school!"

"Yeah, neither did we." I nodded. I went on about the interview, "The principal said that they have a really intense English department head. He really wants to stress grammar, which I can totally do. I often wondered why it wasn't taught as much in some of my long-term sub assignments. It's like it's gone out of style or something." When Rick had made those comments about the department head, I remember seeing Mike, the assistant principal, chuckling as he sipped from his Taco Bell cup. I remember that he and Rick shared a glance and that Rick explained that there were many dominant personalities on campus.

"Probably no one can teach it," my mom said.

"Huh?" I had been lost in my memory.

"Grammar," my mom explained.

"It's really boring," Diane added.

"I know, I couldn't stand it in school." I thought of my seventh-grade English class. That lady could not relate to us. If I get this job, I thought, I would finally have my chance to show that I could teach English better than that lady. "The school is a mid to low socioeconomic level, and most of the kids are Vietnamese," Rick had told me. The next highest population type was Hispanic. "I don't know why he even told me that. I just hope he hires me. It seems like a pretty cool place."

"Well. I hope wherever you end up, you're happy with it." My dad places a strong value in liking what you do for a living.

"I hope it works out for you, honey." That was my mom.

Diane pensively pursed her lips together and nodded in agreement.

The next day brought nothing. I had already sent in all the applications I had ever ordered. I looked through the phone book, and the only district that had not received a copy of the paper form of me was Alum Rock. I contemplated calling them and requesting an application. I walked the halls of my parents' house that afternoon stewing about whether I wanted to make that phone call. Would a job with them be better than subbing again? In my room, I could see the Japan application collecting dust on my cluttered desk. Would I sooner open and send in that application than go work for Alum Rock? I didn't know, but even though this was the only day the whole summer long that I wasn't doing anything to actively search for a job, I still felt the guilt that comes with inactivity. 'God helps the one that helps himself,' my mom always said.

I picked up the Japan envelope, and began to break the seal with my index finger. I saw Rick's business card, also on the desk but on the side closer to my bedroom door. It had his name and phone number in purple ink. I put the Japan envelope down again.

"Not yet," I said out loud.

The next day, late in the afternoon, I was sitting in one of those green chairs watching some talk show. It may have been Montel trying to figure out who was whose dad, or it may have been Oprah who is more than welcome to endorse this book. The soap and juice drink commercials were waking me up, and I was wondering why the commercials are so much louder than the show.

The guests on the talk show annoyed me. Their problems so often come from themselves that you just want to grab them by the shirt collar and say, "Don't stay with this guy if he's beating you up!!" but they all love their abusive husbands. They can change him. Deep down he's a really good guy; it's only on the surface that he smacks them around. The phone rang.

"Hello?" I said.

"Hello, may I speak to Jim Kohl, please."

"This is."

"Hi, Jim, this is Rick, principal of LeyVa Middle School."

"Hey! How are you?"

"I'm fine, thanks, how about you?"

"I'm great." My grandfather always wanted to know what was wrong with you if you were less than great. "What's stoppin' ya from bein' terrific?" he would ask in his Irish brogue.

"Well, the reason that I called, is to offer you a position teaching with us next year. I would like to offer you the seventh-grade English position that we spoke about on Monday. I'm assuming you are still available for hire."

"Yes. That sounds great! Thanks a lot, and thanks for getting back to me so quickly."

"I need someone now, and you are an ideal candidate. And I truly mean that, sincerely. Mike and I talked after you left and we agreed that you seem genuinely to care about education, and you obviously have the knowledge to extend to the students. We think you'll fit in wonderfully around here."

"Thanks. I was hoping you would call." I was hoping anyone would call, but I liked this guy from the start. I held back the screaming excitement that was trying to burst through every pore of my body. No more car wrecks in my gut; the freeway was wide open and I had a Porsche with a full tank. My dad walked into the room while I was still on the phone.

"Connie from personnel will be calling you within the next couple of weeks to have you come in and sign the contract. You do have the job, though, but the district office is closed for the next week or so."

"Thanks a lot." This was all I could come up with in my moment of victory. My lifelong ambition had just been realized, and I just kept thanking this guy over and over.

"Once you sign the contract, I would like you to come down and get your room and meet Craig, our English department chair. He's the intense one that I talked to you about. This way, you guys can get together and plan the year for English. We had really low test scores last year, and we are looking to you to be a key factor in raising them up."

"That's cool." Here were those test scores again.

"Anyway, as I say, Jim, we are really thrilled to have you, and let me know if there is anything I can do to help you out."

"Thanks." I said. We hung up. "He must think I'm an idiot or some sort of cave man!" I thought. "He hired me to teach English and my sentences were no more than two syllables on average!"

I was a fully employed teacher! The whole journey and struggle came down to one phone call. Five minutes ago, I was a slacker watching talk shows, but now I was a professional. It all seemed so easy now. I was not a sellout; I would make a career out of creativity and keep my soul intact. I was a Bohemian-a subterranean straight out of a Kerouac novel. I was going to live by my rules, not the stock market's. I was a true artist, and I would get paid to be one as well.

"They hired me!" I told my parents.

"Good for you, Jim!" My dad shook my hand.

"Oh honey, I'm so happy for you!" My mom glowed with pride. "Do you have to do anything, like sign anything?"

"They're gonna call me about signing the contract." I floated out of that green chair. "I want an apartment now. I have the money saved up to move in, and I have the money for the first two months of rent. I'm going to go and get that apartment down the hall from Mike's!" The world glowed golden and possible.

I went that very second, 5 o'clock in the afternoon, and applied for the apartment in the Cardiff Gardens apartments on Union Avenue in Campbell. I was approved the next day, and I moved in a week later with the help of my sister's boyfriend, Alex, who was my closest friend with a truck at the time. It took us about 20 loads to move my bedroom into an apartment with much more room than I needed. There was one bedroom, a bathroom that was 10 good sized steps deep, a kitchen with a white electric stove, and air conditioning that was effective if you sat in front of it and didn't move at all with a glass of ice water in your hand in the dark. The living room window looked out on the hallway, and all the neighbors looked in at you when they walked by just like you did to them. The bedroom window looked out on the two black and tall office buildings that are the overlords of the Pruneyard Shopping Center's parking lot. I was paying about $700 a month, and my adult life had finally started.

Somewhere in a trash heap, my unopened application to teach in Japan rotted.

CHAPTER XXIII

I had a month until work started. I woke up early each day and worked out. I would then go home and go back to bed. A little later, I would get up and go get some coffee at the Boulangerie in Pruneyard, which was less than a block away from my apartment complex. I could walk to coffee, but I often drove anyway. I would sit for an hour or so and read and re-fill my coffee until I was on the verge of being jittery. This was a life that I could get used to. This was the summer that I had saved for myself by taking this dream job. I wondered what the cubicle people were doing this morning as I returned to my booth with more coffee in my cup and played with the sugar crystals on the table. "What would I do today after coffee?" I wondered-anything I wanted to.

In the second week of August, my mom called over to my apartment and told me that Evergreen had called her house to set up an appointment for me to come in and sign my contract. I thanked her and called them back immediately. Connie, the human resources clerk, told me to come in at 11 on August 9.

After coffee that morning, I drove down to that district office to sign my contract. It was the perfect California summer day, and the sun was in just the right place in the sky. The hills were golden brown, waiting to be turned emerald by the rains of fall. I pulled into the lower parking lot of the Evergreen District office on Quimby Road and slid the CRX into a visitor's spot. "Someday, I'll be parking in the superintendent's spot!" I joked with myself as I headed for the double glass doors of the main office.

The receptionist pointed me in the direction of human resources, and a blond woman, who appeared to have been with the district for quite a while, greeted me.

"Jim Kohl?"

"Yeah." I was shocked to not have to announce myself.

"I'm Connie. We spoke on the phone."

"Nice to meet you." This was it!

Connie gave me a pile of paperwork to fill out. It seemed like the equivalent of all the applications that I had filled out all summer. There was the contract, the health insurance, the dental insurance, and the life insurance.

"Do you have any dependents?"

I didn't know. She could probably tell by the look on my 25-year-old face that I wasn't up on the buzzwords.

"Do you have a wife or any kids?"

"No. I don't even have a girlfriend."

"Okay, so you won't need this form or this form." She took two of the forms away from my pile. "You can go right into this room to fill these out if you like. Did you want some coffee or anything?"

"No thanks." She left me in a small conference room with a table and four cushy leather chairs. The room was air conditioned like the rest of the District Office.

The good thing about filling out 20 job applications in one summer is that you memorize all the possible questions that show up on forms like these. I was able to breeze through the pile of paperwork in about 10 minutes. I saved the actual contract for last. I saw where Rick had already signed it in thick black ink. There was a spot for my signature and a spot for the superintendent's. I read through it, but I already knew what it said. I held that contract in my hand and marveled at it. I had spent a whole summer chasing this thing in interview after interview. I had stuffed many envelopes to get here, not to mention the two years of subbing and one year at National

University. My whole life would change for certain after I put my name on this piece of paper. I was something, finally-I was a teacher, on paper anyway, once I spilled my ink on this. I took that black ink pen and scribbled my name next to the 'X.'

"I think I'm done." I told Connie.

"Let me see." She held out her hand and took my stack of papers. She flipped through them, eyeing them over the tops of her glasses. "Mmm-hmm." She announced. "I noticed you didn't choose a dental plan."

"I wasn't sure which one to choose." The dental papers had confused me with their thous and therefores, so I just left them blank.

Connie reached into a drawer and pulled out two thick pamphlets that described the two separate dental plan options in much more detail than I ever cared to know. It's amazing to me that Americans just don't let their teeth fall out of their head and live off of milkshakes to avoid the headache of trying to understand the dental plan. The stereotype is that people avoid and procrastinate going to the dentist, but the truth is most people get too confused at the choose a plan part of the process to ever proceed. "These will help you make your choice," Connie assured me.

"Thanks." I took them. One was green and one was maroon. I would find a coin later and make my decision.

I found it odd to fill out a life insurance policy as well. I wasn't planning on dying, so choosing a benefactor in the event of my death was surrealistic to say the least. "Welcome to your career, young man, who do you want to have your stuff if you die?" My mom was going to get all that I owned-the CRX, my compact discs, and my half a box of Kellogg's Special K.

I drove out of that parking lot an official teacher. I had already felt like a teacher, but now I was under contract for the 1995-96 school year. Beyond that was undecided. I was what was called a temporary employee. That means that I would have to re-sign a contract every single year until I was granted Probationary status. Probationary meant that I was one year away from getting Tenure, which means that I would be a full-fledged employee of the district. Only employees that are Probationary or Tenured receive health benefits during the summer.

You are supposed to be granted Tenure on the first day of your third year of teaching, but many teachers are not. There are rules regarding how many tenured staff members a district can have at a time, but once you have it, no one can take it away unless you switch districts.

My brain spun around and forgot most of this information on the drive back to my apartment. The summer sun led me around San Jose like a golden-haired love goddess. I had just signed a binding contract that would guarantee me this sort of freedom every summer until I died. I went up highway 101 farther than I needed to and took in San Jose through the rolled down windows of the CRX. The spirit of pure art and music had been set free that day, and I could feel it in each breath of air that cycled through my lungs, see it in every car and tree and beast, hear it in each song on the radio and in the nameless tunes in my head. I wanted to go down so many roads and stop strangers just to shake their hands. From that day forward, we would miss Jerry. My career started the day my favorite band ended.

The phone in my apartment rang a couple days later. It was Rick. "Hi Jim, Connie tells me you have signed the contract!"

"Yeah! I signed up the other day."

"Well, that's great. We truly look forward to working with you this year. On that note, Craig, the English Department head would like to meet with you. Could you come by the school tomorrow morning about 10 or so?"

This was going to cut into my coffee time. "Yeah, I can be there."

"Great. Since you don't know Craig, just come to the front office, and I'll tell him to do the same. When he is done with you, I would like to meet with you too, if you don't mind."

"Sure." He was my boss, but he was so polite about meeting with me. Couldn't he just demand that we meet? He always could, but he never did, and that is one of the things that made Rick a great principal.

"All right great, well, we'll see you tomorrow then."

The next morning, I dressed up in my teacher's costume. I was no longer a student teacher, so the tie would stay in the closet and wait for a wedding or something. I put on a short sleeve button down shirt and a pair of black Dockers. I wore a pair of black Doc Martens, the only shoe that can get me through the teaching day. This would be my uniform for the rest of my life. These were the clothes of Mr. Kohl, seventh-grade English teacher.

I pulled into LeyVa's parking lot about 10 minutes early. On the other side of the parking lot walked a thin man with large mirrored sunglasses like a skier wears. He carried a navy blue duffel bag with cream-colored straps over his right shoulder. He had on corduroy shorts that were faded blue.

We were both heading for the office, and I wondered if this was Craig, the intense English Department head.

He nodded his head up in the formal male greeting, and said, "Are you James?"

James! Not really, but I'll go with it. New job, new identity. "Yeah."

"Craig." He offered me his free hand.

"Nice to meet you."

He nodded. "So, you're going to be teaching English with us this year, huh?"

"Yeah. I'm really looking forward to it. It was my major."

"Oh, you have an English degree?"

"Yeah."

"Cool. Well, that makes one in the department. Let's go in the office for a second. Did Rick tell you about the tests?"

"A little bit." He opened up the office door for me. He led me into a small room that was next to the photocopy machine.

"I wanna see if I can get you one of these." He slapped a copy of a standardized test on the table that took up most of this room. I recognized it as the CTBS (California Test of Basic Skills) that I had to take every year in grade school. It was the bubble in sort of test where you bubbled the answers in on a separate answer sheet with a number two pencil. I remember the teachers would have a big pile of freshly sharpened number two pencils in case you forgot to bring your own. We all wanted to use a new pencil, so no one would remember their pencil.

"Here's one." Craig gave me a copy of the test. I flipped through it and pretended to look at the pages while he talked. "Over the past week or so, I have been taking this test apart question by question. I've been taking notes on the different skills that are on this test." He showed me a pile of papers about 20 thick with carefully scrawled pencil notes covering every possible inch of them. "These guys get crazy with their skills." His eyes were widening with every word. "We all have different feelings about the importance of basic grammar skills; how do you feel about them, James?" He said, at me.

"I think grammar is important."

"Let me tell you, we got our butts kicked up and down the state last year on this test because teachers just don't want to get down and dirty with these kids and get in their faces and teach some skills. Teachers are so afraid of," his voice got high and whiny, "*drill and kill, drill and kill.* They're so damn afraid that someone is gonna accuse them of drill and kill, that they're afraid to do their jobs and make these kids learn this stuff."

Craig spoke a little more rapidly than a machine gun. I was nearly moved to shout Amen. I see why Rick warned me in advance about this, and I had suspicions about him asking to see me after this meeting. Craig was still talking. "I can't handle all these projects that teachers are having the kids do, I mean, no offense if that's what you're planning, I use them occasionally too. I mean, it looks really good on the surface to have a poster illustrating the themes of Romeo and Juliet, but then when you look down into the actual writing on the poster, and the whole thing is nothing but fragments and run-ons, is that good writing?"

I opened my mouth to answer.

"No! No WAY!" He answered. It was clear that my participation in this conversation was not necessary, so I just listened to him go off. "Have you seen your room yet?"

"No."

"I think you're in five. I'm in three, let's go to my room. You can get into yours through mine and at least take a look at it. Probably nothing there though."

I picked up the CTBS booklet and followed him out of the office, across the courtyard, and into his room. All the way, he was talking. "Writing and English is a skill, I don't care what anyone says. Just like any other learned skill, there are basic skills that make up the large skill of writing. Some of these people will tell you, James, that you can't teach someone to be a better writer by teaching skills." He meant grammar rules. "Basketball is a skill. Does the coach say, '*Okay guys, lets just watch good basketball, and then we'll automatically play good basketball.*'" It was the whiny voice again. "No way! He teaches them how to dribble, he teaches them how to pass, he teaches them how to shoot, he teaches them many ways of shooting-he doesn't start with a slam dunk and a shattered backboard-he starts simple, and when the basic skills are learned, he moves on to the more complicated skills, and he drills them. That is the only way that his team can compete. That is the only way that they can stand up and even have a prayer of being successful! And let me tell you something that they didn't tell you in your teacher-training, mate. When it comes to these tests, we are in competition with the other schools in this district and with the other schools in the state! Where do parents want their kids to go? The schools with the high scores. Plain and simple. It all comes down to basic skills! Gotta walk before you run. Gotta run before you win a marathon. I don't care how you get those kids to get the skills, I don't care if you lecture, drill and kill, use a guitar..."

"I sometimes use one." His room was a clutter of boxes, but his voice filled up most of the school.

"I know that's why I said that. The other thing is you gotta be willing to get in their face and show them there are consequences. I hold kids after school every day that they skip their homework. You'll see it when school starts that after school, on some days, my classroom looks like school hasn't even let out yet. It's the same group of turkeys every day that can't learn to do their homework so they can actually go home on time for once in their lives. But I don't care. The reason we stop at stoplights is because if we don't, the cop will be there to write a ticket. If you do go through stoplights, sooner or later you're going to get burned. If you do get burned, wouldn't you learn not to go through stoplights?"

"Ye..."

"Of course you would. Some of these kids, mate, are too stupid to know how to help themselves. So I force them to. People say I'm crazy to keep them all every afternoon, but I say you're not doing your job if you don't." he paused for a second. "Did you want to see your room?"

"Actually, I'm supposed to meet with Rick."

"Oh, I won't keep you then." It had been an hour. "Anyway, go through that test book and take notes on the necessary skills. Glad to have you here."

"Thanks."

I walked out of Craig's room in a daze. I stared straight ahead at absolutely nothing, and watched the heat bounce off the cement. I walked across the concrete courtyard back to the side office door that led into the faculty room. It was propped open as it had been, I'm sure, on the day of my interview to try to get a cross breeze through this tomb of heat. I walked to Rick's office, which was right next to the room where Craig had given me the standardized test that seemed to have taken the place of my manila folder of old.

Rick sat at a large desk neatly organized with carefully placed piles of papers. There was a computer to his right, and the entry door was to his left. His eyes came up from the papers on his desk when I walked in. He looked down at the CTBS book that was in my right hand and grinned, "I see you met Craig."

"Yeah."

Rick laughed. My face probably said it all. "Craig has a lot of factual opinions, that is I mean, he considers them to be facts. Your opinion matters to him as long as it matches. He's a good guy though. He and I can scream at each other for hours on end and still be friends. We truly can; it's not a personal issue at all even though it sounds like it sometimes. There is a lot of that here at LeyVa, and I wanted you to be exposed to it as early as possible."

"That's cool." There is something about being in the principal's office that never left me no matter how old I got or the fact that it was with Rick, a very nice man. I kept expecting him to tell me that my behavior was unacceptable and that he was going to have to call my parents.

"So he wasn't too hard on you then?"

"No. I agree that grammar skills are important, so he was more or less preaching to the choir."

"That's good! Now, Jim, by no means do I expect you to have his sort of…" Rick looked around the room for the right word to fall out of the air while he worked his hands back and forth, "…Mania, I guess, as far as keeping the kids after for skipping homework. I never did that as teacher. No one really does it except him. You're free to do it if you like, but it's not a school policy or anything like that."

"Okay." I nodded and stared at the papers on his desk.

"There is a new teachers orientation that I would like you to attend. There are three other new staff members that you can meet while you are there. It's next Tuesday morning, and I think it goes all day."

"Right on." I felt like I should say something else. "I'm really anxious to meet the challenge of these tests," I flopped the test book around. "I can't wait for school to start. I've never said *that* before in my life!"

"I imagine not!" He laughed, "And to be honest with you, I haven't said it too many times myself. Now did you get a chance to see your room?"

"No."

"Okay, well, let me give you a quick tour of the school and we'll end up in your room. I can't give you the key though. Pat, the secretary, is off until next week, and she would tear me to pieces if I went into her system and gave it to you. If you would like to get in there before that, just find me, and I'll let you in. Or you could sneak through Craig's or one of the other teacher's rooms. There is a center room that all the rooms in your pod share, so you can slip through it and get to your room through any room in your pod. The center room in the English pod is a bit…" again he searched the air for the correct word, and he seemed to find it floating near the clock on the wall behind me, "messy, I guess. One of the teachers has been converting it into a makeshift computer lab using a bunch of old Apple 2e's."

"That's cool." I didn't know much about computers, but I remembered using an Apple 2e when I was in middle school about 12 years earlier.

"Anyway, let me show you around." Rick pushed himself to a standing position and we walked out of his office. He showed me where the copy machines were, where the paper cutter was, where the staff lunchroom was, where the bathrooms were and where the teacher's boxes were. The boxes had no names on them yet, but they eventually would and soon after that they would be crammed with the daily roll sheets and papers selling books and videos.

We walked outside and he showed me the outside of the gym. Finally, we walked back over to the English pod and I was let in to Room 5 for the first time. We flicked on the lights, which showed us aged orange low nap carpet that was new in about 1970. The room was empty except for a teacher's desk and 30 student desks with plastic chairs attached. Some of the student chairs were blue, some were green, some were yellow and some were black. As you entered, to the right was a yellowed curtain wall that could be opened in the center and pushed completely out of your way. If you were team teaching with the teacher in that room, it would be really convenient.

"Who teaches on the other side of the curtain?" I asked.

"No one."

"Cool." I could be as loud as I wanted.

I continued to take in the room. The wall opposite the curtain wall had an old brown chalkboard on it. Directly to the left of the entry door was a broken shelf with metal jacket hooks beneath it. Just beyond that was a window. "I'll put my desk right there by the window." I thought. To the right of the door, a red fire extinguisher hung. I wondered if it worked.

On the wall opposite the entry door was a cabinet about three feet high and nine feet wide. It had light orange drawers on the left half and light orange cabinet doors on the right half. On the far right of that wall was a door that led to the center room Rick had mentioned. On the far left of that room was a tall brown cabinet.

"The books are probably stored in these drawers and cabinets. The school's collection of novels is in the cabinets in that center room. Both the reading books and the grammar books are a bit dated, but we are up for getting new sets in two years. I'll leave you alone to see what you can find in here. I'm going to lock the door, so just be sure it's closed when you leave, okay?"

"Okay."

"Let me know if you need anything."

"Okay. Thanks." My eyes kept darting around the room. This is where it was all going to happen! If I did it right, I would be affecting lives in a positive way right here in this room. This is where I was going to turn kids on to literature and teach them how to write well. This is Mr. Kohl's room.

Chapter XXIV

Looking through the cabinets and drawers of my room unearthed all sorts of treasures. I found 10 posters, of which I used one. It was of the school name and logo, the fierce-looking face of a bulldog outlined in purple. There were about 30 boxes of yellow chalk, a tin of well-used crayons, and a fluorescent orange and purple Nerf football. I kept the football in my desk drawer.

I arranged my desk and the students' desks the way I wanted them. I mapped out in my mind where I would put some posters. I made a list of the items that I needed from the teacher supply store: grammar/writing posters, stapler, tape, red pens, (no teacher should be without them) and trays to organize the mountain of paper that would come my way. My hair lay drenched across my forehead. I wiped it away, swearing that this is the last time I come to this school in anything but shorts on a non-school day.

Back in the center room, there were two file cabinets, a tall one and a short one, with Room 5 marked on them, so I moved them into my room. It was tough moving them around all the antique computer parts that Rick had mentioned. Once they were in place, the heat in the room became nearly unbearable, so I went home. Why couldn't I have been hired at a school with air conditioning?

I took a copy of *Blueprints*, the reading book, and a copy of *Language Arts Today* home with me along with the CBEST test. I would go over all three within the next few weeks to figure out what I wanted and didn't want to teach this year. I was excited that Edgar Allan Poe was on the seventh-grade reading list because I always liked him. My career was off to a good start.

"So how was the school?" asked my friend Martin on the phone.

"They don't have a lot of stuff, including air conditioning, but the principal seems cool. Dude, the English department head is a trip!" I explained Craig's sermon as briefly as possible.

"That's cool. Hey, uh, when do you guys start anyway?"

"I don't know exactly, the last couple days of August, I think."

"But August is supposed to be sacred!" From his tone, you would've thought he was starting school that day.

"I know man, it sucks. It starts earlier and earlier it seems like." We made plans to hang out later that week and hung up.

I walked to my blue-and-white couch, the one that sat virtually unused in my parents' living room for years and was already starting to show the scars of use after less than a month in my apartment. I turned on my TV that sat on an old blue bench built by the grandfather that I never knew, and felt like my life was pretty much perfect. School was all I wanted to talk and think about. I couldn't wait to start.

I looked at the two textbooks and the standardized test booklet that I brought home. My reading material for the coffee shop was set for the next couple of weeks. I needed to figure out which stories to read and whether the grammar book was organized in a way that would work for me.

I thought of Craig and how I needed to go through the standardized test booklet to list the skills my kids would need to pass the test. I had my work cut out, but the test scores were so low the previous year that I didn't think it was going to be that much of a big deal to show improvement. I looked out my window and watched the summer sun lose its hold on the day. The phone rang. It was my mom.

"What's going on?"

"I saw my classroom today, and I met the English department head. He's a bit crazy, I think, but that's about normal for middle school. He's really into these tests. I need to help this school bring up their test scores, which supposedly really sucked last year."

"I'm sure you'll be able to do it, honey."

"Yeah." I sure hoped so. "What's going on with you?"

"Well, I was talking with my friend Monica at church, do you remember her?"

"Yeah." She had taught religion classes to me when I was a kid.

"Well, she was asking about you and Diane and I told her that you had just got this teaching job. She is a teacher, you know, so she asked where. I told her in Evergreen, and she asked me which school. I could not remember the name of your school, but I told her it was a middle school and that the name started with the letter 'L'. Anyway, that is where she works!"

"No way!" I flipped the phone wire around in my hand and looked out my kitchen window at the young woman that lived downstairs. "What does she teach?"

"Eighth-grade English."

"Oh, cool!" It was a comfort knowing that I knew at least one staff member from my former life.

"Anyway, she asked me to give you her phone number in case you wanted to get together with someone to talk about the school."

"That would be great!" I took down the phone number and thanked my mom. I called Monica, and we made plans to meet at a coffeehouse in Almaden, called Our Daily Bread, the next morning. It was a family-owned coffee shop where two of my friends and I had once played music for tips on a Sunday morning.

Mike, from down the hall, pounded on my door.

"Jimmy-James, what's up?" he asked as he barreled in.

"Not much man. I met some of the people I'm going to be teaching with today. What's going on?"

"You wanna go get something to eat?"

"I already ate, but I'll come along and grab a soda and hang out."

We piled into Mike's car and headed off to Kentucky Fried Chicken with Black Sabbath screaming and growling out the soundtrack of our lives.

"Check out this riff right here, man!" Mike reversed the CD a couple of beats. "Right here!" He yelled just under the volume level of the music.

"Cool!" I shouted. I think I had heard what he was talking about, but I could never be 100 percent sure. Mike had the Black Sabbath catalogue memorized note for note. He could point out songs in which Toni Iommi slid his fingers across the strings before hitting the first power chord. You've never heard Black Sabbath until you've listened to them with Mike.

After dinner, we spent the rest of the night in his apartment checking out the newest video games and listening to Sabbath and Jimi Hendrix. Mike was some sort of computer repair guy at the time, and there were chipboards and spare computer parts taking up every inch of space in his apartment that wasn't taken up by a CD or a guitar.

We relieved the world of some excess beer, and at the end of the night, I walked back down to my apartment in the darkened hallway just like I did that night that Mike had moved in and had no electricity. This time, I took out my key and opened the door to my own place. The novelty of complete independence beautified in my slight beer buzz.

I let myself fall asleep in front of the TV in the dark. I was going to meet Monica tomorrow, one more step in my fledgling teaching career.

It occurred to me as I went to the coffee shop the next morning, that I didn't really remember what Monica looked like. I guess I would just hope she recognized me, or I would see someone that looked familiar. In the meantime, I ordered a cup of coffee and sort of hung out, watching the door. Our Daily Bread had self-serve free refills, so I was set for the morning even if I didn't find Monica.

A blond woman about my mom's age came in. I recognized her from somewhere, and I figured this must be her.

"Jim?" She asked, as I approached her.

"Yeah."

"I'm Monica." We shook hands. "So you'll be working with us this year?"

"Yeah. I'm really looking forward to it!"

"Wonderful! Do you know what room you are in yet?"

"I'm in 5, over there towards the front of the school by Monrovia Drive."

"Oh wonderful! I'm in Room 4, so we'll be neighbors."

"Cool!" Monica would be teaching on the other side of the wall from my chalkboard. At least I would have a nearby support group. "She could be my new Lynne," I thought.

"Well, let me get some coffee," Monica said, as she fumbled with her black vinyl purse, "and we'll get a table."

There were two rooms in Our Daily Bread. The room with the cash register was always hectic; we chose a table against the wall in the middle of the quieter room and talked about education.

Monica had been teaching in the Evergreen District since the year that I was born. She started off at Quimby Oak, but moved to LeyVa and would not dream of going anywhere else. She actually knew George LeyVa who named the school after himself in an amazing act of modesty when he became the superintendent of the district. Before she worked for the public schools, she worked in the Catholic schools and was even a principal of one for a while. In those days, the Catholic schools principals still had to teach classes as well as run the school. For Monica, teaching in the public schools was retirement compared to that ordeal.

"Have you met anyone else from the school?" Monica asked with a smile in her voice.

"I met Craig." I studied her face to see if she would tell me anything with it. "He seems pretty...dedicated."

"That he is!" She laughed. "It's tough to get a word in with that guy, but he's a great teacher. The kids really learn from him."

"He seems a little crazy."

"Aren't we all though?"

I nodded. "So what else is the school like?" I was hoping to hear a straight story about behavior and whether I had accidentally landed in a place like the middle schools in Alum Rock.

"Oh it's a great school! Every year we are given the opportunity to transfer out and no one ever does. I think you'll really like it there. They're a bit eccentric, and some are overly opinionated at times, but we have fun. Do you know anything about computers?"

"A tiny bit." This was an exaggeration on my part. I knew how to play video games in Mike's apartment, and I could use one as a really expensive typewriter.

"I'm trying to make a computer room in that center room of the English pod. Did you go back in there at all?"

"Yeah." I smiled picturing those Apple IIe's strewn about in there.

"Then you know I don't have much to work with. Would you know about hooking them all up to printers?"

"No, but the guy down the hall from me in my apartment complex is an MIS guy. He's really busy, but I could ask him if he could come in and take a look."

"That would be great, if he could. Yeah, please do check with him."

"So what about behavior at this school?" I figured I had better go direct.

"The behavior really is not that bad."

"Do you ever write referrals?"

"Oh, a referral is a last-ditch effort. I haven't had to write one in a couple of years. Those are for extreme cases like fights, which we hardly ever have."

This place was sounding great. I sipped at my coffee with the confidence that I would be able to survive.

"The guy whose place you're taking tried to be all chummy with the kids, and so a lot of them ate him alive."

"Oh well," I put my cup down, "I would never do that. You need to have a professional distance."

"Exactly."

"I mean you can be close to the kids, but you still have to teach and they still have to learn."

"Exactly. I'm glad to see that you know that going in. Don't smile until Christmas." This is an old adage among teachers meaning that you have to be strict and hard for at least half of the year. You can always lighten up as far as discipline goes, but it's harder and, in some cases, impossible to get strict after you have started soft. My problem was just the idea of being there made me smile.

"So who else is in the English department?" I asked.

"In seventh grade, David has all of the gifted kids. We don't have an honors English class in the eighth grade, so the gifted kids get mixed in with the normal kids. It's great for us because we really get to have some stars in our classes. I've always thought it was a little unfair to the rest of the seventh-grade teachers that David has all of the gifted kids. Maybe after you have been there for a while, you can try to take one of those classes from him."

"I don't know about that right off the bat." I couldn't imagine going in to a new job and demanding changes. "I was one of those gifted kids as a kid though."

"Yeah, I know." Monica sipped her coffee, and as the ceramic cup clopped back onto the table, she changed the subject. "Shirley is the other eighth-grade English teacher, along with Craig and me. Jacque is also a new English teacher. She's been in our district for a while as a librarian, but they cut the library budget and they her a job teaching English and Social Studies. You'll like her; she's a nice lady."

"That's cool. Maybe I'll meet her next week because I'm supposed to go to some new teacher orientation at the district office." Talking to

Monica had made me feel a lot better, the more people I knew going in the better.

We talked more about the school. We talked about how I was expected to chaperone dances and support the athletic program by either coaching, volunteering to work at events or at least attending them to support the team. We talked a bit about the district writing proficiency test and how Monica was glad that it was not part of the eighth-grade curriculum anymore. "Of course if they fail it in seventh, they have to take it again in eighth." She told me. Its importance was a bit overrated she told me.

"But Craig and Rick seem to think that it's really important." My face twisted in confusion and wonder.

"Craig is just that way when it comes to tests, and Rick really wants to see last year's scores improve because this is his first year as principal. Don't worry about it."

I worried anyway.

Just before we left, I asked, "Are there any at-risk kids at this school?"

Monica smiled and grunted a laugh. "Honey," she said, "they're all at-risk."

I wasn't sure what she meant, but I let it go at that anyway. Monica would become my rock-the person I turned to when things got too intense, the person I would bounce new ideas off of. She was my new Lynne as I ventured into the uncharted and wild territory of LeyVa Middle School.

Chapter XXV

My restful summer life slowly gave way to a hectic career man's life. At coffee at Boulangerie, I no longer perused a book of choice as I filled cup after cup. I looked through the CTBS and made two pages of notes on what I thought were the skills covered in there. I thought of Craig's 20 some odd pages and felt a sense of inferiority and failure, but I couldn't force myself to find more there than I could see. Maybe I was being too general.

I had Craig's home number, so I called him one evening and told him what I had done.

"All I got out of that test book was about two pages, man." I told him.

"That's fine. We'll combine notes when we get back to school." The guy was not a phone talker. The conversation lasted almost two minutes, including the time I spent waiting for him to answer. I put my notes on the CTBS test in a folder, and I put the folder in one of my huge empty cabinets in my bathroom, and they may still be there right now.

I went to the teachers' supply store. I didn't even know there was such a thing until I student taught and Lynne mentioned it at one point or another. Most of the posters that you saw on your teacher's wall as a kid came from a teachers' supply store. The racks are filled with educational and inspirational posters, charts, signs, diagrams, cardboard punch out letters, markers of every possibility, and books.

I browsed through the poster rack and picked up a few that had to do with grammar and writing. I also got one with a pair of hands surrounded by shimmering lights that said, "Hold on to your dreams." I bought a long one that went across the top of my chalkboard with the slogan, "You're not finished when you lose, you're finished when you quit."

I picked up a box of red pens to correct student work. I paid for this all out of my own pocket and couldn't be reimbursed by petty cash from my school because the total cost was more than $25. If I really wanted to fill out the paper work and wait for a month or two, I could have been reimbursed, but it seemed like too much of a hassle, and anything that I got reimbursed for would become the property of the school. That meant that if I ever changed schools, I would have to leave all my posters there and start all over again with nothing.

I was glad I was going to teach middle school because elementary school teachers spend even more money out of their own pocket each year. "It's probably not that the salary is not good." I thought, "It's just that to do the job right, you need to put so much of your own money into it."

My next stop was Office Max where I picked up a stapler, staples, file folders, stacking trays for papers, and a couple of notebooks. That day, I spent nearly $60 just to get my classroom up and running. I kept all of my supplies in the back of the CRX until the time that they would be up on the classroom wall. It was less than two weeks now, and I had the feeling of ultimate excitement mixed with a sense of immeasurable fear. At least I had Monica in the classroom next door for the times when running and screaming down the Capitol Expressway seemed like a logical option.

A few days later, all the new teachers were to meet at the district office for orientation. I went by LeyVa early that morning to hang the posters that I bought from the teachers' supply store. I found an open door and got into my room.

I clicked open my new stapler and loaded it full of silver staples. I put up the four posters that I had bought. I put the poster of the purple bulldog up on the wall directly behind my desk. The walls looked like 20 feet of white sidewalk with three red or blue bottle caps randomly tossed on it. "I might need more." I thought as I looked over my work.

Looking through the center room where Monica was constructing Frankenstein computers, I found a daily schedule that I taped to a green piece of construction paper that I found at the back of one of the drawers in my room. I added this to the wall. Now my vacant sidewalk had four bottle caps. "Well," I thought, "that is how it's gonna be."

Although I had arranged the desks on my last visit to the room, someone had come and "unarranged" them. I put them back the way I wanted them and headed down Capitol Expressway to Quimby to meet with all the other new teachers.

Bowls of small candy bars centered each of the white tables in the conference room where the new teacher orientation would be. Being one of the first people there, I flopped my spiral notebook with my pen jammed into the spirals down on the table and slumped into the chair the way I had all through my career as a student. I brought the notebook and pen just to have something in my hand the way I had never gone to an interview without my manila folder. I would seem prepared and organized to anyone without access to my true emotions and the general cognitive chaos that is my thoughts when I'm starting something new. I unwrapped and ate a candy bar just to have something to do.

Soon, the room filled with mostly women and a few men. They all appeared to be about my age, but some were older. It reminded me of my credential classes. A tall blond guy sat at a table to my right. He reminded me of a GQ model or a giant Ken Doll. I watched all the other tables fill in. Three guys came in together and sat together at a table across the room from me. My table filled in with three women.

The meeting started off with Mr. Smith, the superintendent, Maryanne and Loribeth, the assistant superintendents, Betty, I still don't know what she does to this day, and Cliff, the head of human resources. They introduced themselves, welcomed us, and they all left except Cliff, who piled us onto a yellow school bus to take a driving tour of the district.

The Ken Doll guy sat behind me on the bus. "How's it goin'?" I nodded to him as he walked past me to take his seat.

"Pretty good." He answered. As he took his seat, he offered his hand, "I'm Eric."

"Jim." We shook hands. "So, what are you going to teach?"

"Fourth grade. Cliff just got me in today. I'm going to be at Cadwallader. How about you?" Erik seemed to be in pretty tight with Cliff, whom I had never met. I caught the vibe through the ride that everyone had at least met Cliff before today.

"I've got seventh-grade English over at LeyVa."

We toured the district and stopped at nearly all of the schools. Cliff narrated the ride over a PA system the way a tour guide would. After awhile, all the schools started to look the same. "You see that shopping center to your right?" Cliff pointed, "They had to take all the payphones out of that shopping center because there were too many drug deals going down in there."

Where did I land?

We returned to the District Office and took our seats. "Why don't you guys spend some time introducing yourselves to the people at your table, and then we'll go around the room and introduce ourselves to the big group. You'll find that the camaraderie that you begin building today will be invaluable as your career progresses."

We did that. I was at a table with Krissa, Mary, and Annabelle. They all were going to teach at elementary schools, and Krissa and Annabelle were going to teach at the same one.

"I can't believe school starts *next* week!" panicked Krissa.

"I know! My room is like, in total pieces. Chunks of stuff here and chunks of stuff there. I don't see how it's ever going to come together," added Mary.

"I need to go back to the teacher supply store again," Annabelle complained.

"My room is ready," I said. I squeaked it out about as shyly as I have ever said anything in my life. They all stopped dead in mid-complaint and stared at me. I had to say something. "I told you. I'm teaching junior high, and I put up about five posters and that's about all I'm going to have this year. I figure I'll build as I go."

"Five posters?"

I nodded. They went on with their conversation about welcome signs, red playground balls, boxes of crayons, multi-colored bonded construction paper, posters for each subject, bulletin boards made of fade proof paper, and the borders that go around them.

I sat and listened to them as my head spun on my shoulders. Why didn't I care about any of this stuff? I had planned on going in and teaching. I am my own visual aid. Over the years, more and more would accumulate on my walls, but for now I planned on being a minimalist. Maybe I wasn't doing enough? Maybe I should decorate more. I thought about my five posters-my sidewalk littered with a couple bottle caps-and I started to doubt. Well, I'm here to teach, not decorate. The way the room is decorated now, I can only show improvement in the coming years. The three women rattled on about laminating everything, and I fell into a daze.

When we introduced ourselves to the room at large, I found that the three guys that had shown up together and were sitting together would be working at LeyVa too. One was a jolly looking guy with spiky brown hair. One was a skinny guy with a long neatly captured ponytail. The last guy wore a white shirt and had blond hair and a beard. "I should probably go introduce myself to those guys at some point," I thought.

Cliff introduced two teachers that would be our mentors. We were supposed to call them if we had a question about anything, and they would be offering workshops for us to attend throughout our first year.

The two of them were in charge of all 50 of us. They started telling us all about setting up our classrooms.

"One thing that is a great idea," bubbled the tall blond one, "is to make paper apples out of red and green construction paper. You know, use red for the apple and green for the leaves."

Oh, I'm glad you cleared that up. That whole color thing really had me for a second.

"A lot of times you can use scraps from your scrap paper box, or find a nice teacher at your school that will let you go through their scrap paper box," she continued. "And anyway, make an apple for each child in your room and write their name on it. That way, when they show up to school on the first day, they'll already feel special because something in the room will have their name on it."

"A paper apple!" I thought. It became obvious quickly that this orientation was geared toward elementary teachers. They didn't seem to be concerned with the disaster that would greet me if I were to give each of my 150 students an apple with their name on it. With middle school kids, never give them something to throw or something to hit each other with. Above all, don't give something to a middle school kid that makes them think that you are treating them like a baby. I didn't even have one teaching day at LeyVa yet, and I knew I wasn't going to be passing out any paper apples.

"And it's a good idea to laminate your paper apples so that they will last the entire year." Her voice modulated up and down like she was describing the prizes we won from a game show. I looked around the room as she spoke and watched as nearly everyone scribbled down little tidbits of advice that rolled off her tongue. I stopped listening when she was saying something about making a growth chart with all the students heights at the beginning of the year, which you can then add their heights at the end of the year to see who grew the most.

Don't get me wrong, all the ideas were cute and very nice for elementary, but none of them were geared for middle school. "You know," I said to the people at my table during a break, "they're not really saying much about middle school preparation."

Krissa turned to me and said, "Just put up your five posters and try not to get killed this year. There you go."

"Thanks." I said. I walked over to the three guys who were also going to be teaching at LeyVa.

"Hey guys. I'm Jim, and I'm going to be teaching with you over at LeyVa this year."

"Hey, cool. I'm Steve." The red was really close to the surface of his face as it is in mine, and I wondered if he was Irish. "This is Mark and Roland." He motioned to Mark, a solid looking guy with a blond beard. Roland was a skinny neo-hippie with a long brown ponytail.

"Nice to meet you guys." We all shook hands.

"Nice to meet you too. What are you teaching?"

"Seventh grade English. How about you guys?"

"I got sixth-grade." This was Steve. He was definitely the friendliest of the bunch of us, including me. I nearly had that sixth grade. I thought. It was weird to meet the guy that got the job you almost had. He may have been thinking the same of me.

"That's cool."

"I'm doing seventh grade science and PE." This was Mark. He seemed the PE type-a man's man in the Ernest Hemingway tradition.

"Cool."

"I only work a half day. I'm teaching three classes of eighth-grade U.S. History." Roland said.

"Right on. Man, I don't really feel like anything they're saying here today relates to me and what I'm doing at all." I said quietly to the group.

"I know!!" Steve said. His ruddy face bursting into laughter, "We've been joking about it the whole time." Steve shook with laughter, Mark smiled, and Roland sat quietly as if in deep thought. It was painfully obvious that I was sitting at the wrong table. Roland probably was too.

"Have you guys worked on your rooms at all?" I asked.

"Yeah, mine's just about done." Mark said as he popped one of the candies from the center of the table into his mouth.

"I only have about five posters, man."

"I think I might have seven, but maybe less." Mark and I were on the same page, anyway.

"I do not have too many things either." Stated Roland.

"I got a lot of junk, but you know, my sixth grade is self contained, so it's supposed to look more like an elementary room." Steve said, "I'm nowhere near set up."

"I put up about five posters, and I feel like I'm pretty much done. The people sitting at my table over there are freaking out on me. I think they're going to spend the rest of the week until school starts laminating paper apples!"

"With names on them!" Steve's eyes teared up he was laughing so hard. Roland contemplated the room, and Mark half smiled while watching Steve.

These all seemed okay. Steve seemed really cool. I felt better about my five posters, and I felt a little more at ease in general knowing that these guys would be new at LeyVa with me. It was seven days until the first day of work where we would all meet back at the school. The kids would start the next day. The eve of my professional life had arrived.

Chapter XXVI

My eyes opened far before my 4:30 a.m. workout alarm screamed on the first day of work at LeyVa. I lay in the dark and wondered what my life was about to become.

I went to the gym and finished up there at about 6. I showered there for the first time because today there would be no going back to bed. Today, I would become a part of the work force in a way that I never had before. My life's work would begin today, and I would never be quite the same again.

I dressed in the gym locker room and put on jeans and a T-shirt. This was my last day to dress relaxed for a while because tomorrow, when the kids would be at school, I would wear my teacher costume. I found a nearby 7-Eleven and bought the biggest cup of coffee I could find. Then, the CRX, my coffee, the textbooks I had taken home ages ago, and I headed off to LeyVa.

The small parking lot was much more full this morning than I had ever seen it. I would have to get here early every day if I didn't want to use the far lot and walk the length of the campus. I pulled into the second to last open spot in the lot and headed to the front office.

Rick stood in the hall by the teachers' mailboxes slipping a piece of paper into each one.

"Good morning, Jim." He said. "Have you met Dolores yet?"

"I don't think so."

"She's one of our assistant principals. Let's see if she's available." Rick led me into the Student Center where I had interviewed with him and Mike about a month earlier. The lights were on today, and two female clerks sat behind a desk. They filed papers and answered the constant ring of the phone. Rick brought me to a small office not five feet from the counter where the two women bustled away the last bits of their summer. "Dolores," he said, "this is Jim Kohl, our new seventh-grade English teacher."

"Nice to meet you." Dolores was a petite Mexican woman with short dark hair. "Do you have time to sit down for a second?" Dolores motioned to a chair in the cramped office. I sat.

"Once again, Jim, welcome to LeyVa. Now if you two will excuse me…"

"Sure. See you later Rick." Rick headed off in about 10 directions.

"So you were an English major?"

"Yes."

"Do you do any writing at all?"

"Yeah. I have written some stories, lots of poems, and some songs. I published a couple poems in some small literary magazines."

"That's great. I write as well."

"Cool!"

"I've written a couple of children's books. It's tough to get published though."

"It sure is." That truth hung in the silent air.

"Do you have the seventh-grade novel list yet?"

"Is that the one with Edgar Allan Poe on it?" My eyes darted around the office as we spoke. Dolores had a son about 5 years old if the pictures that were everywhere were new.

"I think so," She said. "It's this one." She reached into a drawer and handed me a sheet of paper. I read it over.

"Yeah, I did get this. I have pictures that I took of Edgar Allan Poe's grave when I was in Baltimore that I'm planning on using in class."

"Oh, I think the kids would really like that. Anytime you can make something more real for them, it's a good thing. Here's a copy of the eighth-grade novel list just so you have it. You can't teach anything that is on it, but it may be helpful to at least know what is on it. District policy is that you can teach down, but you can't teach up. In other words, an eighth-grade teacher can teach something on the seventh-grade list, but you can't teach anything on the eighth-grade list." She paused and looked at me as if she were trying to read my reaction to this. I didn't care. "I think Monica, for example teaches *The Pearl* by John Steinbeck even though it's on the seventh-grade list. If you decide to teach it, it would mess up her program."

"That's fine." I was so happy to have a job, nothing was going to upset me-even if it did seem like a slightly unfair policy.

"Well, I won't keep you any longer. There is supposed to be a big meeting at Chaboya, one of the other middle schools, with all the district employees. I think that starts in about a half-hour. I'm glad you'll be working with us Jim."

"Thanks. I'm really glad to be here."

I left Dolores's office and headed for the teacher mailboxes. I found mine. There was a little white paper tab that said, 'James Kohl 7th Grade English.' I reached into the box for the first time and pulled out a pile of papers and pamphlets. There was a green itinerary sheet that outlined the whole day for me. There was going to be a district meeting at Chaboya at 9. Then, there was a LeyVa staff meeting at 11. Then I would have some time to get lunch and work in my room. At 1, there was a meeting with Dolores and all of the new teachers.

I still didn't have a key to the room I realized as I tucked the papers under my arm.

Pat was a blond secretary. She assigned my room key to me and also gave me a key to the file cabinet that was in my room. "You need to sign this so we can keep track of where the keys are."

"Sure." I signed it, handed it back to her, and I never saw it again until I signed the key in to her the following June.

I went to the closet in my room and took out a box of yellow dust free chalkboard chalk. It was amazing to me, throughout that first year, how many times my clothes were coated with dust free chalk dust at the end of a teaching day.

I wrote the word Homework at the top of the far right side of the chalkboard and drew a line, making a column. I would list homework there everyday. Just to the left of that, I wrote the date of the first day of school right below my name, Mr. Kohl. My career became more real every second.

On the far-left side of the chalkboard, I made a daily agenda, an idea I had stolen from the sixth-grade science department at Cabrillo. The agenda had three branches stemming from a box in the center. One arm branched diagonally to the right and one branched diagonally to the left. The third arm branched straight down.

In the center box, I wrote the main focus of a day's lesson, such as Nouns. Underneath the arm on the right, I listed everything the students would do that day such as, Take Notes. Underneath the arm on the left, I listed everything I was going to do that day such as, Lecture. The arm on the bottom had any group work involved in the days' lesson listed next to it. This was the greatest because it eliminated the "What are we going to do today, Mr. Kohl?" question. It also showed, graphically that we were all responsible for part of the learning process.

"How are you doing?" It was Monica coming through my door.

"So far so good. I'm ready for the kids, I think."

"Well I would hope so, Kohl, they'll be here tomorrow!"

I glanced at my watch. "Are you going over to the meeting at Chaboya?" I was hoping I could bum a ride or at least offer her one because I had no idea where Chaboya was.

"What meeting?" She wrinkled her face as she asked me.

"You know, this district meeting that we're supposed to have at 9." I walked to my desk and showed her the green itinerary sheet. She paused and shook her head.

"I don't think this meeting is going to happen."

"What do you mean?"

"Well, we have been working without a contract for nearly nine months, and to show our disapproval with the district administration, most of the teachers that have been here for a while are boycotting the meeting. I heard they were just going to cancel it."

I didn't understand one word she said. "What do you mean you guys have been working without a contract? I signed a contract less than a month ago."

Monica explained that all the teachers in a district work under an identical contract. Tenured teachers work under the same contract. The main difference is that temporary (new) teachers do not have health coverage over the summer months. "That contract has expired. In this district, we have to renegotiate a new contract every three years." Monica was quick to justify this, "That's better than most because in some districts, they go through negotiations every year."

Negotiations didn't sound so bad-we give a little, they give a little. Sesame Street must have planted that definition of negotiation in my brain. "What do you mean negotiations?"

"Mainly, we're trying to get a raise. He only gave us a 2 percent raise over three years last time." By "he," Monica meant Mr. Smith, Evergreen's superintendent. Monica continued, "No one is going to expect you to do anything, but our staff has a reputation as being sort of…ugly during negotiation time. We're pretty radical when it comes to our opinions." Her voice took on a nurturing mother's tone, "You're going to hear a lot and see a lot until this is over. Try your best to ignore it."

I could hear Lynne's voice: *You're here for the kids.* I looked at the paper that still pretended there was a district meeting today. "You, know," I said, "I got a huge raise just by being hired."

"Yeah, but you'll want to support what everyone else is trying to do because you'll want a good raise the next time too. You may even want to join the union some day. I dropped out of it for personal reasons.

Right now though, no one expects that you'll do anything. You could be fired if you do."

I felt my face grimace. Unions were a necessary evil, I guess. "So anyway," I started, "I need to get some scissors, do you know if there are any pairs lying around?"

"One thing, Jim, there is never a spare anything just lying around at this school. We're sort of hurting for supplies. I have an extra pair of scissors that you can borrow until you get your own." I followed Monica next door into her room. It was still in a crazy state with posters and charts piled randomly on student desks and papers piled everywhere else. Monica rummaged through some things and came up with an old looking pair of scissors with black handles. The black paint on the handles was randomly chipped, and Monica's last name was written along one of the blades in faded black marker.

"Thanks!" I said. "This'll save me a couple of bucks."

"Is there anything else you need? That pile of posters over there is heading for the trash unless you want any of them." She pointed to a pile of posters that was nearest the door.

"Cool! Thanks!" I went to the pile and started foraging. I would become an expert at foraging for supplies. There were a couple of posters having to do with the writing process. I took them, and now the grand total on my wall was seven! Monica also gave me an entire unit on comparative mythology. It had creation myths from all over the world, and they were interesting in that they all were developed about the same time in totally isolated sections of the world, yet they were eerily similar. That could be good in a class.

I thanked Monica and headed back into my room to tinker around. I took all of the textbooks I would need from out of the cupboard and stacked them on a shelf, then I arranged the student desks one more time and pictured what the full classroom would look like.

My overhead projector had no screen so I used the back of a map of Africa I found in the center room. My pencil sharpener had no handle, and the shelf by the door was broken on the side nearest my desk. Reality was slapping my utopia, but only in a playful way.

"Staff," Rick huffed into the PA system. I jumped-the speaker had never come on before, and it was a bit louder than I had hoped. "If you could please head towards the library, we want to start our staff meeting in about 10 minutes. Again, please start heading to the library so we can get started shortly. Thank you."

I figured I had better tell Pat, the secretary who had given me my keys, about the pencil sharpener and the shelf. I stopped by the front office.

"Um…The pencil sharpener in my room doesn't have an arm attached, and the shelf by the door is broken. I think the whole thing would fall down if I put books on it."

"Then don't put books on it." She answered deadpan. I couldn't tell if she was joking. I just sat there not knowing what to do. After what seemed like about a century, she added "I'll have Al fix it."

"Thanks." I said and escaped into the library.

The library was filling up with a bunch of strangers. Monica was not there yet, and neither was Craig. I didn't see any of the guys from the new teacher orientation either. I took a seat at a table with a blond guy who combed his hair like Elvis and a tall dark-haired man, both of whom looked like they had been teaching about 20 years. Another joined us, and the table was full. I had this strange feeling I had accidentally taken someone's chair.

"How long is this thing supposed to go?" asked the dark haired one.

The blond one shrugged.

"Well, at least David isn't running the meeting. Remember that volleyball speech he gave at last year's recognition assembly?"

"Hey!" interjected David, the last one to join the table, "It was a great year. Those girls deserved the recognition I gave them."

"We recognized them already! We saw them at school everyday. How could we not recognize them?" I was Alice at the tea party; I had no clue who these people were or what they were talking about. The blond guy remained silent and made faces in reaction to the bickering of the other two.

Finally, the dark haired one turned to me. "You obviously are new. I'm Lou. This is Mike and David."

"I'm Jim. I'm the new seventh-grade English teacher."

"Oh you took Frankman's place?" David asked.

"I…guess."

"Yeah, Frankman was a weird guy…a weird guy!" David explained. "I'm a colleague of yours. I teach the gifted seventh-grade kids."

"That's cool. I was one of those."

"Have you met Craig yet?"

I nodded.

"Lou…He's met Craig!"

"I'm sorry for you," Lou sympathized.

"Did Craig talk to you about test scores?" David asked.

"Yeah. Rick did too."

"YO!" David yelled as if in pain. "We have to talk…we gotta talk. The test scores…" David threw his hands in the air. "I wish I had met you before Craig."

Rick called for attention and the staff shouted out last minute comments and such like a bunch of unruly middle school kids. It was a fun environment-a little wild for a workplace, but fun.

Rick welcomed us all back and thanked specific staff members for their help and efforts before today. Rick went over his goals for the year. He introduced the new staff, and I had to stand up and blush as Rick talked about my talent and potential. Next, he talked about his philosophy of education.

"We got our share of the California lottery money for this year." Rick continued. Most of the room laughed. Rick smiled. "We were able to pay for almost half of a copy machine." The room roared with laughter and sarcastic comments.

"Thanks California!"

"Our schools win too!" This was the slogan used to push the legalization of the lottery on California voters. "I think I won more this last year personally than the school got."

"And the state got more than that!" jeered someone else.

"Okay. Come on, let's get back to the meeting." Rick introduced Dolores who told us to go to the back of the library to pick up our class lists after the meeting. The meeting ended, and Rick and the assistant principals left the library. I stood to leave, but sat quickly when I noticed no one else was getting up.

"What's going on?" I asked.

"ETA." Lou told me.

I looked at him with pure confusion.

"Union."

"Screw this, I want to see who my kids are!" complained David. I felt the same way.

"I would like to make it clear that if we are going to keep this telephone tree…" said a woman with short blond hair. All I could see was the back of her head. She continued, "That we leave messages for each other. We had an incident where one of the staff members called my house and refused to say what the message was to my son. The staff member got rude when my son asked what the call was regarding, which is what I have taught him to ask…"

"Jan!" came a shrill shout, "It was me, why don't you just come out and say it. I have no shame in the conversation that you are referring to!" The woman's eyes were fighting huge.

"I just feel like we shouldn't be rude to each other's families." Jan stated.

"I shouldn't be expected to tell a child what the state of the contract is!"

"My child should not have to take your verbal abuse on the phone!" Jan's voice rose for the first time during this exchange. I could see the skin on the back of her neck redden as she spoke. The other woman glared at Jan, and I imagine Jan returned the glare although I could not see her face.

"Who's that woman that's doing most of the yelling?" I asked David.

"That's Shirley. She's in the English department."

"Great." Where did I land, anyway? What planet is this? I had never seen two staff members scream at each other like this, and this was the first day of work!

The focus of the meeting went to a man with a brown goatee and Birkenstocks. He started talking about how the district's administration was not willing to accept an offer that the union gave them for a settlement. A lot of yelling filled the room after he got that one sentence out. Chaos was the only order in this meeting.

"We gotta strike!"

"Work to rule!"

"...march down to that office and picket him every day!"

"We need to get parents involved!"

"Wait...Hold on...I only have a few more things to say, and then I'll be more than happy to take your comments." The man stood in the front of the room holding up his hand as if he were trying to grab the group's attention out of the air. They allowed him to talk, but I didn't understand a lot of what was being said. He was interrupted every sentence or two by quick explosions of sarcasm. He was the union president, and he couldn't please anybody anytime in a negotiation year.

Finally, the meeting lost momentum, and we headed out in separate directions. I ran into Monica on the way back to the room. "So, what did you think?" she asked me.

"It seems like a lot of people here hate each other."

"Oh, no! You're getting the wrong idea. We're all very supportive of each other, it's just that everyone is really angry because of the contract." We stopped by the parking lot near our rooms.

"Everyone seems to be doing a lot of yelling. I can't feel the way they feel because I did get a raise. I went from making nothing to making something. I can afford my own apartment for the first time in my life." I wished I were there right now watching the alcoholic across the hall stumble down the steps with a cup of bleach in his hand as he headed toward the laundry.

"Once you've been here a few years, you'll understand where these people are coming from. They're not bad people, they just have strong feelings." Monica stared at me hoping I would see the truth in her eyes.

"They're yelling at the wrong people. It doesn't look good to new people if the union doesn't even seem unified." I paused for a second and thought of Lynne. "I just want to teach."

The union president walked past us toward the parking lot. "Art," called Monica, "this is Jim Kohl, our new seventh-grade English teacher."

"Art is the president of the E.T.A.-the union."

"Oh, that's cool." I'm sorry for you man!

"So let's see Jim," Art said, looking up to the sky as if he were calculating, "in about three years, when you get your probationary status, you can join the ETA if you choose."

"Oh, yeah." I said. Yeah right!

Monica and I rounded the corner and walked past the vacant room 6. We didn't speak. My room was next.

"What more do you have to do today, Jim?" she asked.

"I'm going to make some seating charts. I figure I'll put them in alphabetical order so I can learn their names faster."

"That's what I do too. Somehow, God separates the bad ones that way too. Kids that are a bad combination in a class are seldom close together alphabetically."

"Cool. Well, I'll see you later." She said goodbye and reminded me that if I needed anything she was right next door. I turned the key in my room's door and went in. This place was mine. I had control over the events. In this room, no one would ever bicker about the union. "Union-what an ironic term for what they have here!" I thought. The unity had left their union.

It didn't matter. I was here for the kids. Lynne had taught me well. I sat at my desk and made alphabetical seating charts on overhead transparencies. I had five classes with 30-35 kids in each one. It was roughly 150 kids, but I never really counted.

I drew a grid on the overhead transparencies and added each of their names in the squares. Rowena, Joseph, Stephanie, Jolly, Jessica, Monique, Hipolito, Ruthy, and Elizabeth-all the names sat quietly and calmly in their transparent squares, but what would tomorrow bring?

I met with Dolores and the new teachers at 1 o'clock. She showed us how to fill out the school's roll sheets, and she gave us copies of the student handbooks that would be distributed during first period. "Whenever any major information needs to be distributed, we do that through the first period classes. Tomorrow in first period, you will give each of your kids their locator cards-their class schedules-and you'll also give them two emergency cards. The cards have all of their guardian's contact information, and both of them have to be returned to school. One is for the nurse, and one is for the student center." The student center is where bad kids were sent, and it's also where my interview had been. "Jim, you have first period prep, so you don't need to worry about any of this stuff, but be aware of it because you may need to do it next year."

The meeting ended, and overwhelmed, I got in my car and drove to the sanctuary of my apartment. Tomorrow was for real.

CHAPTER XXVII

The sun glared onto my windshield. Who needed such warm weather on the first day of school? I pulled into the small LeyVa parking lot at 7:15 that morning, 15 minutes before the contract said I had to be there, and found a prize parking space not 10 feet from the door to Room 5. I had decided it would be a good idea to make a sign for my door, so on a big sheet of green paper, I wrote as neatly as I could (which was not very neat) "Mr. Kohl" and underneath that, "7th Grade English."

I taped up my new sign and went to prop open the door. The door had a little latch that could be flopped down to hold it open, but the rubber doorstopper was gone. It had been there yesterday. I went to Room 6, an empty room, and took the rubber stopper from that door. "I'm reduced to being a scavenger!" I said out loud to myself.

I sat at my desk and looked over the yard duty schedule and memorized my post. I had after-school duty this week and had to watch kids until they got on the bus. I looked over my seating charts again. Kids started walking by my door more and more frequently as the clock passed 7:30. Busses started arriving and dumping hordes of kids into the schoolyard. A group of them passed by my window and looked in at me. I just looked at them. I couldn't even get my senses together to smile.

"I wish Mr. Frankman was still here. He was so nice," purred one. "The new guy looks mean."

"Good," I thought, "let them think I'm mean." I had planned on coming off as all business today so the kids would get that impression of me.

No kids came into my room before school. I didn't have a first period, and no one knew me, so there was no point to go and see the new guy. The bell rang, and my heart jumped, but it was only a bell signaling that there were five more minutes left until my prep began. Monica stuck her head in my door.

"How you doing?" She asked like a walking smile.

"I'm okay. I didn't sleep much last night."

"I still can never sleep the night before the first day of school. Are you going down to the office?" Monica had first-period prep too. Craig and Jacque, the other seventh-grade English teacher that I had not met, had it as well.

"Sure." I pushed back from my desk and headed down to the office with Monica. Kids were all over the place. Many of the girls were overly painted up-black around their eyes and brown lip liner. Some of them had the old "Hair Bear" look where their hair stood a good 5 or 6 inches above their heads. A lot of them wore flannels. The guys had baggy pants and shirts. All the kids were in groups of between 5 and 15. They had areas that were theirs to stand in.

"Good morning, ladies," Monica said to two girls as we walked by them on what seemed to be the longest 100-foot walk of my life. I was a stranger. I didn't know any of these people. Where were Jessica C. and Steven?

The staff room bustled that morning. People were welcoming each other. There were donuts. The orange walls seemed to hum that morning as if they had missed the staff as well. People brushed past one another in the crowded room on their way to class. They had less than five minutes. The room emptied out, and by the time the 8 o'clock bell rang, Monica, a woman with brown curly hair, and I were the last three people left looking over the ravaged boxes of donuts.

"How are you doing?" The woman asked Monica. They hugged. They exchanged how their summers had gone.

"Jacque," Monica said, "this is Jim Kohl, our new seventh-grade English teacher."

"It's nice to meet you. I'm going to rely on you to tell me about grammar." Jacque said as she shook my hand.

"Oh, I'm sure you won't need my help," I said with a laugh. She was an English teacher, after all.

"No seriously. I'm a librarian by training. I have a credential, but the only reason I'm here is because the district has cut back on librarians, and I have tenure so they had to find a place for me."

I looked at her.

"Don't get me wrong. I want to teach, and I'm looking forward to working with the kids and making a difference in their lives, but I don't know much about grammar."

"That's cool. Just let me know what you need." I said.

The three of us sat down at a table. Jacque started showing Monica her plan book for the year.

"I thought I would start off with Greek Mythology and have them do a report on the Greek god or goddess of their choice. Then I figured we would move into fables because I feel very comfortable with those. Next…"

Jacque had the whole year sketched out in paper in front of her. The more she talked the less prepared I felt. Every word she said was a twist in my stomach like when you have not studied for a nearly impossible chemistry final. I knew what I was doing this week and part of next week, but beyond that I had no plans. A burst of honesty overcame me.

"You know," both of them looked up from Jacque's future, "I don't have a clue what I'll be doing nine days from now. I feel like I'm an idiot right now."

"Oh don't feel that way!" Jacque reassured me with the tone of a newly made best friend. "I'm just a really anal planner. I need to have it all out on paper for me or I can't see that it will work. No, don't feel bad. I think most new teachers are like you."

"I only know what I'm doing because I've been doing it for so long." Monica volunteered.

"That's cool then." I did feel better.

"What are you planning on reading with them first?" Jacque asked me. I fidgeted on the brown table.

"I know we have to read one novel, and it looks like the only one on the list that we own is *A Boat to Nowhere* so I thought I'd get that out of the way first. I'm going to teach Poe too."

"Excellent! These kids will really like him."

These two would become my support group, and I would support Jacque as well. First period everyday we shared our triumphs and catastrophes. It was good to have reliable people to lean on when I needed it.

The bell rang.

"Well, we're on. Good luck, you too. You'll do fine." Monica scooped her things into her arms and led us out into the hallways already crowded with students trying to find their way to the next class. This was it-one of those moments I had been waiting for all of my life. I turned the corner with Monica and headed to Room 5, which already had a few kids waiting at the door. "Have a good day, Mr. Kohl," called Monica without looking back.

I unlocked the door and went in. No one followed me in. I was glad because this gave me a few seconds to set up my life. I put the transparency with the seating chart on the overhead and went back to open the door. They all looked at me blankly.

"I have a seating chart on the overhead. Please come in and find your name on the chart and find your seat. The top of the chart is the front of the room. The left side of the chart is the side of the room with this door." I tapped the door twice to be sure they knew which door I was talking about. "Okay, come on in."

They all stood and pointed at the chart trying to find their names. Slowly, many of them started taking their seats. There was some confusion, and I helped those that didn't know what they were doing. It was taking too long! Why didn't they just sit down? How hard could it be? Five or six of them were still wandering around the room, and class had officially started four minutes ago! This chaos was unbearable.

Finally, the last of them had found their seat. They stared at me blankly if they looked at me at all. Many of them wore red. It looked like the crowd at a 49ers game in my classroom, but from facial expressions, it was one of those games that the Niners were losing.

"Okay, let's see how you did. I'm going to call roll, and since you're sitting in alphabetical order," there was a groan, "you should be sitting in the order that I call your name. If anyone is in the wrong spot, I'll rearrange you during this time. Please say 'here' when I call your name, and if I pronounce your name incorrectly, please tell me the correct way to say it at that time." I kept my tone serious and precise.

Most of them said, "Here." Others grunted, and the boys in the baggy pants barely flipped their hands up at me at the sound of their names. That was a good start! I was still alive.

"My name is Mr. Kohl, and this is seventh-grade English. I have a handout for you, which deals with my rules and my expectations in this class. We will go over this as soon as everyone has one." It was a two-page class description that I had made copies of and stapled together for the better part of an afternoon. I didn't want to pass a stapler through a crowd of kids that I didn't know. I walked across the front of the room counting the number of people in each row and giving the first person in the row enough papers for their row.

"Mr. Kohl, I didn't get one." The girl had her hand up, but finally called my name when I didn't see her. She was a strikingly mature Mexican girl with thick, long, black hair in the back row. She wore nice clothes like those of a young female executive. She looked too old to be here, so much so that I checked her birth date in the office-she was normal age.

"I'm sorry. What was your name?" I asked, as I walked to the back of the room to hand her one. I learned their names by having them say it to me each time they spoke.

"Alicia," she said, with confidence.

"Alicia," I repeated to her. "I'm trying to learn names as quickly as possible." She smiled. It was the first smile in my professional teaching career.

We went over my rules and my academic expectations. "In my class-room, one person talks at a time whether that is me or one of you." At this time, it didn't look like that would ever be a problem. I feared that I would be the only one talking-ever!

"Late work is accepted, but you lose 10 percent of the points per day that it is late. This does not apply to late work as the result of an excused absence. You have as many days as you were absent to make up work you missed while you were gone. Next semester, I will only take late work from those with excused absences. If you skip homework next semester, it's a zero, except in the case of the excused absence. Why do I do that second semester?" I asked rhetorically, "Second semester is the next level. Just like in a video game, the next level is always a little harder." They had heard it all before because this was second period. Every teacher in the school was doing exactly what I was doing today. They tolerated me. At certain points I would stop and ask, "Are there any questions?"

No response. They just stared at me, or the wall, or at nothing.

I showed them the major points in the room. I pointed out the agenda and the tray where they would put completed work. I showed them where the homework assignments would be written each night and explained that they would be responsible for writing them down. I told them I would be checking homework at the beginning of each class period, but that I would not necessarily be collecting it each day because a lot of the homework should be stored in a notebook and used for studying for tests. I would be checking the notebook once a quarter. "Any questions?"

Nothing.

I explained how my grading worked. It didn't seem to matter.

I gave them each a grammar book. The books disappeared into their backpacks. "You don't need to carry them back and forth to school every day, they are really just for homework." Who cared? I did.

I explained about the writing proficiency test and the "bubble in the correct answer standardized test" and received the same reaction I would get if I were explaining a hole in my pocket to an average person. "This school has a lot of sports and these tests are the way that we compete with Quimby and Chaboya in the classroom. They have been beating us year after year, and this is the year when we can beat them." Cheerleading did not get a rise from them, and I disgusted myself for doing a poor imitation of Craig.

"When you write essays for me in this class, I ask that you use blue or black ink, or that you type it. I will not accept a paper written in red ink."

"Hey, 'ow come we can't write in red?!?" It was a loud female voice from the front of the room, and isn't it always? I looked at her. She had thick black hair that was parted in the middle and draped straight down. It covered most of her shoulders. She looked Mexican with a hint of Native American. She had big brown eyes that stared at me like I was a welcome corpse. She wore a red flannel, and she had XIV written in red ink on her right hand between the thumb and first finger. Her eyes pierced me, waiting for the answer to her question. They were masked in hate, and should my answer be incorrect...

"It's because I correct in red, and if you write in red too, you're not going to be able to see what mistakes you made." She seemed okay with my answer, but stared hatefully at the top of her desk. I checked the seating to get her name-Elizabeth.

"Well, if there are no more questions, I would like you to fill out this survey the best you can. If there is something you need me to know, such as you can't see from your seat or something like that, please write that on the back of your paper."

I passed out the survey that Monica had given me. "It's a good filler for the first day, and it also gives you an idea who your kids are," she had told me. I already knew who Elizabeth was. She would borrow your knife to stab you with it. It wouldn't matter if your blood got on her clothes because they were red anyway. I looked around the room as they filled out their surveys, but mostly, I looked at Elizabeth. The bottoms of her pants were frayed. She was rugged as they came. She was the last Chola.

The bell rang and I dismissed the class. Third period showed up and found their seats in the same chaotic way as second period. This class was full of Raiders jackets. There was an African-American boy in this class who was older than the others. He looked like he was about 15. I started my routine and speeches that I had given to second period. It was a complete re-run of what I had said an hour before. I knew it would be, but until you've done this, you don't truly realize the strangeness of making the same presentation five times in a day.

The African-American boy raised his hand. "So...uh...this is English class?"

"Yeah." I had been talking about that for the last 10 minutes.

"So...uh...what do we do in here?" The class laughed, and a smaller African-American boy laughed shrill and the two made fists and hit each other on the top of the fist. Stupidity was a high form of comedy for this class. God had played a joke too and placed two kids that should never be near each other in close alphabetical proximity.

"I've been explaining that for the past 10 minutes." I said factually. "What was your name, please?" Why did this kid look so old? I would have to find out later.

"Troy. Oh, sorry...uh...please continue." His little sidekick and he did the fist thing again. The little sidekick laughed at everything that came out of the older boy's mouth. I knew two names by the middle of the period, Troy and Charlie.

I would have to talk to the office about these two and see what the deal is with them. It was clear that Troy was the master of acting stupid to draw attention to himself. His mode of operation was to ask questions like "Do we need a pencil?" seconds after I told them they needed one. It was ingenious class disruption, really, because the question was legitimate and always spoken in a polite tone. It also got the effect he wanted-everyone's laughter and attention.

When I finally dismissed this class on the first day, a quiet girl named Evelyn came up to me. "I don't know how you're going to handle the year with Troy in here." She smiled.

"I've seen worse," I told her, and her eyebrows lifted high above her brown eyes.

One more class, and then I would get to talk to adults in the staff room. Fourth period came in quiet and timid. It was a nice break after the jabbering of Troy. I was still getting over him when they walked through the door and tried to find their names on the seating chart transparency.

They were the shyest class I had ever taught. They hardly looked at me. They didn't even talk to one another. Instead of the apathy of second period or the rude wannabe gang glare of third, they seemed terrified.

The bell rang, and I released them to lunch.

"How's it going?" asked Monica as I was locking the door to my classroom.

"It's all right. My third period seems like it's going to be a bit...challenging. The rest of the classes seem great. Fourth is really shy."

"They usually give you their best impression on the first day." Monica explained, "They sort of feel you out for how much they think they can get away with." We headed down to the staff lunchroom as we talked.

"Do you know a black kid named Troy?" I asked her.

"No. Why?"

"He's a pain in the butt. He and this other kid are already messing up my third period." I didn't want to come off as a bitter old teacher on my first day, but I didn't know a politically correct way of expressing this.

"You should talk to Mike, the assistant principal. See if he can help you out at all. He may be able to give you some insight as to where the kid is coming from."

I got my lunch out of the refrigerator and took a seat at the long table. Monica sat diagonally across from me. A Vietnamese man sat directly across from me and prayed over his food. When he finished, Monica introduced him as Mr. Dang, a language acquisition aid. He spoke seven languages and worked with all the ESL (English as a Second Language) kids. That acronym was current at the time, but it changed many times during my teaching career.

Craig put his lunch bag down a couple seats to my left and ran off to the bathroom. A large man with gray, tight, curly hair sat at the other end of the table from me.

"Are you the new teacher?" he asked.

"Yes. I'm Jim. I'm the new seventh-grade English teacher."

"Why would you even begin teaching with the world the way it is today?"

"I want to." Who the hell was this?

"I've been teaching for 30 years. Teachers used to have respect. It used to be considered a profession. You couldn't work without a coat and tie. Now everyone just walks all over us. I can't believe young people are bothering to get into it."

"Well, I am." This guy was a real inspiration. Someone else started talking to him, and I was excused from his whining.

"Hey, I'm Martin how are you?" asked a blond, ruddy man who sat down next to me.

"Jim Kohl." We shook hands.

"So are you a liberal or conservative?" He looked me in the eyes and seemed to truly want an answer. I just met this guy, and he's hitting me with politics. He must be real popular in bars.

"I'm Generation-X." I told him. "We hate everything."

His lip curled and he got up and left the table.

The lunchroom was filling up with people and their conversations.

"…yeah, but wouldn't you agree that it's like basketball, you have to learn the skills to play the game. If the name of the game is writing, you better have those grammar skills intact."

"…But I've been teaching for 30 years…"

"I can't believe that people would touch a doorknob and not wash their hands!" I had to see who this was. She had long gray and white hair and seemed to speak through her nose. She went on, "Germs are passed by hand to hand contact. Can you believe the amount of hands that touch a doorknob per day? Do you think anyone ever cleans the door-knobs?"

I waited for a break in Monica's conversation. As I waited, Jacque walked through the room, waved and mouthed "hi" and went out the other side. I wondered where she eats lunch. "Monica," I said quietly, when she had a break in conversation. "Who's that old guy down there on the end?"

"Oh that's Leon. Why?"

"He was asking me why young people would get into teaching. If he feels that way, what is he still doing here?"

"Oh, Leon's harmless. He's been teaching for…"

"Thirty years?"

"Yeah." She looked at me in shock. "He probably thinks it's great that you're doing it, but when you've been doing this as long as Leon has, you see what you believe to be…deteriorations in the profession. You think it's great right now, but once you've been anywhere long enough, you long for the good old days, to use a cliché."

This made sense. I nodded. "I hope I get out of this before I feel that way."

"Well, you got a long way to go, Kohl."

I tried to imagine 30 years from now, which was not easy because I didn't even have 30 years of life yet. I probably would look fondly on the beginning of my teaching career, but would that mean that I would have to look down on the current state of the profession? I hated the thought. It would be a disservice to the kids, and as Lynne's voice in my memory constantly chanted, they were the reason I was here.

The bell rang, and the staff that remained in the room grumbled the same way the kids probably did outside. I headed back to Room 5 to see what I would have next. I hoped, to have at least one class that I really liked and that I really connected with. Maybe this would be the one.

I went through my normal routine with the new group. I had the door open, but it was still getting very hot in the room. The sun was directly outside my classroom door after lunch, and the 34 bodies in the room generated about 10 extra degrees. They had all been eating lunch outside, and they felt the heat too, and watched politely as I went through my speech. Sweat collected on my forehead, and I thought of Cabrillo with its air-conditioned rooms.

After I had been through my rules, and policies and the course description and after I had done my cheerleading act about the two standardized tests, I asked, "Are there any questions?"

A hand went up! I couldn't believe it! I tried to act like it was a normal occurrence, but it had happened so infrequently that my heart raced. It was a Samoan girl who had landed in the back row alphabetically.

"Yeah," I pointed to her, "Tell me your name please."

"Jolly."

"Jolly." I repeated, trying to make the name and the face stick in my brain. I walked towards her and nodded to indicate she should ask her question.

"Can we drink in here?"

"No." The question annoyed me. They were trying to take advantage of me because I was the new teacher. No one was going to walk all over me! Jolly just looked down at her desk. "You just finished lunch, and you should've had plenty of time to drink."

"Are there any other questions?" I returned to the front of the room with full confidence that I had played that correctly.

A boy in the front row raised his hand. "Yeah." I said, nodding to him. "Tell me your name?"

"Hipolito. Yeah, like you know how this is English class?" The boy was a ventriloquist with no puppet. His mouth sat open about a centimeter, and the words came out in a garbled rush. He forced you to listen carefully, or you would not understand.

I nodded, indicating to him that I was aware that it was English class.

"Well, like are we gonna learn about Old English?"

I looked at him like I looked at many kids that year. I looked for a hint that he was trying to mess with me. I looked for even a hint of a smile that would make it clear that he was kidding around. He just stared at me with his mouth open a centimeter. His slick backed hair, I noticed for the first time, was only on the top of his head. Both of the sides were shaved to the skull.

I walked back and forth a few steps trying to figure this kid out. Did he mean Old English the font, or was he making a reference to a malt liquor? The more I studied him, the more I got the sense that the question, in his mind anyway, was a legitimate one.

"No." I said, finally. He was visibly disappointed. "Any other questions?" I looked around the room. People just stared at me through the heat. I passed out the survey, and sat down at my desk.

Sixth period finally roared through my door. The room was still hot from the fifth period bodies. The sun sat right outside my door, and sweat dripped off my face.

Not even halfway through my talk, before I asked for questions, I started getting them. "What was your name?" I asked a thin girl with black, shiny hair.

"Monica."

"Monica," I repeated. "What's your question?"

"Are you married?"

"We're not here to talk about that." This was my standard answer to questions that are not on the subject.

"Do you have a girlfriend?" Monica didn't wait to be called on this time.

"Monica, I told you that we are not here to talk about these things. If you want to stay after school, I'd be glad to answer these questions for you."

"I can't today." she told me, as if I had just invited her over for a barbecue.

A hand went up in the back. "Yes," I said. "Your name please."

"Jessica." Her voice scratched like a smoker's. She had a thin Mexican face and wore a sweatshirt even in the heat.

"Jessica," I repeated.

"But seriously, do you have a girlfriend?"

"Jessica!" My tone got stern at this point. I was determined that these kids not know about my personal life.

"Well, what do you do on the weekends then?" she asked with desperation in her voice.

"Does anyone have a question about the class?" Choosing to ignore inappropriate questions normally will end them. Sure enough, not a single hand was raised at this point.

In the front row, sat a large boy with an even bigger smile. "I have a question, but it's not about the class."

"Then I would rather you not ask it. What is your name?"

"Shane." Shane sat with his hands on his face and looked at me from between his fingers. I could tell he was going to ask his question even though I asked him not to.

"Shane, we really need to use class time for English related topics."

"My question is in English," he volunteered.

I shot Shane a look that raised the temperature an extra 10 degrees.

"Sorry. I mean it, I'm really sorry." His voice tapered as his apology continued. "But I want to know."

"After class."

"What kind of music do you listen to?" The question exploded uncontrollably from his mouth.

"Shane…" I realized how much class time I was wasting refusing to answer these questions. I needed a different tactic, but I would stick with this one for today. "This is not the time for this."

"Country!!" he shouted, pointing at me. "I bet you listen to country, don't you?!" His smile nearly broke his face in two.

"Shane!"

"I'm sorry, I'll be quiet now." He looked down at his desk. "Country." He giggled to himself.

Somehow I got through the rest of my presentation that period. When the bell rang, I let them leave and fell exhausted into my chair. Day one was over, and there were only 179 to go, but for now, only tomorrow mattered.

Chapter XXVIII

I needed to find out more about Troy. Between him and his little buddy, I felt the class would suffer in a constant battle for control. When I was in seventh grade, I would listen to the class clown over the teacher any day of the week, and I was pretty confident that these kids felt the same. Troy had leadership qualities simply because he looked so much older than the rest of them.

I found Jacque early one morning. "How's it going, Jim?" She asked.

"Pretty good. How about you?"

"I'm alive."

"Well that's good," because I need your advice. "Jacque, do you know a kid named Troy?" This was the first of many conversations that Jacque and I would share that began this way. We both had seventh graders, and she had one seventh-grade social studies class, so some of our kids overlapped.

"Black kid, real obnoxious?"

"That sounds like the guy."

"What about him?"

"He and his little buddy Charlie are screwing up my third period." The action I saw on the first day of school had escalated over the first week. I got less done in third period than in any other class. I was starting, already in the second week of school, to worry about the test scores that they would get in February.

"Have you looked in his Cum. File yet?" It sounded like "Kyoom."

"What's that?"

"In the office in the small room next to Rick's office is a room with a huge file cabinet. In the file cabinet are the cumulative files for everyone that goes here. It helps to get to know where the kids are coming from if you go through these files."

"That's cool." We had been standing in the parking lot and started heading toward the office.

"Also, you should talk to either Mike or Dolores about them and see if the office can back you up at all."

"Thanks."

"Have a good day." We split from each other after we entered the office. I headed to the right and found the room with the file cabinets that she had been talking about. There was a sign written in black marker on an orange piece of paper warning us not to open more than one drawer at a time because the whole cabinet could topple forward.

I found the seventh-grade cabinet and Troy's file. There were school pictures of him all the way back to kindergarten on the cover. Troy had started out looking like a very happy 5-year old. In first and second grade, he had some teeth missing in the front just like anybody else. He used to smile big in his pictures, but the smile went away in the sixth-grade picture.

I tried to make some sense of the pile of papers, but they may as well have been medical records written in Ancient Latin, I didn't even know what I was looking for. I thought back to my credential program classes and wondered why they taught me how evils phonics were, and why they never taught me how to read Cum. Files. I slid the papers back into the file and shoved the drawer shut.

I went to the student center to see if I could find either Mike or Dolores. I may not be able to read a Cum. File, but I could talk to one of them.

Dolores stood in the student center behind the counter that late students report to. She was looking at the master scheduling board, a bulletin board with all the teachers' names on it as well as the number of students in each class listed by period. Many teachers on the staff complained when their numbers were too high, especially during a negotiation year.

"Dolores?" I meant to say it, but I am easily intimidated by authority, so it whispered itself.

"Oh, hi Jim." She greeted, looking away from the schedule board.

"I have a problem. Do you know a kid named Troy?"

She nodded her head and rolled her eyes. "Very well."

"He's really messing up my third period. He's got almost an artistic way of disturbing classes. He'll ask me stupid questions that are on the subject, and the other kids think that he's so funny. There's this one kid, Charlie, in there that worships him every breath the guy takes."

"I know Charlie too." If the vice principal knows you, of course, that either means that your parents are active in the school, or you're a problem on campus. I hadn't seen Charlie's or Troy's parents around.

"Do you have any suggestions about what I could do?"

Dolores thought for a moment. Her lips pursed and her eyes worked. "They are not sitting near each other, obviously, right?"

I had moved them to opposite corners of the room on the second day of school. "No. But that doesn't stop them from yelling across the room to each other. At least I don't have to watch them take turns hitting each other on top of the fist anymore."

Dolores just looked at me. She shook her head. "Those two should not be scheduled together." I couldn't believe what I was hearing. "I'm going to call them both in this morning during first and see what we can work out." She looked at me and put her hand out with her palm toward me. It's not just you that has come to me about them."

"Thanks." I would get rid of one. That would be half my problem in the worst class I had! I was thrilled but didn't show it. "While we're on the subject, why does Troy look so old?"

"Because he is." She was blunt, and you could hear a hint of frustration in her voice. "He failed seventh grade last year, and we have a retention policy in seventh grade, so..."

I looked at her with my forehead wrinkled.

"If a kid doesn't have a 1.5 GPA in seventh grade...cumulative GPA, I should say...then the student repeats seventh grade. It's the only grade we do that in. You have Troy on his second time through. If he gets a 1.5 GPA by the quarter, we can move him up to the eighth grade."

All of this sounded encouraging to me. I thanked Dolores and left her to her schedule board. Maybe Troy would be out of my class today! Maybe he would make it out by the quarter. How hard could it be to get a 1.5 GPA? Soon, I would find out-over and over.

I realized I had forgotten to ask Dolores how to read a Cum. File when I was halfway back to my room with my roll sheet in hand. That could wait.

During my prep, my private intercom buzzed, and through the static that was always on the line, Dolores told me that she had moved Charlie. "To his credit, he admitted that having Troy and him in the same room is not a good idea," she said. I thanked Dolores and dreamed of a better third period.

My dreams didn't last long.

One day as I spoke, Troy raised his hand. I had taken the advice of some of my colleagues and started to ignore him when he raised his hand because he had yet to contribute anything meaningful to the class.

"Damn, my arm's gonna fall off." I heard him say. The people around him laughed.

"Did you need something, Troy?"

"Ah...I was jus' wonderin' if I could sharpen my pencil." We were nearly a month into school, and it was common knowledge that the office still had not fixed my pencil sharpener or that shelf by my desk, but that's another story.

"Do you have a pencil sharpener?" I asked.

"No. Can I use that one?" He pointed to the handle-less pencil sharpener four rows over to his right.

"That one doesn't have a handle, Troy." I breathed deeply.

"Can I try it anyway?"

"No."

"Oh, man, that's messed up."

I shrugged. "Does anyone in this room have a pencil sharpener that Troy can use?" I looked over the class. Evelyn reached into her backpack and pulled out a hand held pencil sharpener. She passed it to Roxanna, who passed it to Troy, who ground his pencil into the sharpener. He pulled it out and inspected it. "Hmm," he said. He stuck it back in the sharpener and repeated all the steps a little louder. The third time through the routine was even louder. Troy's crowd laughed.

"Stupid!" Some of them said as they laughed, but stupid was a popular and good thing to be. Troy strived for stupidity and hit his mark on a daily basis. His peers even said so as they laughed.

"Troy, I'll see you after class," I said.

"Why, I was just sharpenin' my pencil." His look of innocence was all part of his act, as was my attempt at stopping the situation.

"We'll talk after class."

"First person to ever get in trouble for sharpenin' a pencil!"

"That's enough, Troy."

"Sorry."

I went on with the rest of the class. Troy had done his performance, and he knew that any more antics would just make me talk to him longer, and he really didn't like talking to teachers much without his fans in the room. Class ended, and he stayed. A couple of his groupies, Lawrence and Joseph, waited for him and refused to leave, so I took him in the back room. I could've talked to him about disturbing the class. I could've told him how unfair it was that he was interfering with others that cared about their education. He had heard all that before, I was pretty sure, so I tried something else.

"So you've been in seventh before."

He had been looking at the ground and was shocked enough to look up at me. This was not what he thought he would be hearing about. He didn't answer.

"That's true, isn't it Troy? And you can lie if you want, but I've already looked it up."

"It's true." I had never heard him speak so softly. "Same wit' Lawrence and Jose, though." Those were two other kids in my third period. I would have to look that up now.

"Yeah," I said, acting like I already knew this, "but, you see, the only one you need to worry about is you." Geez, I sound like my mom! "You know, if you get a 1.5 GPA-which doesn't take much, by the way-you can move up to the eighth grade where you belong. Do you like hanging out with all these little kids?"

He shook his head. He looked at the ground the whole time.

"Is it a goal of yours to try to make it into the eighth grade?" I was hoping it was. I knew I wanted him in the eighth grade, even if it was for selfish reasons.

He nodded, still looking at the ground.

"Well, then I'm willing to do whatever it takes to help you reach that goal. You can come by this room anytime for help in any of your classes." I didn't really know if I really meant this. "I'll see you tomorrow."

Troy left.

As time went on, his behavior stayed the same, and he didn't do any schoolwork. He failed five classes, and he usually got a C in PE. Each day during second period, the school would deliver an absence list to our classrooms, which listed all the kids and teachers that were out on a par-ticular day. I would scan the list in hopes that Troy would be out. When he was gone, I would get things done in third period. I sent him to the office when I could, but he was careful to be obnoxious within the rules. I was finally able to give him a referral for refusing to spit his gum out.

It was open defiance to a reasonable request from me, and gum chewing was a major pet peeve of our Rick's.

One day after report cards came out, I asked him to stay after class for a few minutes. He had his usual 0.5 GPA. He stood in front of my desk. I was fed up with him at this time. "Do you like seventh grade, Troy?" I asked.

"No!" He sounded disgusted by the question.

"How about this class, do you like this class?" I knew what the answer would probably be.

"No!" He looked me straight in the eye, hoping this would hurt my feelings.

"Then why don't you do something to get out of both of them!? You are one of the only kids in this class that hates it and *can* get out. Why can't you do that for yourself, Troy?"

No response.

"What do you want to do, stay in the seventh grade until you're sitting in the same classroom with your kids? I've offered to help you, and I know that other teachers probably have too. You claim to be unhappy in this situation, but you do nothing about it. This world is not going to do things for you."

"I ain't got no kids." This was all he could argue, I guess.

"See you tomorrow, Troy."

Troy left.

Then a miracle happened. Troy left LeyVa one day in late November. He was going to live in Mountain View, I think, but it didn't matter because he was going to be someone else's problem. I had failed him. That's what I disliked about Troy most of all. He was an at-risk kid that needed my help, and I couldn't do a thing for him. Troy was a personification of my failure as a teacher.

Life went on at LeyVa, and my third period continued to think they were tough and act like little gangster rappers, but I grew to like them. With Troy gone, I was able to direct attention to other kids in the room.

When I became engaged to the woman that is now my wife, it was third period that threw me a party.

"You seem much happier with Troy gone," Evelyn observed.

"I didn't hate him. I just didn't like the things he did." This was the story I was sticking to.

"What's the difference, Mr. Kohl?" Evelyn asked me with genuine confusion in her eyes. I love it when they are all profound and you have to go to your desk and sit and think.

One foggy morning in February in the parking lot, I ran into Jacque. We said our ritualistic good mornings. "I have some bad news for you."

"What?" I asked as I tried to juggle my freshly photocopied papers and my roll sheets.

"Troy's back."

I felt my world sink. "Maybe I won't have him again." I hoped out loud.

"He's back in my Social Studies class, and I'm pretty sure they're giving him back his original schedule."

"How do you know this?" I had made such progress with my third period, and it didn't seem fair that he should be allowed back in to mess them up right before the writing proficiency test. The test was about a week away.

"I was in the office yesterday afternoon when his mom or aunt or whoever she is was checking him back in."

"Well, there go my proficiency scores."

"Are you still worried about that stupid test?" Jacque asked.

"Aren't you?" I asked.

"There's no way they'll get rid of us-any of us. Do you think there's a line of people dying to do what you're doing?"

I looked at her to see if she was kidding. The morning breeze blew past us and the glare of the sun was just cracking the clouds. "I'm dying to do it," I said about as shyly as anyone has ever said anything.

"I know. That's why the kids are lucky to have you."

That made my morning. Even if Troy was back, and he was, at least one person thought I was contributing something of value to the school and to these kids.

Break came right before third period. I walked down to the office to take care of something. Evelyn stopped me on the way. "Mr. Kohl, did you hear that Troy is back?"

"Mm-hmm." I said, playing it off that it didn't affect me one way or the other.

"He's in our class again." She added.

I turned to face her directly. "What exactly would you like me to say about this, Evelyn?"

She looked at me. Kids walked by us on either side.

"I'll see you in class." I walked away.

Troy slouched and bounced into my room the like a rapper on a stage. He looked from side to side and flipped a paper on my desk. I needed to sign him back into my class. "I would give you some books," I told him, "but you never gave back the ones you originally had."

He just looked around, keeping his street pose. I showed him where to sit. It was February, and there was no chance of him moving to the eighth grade this year; he had flaked his way past the cutoff. There was no longer a goal that he could accomplish. Even if he got a 4.0 from this point on, his overall GPA would not make the 1.5 requirement. He was a space taker in the room, and that was about it.

I started off my lesson. I was teaching about the life of Edgar Allan Poe. I talked about his pitiful existence and the tragedy that followed him everywhere. The kids sat and listened with a mix of sadness and giggles at the string of horrible events that was Poe's life. When I had been talking for nearly 20 minutes, Troy raised his hand. I ignored him. I liked teaching about Poe, and the kids seemed to be into it. "Let him lose circulation in his arm and complain about it," I thought, "That'll give me an excuse to throw him out of here."

"Da-yam," Troy said in his normal drawn out way whenever he thought his hand had been up too long.

"Watch your mouth, Troy." I said and continued on with my lesson. I couldn't figure out what felt different.

After another two minutes, Troy said, "Mr. Kohl, I have a question."

I took a deep breath. "What is it, Troy?" I stood at the board and looked at him. He sat in the third seat back near the middle of the room and looked back at me. It was a passive aggressive confrontation.

"Who is Edgar Allan Poe?" It was the same old Troy show. He was trying to stop the flow of my lesson by asking the obvious while still being within the school rules. There was a difference, though, and this time I noticed it. No one laughed!

I looked at him. "Troy, that is what I've been talking about for the past 30 minutes. I'm going to see if anyone else in the class can answer this for you. Can anyone tell Troy anything about Poe's life?"

Hands went up all over the place. Troy looked around and appeared betrayed.

"Joseph?" I said.

"Mom died of TB."

"Good. Evelyn?"

"Got adopted, and his adopted father didn't like him."

"Great. Sheree?"

"His adopted mom died of TB too."

I watched Troy as his once-loyal fans provided fact after fact.

"I did not know that." He tried a couple of times. "News to me." He tried a few more. No reaction. I just kept calling on kids and they kept answering my questions.

"Great job, guys." I wanted to hug them all. "Troy, you were gone a long time. All the way from November to February. It looks like you've gone out of style, man."

He just looked at me.

It wasn't much longer until he started getting in fistfights. He was suspended a few times, and they finally expelled him. Jacque told me he and his buddy, Charlie, once showed up at a LeyVa basketball game stinking of alcohol. They got thrown out, and a lot of the kids there didn't even know who they were.

Troy was a failure of mine, but from him I learned that you can't save everyone, and you can't help those that won't let you. Despite how many times I had to watch, it never got any easier watching a kid self destruct.

CHAPTER XXIX

I met the LeyVa staff in the middle of an ugly contract negotiation between the union representative and Mr. Smith, the superintendent. Every three years, the contract comes up for renewal in the district, and every three years there's a fight over the raise that teachers will get. Three years prior, they got 1%, and everyone at LeyVa was still angry. Monica told me that LeyVa had the reputation of being the most militant during negotiations, and I was about to see that first-hand.

We had a staff meeting one Wednesday afternoon near the beginning of the year in one of the portable classrooms. The portables were the only rooms on campus with air-conditioning. Traditionally, after Rick and the other administrators finish their business with us, they leave the meeting, and the ETA business begins. I was not a union member because you can get fired for being active in the union when you have temporary employment status. I would be risking my job by participating in any of the union activities except sitting and listening at their meetings.

As the ETA president, Art started the meeting off. "Negotiations are not looking good at this point. We still seem to be nowhere near an agreement. Mr. Smith will not give us the 5% raise that we are asking for, and he's not willing to even discuss that amount."

"He gave himself a 6% raise!" yelled Rich in the gravel scratch voice of a smoking PE teacher.

"If I could just finish my comments before we open the floor, I would really appreciate it." Art knew his audience, and showed great patience.

"Open up to the floor!?" shouted Bert, the science teacher. "When's he gonna open up his checkbook!"

"Okay, Bert, let me just get to it." Art continued. "We have decided to picket the district office next Thursday evening during the board meeting. There's been talk of a 'sick out' where we all call in sick on the same day, but the union does not back or authorize that particular tactic."

"Damn liberals!" shouted Martin. "Our hands are tied by our own organization. They take money from our checks and tell us what to do." Martin taught PE and leadership, which organized all the school dances.

"I've expressed your opinions to the union representatives. They know how you feel, but we need to make sure that the CTA backs any action we take or we'll all lose." CTA was the California Teachers Association, which was the main union. Our teachers joined the ETA, Evergreen Teachers Association, which was the local branch of the CTA.

Bert stood up, shouting, "Well the CTA better approve of some strategy that works because we been without a contract for over a year now! Any other district would be on strike already! Screw the 'sick out,' I say we walk out right now!"

"Hear, hear," said Craig.

Art stood in front of us behind a wooden podium and shook his head. "You guys know we can't vote for a strike in this room."

"Art!" Jan, the sixth-grade teacher called out with her hand in the air. She was the only one who asked for the floor during the meeting. "We have Back to School Night coming up. Couldn't we picket that?"

"Yes, I was trying to get to that." Art shot Bert a look. "It has been approved for us to picket the Back to School Night next Wednesday evening. Those that want to participate can stand in the main quad area carrying signs and passing out ETA literature regarding the grievances we have with management. This boycott is not mandatory, and of course, you shouldn't participate unless you are at least probationary status. Which brings me to my next point. I need people to go to Mt.

Hamilton and paint signs so that we have enough to picket with. Any volunteers?" Art took down the names of people who raised their hands.

A few more people, mostly Bert, Martin, and Rich, yelled and screamed a bit more before we left the meeting. They seemed to be most agitated by people who were not union members. "I'm sick an' tired of working my butt off for a bunch of people that won't join the union," Bert went off. "Why should they have the same raise I get if they don't even join? Anyone not in the union is a scab, an' we should treat 'em like scabs!"

I wondered if this guy knew that some of us couldn't join the union. I thought about this all the way out to my car. Monica assured me that everyone knew the position that new teachers were in and that no one expected us to join the union. This guy didn't seem to understand anything except that he hated Mr. Smith and non-union members. He had called me a scab as far as I was concerned.

I went to Craig the next morning with that very question. "Dude, what's the deal with that Bert guy?"

Craig turned from the chalkboard where he was writing the lesson outline for the day. "What do you mean, James?"

"I mean, why should I join an organization just because they say I'm a scab if I don't?" I took a seat in a student desk near the front of Craig's room as if I was there to be taught. "Those guys yelling at the meeting yesterday are a bunch of whiners. I don't know if I want to be in an association filled with people like that. It really doesn't say much for the organization if the main focus seems to be to interrupt and yell a bunch of suggestions that they're probably too scared to try for real anyway. You guys don't seem unified if they can't even listen to the president."

"Those guys just like to stir things up," Craig began. "And I think you're right about not being unified. I lived in Australia for a couple of years and over there the union is everything. If the steel refinery goes on strike, then the teachers go on strike on their behalf. So do the dockworkers, and any other group of workers that are around. That's a true union, mate, they'll shut the whole country down to make sure that people are paid fair. I mean 100%, James, they'll burn your house down if you cross a picket line over there." Craig blew a hard "p" sound through his lips and continued. "Cripes, over here even if we got the guts up to walk out, I'll bet about a third of the staff wouldn't even bother. And it would be all women crossing the line. That's the problem with teaching, most teachers are women and women won't stick up for their rights because they got some man at home bringing home enough money for them anyway."

I couldn't believe he just said that. These were the politically correct '90s.

"Wouldn't you agree, James, that you and I deserve to be paid as much as any of these high tech people here in Silicon Valley? Don't you think that we have as much if not more training than any of those guys that started making at least 50 thousand right out of college? We did a whole year or more extra to make a lot less than any of those guys. My stepson just landed a job as a technical writer, and I'm pretty sure that he'll be making more than me within three years, and I've been working for 20 years!!"

I took what Craig was saying to heart because I felt like I needed a variety of opinions on the subject. I headed back to my classroom, shut the door, and taught.

A week later, it was the Wednesday of the big "Back to School Night Boycott." As far as I could tell, four of us would be in our classrooms that evening: Steve, Roland, Mark, and me. The rest of the staff was tenured, or at least probationary, and they were going to be carrying signs in the courtyard like many of them probably did in the '60s. Craig, with his opinions, had certainly been a part of many protests in his time, I imagined.

Roland happened through my room early that morning before school.

"Hey, Roland."

"Hello." This guy seemed almost robotic in his language. He never used contractions in his speech, and he always said 'television' instead of TV.

"Hey, man what do you think of this whole union thing?" I was desperate for viewpoints because I truly didn't know how I felt about it. I was at the school for the kids and to teach, but I didn't like that the district administrators were taking advantage of teachers. I also didn't like the vibe of the few ETA meetings that I had sat in on; why would teachers attack their own? That is exactly what the district administrators would use against them. Nothing's weaker than a union that is not unified.

"Gee, I have not really thought about it at all. I am trying to get a hold on my new career, and I do not have the time to really take a stand on the issue. Surely, I would support the teachers' point of view, but currently I am not in a position where I can take a stand."

"That's cool." He left. I didn't really want his prepared statement, I wanted to know how he felt about being one of four classrooms open for Back to School Night. I knew I hated it, but I didn't know how much yet.

Back to School Night at LeyVa is a night when the parents come and spend 10 minutes in each of their children's classrooms. They follow the same schedule, so they go to first period for 10 minutes, and when a bell rings, they go to second, and so on until they complete six-period school day in about an hour. With the boycott in effect, the problem was obvious-the schedules couldn't be followed, and the parents would have four rooms to choose from. Mine was one of them.

I taught through my classes with that reality stabbing me in the back of my mind. "Mr. Kohl, what are you staring at?" asked Jennifer in fourth period.

"Nothing."

By the time lunch came around, I was already scripting what I might say that evening. I would tell the parents that I support the teachers in what they are doing, but that I am a new teacher. I would tell them that the staff was not divided, so that they wouldn't think that their children go to a school where the staff is in turmoil. I would then explain the program that I had for their children this year and hope to God that the 10 minutes I had to spend talking to them would pass quickly.

The lunchroom was jammed with commotion that day. It seemed more crowded than normal. I took my regular seat across from Mr. Dang and Monica. Craig was to my left, and the door to the room was on my right side.

It wasn't long before the subject came up, and once it did, it wasn't long before its escalation got crazy. I heard bits of it throughout the room.

"I've been teaching 30 years, and I've never seen education…education is in a deplorable state right now…"

"…they don't think they have to respect us…"

"If a basketball team wants good players, they have to lay the money out…"

"Smith just wants the money for himself…just got married, you know"

"…doesn't care about us…"

"We gotta support the union or we're nowhere."

"Thirty years ago, when I started, teaching was a profession, and they've turned it into a job. And we let them do it."

"This will be your fight one of these days, Kohl," Monica told me. "We've all worked hard to make sure you could start at the salary you're getting right now. It will be your turn to join in the fight next time." Monica wasn't a union member, but she planned on boycotting that evening.

"I'm sick and tired of working my tail off for all you people that won't join the union and end up getting a raise and a better life for all my hard work!!" This was Bert. Until then, I had kept my eyes focused on my turkey sandwich and let my ears wander around the room to take it all in, but his outburst made me look. He stood in the middle of the staff room screaming and red faced in a green polo shirt. Al, the art teacher, shut the door between the staff room and the main office. Bert went on ranting and raving and screaming, "You fat lazy scabs don't deserve anything! We do all the work and you get the same raise! Tell me how that can possibly be fair? I'm not a charity worker! I'm gonna slash the car tires of anyone that doesn't join the union."

The bell rang for lunch to end. Monica and Craig kept telling me that no one expected me to join the union, but this guy didn't seem to get it. If my tires got slashed, I would kill that guy. I made the vow silently to myself on the way back to fifth period.

I walked towards fifth with a cloud hanging over me. Why should I support some jerk that threatens me if I don't? If they want young teachers in this organization, they shouldn't alienate us by screaming about how we're a bunch of scabs. I was weighed down with this baggage as the bell for fifth period rang. That jerk better hope nothing happens to my tires.

"Here's your opener." I turned on the overhead and shined the two sentences that they needed to re-write correctly on the screen/map. "Re-write these sentences correctly, and I want to see last night's homework, the five similes, on your desk. I'll be with you as soon as I take roll."

Jolly raised her hand. I nodded to her. "Are you in a bad mood or something?" She had a mix of concern and annoyance on her face.

"No, I'm fine." I snapped it at her. 'I really like her.' I thought to myself, 'She is a cool and smart kid, and I'm snapping at her because one jerk messed up my lunch.' I needed to rise above this. I was here for the kids.

"Just asking," she sighed.

"'I' seem like you inna bad moo'." Hipolito stated from the front row.

"Well, I'm not, Hipolito, and you're too busy right now to spend time wondering what sort of mood I'm in. Do you have your homework?"

"Uh-uh."

"See what I'm talking about?!" I was on a warpath and these kids were taking the brunt of my lunch anger as well as the experience that I imagined for myself later that evening. It wasn't their fault, but I couldn't shake it, and I'm sure they all breathed a sigh of relief that day when the bell rang and they got to leave.

Sixth period asked me if fifth period got me in this bad mood. I told them I wasn't, but they knew better.

"Sure, you're not in a bad mood!" called Shane from the front row.

I got through sixth period and tried to straighten up my room the best I could for the night. I went home, ate dinner, and headed back to the school, dreading each inch of road. My classroom was at the front of the school. I would be the spokesperson for why the teachers were not in their rooms. I would have to speak for Bert, the tire slasher.

David, the tall, white-bearded English teacher, greeted me as I came through the gate about 20 minutes before Back to School Night was slated to begin. He carried a sign that said, "Evergreen Teachers Deserve a Fair Contract."

"Hey," I said.

"How you doing?" he asked.

"Look man, you know, I'm one of the only guys that's gonna be in a room tonight, and I want you to know that I'm not anti-union or anything. I'm not an enemy of the cause, you know."

He put his hand up. "You have to do what you have to do. I would much rather be in the classroom greeting parents tonight. I have to do what I have to do also." He let that hang in the air. "Did you open your room yet?"

"No."

"You should get in there and open all the windows and doors. It was hot today, and if the room has been closed up for a few hours, it's going to be really uncomfortable. If you have a fan, you should turn it on. I used to have that room until everyone refused to teach on the other side of a curtain from me. Carl was the last one that tried." David had the stage voice that came with his drama degree. His voice boomed with enthusiasm, and on this night, he made me feel okay about being the odd man out-the one with an open classroom.

I opened the room up the way he suggested, and left the lights off until people came. I was reading from a Robert Frost poem book to kill the time and to hopefully find some order in all of this. I could see teachers arriving bearing signs on their shoulders. Some of them looked like they would have been glad to carry two. I spent a half hour trying to get through one of Frost's poems that I had read countless times before- "The Road Not Taken." The four stanzas stood on the page and I looked at the words but didn't see them.

The PA system announced the official beginning of Back to School Night. Rick sounded heavy of breath as he instructed parents to head to their child's first-period class.

First period was my prep period, but I had a feeling that I wouldn't have an empty room because the parents would have nowhere else to go. I had all the texts we were using that year lined up on a dark brown table at the front of the room. I thought about Steve, Mark, and Roland and wondered what was going through their minds. I would try to avoid the topic of the boycott. Seconds later, my room was filled with parents and students from all of my classes. I invited them in and told them to have a seat.

"I'm Mr. Kohl, your child's English teacher. I want to talk a little bit about my class and show you what we plan on doing in here this year." One man came into the room and slammed into one of the desks. Others scowled around the room. Others seemed fine with just listening to me.

I talked all about my class, and the bell rang. "Thanks for coming." I said, as they got up to leave. A few stayed behind to shake my hand and talk with me.

"How come you're in your room?" one father asked me.

"I'm new. They can fire me if I don't open the room. I support the teachers, but I honestly don't completely understand the issue here-other than money." It made me sick that teachers could be so greedy. I didn't get here to get rich—I wasn't a corporate scum. My answer seemed fine with him. Relieved, I planned to use that exact statement as the night went on.

The Back to School Night was supposed to go from 7 until 8. Until about 7:30, my room was filled with parents that ranged from irate to simply wanting to know about the new teacher. My formal presentations had stopped, and groups of parents dropped in and out of the room at random. Rick still had the bells ringing every 10 minutes to present, I guess, some semblance of order. I was talking with a group of parents about the class when the question came up again.

"How come you're in your room?" By this time, I had answered the question about four times, so I let the answer roll off my tongue:

"I support the teachers that are out there, but because I am new, I would be putting my job at risk if I didn't open my room tonight." It was a more brazen version of my statement, and it wasn't as popular.

"Well I *was* just about to congratulate you on having the guts to stand up for your own beliefs and not screw the parents the way the rest of the staff here has, but you can forget that now." He was yelling. He had a right to be mad. Time is a precious thing, and when you take time to go to the school for this sort of an event, you don't want to feel like your being messed with. I just nodded. Inside, I could hear the voice of Bert screaming about slashing my tires. It was mixed with this father's voice. I was yelled at from both sides of the argument on the same day, and my patience had gone. Both voices replayed in my mind. I could see both red and infuriated faces screaming in my face. It was my turn to become red and infuriated.

I kept it cool while all the parents were in my room. When they left, I walked out to the courtyard and saw all the teachers carrying their signs and handing out brochures. I had taken their bullet, and I didn't like or want to defend or deflect anything from these people ever again, and I planned on making that painfully obvious within the next three minutes.

Craig was the first familiar face I saw, so he was going to get it. "Craig." I said as calmly as an insanely angry 25-year-old can, "I got something to say."

He looked at me, and I saw his face change. He wasn't going to give me a basketball metaphor this time.

"I get screamed at in the lunch room by that one bastard-whatever his name is-for not being in the union, and I just got screamed at in my classroom by a parent for the exact opposite reason!"

"Wait a second," Craig said. "You're telling me that a parent just yelled at you for not being out here with us?"

"No!! Listen for once! He yelled at me for saying I support you jerks! You guys don't deserve a raise. None of you are teachers, you all suck! Teachers care about education and support each other! You guys only care about money! I'm not going to be threatened by members of this staff! I'm too good to work here, and you're lucky you even have me!" I motioned to the staff as they picketed about like geriatric hippies, "I don't see a teacher out here! The real ones were in their rooms where they belonged! You guys are a bunch of whiners." I had exploded all over Craig, and I was loud enough to gather a crowd. I had the attention of about 25 people. "Why should I join some organization that uses threats to recruit people?! I've lost all respect for you guys as people much less professionals! No wonder the administration walks all over you!"

"Hey man, take it easy." Craig told me. "Obviously, you've had a rough night."

"Yeah, taking bullets for you guys while you hang out in the quad skipping around the May Pole with your signs in your hands!" I shouted.

"Okay, all right," Craig tried again. "You need to keep it under control, and I can see that you're not the type of guy that takes a lot of crap."

Monica was there by now and heard most of what I was saying.

Mike, the blond haired math teacher with the Elvis haircut, walked by.

"Hey Mike," Craig called out. "Can you talk James down?" Craig turned his face back to me. "It's pretty clear to me that you're the type of guy that is really easy going to a point, but then you explode. There's not much of an in-between for you. Mike here has never been outwardly angry."

"What's going on, coach?" Mike asked me. His voice was sedate and level.

I gave him a quick rundown.

"Whoa, coach. Who's gonna slash your tires?" Mike started walking me away from the scene that I had created. Evidently, this staff, for all its screaming and yelling, had no idea what really pissed off looked like. I taught them.

"Bert." Craig volunteered from about three feet away.

"Dude, I really don't think he'll do that. People get all uppity around this whole contract thing, you know? None of it's real. You wanna go for a beer or something?" The more he talked the calmer I felt. It could be his sedate manner, or it could be that I had exploded and there was nothing left.

"No thanks, man. I'm going to head home and teach the kids tomorrow because that's all I care about." I was tired, and we were getting close to my car.

"There you go!" said Mike, and he pointed at me as he walked away. "See ya tomorrow."

I drove home, knowing that I had the right job, but doubting whether I was at the right school. What could drive adults, including myself, to this sort of behavior? What would make a grown man so emotional that he would threaten people he worked with-people who had the same goal as him: a raise?

When I look back on it now and think about all the politicians who are going to improve education by passing legislation to raise test scores, I get sick knowing that the politicians will probably never pass the legislation that will take some of the insanity out of the profession. They'll never pass the legislation that will relieve some of the tension on the backs of teachers. It's simple: Teachers are educated professional people, and they should be paid as such.

Chapter XXX

"What do you do on the weekends, Mr. Kohl?" I had successfully made it through many months without answering the question, but it still came at least twice a week. I told them nothing about my personal life. I made up stories about my life to illustrate points I was trying to make or to lead into a grammar lesson. I told an elaborate story about my rich friend in San Diego whose house overlooked the beach. He ordered a huge window so that he could see the ocean better, but on the day it was delivered, it was raining and the deliverymen dropped it and shattered it. They picked up the biggest piece and headed up the hill. This kept happening until they only had one small piece left, but they still tried to collect the money.

"That's a ripoff, Mr. Kohl. You don't have to pay for a piece of a window!"

"You mean you don't have to just settle for part of what you wanted?" I baited.

"Yeah!"

"You see, I agree with you. That's why I feel ripped off when you write sentence fragments instead of full sentences. I want the whole thing, and some of you are only giving me a piece-just like the window. Here's how you avoid fragments." I then explained the whole process. One of my classes actually applauded that story.

My friend in San Diego was a pizza deliveryman with barely enough money to buy a soda at the beach when I used to tell that story.

"What are you doing this weekend, Mr. Kohl?"

It was early October when the question came this time. I didn't want to talk about what I did on the weekends because what I was doing was a lot of partying-responsible partying, mind you. "I'm going to do the same thing I do every weekend," I started. The room diminished to a noiseless vacuum waiting to see what that activity might be. I'm sure they all had their theories. I looked around and loved seeing the anxious faces that believed they were finally going to get the scoop. "I'm going to sit at home and read the dictionary."

The room gasped. Some of them clearly didn't believe me. Some were all too worried that it may be true. "You're gonna read the dictionary!?" asked Martin, the hyperactive child in the front row of third period. "That's boring, man!"

"Well, I like it." I acted offended. "I don't tell you what you should do on the weekends." I paused for a couple of seconds. "This weekend is going to be really cool because I'm starting the 'O' section."

"I can't even believe this," someone said. The rest of them winced and moaned in agony.

"Mr. Kohl, don't you think you would like to get a lady?" asked Joseph, who sat in the back row and was very worried about such issues for himself.

"Do you think that would be better than reading the dictionary?" I asked with schoolboy naivete.

"Stupid!" someone said.

"My cousin is single," volunteered Evelyn.

"No thanks. I'll stick with my dictionary." All this was going down in the final seconds of the period, and I couldn't wait until the bell rang. I hadn't had a "lady" in five years, and I didn't need these guys knowing anything about my personal life. It was not what we were here to talk about.

That day at lunch, Jacque stopped by on her normal sprint through the lunchroom. She leaned across the table as I sat in my usual seat by the door. Her voice was low, and her eyes overflowed with what looked like deep concern. "The kids say that you need help," she told me in a grave whisper.

"That could be true, but I'm probably beyond that."

"That's what I told them." I always enjoyed Jacque's quick wit. "They say that you spend the whole weekend at home reading the dictionary, and that I need to talk to you about what boys and girls do."

"Dude!" I said because I wasn't sure what else to say, "There's no way they really believe that!"

"Yes, sadly, some of them do. I just thought that was hilarious! You crack me up!" We shared a laugh, and she left the staff room.

The last bell of the week sounded and I was as excited, if not more, about the weekend than any of the kids. I couldn't wait to get home to that dictionary, which on this particular evening, was a bar-hopping expedition in Los Gatos ending up at Mountain Charlie's and some live music. Mike down the hall and my friend Rob and I had been planning this. Normally, things just happened; I had just turned 25 and lived moment by moment, page by page in the dictionary of life. I had no idea that on this night, I would define my life.

Sometime after dark, Rob came to my apartment and we put on some Grateful Dead while we waited for Mike to call. I was wearing Dockers and a button-down shirt-teacher clothes. I just felt like doing something different than the T-shirt and jeans that I almost wore as a weekend uniform.

Rob and I blabbed about nothing for almost an hour, trying Mike's number every once in a while. Mike sometimes plays his Black Sabbath too loud for the meek ring of a phone, so we took a walk down the hall to see if he was home. Four apartments away, we knew he wasn't there because we didn't hear the tell-tale distorted guitar riffs.

"What's up with Fuzz, man?" Rob asked, using the nickname that Mike gave himself that I ignore. Fuzzdink is the full nickname.

"I don't know, dude. Let's give him about a half hour and then just head to Boswell's. How's that sound?"

"Cool."

Boswell's was across the street from where I lived. We could walk there. It was a small bar with live music.

The half hour went by, and Mike never called. We walked by his place one last time on our way to Boswell's.

Music purred out into the courtyard of the Pruneyard. The under-21 crowd grabbed some of it as they sat at the outside tables of a coffeehouse and smoked. The night was a little cold. Maybe I should have worn a jacket. I couldn't afford to get sick. My classes had testing in four months.

Rob and I squeezed through the door.

"You gotta check out this one beer I just found out about." Rob and I were beer snobs and were constantly turning each other on to the darkest, richest brew we could find. "It's called John Courage. It's not dark, but it's real good."

Rob and I got our John Courage and stood in front of the band, Lulu and the Atomics. The band had a female singer, and they were doing '80s music like Blondie and Joan Jett songs. My eyes glanced across the dance floor, and I noticed a beautiful Mexican woman. Mainly it was her eyes that I noticed-they were pure. "Oh, there's my wife over there." I thought.

What did I just think!! I had dated a bit recently, but I didn't like those people enough to marry them, and they didn't like me that much either. In between sips of beer, I kept sneaking peeks at this woman as she danced. That was her all right. I was obviously an insane man because you can't walk into a bar one random evening and know that a woman is your life partner and true love without even talking to her. But, I did know.

The music was too loud for Rob and I to do a lot of talking, so I didn't feel the need to let him know all that was going on in my head. This was good news because getting hauled off to the loony bin would've ruined my chances of ever talking to her. I was too shy to talk to her anyway; she was too pretty for me.

A few more beers into the night, Mike showed up. It was then that I realized that my beautiful Mexican lady was hanging out with an on again off again girlfriend of Mike's. Her name was Joanne. I had pissed her off the last time we had met by speaking the truth about her blond friend. My diatribe had been out of line, so I went up to her this night to apologize.

"Hey," I yelled over the band.

"Hey man, what's up?" She said without really looking at me.

"You know, I'm sorry for saying all that stuff about your friend that one night. It wasn't cool."

She looked at me in shock. "Right on man! Thanks for saying something."

"Right on." I paused. I had to make what I said next as casual as possible for a guy speaking with his heart in his throat. "This isn't why I apologized, but I think your friend is really pretty."

"Which one?"

"In the white sweater."

Joanne looked over at the table where the girl sat with another woman in black. There was a drink in front of her. The one in black drank a Budweiser.

"Her name is Kristin. She's single, dude."

"Cool." I had had many girlfriends with that name and always thought that since I was attracted to women that ended up having that name, that I was somehow destined to end up with one Kristin or another for a wife. I walked toward the empty chair next to her hoping that she would at least go out with me.

I sat down with Rob to my left and Kristin right in front of me. It was nearly midnight, and Lulu and the Atomics were still going strong. "Hi," I said and her glance came right into me and curled around all over my insides.

"Hi," she answered.

"Uhm, I'm Jim, and this is Rob." I think we shook hands.

"How's it going?" Rob asked and shook her hand.

"This is my sister-in-law, Anna."

The girl in black said hi to us and sipped on her Budweiser.

"What is that you're drinking?" I pointed to Kristin's drink-desperate for conversation.

"Bailey's and coffee."

"That's cool."

"So what do you do, Jim?"

I almost wanted to lie, money being what it is, but there was no way I could to those eyes-ever. "I'm a teacher."

"Oh, what do you teach?"

I looked at her. She really looked like she was interested. "Seventh grade. English."

"Wow that's cool. I used to teach pre-school. I stopped when I wanted to ring their little necks." She smiled, beautifully.

"That's a good time to stop." I said.

Rob agreed.

The conversation was smooth and easy from that point on. We talked for nearly an hour about small things. She was funny and interesting and beautiful-inside and out. I had to ask for her number, but I hated that move because it made me nervous.

"I was wondering if I could get your number."

"You want my number?" She sounded surprised. I probably wasn't good enough for her.

"Yes, please."

"Okay." She got a pen from Anna. She wrote her pager number on a bar napkin. "Whenever you page, put in your number and 77 at the end so that I know it's you." She looked over and said something to Anna. Anna nodded. "Here's our number. I live with Anna." She wrote a second number on the napkin.

"Man, you're gonna be able to get a hold of her 24/7!" commented Rob.

I smiled. She smiled. She had such pretty eyes.

It got late and the band stopped.

"Well, I will call you within the next couple of days," I said.

She looked into my eyes. "Great," she said. I put my hand on her shoulder as she walked away, and felt the material of her white sweater.

It had come out earlier in the conversation that I lived close by and that Rob and I had walked over. Mike was trying to hit on Anna, so he wanted them to come back to my place because it was the cleaner of the two apartments. I felt sort of weird about that considering that I had just said goodbye to Kristin. What if she liked me so far, and then when she saw me in a lighted apartment she didn't like me anymore? What if I said something stupid? I almost wished that I could go home alone and just dream of the next time I would get to see her. They were coming though, so there wasn't anything I could do about it.

Mike, Rob, and I sat in my apartment waiting for them. Anna and Kristin came about five minutes after we got there. Kristin was even more beautiful in the light, and I hoped to God she at least thought I was okay. Kristin and I sat across the room from each other that evening. I was on the couch, and Mike sat at the other end of the couch. Rob took a chair. Anna said she wanted a smoke, and Mike started flipping cigarettes at her from across the room. She didn't seem impressed and commented about how old she was.

Kristin had a miniature Etch-a-Sketch on her key chain. Going to look at it would give me an excuse to get near her. I went across the room and kneeled in front of her to play with it

Mike continued flicking cigarettes across the room at Anna.

We talked for another hour or more, and then they left. I looked forward to calling Kristin in a couple more days.

The next morning she called me. Our phone conversations were like two old friends talking with one another. "You know what the craziest thing is?" she asked. "We weren't even supposed to go to Boswell's that night. We were supposed to go bar hopping in Los Gatos and end up at Mountain Charlie's."

"Me too."

The next week we went to Capitola and saw the Monarch butterflies. We had coffee on the balcony behind Mr. Toots, stared out at the waves, and fell in love.

Two weeks later, we were living together. My friend Martin called me one evening. "Hey man, no one has seen much of you lately, what's going on?"

"Nothing." I didn't know what he meant.

"Uh, I was at Mike's the other day, and I walked down to see if you were around. You didn't answer the door, but I saw that picture you guys took hanging on the wall of you and her and her two kids. What's going on?"

"Nothing, dude." It wasn't like I was married or anything, but actually it was exactly like I was married. I had never been happier. The two kids lived with us every other week. They lived with their dad on the alternate week. We only had a one-bedroom apartment. We slept together on a twin bed, and the kids split the couch. There was not enough room in there, so we got a new place that following January.

The new place was $500 more in rent, but it had two bedrooms. We got the kids bunk beds.

A month later, on February 12, I got down on one knee and asked Kristin to be my wife.

The next morning, I went into school and started class like I always did. After they had done their opener for the day, I said, "I normally don't tell you anything about my personal life, but I got engaged yesterday. Anyway, if you could take out your homework, which was page 146 in the orange grammar book…"

"Wait!" shouted Monique.

"What choo say?" asked Elizabeth.

"I thought you did nothing but read the dictionary on the weekend!"

"What's 'er name?"

"Kristin."

"What's 'er last name?"

I told them.

"She's Mexican?"

"Yes." I had no idea how this would influence their opinion of me.

"How'd ya meet her?"

"Does she read the dictionary too?"

"Look guys, I don't really want to talk about this in any more details than I have already told you. If you really want to know about this, I'll be glad to talk to you after school or at lunch."

"Are we gonna get to meet her?" asked Joseph.

"Maybe."

"Good, cause I gotta tell you if I approve."

"I knew homeboy wasn't reading no dictionary."

That was the last class that I had to announce it to. The rest of my classes announced it to me.

My third period threw a surprise party to celebrate a few days later. I never gave parties because I didn't want to clean it up, but they handled it all. The party was really for them. All my other classes worked that day, but I still have the little plastic bride and groom that they put on my cupcake.

Bringing my personal life into the classroom worked. These kids cared who I was and wanted to know who I was and what sort of things I liked. They would listen to me if I was more of a real person to them. They didn't want a robotic emotionless teacher, they wanted a real person with a real soul that had respect for them and that cared about them. They would learn from this sort of teacher. I could be that sort of teacher.

CHAPTER XXXI

As a teacher, you need to find and define your classroom persona. Because you are constantly in contact with a group of people, you need to create yourself, almost like an author creates a character, and how you will behave toward the kids.

I had made the decision going in that I was going to be all business. I was going to work them hard and wouldn't listen to any excuses for not completing assignments. I was never going to have a personal rapport with any student because they might misconstrue it for an excuse not to work.

Although a teacher once told me that humans have logical minds that strive for order, the truth is the more we strive for order, the less likely we are to achieve it. The more people you get together to do something, the more chaotic the task becomes. Think about meetings that you've had at work, or as a student at school or about group projects you have done. When you try to get something accomplished in a group like this, how much time is spent off task? How many people actually do the work? I had chaos smack straight into my orderly plan of self-definition as a teacher. Chaos wore red that year, and her name was Elizabeth.

She was the girl who wanted to use red pen and thought that I was "dissin' her colors" by insisting on black or blue ink. Elizabeth liked red because it was the color of the Norteno gang that her brother was active in. Elizabeth, to my knowledge, had never been "jumped in," (beaten up as part of gang initiation) but she hung out with a lot of gang members and felt a loyalty toward them.

On the LeyVa campus, you didn't mess with Elizabeth. Even though she was in seventh grade, the eighth-grade girls and most of the boys knew that she could beat them up and feared she may even kill them. She was a big, solid girl with long, straight, black hair and eyes that stared through you with hatred on a good day. She always wore a red flannel pendleton. She had XIV representing N-the 14th letter of the alphabet and the first letter in the word Norteno-written in red pen on her hand in the space between her thumb and first finger. She hated all the adults on campus. She hated life. She would kill for her family and friends.

"Do you have your homework, Elizabeth?" I asked as I came around to check off homework.

"Nah." She slouched in her seat in the back of my room. The seat that I assigned her was in the front, but she wouldn't sit there.

"Your seat is not back here; it's in the front-over there." I pointed to the empty seat in the front of the second row of the room.

"This is my seat." She informed me in her loud voice. She stared at me like this was the most important argument she had ever been in. She had everyone's attention, and I, being a new teacher, had to establish my authority.

"It's not your seat. I need you to move to the front of the room, now!" My voice was rising. I could feel my face burn.

"I don' gotta sit anywhere I don' wannew!" Elizabeth was pumping up with hate and anger. Her friend, Ruthy, was laughing.

"You're either going to move to the front of the room, or you're going to move down to the Student Center!" This is where the bad kids went with referrals. Elizabeth was a regular guest down there.

"Fine! Sen' me down there. I don't give a…"

The class "ooooohed" at her profanity.

My hands shook as I wrote up the referral. She made me so angry! She always chose the Student Center because it was a way out of class and, sometimes, a way out of school for the day. It was common for her to escalate her behavior until she would get sent home.

It became obvious, quickly, that Elizabeth was about respect for those that respected her. She was proud of who she was and what she was. She was proud of her friends, and she was proud of the gang that her brother was a part of. What you were and did was fine as long as it didn't interfere with who she was. In school, this sort of attitude didn't mesh well because things like homework and rules didn't fit into the world that Elizabeth lived in. Soon, she started skipping school about two days a week, but her mom always wrote her a note.

She was late for my class a lot and many mornings would be walking down the sidewalk that was on the other side of the school fence from my classroom door. She used the stroll of a tough girl with her head tilted slightly back and would whistle to Ruthy as she walked by my door on her way to the office, where she had to check in before she went to class. Ruthy would wave or just laugh; it was enough to mess up my lesson for a few minutes.

Because she was a chronic tardy, the office almost always held her for about 20 minutes, which meant that she would saunter into my room with about five minutes left in the period, if that. Many days, they would talk to her about her tardiness, and it would become a confrontation and they would send her home.

I had already talked to Jacque about Troy, and she had told me to look at the cum. file, so I figured I would start there with Elizabeth.

Elizabeth, like Troy, smiled in all of her young pictures. She even wore colors besides red. She had a nice little smile in first grade with her hair in pigtails. In her sixth-grade picture, the smile was gone, her hair was the straight, tough girl way that it was now, and the red flannel was in place. I had to try to decode what happened to her between the pigtails and the scowl by looking at the papers in this file folder. I sat at a table in the file room and opened it up. I was better at reading these things now, but I don't think very many people ever really master the art of cumulative file reading. I question whether those that have "mastered" the craft can really tell you much about the student that the folder supposedly summarizes.

Her main language at home was Spanish. She had okay grades as a young student, but they got progressively worse through the years. In English, in sixth grade, some teacher had taken the time to give her an F minus for a semester grade. Elizabeth actually did a little worse than failing. I understood. Elizabeth hadn't handed anything in to me and it was November. Coupled with the attitude, her sixth-grade teacher probably felt the need to make a statement.

"Do you have a girl named Elizabeth?" I asked Jacque. She was running through the lunchroom as usual, but I caught her attention and she sat right across from me at the table to talk about this girl.

"Really tough Mexican girl that looks like she'd like to kill you-unless she's asleep in your class?" Jacque asked.

"That's her."

"I have that girl," said May, the math teacher. "She doesn't do anything."

"That girl is garbage," said a female voice down the table. I had to agree.

"She argues with just about everything I say. She yells at me in class, and she never does her homework on top of all that," I said. I really had never seen anything like Elizabeth. Not many at LeyVa had, despite some of the stories that older teachers told about how rough things used to be.

"Who's this?" asked Craig as he plopped down in the seat next to mine and started to unwrap his peanut butter and jelly sandwich.

"Oh, just this girl I have." Craig didn't hold a grudge about the night I screamed in his face about the contract dispute. He was a good guy. Once he found we were talking about a kid he didn't know, he focused his conversation elsewhere.

"Have you looked at the Cum. File?" asked Jacque, just like I knew she would.

"Yeah," I nodded and I bit into my apple.

"Did you find out anything interesting?" May looked over to see if I was going to provide any insight.

"I found out that she speaks Spanish, she smiled in school pictures until last year, and in sixth-grade English, she got an F minus."

May laughed out loud and struggled to hold her food in her mouth.

"An F minus!?" Jacque thought I was messing with her.

"Swear to God," I said.

"I can't believe someone would take the time to fill in the minus on the scan sheet," said Jacque, referring to the bubble-in-with-a-number-two-pencil-forms that we filled out in those days to report grades.

"I can," May added out the side of her mouth.

"Isn't an F low enough?" Jacque asked.

I shrugged. "This girl is out of control. We hate each other, I'm pretty sure. But I'm sure I'm not the only person she hates, and I've been hated by more important people." The truth was, it really bothered me that I couldn't reach her. I was in the process of blowing it with Troy, and it was people like Troy and Elizabeth who kept me awake at night. You end up trying to find a strategy, something that will hook them and save them from their self destruction. You'd like to watch a life turn around to restore your faith in humanity once in a while. Sometimes, you want to live in the movie of the week.

About a week later, I was out because of illness and had a young substitute named Julie. Julie was a blond, blue-eyed teacher, whom Mexican girls at LeyVa hated because they considered her a "Barbie type." She had that going against her the moment she set foot on campus. As bad luck would have it, the day Julie was in was one of the few days in that particular week that Elizabeth came to school.

I don't know exactly what happened because you never do when you come back and a sub has been there, but Julie left me a full two-page report on just Elizabeth. According to the note, Elizabeth had come in late and made a loud entrance, saying something in Spanish when she saw that I was not there. She had written a note to Ruthy, and while she was trying to pass the note, Julie saw it and asked for it. Elizabeth refused to surrender the note. Julie asked for it a second time, and then a third. Both of them yelled, and Elizabeth eventually was kicked out.

As it can, the confrontation with Elizabeth ruined the rest of Julie's day in my classroom. Her note to me was really a bit of a catharsis for her, I believe. I read the note twice, sat at my desk and stared at the wall. What was I going to do? I couldn't ignore it. I was going to have to say something to Elizabeth, which of course, would undoubtedly end in a huge argument where my blood pressure would be up through the roof. I hated it when I came back to a bad note. Why couldn't she have been absent yesterday?

On the day I came back after a substitute had been in, I always had the students write a paragraph describing what the experience was like for them. Did they get work done? Did the substitute treat them fairly? Were there any questions about what the substitute presented to them? After they wrote for 10 minutes, if a student had ended up as a feature in the substitute's note, I would ask that student for his or her side of the story and decide whether I was going to give them detention for the behavior. In rare cases, the kid would say, "I was disrespectful. I deserve the detention, Mr. Kohl." But in most cases, I allowed them to talk their way out of it. I felt that just the discussion held them accountable most times.

All during first period, I sat at my desk staring out onto Monrovia Drive and visualized the conversation that I would have with Elizabeth. I remembered some of the terrible experiences I had as a substitute and felt horribly that someone had that sort of experience right here in my room where I was in control. The leaves in the trees outside my window moved a bit with the light breeze, and now and then one would jump down to the lawn just for kicks.

The bell rang for second period to begin. Show time. I plopped the writing prompt about the substitute down on the overhead projector and pulled down my map/screen to cover the brown chalkboard. This was it. If she was here today, she'd surely be screaming at me within 15 minutes.

The kids started filing in.

"You're back!" They always seemed so surprised.

I nodded.

"Where were you yesterday?" asked Rodolfo. He was a little kid with a thick Mexican accent who sat by the door and never seemed to understand or believe anything I said.

"None of your business." They knew by now that would be my answer, but they always asked anyway.

"Oh, man!!" Whined Rodolfo.

The room stirred with the sounds of talking, laughing, flopping into desks and unzipping backpacks.

The bell rang-no Elizabeth. Maybe I would not have to have this confrontation after all. She might be out for the next two or three days, and by that time, talking to her about something that happened with a sub would be pointless. There would probably be new problems to address by then.

I took roll and hung my roll sheet on the clip by my door. "Get out your homework so I can see it, please. You were supposed to write five different examples of personification, metaphor and simile."

"Homework?" asked Rodolfo.

"Yes, Rodolfo."

"Oh, man!!" This was his whine each time I asked for something he didn't have. I heard it several times a day.

I was standing in the middle of the room when the door opened. My body chilled. I looked up. A girl's hand reached in and took the roll. It was nearly 10 minutes into the period when I was done checking homework. She probably wasn't coming. It's a good feeling to be stood up by someone you didn't want to see in the first place.

I started the discussion about the substitute. No one liked her. Rodolfo didn't like her because they had to work. Ruthy didn't like her hair or just anything about her at all. I listened to these trivialities for a minute or two, and then I asked, "Did she treat you the way that you deserved to be treated?"

Alicia raised her hand. She had impressed me on the first day of school with her professional dress and maturity but since then had fallen in with Ruthy and Elizabeth. She was sporting a flannel now but was red free for the moment. "I shouldn't be talking because she's not here, but she wasn't fair to Elizabeth."

"Stupid!" hissed Ruthy.

I let that all hang in the air for a second. "The sub mentioned some things about Elizabeth, but those things shouldn't be discussed without Elizabeth being here." Almost as if on some sort of cue, the door opened, and Elizabeth made her entrance. She handed me a slip they had given her in the Student Center and headed toward her sanctuary at the back of the room. The class was silent.

Ruthy whispered something to Elizabeth, presumably telling her what we'd been talking about.

Elizabeth looked up at me with her eyes clenched and shouted, "Hey, I didn't do nothin'! She had a problem with me when I walked in. But I know you're gonna take her side cause she's a teacher, but I don't care!"

I stayed calm. "I want to know what your side is." I said it as deliberately as anyone could with a nearly crazed 12-year old street kid yelling at him.

"As soon as I came in, she gave me her attitude!"

"What do you mean, exactly?" She paused to let me talk. This was huge progress. I thought I would push the envelope. "Also, I want to talk about this, so let's not yell please." I kept my voice at a near monotone. I sounded like someone trying to soothe a screaming baby. She was excited enough. I didn't need to set her off worse.

"You know, she gave me a dogged look." Her voice actually reduced to a conversation level. "An' I said, I don' think so, not from no Barbie!" Well, she stopped yelling for one sentence anyway. The class laughed at the Barbie reference, but Elizabeth wasn't trying to be funny. "An' I know you ain't gonna believe me, but I didn't do nothin'."

I tried to think of a reason why the 'dogged look' was given, if indeed it was. "Did you come in late?" I asked.

"No!"

"She was about two minutes late," Alicia volunteered. Elizabeth shot her a look and Alicia was finished talking for the rest of the period. I looked around the room and people nodded that she was only about two minutes late.

"Were you about two minutes late, Elizabeth?"

Nothing.

"Cause, you know, two minutes late is still late, but it's pretty good…for you." This was true.

Elizabeth looked up from her desk and right at me. She was out of her element, all of a sudden. She looked at me with those brown eyes, and they didn't want to fight. She looked like a little girl. I could almost picture the pigtails and the smile. "That's what I'm saying," she said.

"Now what's this about a note?" I asked her.

"Oh! She tried to take my note away, and she said that I better get up an' take the note to her or else she'd kick me out." The little girl was gone again. "I'm like, 'Fine then kick me out,' cause she ain't getting' my note, that's my business, an' she has no right to be getting' in my business! I told her I'd put the note away, but she was like yelling about me bringin' her the note right now and this and that, right? So, I'm like," She made an 'F' sound with her mouth and stopped herself, I wondered quietly if that was why she earned an F-minus. "No way, you know? So then she thinks she's all big and bad cause she writes me a referral, an' sayin' how I'm gonna have to give it to the vice principal, yeah right! I spend the rest of the period in the Student Center."

"Did you give them the note?"

"No! I to'd them I didn't have no note." She looked up at me in her normal hard way. I looked at her detached-just getting the facts.

"Then what happened?"

"They didn't do nothin'."

I waved my hand back and forth at chest level as if I was erasing the comment. "Anyway," I said, "why do you think that she was being unfair?"

"Because," Elizabeth wrinkled her face in disbelief that I could be so stupid that I would need this explained to me. "I told her I'd put it away, an' she just thinks she's all that."

"Do you think that it was a bad idea to try to pass the note to Ruthy at that particular time?" I braced myself for the response because my question would more than likely be considered an attack by Elizabeth.

There was a tense moment where I thought everything might erupt, but then, she nodded! I couldn't believe that she was admitting that she made a mistake! This was huge! This was the most progress I had ever seen from her. "But she was more wrong! And she gave me a dogged look as soon as I came in the room!" Her tirade went on, but I stopped listening because I was still in shock at the admission of poor judgement.

When she took a breathing break from her rampage, I asked, "Do you think you deserve detention for this?" Elizabeth had the system figured out. If I gave her a detention, she would skip it, and then she would have an hour of school detention. When she skipped that, they would give her a Saturday School, which she would also skip. The end result would be a suspension, which is what she really wanted anyway-a day off from school.

"Whatever!"

"Well, I don't." She was visibility shocked. Ruthy, who had put her head down minutes ago, looked up at me to see if she had heard me correctly. I shook my head. "It sounds like you two had a misunderstanding, and she handled it, so in my opinion…it's over."

The class didn't really know what to say to this. They didn't really know what to think about this either. Elizabeth started to say something more about how she'd better never see that sub again, and I asked her not to talk about it anymore because I needed to get to the lesson.

"I'm just saying…"she said.

"I know."

I know that some of my colleagues at the time would have thought I was being too soft, but I found the admission of guilt much more effective than a detention that she would probably skip. I never dreamed the admission would come, but the fact that it did made me begin to think that maybe she wasn't as misanthropic as I thought. Maybe there was a heart beneath the red flannel.

I went to the office to talk to Mike about Elizabeth a few days later. Even though she seemed to have exhibited a hint of morals, the two of us would still get into it over one thing or another. She often would disagree with the way that I insisted another student do something like, schoolwork, for example. She would tell me that I shouldn't walk around thinking that I'm all "high society" when I would mention that the word "ain't" should be avoided in a formal essay. I had reached the end of my rope with her, and it was only her frequent absences that kept me going.

Mike had a corner office in the Student Center, the one closest to the door that students entered through. He towered over his desk even when he was sitting down. He pushed papers from one pile to another as I stood in his open doorway. "Oh, hey Jim." He said when he finally noticed me. "What can I do for you?"

"I have this kid," I said as I took a chair in Mike's office, "named Elizabeth."

Mike said her last name.

"Exactly. I don't know what else to do with her. I don't kick her out as often as I probably should, but she really needs to be in class even though she doesn't do anything when she's there." I grimaced. "She doesn't do any work at all ever, and she's rude. She threatened my substitute one time, at least the sub wrote that she felt threatened in my note."

Mike thought for a second. His face had hardened to the point of disgust as I explained the situation to him. "We're planning an SST for her in January." An SST was a Student Study Team meeting where one student's problems are focussed on by the SST committee. The student and parent are requested to attend these meetings, but many of them do not show up. The goal of the meeting is to address whatever difficulties the student is having at school and come up with solutions for those issues. Ideally, some of the solutions are supposed to be enacted by the student, some by the parent, and some by the school. It usually turns into "What are you guys gonna do for my kid?" with the school taking the grand share of blame for the kid's problems and the responsibility for repair. "The main focus of the SST is going to be her attendance, but you should really bring up all of the points you just made at the meeting as well."

"That's cool." But January was a month away, and I needed a solution sooner than that.

"In the meantime," continued Mike, "send her out of the room. She's beyond deserving chances. Yours is not the only classroom that she tries to sabotage; she's in here all the time. She's at the point of zero tolerance, so throw her out of the room and send her up here without giving her a warning. Everyone up here will support you on this. Elizabeth is making it impossible for you to do your job, and that is against the mandatory education law. The other kids deserve a chance to learn."

I thanked Mike and left his office.

It was not long after that day, somewhere near the beginning of December, that I assigned an autobiographical incident essay to the kids. It was in preparation for the writing proficiency test. The essay had to include certain components that sat in purple on a bulleted list on my wall on an enlarged recipe card:

Dialogue

Movement and gestures

First person narrative

Emotions that were felt

Must describe a true event from the writer's life

The significance of the event had to be plainly stated.

Once I had taught them what all of that meant, I let them loose on topic selection and the beginning of a rough draft.

I wandered about the room as they began this process, hopping from desk to desk to offer suggestions, help and moral support. Eventually, I ended up at the back of the room with Elizabeth and her crew, and I knew I would probably need to nag them to start something. It's easier to motivate a B student into an A student than it is to motivate an F student into anything.

"What are you guys doing?" I tried to hide the dread from my voice, and I knew that they knew it was there.

"Uhm…We're workin' on this thing. What is it again?" Elizabeth was always their spokesperson.

"The autobiographical incident essay?" I asked, hoping that it would ring a bell.

"Oh, yeah. We're workin' on that."

"Oh good," I said, doubting every word that came out of her mouth. "What have you guys chosen as topics?" They all had one except for Elizabeth. "What about you?"

"I was thinkin' of writing about the night my big brother got shot." I was floored. I was a big brother, and I had never been shot, but she said it like every big brother in the world gets shot at some point. She sensed doubt in me, "No for reals, he got shot in the arm. Like about a month ago."

"Geez! Is he allright?"

"Oh, yeah, he's cool." She was sitting right in front of me as I stood to her left. We were close enough to shake hands, but it was clear we knew nothing at all about each other's worlds.

"Okay, well…That sounds like a great topic. All you have to do is write it now."

"Yeah, but I don' know how to start it. You see, me an' my sister were sitting in the house one night listening to oldies, an' you could hear the cops in the helicopter, an' they were calling out my brother's name on the loudspeaker. All of a sudden, the door busts open an' my brother comes in and he's sweating an' breathing hard an' this an' that, an' then we told him, 'You all right, Fernando?' an'…"

I put my hand up and waved it back and forth. "You know, it sounds to me like you have a pretty good idea how to start it," I said.

Her mouth dropped. "You mean…Write it just like I was tellin' it to you right now?" This had never occurred to her.

"Yeah. Add how you felt and the rest of that stuff." I motioned to the recipe cards on the wall, the purple print on them seemed so silly compared to the beginning of the story I had just heard. "And I think you'll have a great essay." She had hooked me with her storytelling ability. I was picturing everything she said, and she didn't even "know" anything (according to standardized tests) about making a narrative. "Could you do that?"

"Yeah." She looked at me with a wrinkled forehead. "Just like that?"

"Yes." Maybe I would see this essay.

Three days later, Elizabeth proudly submitted three pages detailing the events of the night that her brother was shot in the arm. It was in pencil, and I had made it a policy to only accept ink or typed papers, but it was turned in, and it was complete, and it was the first work I had seen from her in three months of school. There was no way I was going to deprive her and myself just because it was in pencil.

I took it home that night in the pile of 150 essays and flipped right to it as soon as I unzipped my briefcase. I sat on my blue and white couch next to Kristin and read about the boy being chased by police from the scene of a fight involving a gun. I read about the helicopter police calling his name. I read about how he stormed through the front door with blood pouring from his arm, and how Elizabeth, her sister, and her "brother's ol' lady" tried to clean him up and treat the wound. They couldn't go to the hospital. The cops finally came to the door with a warrant and took him away a few hours later.

"Geez." I put the A on the paper, and put it down. The grammar was off, and she wrote exactly the way she talked, but her detail was good, and she had a natural ability to carry you into the story and hold you there. "If we could just tame the grammar, she would write a best seller someday." I thought.

"Check out this paper, honey." I only gave Kristin the really good essays to read, and in a period of five years, I think I gave her four.

"Wow," she said as she finished it.

"I know. This is the first thing she's ever given me."

"She's got a lot of baggage for a 12-year-old." Kristin's upbringing was similar to Elizabeth's, but she never had the gang element in her immediate family.

"I know." What could I do for this kid?

On an afternoon in January, the SST that Mike had spoken of was starting up. All of Elizabeth's teachers, Pam, the school psychologist, and the faculty all headed down to the school library to share anecdotes about Elizabeth. Dolores, the vice principal who ran the committee, talked to me earlier in the day about how she dreaded this one because she felt it was going to be really negative. "The girl doesn't give you very much to like about her," Dolores told me. "I've never wanted a kid out of the school before in my life."

Since Elizabeth had turned in her paper, she had continued to come to school late, if at all, been thrown out of numerous classes numerous times (including mine), threatened many students, and been in a physical altercation with an adult yard supervisor who, Elizabeth decided, needed to be slapped across the face. It had been a busy two months, and the chances of this SST being very negative were pretty much 100%.

We gathered in the library. Jacque was in there, and I took a spot around the rectangle table next to her. Pam sat to my right, and the rest of the SST committee and Elizabeth's teachers filled in around the table.

I didn't really know Pam, but she was at other SSTs I had been a part of this year. She was loud and had a great scratchy laugh like Janis Joplin's. Pam was a student advocate, and there was no kid, no matter how bad whom she was ready to write off.

"Are the parents coming?" someone asked.

"I spoke with the mother this morning, and my understanding was that both she and Elizabeth would be here," Dolores answered, as she flopped Elizabeth's cumulative folder on the table.

"I gotta see this F-minus!" whispered Jacque as she reached for the folder.

I smiled.

We all waited in the semi-lit room, but Elizabeth and her mother were beginning to look like no-shows. Someone called the house, but no one answered.

"So typical!" complained one teacher as he shook his head and looked at the floor.

"Well, we need to proceed with this meeting as if they were here, and with any luck, maybe they'll show up in a couple of minutes." Dolores began, trying to keep things positive. "As many of you may know, one of the many problems that we're having with Elizabeth is attendance. It has become necessary to refer her to SARB," Dolores looked over at me and decoded the acronym, "Student Attendance Review Board. This is the first step in placing Elizabeth in some sort of an alternative program where she may be more successful."

Normally, at an SST, teachers list the students strengths and weaknesses, and then we try to list solutions to help the student be more successful in the school they are in. This was different. It was a formality on the road to making Elizabeth someone else's problem. We were dumping her.

We went around the table and everyone shared similar stories about Elizabeth continually running the gamut of behavior between rude and threatening. There was a great amount of discussion surrounding her hitting the lunchtime yard supervisor. Above and beyond all of that, she was failing every class. She didn't even show up enough to pass PE.

"Well, we've heard a lot of the bad things about Elizabeth…" It was Pam. "Doesn't anybody have anything nice to say?" She cackled like Janis Joplin as she said the second sentence, but when I looked at her, she had a tear in her left eye.

The room fell silent. Everyone just looked at Pam.

"I mean sure, you all hate her and…"

"We don't hate her…" someone said.

"Oh, but I think you do," said Pam, "I know what it's like to go to a school where you feel like all the adults there hate you. It doesn't feel good!" Pam's laugh again. "Why should she come here when everyone hates her? Why should she do your work when you all hate her?"

"I don't hate her," said Jacque, "But, Pam…She is a lot to deal with."

"I know! I have her in my office sometimes the whole friggin' day, and let me tell you, her perception is that all the adults on this campus hate her." Pam tapped the table with her index finger to emphasize her point.

"But she brought this on herself. If she wasn't the way she was, no one would have a problem. Why should we bend over backward anymore for one punk kid?" This was Shirley, Elizabeth's Quest (peer pressure and teen problems) teacher.

"That is a chicken and the egg question, Shirley. It's up to us to be the adult in relations between us and students," said Pam.

Suddenly an idea blossomed in my head. I never spoke at these meetings but I had to this time. "Elizabeth has turned in one writing assignment to me this year. It was great. I think she's got a lot of potential as a writer. It's raw as far as grammar goes, but her writing stirs emotions." I had everyone's attention. "It's obvious to me that she's never going to do any homework the way we would like. If it's okay with the office," I nodded to Dolores, "I would like to allow her to get a grade based only on writing that she'll do for me in class. She won't need to listen in class unless she wants to. I'll grade her based on the number of pages of writing she gives me per quarter. They have to be quality though-it can't just be a bunch of words."

I had silenced the room.

"What a beautiful suggestion!" Pam said after about a minute. Pam was obviously a genius.

The rest of the teachers in the room just looked at me. Tony, the computer teacher who was a member of the committee, looked at me pensively and nodded. Other teachers dropped their eyes when mine met theirs.

"If you would be willing to do that, Mr. Kohl, the office would certainly back you on it," Dolores said. The meeting adjourned a short time later, and I headed home.

Kristin and I went out grocery shopping that evening. "I need to buy two notebooks." I told her.

"Why?"

"Remember that kid that wrote about her brother being shot? I'm going to put her on an alternate program where all she does is write for me." My idea was that I would give her a notebook that would never leave the classroom and one for her house that she could write in at home and bring to me for credit as well. I figured I would give her one point a page.

"Aren't the other kids going to think that's not fair?"

"Probably, but the office is backing me, and the only way they can get on that sort of program is to have an SST. None of them are going to want that."

We had reached the stationery isle. I looked at all the notebooks. Some of them had cartoon characters on them, and that definitely did not say "Elizabeth" to me. Finally I saw the one I needed. It was bright red and about 300 pages thick. I picked up two of them.

"These'll match her clothes." I told Kristin as I flopped them into the cart.

I left for work the next morning with the notebooks under my arm. I couldn't wait to see Elizabeth. I was anxious to see what she would say about this new plan. I pulled into the parking lot of the school and carried my stuff over to Room 5. "I hope she comes today!" I thought.

In the office, I saw Dolores by the teachers' mailboxes. "I'm going to give Elizabeth her notebook today so she can start writing for me."

"Yeah? Good luck with that. I hope it works for her." Dolores lowered her voice to a mumble, "Not much else has."

"It will." I told her.

Elizabeth was there that day. She came into the room right at the bell and went to the back of the room. She nodded to Ruthy.

"Okay, your opener for the day is word roots. List as many example words as you can for these two roots." I flipped on the overhead projector and shined the two roots on the map/screen. "Get out your homework, the rough draft of the Emotion Paragraph, and let me see it as I come around. I'll be with you in a couple of minutes." I paused and took three steps towards the back of the room between the first two rows of seats. "Elizabeth," I said in a voice a shade quieter than the one I used to address the entire class, "I need to see you for a couple of seconds, please."

"What'd I do now?" she attacked.

"Nothing. I want to tell you something." Her curiosity must have been too much for her to handle because she got out of her seat and followed me back to my desk without saying anything.

"We had a meeting about you yesterday. You were supposed to be there."

"My mom couldn't get off work."

"Oh." I nodded. I sat at my desk, and she stood in front of it. "Anyway, at this meeting, the office gave me permission to try something new with you." She looked interested. We weren't yelling. "You're a good writer. I told them all about the essay you wrote about your brother."

"You told them about that!" Her eyes widened.

"I just said it was good. I didn't say what it was about. Anyway, so…what I'd like you to do is write for me. Everyday, you'll just come into class and write in a journal for me, and I'll give you a grade based on how many pages you fill with quality writing. Quality writing means it has to say something. It just can't be a bunch of garbage and scribbles, do you get what I mean?"

She nodded.

I reached into my desk drawer. "I bought you two notebooks. You can take one home, and the other has to be turned in to me every day for a grade. The one you take home you can write in it, bring it in and show it to me, and I'll give you credit for that too."

"You bought these for me with your own money?" She took them from me and looked at them.

"Yeah. I got you red ones because…" I motioned to her clothes "You seem to…like red." I loved acting stupid.

She snickered. "Thank you." I nodded, and Elizabeth looked at the ceiling for a second. "I don' gotta listen in class no more?"

"If we're doing something that you want to do, you're more than welcome to join us on those days. Other than that, you only have to write. Do you think you can do this?"

"What do I gotta write about?"

I don't think she believed the freedom I was giving her. I think it may have scared her a little. "Write about whatever you want. Write about what's important to you. Do you think you can do this?" I asked again, praying that she would agree to it.

"Yeah."

"Cool. Well, start today."

I taught the class that day, but I was on automatic pilot as I watched Elizabeth fill a couple of pages in her red notebook. I couldn't wait to read what she was writing. Besides the essay on her brother, she had never done any work in my class until now. This was the sort of victory that teachers dream about-I had engaged the apathetic student.

The class ended, and the kids headed toward the door. A few of them had questions and made a half circle around me as I answered them. Elizabeth stood behind the half circle. "I'll put this on your desk," she mouthed to me while motioning toward my desk with her notebook.

I nodded.

There was a short break between second and third period everyday. It was more or less time for anyone who needed to make a run to the bathroom. I ran to the notebook instead. I opened the first page, which was filled with red ink, and read the first line, "I wasn't always like this."

The page went on to talk about how she knew that all the teachers at LeyVa thought she was a scummy person, but that didn't matter. She knew that at her old school, she had been taken to the Young Authors Fair. She had been school president. She had delivered a speech at graduation that made people cry.

"I'm not sure how I got this way." The page went on. She began to ponder this when she wrote, "Well, the bell's gonna ring. I'll tell you more tomorrow."

I picked up one of the many black pens off my desk and wrote, "Nice job for the first time out! I really like what you wrote; you have a knack for storytelling. I look forward to reading more from you."

And so began the dialogue between Elizabeth and me. We fought out loud all year, and became friends in the quiet of correspondence. Each day she would tell me what was on her mind, and each day I would encourage her writing and ask questions.

Elizabeth couldn't see how she "got this way," but it glared off these pages. Her dad had been physically abusive to her mother, and he was no longer in the picture. He came around occasionally, but not since Elizabeth had become "big enough to throw him out." Her brother was 20, in a gang and in and out of prison. He was sent to San Quentin that year. He punched Elizabeth once and I called Child Protective Services, but the incident had already been reported. Her mother spoke no English, and didn't understand the school when we would call and talk about a lack of homework. She pretended to understand, and it wasn't until halfway through the year that we realized that only a Spanish-speaking school representative should call the house.

Elizabeth spent a lot of time with her friends hanging out in the street. She came home late a lot and had a hard time getting up for school after being out until 1 in the morning. Bullets had missed her in a recent drive-by shooting. Her mom worked late hours, and it was either stay home alone and be bored or find something to do. She chose the latter. At least out there, she felt like someone had the time for her and cared.

She knew the teachers hated her and she didn't care. She hated them too. There was hardly a teacher or administrator whom she didn't think deserved to be "beat down" at one point or another for something they did to her like trying to take away one of her notes or disciplining a friend of hers. Elizabeth saw herself as a motherly figure to all of these girls like Ruthy and Ruby (they were twins) and Alicia. She was there to defend, and she "didn' want no Scraps in her school." "Scraps" was the word the red gang called the blue gang. Woe to the new LeyVa student that came in wearing too much blue!

"I wear a lot of blue," I wrote to her once.

"Ah, Mr. Kohl," she wrote back, "You ain' no Scrap. You're down for your own." I used that line any time a kid joked about my blue wardrobe.

I knew we were getting close when one day, a kid asked me about my wife's ex-husband. I had started talking about my personal life a little by this point. "We don't get along. He threatens to beat me up all the time."

Everyone laughed.

"I got your back, Mr. Kohl." Elizabeth said.

No one laughed.

"Thanks," I said. I have yours as well, I thought.

Elizabeth raised her grade from an F to a C+ in my room with this new program. She had F's everywhere else, so she didn't graduate to the eighth grade. You're not supposed to have students two years in a row, but I asked for Elizabeth. We had another year together, and she still didn't graduate, but she did a larger amount of conventional work than the year before.

"Elizabeth only comes to school to be with you," Pam told me one afternoon with a tear in her eye. A lot of days, I only came for her too.

They kicked her out two weeks before the end of my second year with her for something she did, and we were robbed of each other earlier than expected.

I learned more from Elizabeth about being a teacher than I did in any of those expensive college courses. Some kids will be successful. Some kids will be unsuccessful. Some kids you can make successful if you just open your mind to the possibility that not everyone can function in a traditional school environment. Any teacher will tell you that students are people, and not all of them are perfect, but we all forget that even the far from perfect ones are still people and still have the potential to be good. We also forget that our impact is severe whether it be positive or negative. We have no idea how we affect the lives of the kids. They have no idea how they affect ours. I wanted to be all business coming in, but all business doesn't allow you the pleasure of the kids.

Elizabeth gave me the confidence to know that the next time I saw an Elizabeth come into my room, I could handle it. But in three more years of teaching, I never saw another Elizabeth.

Chapter XXXII

Summer came. My life had been regimented to moving when a bell sounded, and then all of a sudden, there were no more bells and there was nothing to do. I had signed a contract for the following year because I was still a temporary employee, so I had a job starting in fall, but my health and dental benefits were my own responsibility until then. I had chosen the 12-month pay plan when I got hired so that I would still receive my normal check each month.

I packed up my classroom and took all the stuff off the walls. By the end of my first year, I had about 10 posters-they multiply somehow in the course of a year. I walked down to the office and gave my key back to Pat.

"Here you go," I said as I handed the key to Room 5 back to her.

"Do you have the key to the file cabinet?" she asked.

I thought for a second. "It's in the room in my desk." My desk was a jungle of all the things I owned. All the pen holders and coffee cups that appear on teachers' desks were stacked every which way in the drawers, and I knew the key was in there somewhere, but it would take me the better part of my life to find it at this point.

"That's fine. Did you give me a copy of your grade book?"

"No." They had handed me a ream of paper describing procedures for the last day, but I didn't remember reading that anywhere.

"I need one. You'll need to make a copy of it before you go." Pat motioned to the copy machine.

I waited in a line of people that were copying off their grade books for Pat. Finally, it was my turn, and as the last copy clicked and whirred out of the machine, my first year officially ended. It was summer time, and I was a kid again. I drove home from work with Bruce Springsteen on the radio and thought back about a day about six months earlier.

I had picked up Kristin after she got off of work. We only had one car at the time, so I was in charge of dropping everyone off and picking everyone up every day. "I know a guy that knows a guy with a two-bed-room condo for rent," she announced. We both knew that we needed more room and that the kids could not sleep on the same couch forever, but money was tight. Kristin made $10 an hour back then, and I was able to bring home about $1,800 a month that year. Rent for the one bedroom we were living in was $700, and we ended up with about $400 after all the bills were paid.

"That's cool," I told her. "How much is the rent?" The side of Highway 101 blurred past us as we discussed our possible future home.

"It's $1,100."

My jaw hit the dashboard. One more bedroom cost $400! "That bet-ter be some bedroom," I thought. "We'll get to see it of course?" I said. I didn't want my concern for the money to be too obvious. We were already barely getting by as far as I was concerned. We could never afford to put any money away in a savings account. We spent a lot of money foolishly, as all couples did, and if we had this much of a rent increase we may never be able to spend money on anything but necessities again.

"Yeah, we can see it. I have the address right here." Kristin reached into her bag and pulled out a piece of paper folded in fourths. She read the address to me. "We could drive by it on the way home. So what are you thinking?"

"Sounds pretty cool. I'd like to see it though-I mean on the inside too."

We drove by the place that evening because we couldn't find it on the way home. It looked like a nice area, and the actual condo looked really nice. It was peach stucco and had the look of a row of adobe houses. It looked like it should've been built closer to the beach.

"I love it! Don't you love it?" Kristin asked as we drove back from looking at it.

"It looks great from the outside," I agreed. We didn't talk about the condo anymore that evening. I was relieved because I really needed to sit down with the numbers and see how our combined salary would stack up against the rent we would be paying and so on.

That night, I didn't sleep much. I kept imagining the numbers in my head, and I didn't think this move was financially possible. The more I thought about it, the more I was unsure that we could pull this off. For the first time, I started to understand the anger and the frustration associated with teacher negotiations. When negotiations had been going on, I had no family to worry about. Although we weren't married yet, I pretty much had a family now, and the money they were giving me for my college degree plus an extra 30 units-the equivalent of a graduate degree-seemed a little low. Would I be renting forever? Worse yet, would I end up on the street? In the dark, the uncertainty stacked itself upon itself in my brain until I had no room in my head for sleep.

The next morning, It was a nice twenty minutes before she started talking about the condo again.

"So, do you want me to make an appointment so we can go see the condo today after work?" she beamed. I loved it when she was happy and would do just about anything to make her that way. That's why I hated what I said next.

"You know honey, that's a lot of rent, and before we really move forward with this, I'd really like to sit down with the numbers and make sure it's all going to work." I watched her face sink the way a child's does when their scoop of ice cream rolls off the cone and lands in the mud. There was a toxic silence that seemed to last five minutes. I stood and looked at her as she continued putting on her makeup.

"You know," she finally said, "it's all real fun and cute to play house, but when the heat starts coming on it's not fun and games anymore, is it!"

"Honey, I just want to make sure it's going to work."

"You don't think it's going to work because of me and the kids!! You could afford everything just fine if you were alone!"

"All I'm saying is that we need to look at the finances before we make this kind of a jump."

"I don't want to talk to you right now." She wouldn't look towards me.

"Honey," I touched her shoulder, but she shrugged my hand away.

"I said I don't want to talk to you!"

She didn't want to talk to me on the entire ride to work either. We dropped the kids off at the babysitter's house and pulled into the dark street back toward the freeway. The fog obscured everything that morning. I thought that I might crash at any minute because nothing could be seen on the other side of the wall of fog. "So what if I do?" I thought.

I left Kristin out in the parking lot of her job, and she didn't say goodbye to me. I headed back to the school.

The fog was so thick you couldn't see across the courtyard as I stood, freezing on yard duty that morning.

"I feel so safe knowing that you're out here, James," Craig said to me as he huddled into his coat.

I nodded.

"You know all those programmers out at IBM are out on yard duty right now too. We're professionals just like they are. Yeah, right!" Craig continued on to the office.

The bell rang. The show must go on no matter what mood you're in. I was glad to have the first-period prep where I could sit alone in my room and mope.

Fog is great weather to mope in. It chilled my face as I turned the lock in my door and went in. A cockroach scurried off to somewhere, and I silently thanked it for not making an appearance during class. The kids go nuts when one little cockroach shows up in their classroom. Imagine that!

I sat pretending to grade a mountain of essays when the intercom in my room buzzed. I picked up the phone and said, "Hello?" Static crammed my ear shut. "Hello!"

Through the static, I could hear Pat's voice, "Mr. Kohl, you have a phone call down here in the office."

"Thanks! I'll be right down!" I headed down to the office. The fog was starting to break up by now, but the cloud cover still gave California that winter feel. The silver doorknob to the office was cold.

"Oh hi." Pat said to me, "You can take it in there." She pointed to a small side office where the secretaries had a coffeepot with a strict warning on it concerning drinking any if you weren't one of them. "It's line 4, Jim."

I picked up the phone and pressed the flashing button.

"Hi sweetie." Her voice sounded so small.

"Hey, I'm so glad you called!" I was melting on the inside, warm enough to clear the rest of the fog.

"Me too." I waited to see what she would say. "I'm sorry we fought."

"I don't understand why we're fighting."

"I was talking to Joanne and some other people over here, and they all say that you're just one of those people that has to plan things out when it comes to money. I'm not that way. I thought you were trying to say that our relationship wasn't working. Of course we can sit down and go over all the rent and our two salaries and make sure we can afford this."

"That's all I was trying to say." I held the phone in my hand, and I felt my face heat up as Carmen came in for a cup of restricted coffee.

"I know." Her voice smiled. "Joanne said I better call you fast before you get in class and take this out on all the kids."

We talked a bit more and hung up. I was still worried about the money, but at least my mood wouldn't interfere with my teaching. Regardless of my personal life, in Room 5, I always had to be Mr. Kohl.

We ended up getting that condo, and as I feared, money got tighter. We were trying to save for a wedding and raise two kids. I didn't work that first summer, but I still got my check at the end of each month. It may have been easier if they paid teachers more than once a month.

"Things are a little tight, but as long as we can afford rent and our bills and get food, we'll be fine," I told my mom on the phone one day. I stood in my kitchen and looked across the living room out the sliding glass door that looked out onto our patio.

"Is that how you always want things to be-living from check to check?" My mom asked. You could practically see the concern coming through the phone.

"Well of course not, but that's just the way things are right now."

We had no savings, and we had large balances on credit cards with not so friendly interest rates. We just kept paying the minimum, and I knew that sooner or later it was going to catch up with us.

We were doing all the things that new couples do. We ate out a lot. We bought things that we didn't really need. We kept piling the debt on the credit card that was hot from being swiped through the magnetic bar readers of every store in San Jose.

"We work hard," Kristin would say. "We deserve to have fun too."

We started shelling out a lot of money for our wedding. I don't even know how much we spent, but it was well into the thousands of dollars, and we had a relatively inexpensive wedding. Most of the money, as usual, was on the plastic. We planned a honeymoon to Disneyland. Kristin loves Disney stuff, and it was one of the more affordable options. We paid by credit card for that too.

The day we were supposed to pick up the tickets for our flight to Disneyland, I picked up Kristin from work like I always did. She slid into the passenger seat. Her eyes stared forward, and although she seemed glad to see me as always, she was silent. Normally, I would have been hearing all about her day and about who was a freak at the office and who was a jerk, but today it was nothing. Something was wrong.

"We're supposed to go pick up the honeymoon tickets today. I figured we could get them before we go home." I said as we pulled onto the freeway. I looked over at her. She still stared blankly forward, holding her purse in her lap. "Honey?"

"Oh…I'm sorry, sweetie, what'd you say?"

I repeated it.

"Yeah, if you want to that's fine."

If I want to!? This was Disneyland we're talking about! This woman has since tattooed Mickey Mouse on her ankle, and all she has to say about getting the tickets is 'fine if I want to?' "What's the matter?"

"Nothing," she said without convincing me even a little, "I'm just sort of tired. That's all."

We drove the crowded route down Highway 87 in silence. The afternoon commute in San Jose gets worse each year, and it was unbearable that afternoon in mysterious silence. What had I done?

By the time we got to the Santa Teresa exit, I had convinced myself that I must've done something, or that she had another boyfriend. We pulled into a parking spot in front of the Travel Agency. Kristin's pager sang to life. I watched her pull it from her purse strap and press the button to see who it was. It was him probably, whoever this new guy was she was seeing.

"Who is it?" I asked, trying to remain composed.

"It's the work number. It's probably Samantha; I told her to page me if she heard anything." She put the pager back on the purse strap.

"What do you mean 'heard anything?'" This did not sound good, but at least she didn't have another boyfriend.

She looked over at me, her face framed by the sunlight coming through the window behind her. "The rumor around the floor is that there are going to be a lot of lay-offs tomorrow, and I have a feeling I'm going to be one of them. Samantha works in the front office, and she said if she heard anything that seemed certain, she would page me."

My body became so heavy in the driver's seat that I'm surprised I didn't bend the car's frame to the ground. I felt like my cheeks were being pulled down off my face. "Well you know," I finally said, "these are just rumors, and they may be completely wrong." I knew all about rumors from working in the schools.

Kristin shook her head. "I'll go call Samantha on that pay phone over there." She motioned behind me with her eyes. "You go in and get the tickets."

So while I was picking up expensive airline tickets, Kristin went to the phone and found out that the rumors about the lay offs had been confirmed. No one except upper management knew exactly who was going to go, but Kristin had only been with this company for five months. The proverbial ax had missed her on two previous swipes, and it didn't seem good this time. Luck could only last so long. It was 1996, and the manufacturing industry was down.

I didn't like the reality of the situation, so I tried denial on for size. "Still," I said in response to the update Samantha had provided, "we don't know anything for sure yet. It could be that nothing happens." We put the honeymoon tickets in the glove compartment, and I was angry that we couldn't even be excited about the trip now. Instead, I found myself thinking we should cancel and try to get as much of the money back as possible, but the thought of that depressed me even more. I was a professional, and my job didn't pay enough to afford a simple trip to Los Angeles without a second income.

The next morning as I dropped her off at work, Kristin handed me the pager from her purse strap. "Keep this with you today. I'll page you if they lay me off before the end of my shift." I took the pager from her hoping that it would never go off that day.

The morning clouds were still keeping us shaded as I drove from Sunnyvale to Campbell to get a cup of coffee and read. The radio played something, but all my focus was on the pager in my left hip pocket and how I didn't want it to start vibrating.

We were all caught up on the bills, but we were just sending the minimum on the credit cards, and that was only taking care of the interest.

I knew as a teacher that I would never be rich, but I still believed that at least I should be comfortable. With my gross pay of $32,000 a year as our only income, my family of four would be in a great deal of trouble considering that 40% of that was already going to pay our rent. Buying a house was out of the question in Silicon Valley's inflated housing market. The wedding was a month away as well. We had no DJ for the reception and no food for the guests. We also were $20,000 a year poorer if this pager in my pocket went off. I turned into the parking lot of Boulangerie in the Pruneyard wondering if I should spend the dollar on a cup of coffee.

I sat down with my coffee and my book. I looked at all the words for about 10 pages but suddenly realized I had no idea what was going on in the story. The pager remained still in my pocket and Kristin had already been at work for an hour. "Maybe all this worrying is for nothing." I thought as I filled my green mug one more time.

Two more cups of coffee later, I was browsing around the Barnes & Noble opening up random pages of Jack Kerouac and Allen Ginsberg, hoping that there would be a line or two there to set my mind at ease. These two knew about poverty, and they knew about getting out of it as well. I found nothing that even pretended to help.

I had left the poetry section and was heading toward the music books when the pager went off. Still in denial, I thought that maybe she just wanted to talk to me. I found a pay phone and flinched as I dropped another 35 cents. I would be watching every penny for a while now-maybe forever.

"This is Kristin," she said when they transferred my call to her.

"Hey, honey."

"You need to come and get me now." It was a factual statement that foreshadowed so much hidden pain and difficulty I could hardly believe the anti-climactic way she reported it to me.

"Okay, I'm leaving now." I hung up the phone, found my way out of Barnes & Noble and headed to my car.

The drive back to Sunnyvale seemed instant. I pulled into Kristin's company's parking lot where I had waited for her many times before. There were about 30 people standing by the curb to my left as I drove around towards the back of the building where I normally picked her up. All of these people were unemployed now. The slowdown in the industry had affected their lives and the lives of their families, and the owner of the company had no remorse for dropping any of them to save his own. This was the corporate heartlessness that I had avoided by becoming a teacher, but I was smacked down by it anyway now.

I saw Kristin standing about halfway to the back of this line of corporate refugees. She gave a couple of people hugs and headed over to the passenger side of my car.

"Hi honey!" she chirped to me, leaning over and kissing my cheek. Her spirits were incredibly high, considering we were financially decimated.

"Hey." I was as angry as I ever had been. I wanted to smash the company's front window with a brick coated in burning gasoline. I pictured the place in flames, and it nearly satisfied my testosterone-induced fantasies. "I can't believe they did this to you when they know you have a wedding coming up in a month!" I was yelling at the wrong person, but when it's a corporate scum lay off situation, no one is to blame because it's no one's fault. They're all just doing their jobs-too bad if part of the job is crushing you. Since no one is to blame, I have no problem blaming and hating them all. Unfortunately, the only person who could hear my anger was the one person who was probably more hurt by this situation than I was. A few minutes into my tirade, I had destroyed Kristin's optimism.

"You know," she said after listening for a few minutes to my anti-corporate diatribe, "I'm the one who lost my job! I was trying to keep a positive attitude, but you make me feel like there is no hope! So much for trying to stay positive!"

The rest of the ride home was very quiet and long. The clouds painted our world gray, and the car hummed along the empty Highway 87 back toward the condo. We wasted these moments together because of money. We could've laughed or talked or enjoyed that we were alive together, but the money problems hit me hard and I was no good at being anyone's friend just then. The wedding loomed. The honeymoon tickets still sat in my glove compartment-we had no business spending that sort of money. My next check was half a month away.

Chapter XXXIII

We were married that August, and we took that honeymoon. Kristin got a job just before we left and spent only three weeks out of work. We survived our first major hardship before we were even married. Of course, the three weeks had taken their toll on the enormous credit card bills. We were late on a few other bills, but the kids never went hungry, and now that Kristin had a new job with a company called Microbar, we knew that we would eventually catch up. That's what we told each other.

Money was still tight even a month or two into Kristin's new job. There were many times when we only had $100 to last us for two weeks. That's almost gas and food, and doesn't come anywhere near covering the unexpected expenses of having kids. School had started again and they needed $5 here and there for things like craft supplies and field trips. I knew that their teachers were already spending money out of their own pockets to get classroom supplies because so was I. I resented spending my money for their classes as well. In my teaching career, I had never asked my students' parents for a single cent.

We were given a yearly budget at school of about $150 for supplies. My first year of teaching I eagerly filled out the order form to get chalk, a stapler and staples, tape, markers, paper, and other items necessary for a successful classroom. The order came back-I received two boxes of rubber bands. I didn't order rubber bands. My budget was charged for the items I ordered, and I never saw any of them. I asked about this and Craig told me, "They may have been out of what you ordered. It might come through in the next delivery." That was a month later. My supplies still had not shown up on my last day of teaching three years later.

No matter how bad things got with money, Room 5 at LeyVa Middle School was my sanctuary. It was my own environment that I could alter and control in the way I saw fit, a microcosm that I could get my creative fists around and make a difference in. I could shut my door and all my debt and worries would have to wait outside and look in through the window because they couldn't hold me back in Room 5-not in my world.

I had become more open with the kids and, therefore, closer to them. I was a more successful teacher as well. They started listening more because they wanted me to be happy with them. I had stopped eating lunch in the staff lunchroom, which always just brought me down, and started eating lunch in my room with kids like Amber, Katrina, and Shelene. The three of them were like my nieces, and they brought their friends. Soon, I ate lunch in my room with about 30 kids each day, and my fifth period benefited from my avoidance of the bitterness and sometimes downright resentment of children that flew around the staff room. The kids knew enough about my personal life to realize I was human, and more important, they knew that I knew I was human. Humans make mistakes, and my admission that I was human allowed them to make mistakes, which gave them the freedom to experiment intellectually in my room with no penalty.

I became more tolerant of kids not doing their homework. I wanted them to do it because it makes them more successful, but I was not going to yell about it anymore. For the first time I had been late on bills, and creditors were on the phone. They never yelled at me, they just wanted to know when they would get their money. Eventually, if I didn't get the money to them, they would refer me to a collection agency, but they gave me plenty of chances before resorting to this. I gave my kids plenty of chances to turn in late homework. If they missed the final deadline and were missing a lot of work, they failed the class. There were no hard feelings or yelling. I was still a good teacher-they were just bad students right now the same way that I was a bad bill payer right now. Some would argue that I wasn't preparing them for the real world with this sort of leniency, but the real world, whatever that is, gave me plenty of chances. My class was more like the real world than most.

I decided that learning was going to be fun in my room-even if I was the only one having fun. I was a lot happier at work because it was a combination of playing and teaching and discovery.

"Mr. Kohl, you shouldn't be a teacher," Katrina told me one morning before school.

"Why?"

"You're too fun for this job. You should be a game show host or a camp counselor or something." Katrina always made me laugh.

It had always been fun for me to teach and learn about Edgar Allan Poe. It had come to the point where I needed almost two complete class periods just to talk about his life.

It was easy to make literature fun. The real challenge was making grammar fun. I used mind games to do this.

I stood in front of the room one day to talk about verbs. It was my third year teaching, and I still, occasionally, would get hit with new ways of talking about something right on the spur of the moment. It was third period that day when just such a lightning bolt hit me. I was flipping a dry erase marker (from my brand new white board-gone was the ancient brown chalkboard) up in the air and catching it.

"You know," I said, "English is your most important class." Looks of shock! How dare I! "Well, let me explain. What language do you guys speak in Math class here at LeyVa? How about Social Studies?"

Katrina laughed. Shelene, who sat behind her, rolled her eyes and smiled.

"I mean, it's true, isn't it Alex?"

"I…guess," he quietly said from the back row.

"You're right!" I said throwing up my hand that held the purple marker, "Of course, I wouldn't say that to my math teacher if I were you, but you're right. And this, of all days is the most important day in the most important class because we're going to talk about…verbs!" At that point I switched on the overhead and shined the word "Verbs" in bright red directly on the white board.

There was some grumbling and exasperated "Oh my God's."

"Are you excited, Rose?"

She sat and stared at me.

"You're not excited?" I asked in a sad voice. I pretended to be tearing up around the eyes.

"Yay," she said with the sort of sarcasm that only a 13-year-old could create.

"Well you should be, because without verbs we would have nothing."

The stunned faces looked at me wondering what the heck I was talking about.

"You see, without verbs, you wouldn't be able to see me or hear me right now because both see and hear are verbs." There was some excitement about how cool it would be if they couldn't see or hear me at the moment. "However, you also would not be able to talk, because talk is a verb as well."

Some of them smiled at the crazy trip I was on, and some looked like they didn't get it.

"You could never go to school," I continued, "but you couldn't stay home either because both go and stay are verbs."

Katrina raised her hand high. I nodded to her, which, of course, I would not be able to do without verbs. "But Mr. Kohl, wouldn't we just make up different words for these things."

"Ah, great question! I'm not talking so much about the words-I'm talking about the actions. I'm talking about the concepts that the words describe. If those concepts didn't exist, we would have nothing."

Katrina nodded.

"Taking it further," I said, "we would not be able to laugh, but we wouldn't be able to cry either. We wouldn't be able to die, but we also couldn't live."

"What would we do, just sit here?" asked Rose.

"We couldn't sit" I explained. "Oh, but we couldn't stand either."

"That would suck," said someone.

"We wouldn't be able to complain either," I said.

"Could we just be?" asked Katrina.

"I'm afraid not." I shook my head. "Be is a verb too."

"So we couldn't do anything?" asked Shelene.

"We couldn't even do." I explained.

"Stop, you're hurting my head!" cried Anthony.

The class laughed as Anthony grabbed his head and writhed around in agony.

"Lucky for you there are verbs, so I can stop."

"Mr. Kohl!" Katrina said, laughing.

From there we went on with the lesson and I had them take notes. I had anesthetized my mind and crushed the reality that I had no money for another day. Without the classroom and my kids, I would have wallowed in self-pity and depression. My family all needed new clothes, and we hadn't gone out to do anything fun in many months, but each day I had 150 kids pass through my room that reminded me how to laugh and were willing to play and learn with me.

Chapter XXXIV

The phone rang one evening, and Kristin got it. I didn't really pay much attention to what she was saying, but then one remark grabbed my attention. "Well," she said, "it's your place, I mean, thanks for asking me, but you can sell it if you want to. We wouldn't be able to stop you." I knew who she was talking to, and I knew what she was talking about-our landlord was selling our place right out from under us!

Now what? We had been looking for a new place but had decided not to move because rent was too high. At $1,100, our two-bedroom condo was a deal. Now the decision to move was being made for us.

"That was Alan," Kristin said as she flopped the cordless phone on the coffee table.

"Yeah, I sort of figured that it was." I didn't know what to say. I was panicked but didn't want to fly off the handle the way I usually did in these situations. It was going to be another form of money trouble. "Well, I guess we should start looking through the paper for a new place. It's going to be hard to find one that's less money or the same money as this place-we already looked." I threw my hand in the air.

"Alan said his realtor knows some guy at a property management place that can probably find us a place pretty quickly." Kristin always seemed to have a plan ready. I was nearly ready to jump in front of a moving bus, but she had a less painful plan. "They want us out of here by the end of the month. They'll get us that guy's number, and we'll see what he can get us. Sound like a plan?"

"Sounds good." My face wrinkled in disbelief. "I can't believe he's selling us out into the street." I looked around my living room and realized for the first time that it really wasn't my living room. The only things I had were furniture and a family. I never even owned a wall in my life; I only paid for the right to use other people's walls. When will I be able to get my own place? I...

"Oh honey," Kristin said, interrupting my internal whining, "we're not going to be out in the streets. You're so dramatic."

"I know, but...my God, honey! We really don't need this right now." I had just taken a student loan of $4,000 and returned to school to get my master's degree in English. I had aspirations to go on and teach at the junior college level and eventually to complete my doctorate and teach at a university. Although we didn't need to pay that money back immediately, it was still debt. Kristin had recently gotten a raise at work, but we used that money to get her a white mini-van so that I wouldn't have to drive everyone everywhere anymore. "How are we even going to afford a deposit right now?"

"I don't know," she said. We sat on the couch shaking our heads as night darkened Alan's windows. Deposits were normally the same amount as the rent, so in order to move in someplace, we would have to come up with twice the amount of the rent. We knew the rent would be more than $1,100, so the deposit would tower over $2,200. "We'll get in touch with this guy from the property management place and see what he can do for us."

In the back of my mind, a new worry was brewing. I had a teaching credential that was going to expire in two more years. In order to keep the credential up to date, I needed to take three more classes-a computer class, a health class, and a class on mainstreaming, which dealt with having special-needs kids in a "normal" classroom. I hadn't looked into these classes because I knew they were expensive, and I was much more interested in completing my master's because I felt that it held higher esteem. But legally my credential would disintegrate in January of my fifth year of teaching unless I had completed them. Then what would I do? I would be jobless and married with kids. I woke in the middle of the night quite often and lay there with this burden. I would have to look into those classes, and I promised myself I would over and over until my mind let me sleep.

The classroom still let me escape. Eric, whom I had met at orientation on the bus my first year, was now teaching in the room next to me. We opened up the curtains between our two classrooms during lunch each day, and I taught him how to play guitar. As long as I had teaching and these social distractions to keep me going, I was making it.

Within a week after Alan's phone call, we got in touch with Mike from the property management company. The realtor and Alan had both put in a good word for us. He wanted to fax us a list of available rentals in the area and go from there.

"I don't even know if we have a fax machine at the school, much less one I can use. It might be like the secretaries' coffee pot," I said to Kristin after I hung up with Mike.

She laughed. "We have a fax machine at work."

"And they just let you use it, huh?"

"Yeah. And we have coffee that I can drink anytime I want."

"Bragger!" Poverty was easier to take with a best friend like my wife.

The next day, I called Kristin during my prep period. We had real phones now. The district put them in during the summer separating my second and third year. Because Kristin worked in Sunnyvale, about 13 miles from San Jose, the district considered the call long distance and blocked it. I had to use a calling card to call her. This adds up after a while.

"Did that dude, Mike, fax you the list?" I asked.

She had received it, but the most inexpensive place on the list was $1,400 a month. That was $300 more than we paid now, and we were barely getting by! It had three bedrooms though, which was good because each of the kids got to have their own room. Dominique, my stepdaughter, would soon be coming to the age when privacy from her little brother would be important.

"That means the deposit will be $2,800!" I was a genius with math.

"It won't cost us anything to just take a look at it," Kristin told me.

"Not until we see it and like it-plus it's not like we have the opportunity to be real choosy right now." I thought. We had 15 days to get out of the condo.

One evening after Kristin got home from work, we drove to meet Mike at what would soon be our new apartment. Mike had a black BMW and showed up a few minutes after we did. "Jim and Kristin?" He asked as he got out of his car.

We nodded.

"I'm Mike." He shook hands with us. "Well, let's take a look at the place." He led us down a paved path that had apartments to the left and a well-tended lawn to the right. At the end of the pavement, he worked the combination lock box that hung from the doorknob of the empty unit and allowed us to enter before him.

We were in a living room with a fireplace. The carpet was beige and new. The kitchen was to our right, and to the left was a hallway that led to the bedrooms.

"What do you think, honey?" Kristin asked after we had taken a look through the whole place. Mike looked at me.

My dad had installed this belief that you never say what you think about a place or a car that you might buy (or in this case, rent) in front of the person who is trying to sell it to you. "It's okay, I guess." The fireplace was gas and was activated by a light switch on the wall. It hasn't worked since we moved in, but it seemed like a really cool feature on that first day. "Can we call you about this tomorrow?" I asked Mike.

"Sure." He knew our situation and that we were in sort of a hurry to get a place. If we didn't take this apartment, we were back at square one.

"Cool," I said. "We'll call you tomorrow and let you know."

We left.

"What did you think?" Kristin asked. It was clear that she was excited about it.

"I really like it. I really do. I think it would be great for us." We headed back toward the condo.

"It sounds like you have a 'but' attached to that sentence there," said Kristin.

"I don't know. Can we afford $300 more a month? We're barely scraping by." We had $40 to last us four more days.

"We're going to have to afford it. We don't have a place to live right now. Nothing is going to be as cheap as what we've been paying."

"$1,100 is not cheap, honey."

"You know what I mean," she said, sounding a bit irritated. "You saw what was out there when we were looking-it's all in this price range unless you want to settle for a complete dump." She was right. The only way that we could get a better deal than this was to leave San Jose entirely, and since we had joint custody of the kids with their father, we weren't supposed to move out of Santa Clara County. The divorce papers explicitly stipulated that.

I knew what I had to say. "I still have $3,500 of my student loan. We can use $2,800 to move in, and when we get the deposit back from the condo, we'll be able to pay most of it back. I don't want to have to drop out of school though."

"And you won't have to. I don't want you to have to. We'll still owe ourselves $600, and that will be easy to pay because we'll just put in a little every month."

"It's $600 if we get back the entire deposit." We only got a third of our deposit back from my one-bedroom apartment, and Kristin's sister spent an entire day cleaning that place.

"Oh, we should get back the whole deposit. Alan is afraid of me." We laughed. "Besides," Kristin continued, "we'll clean it really good, and we haven't messed it up at all. That place is in great condition."

I wished I had her confidence. "That's cool." I said. What else was there to say?

We made that deposit payment and moved our things to the new place in about 30 trips with a pick-up truck. The kids each had their own rooms for the first time that they could remember. It was a nice place, and the extra $300 was hard, but it was the only choice we had. We lived from paycheck to paycheck like we always had, but now sometimes we had no money at all for a few days.

Martin called a couple weeks after we moved. "How's the new place going?" he asked.

"Oh, it's great." I told him.

"Do you guys feel like doing anything this weekend?"

"Dude. I can't afford to do anything. I can barely afford to even think about doing anything. We have no money at all until the end of the month, and most of that is going to bills and rent." I was dumping all over this guy. He asked me the wrong question and set me off more than I realized I was even going off.

"Okay, okay," he said, cutting me off as I explained just how poor we were.

"Sorry, man. You can cruise over this weekend if you want. We can barbecue or something."

Money kept getting tighter. The credit cards were getting full, and we were starting to get letters telling us that we were over our limit and that we needed to send in almost $400 before we would be allowed to use our card again. We had two cards that were very near their limit. We had the student loan. We had the car payments. We had more rent to pay than before. I had those three classes I had costing $1,000 total.

"I shouldn't have been a teacher," I said to my mom on the phone one day after school.

"You love teaching," she said.

"I know, but I'm completely broke." I watched a cockroach crawl across my classroom floor as I talked to her. "Getting my master's is only going to give me an extra $1,000 per year. Kristin is making as much money as I do, and she didn't even finish high school. I wasted my time in college. I hope my kids don't get an English degree."

"Now wait a second!" She sounded mad. "You have prepared yourself very well for this life. You have a good, strong education behind you. I don't ever want to hear that you wasted your time getting your degree. You studied what you loved, and you're doing what you love. At the beginning of your career you married into a family, and that's why you're struggling right now. You and Kristin are new in your careers, and you have two kids. Most people are more established before they have kids. Where is their father in all this? And I know that sounds like a selfish thing for me to say, but you are my child, and I'm worried about you."

"Kristin says I could make more money doing something else. I want to teach though."

My door opened. "Mr. Kohl?" It was Amber and Shelene.

"I have to go mom, I have kids here." We hung up.

Amber needed help with her math. I wasn't a math teacher, but she didn't understand when the math teacher explained things. I worked through a couple of problems with her until she knew what she was doing.

"Were you talking to your mom when we came in?" asked Shelene.

"Yeah."

"You looked upset. Is everything okay?"

I looked from Amber to Shelene. Then I looked down at the math that I helped Amber to understand. "It is now," I said.

About a month after we moved into our new apartment, we were coming home from somewhere. The four of us were in the van, and Kristin kept saying that she was really hungry. Even though it was a bad idea financially speaking, we decided to go to a local buffet-style restaurant. "I need an all-you-can-eat place," said Kristin. "I'm starving for some reason. I feel like I can never get enough to eat lately."

Dominique loves buffet restaurants because she can go from dish to dish and fill her plate with whatever she wants. The kids ran wild and came back with mountains of French fries, fried chicken and whatever else looked good to them at the time.

The four of us found a table and started eating away at our piles of food. I was hungrier than I had thought. I looked up from my plate after about four minutes. Kristin had her head in her hands, and her plate was still full of food.

"Are you okay, honey?" I asked.

"I feel sort of sick. This food is making me sick."

"But, you were so hungry." I said, shaking my head and wrinkling my eyes. "You even picked this place."

"I know. I'm sorry. It's just really disgusting all of a sudden."

The kids left the table to go get a round of ice cream. They came back with bowls overflowing with hot fudge, cookie crumbs, and all sorts of sprinkly candies. They spooned away at their creations as Kristin pushed her plate away. I put it on a nearby empty table.

"Thanks," she said. "Even the smell of this food is disgusting. Can I go wait outside? I think it will be better for me out there."

"Sure. I'll sit with the kids until they finish their ice cream. I might get some too."

"Thanks. I'm sorry, honey."

"That's okay. I'm sorry you don't feel good." She kissed my cheek and headed for the door, weaving around the tables as she went.

"What's wrong with Mom?"

"The food made her sick I think. Hurry and eat your ice cream so we can get her home."

Kristin was standing by the van when we came out of the restaurant. She looked a lot better than she had at the table. The outside air seemed to have done her some good. It suddenly occurred to me what might be happening.

"Honey," I said, "maybe we should stop on the way home and get a pregnancy test."

"I'm not pregnant," she said. It was clear she thought I was insane.

"All right, so it'll be another negative test. There's a Safeway up the road a bit. You can circle with the kids in the van, and I'll just run in and get one real fast."

"Okay," she finally agreed, "But it's going to be a waste of money."

We had bought countless pregnancy tests before. I knew where they were in the store without even having to think much about it. We had used nearly every brand that there was. I found the least-expensive one, and took it to the counter.

I waited in front of the store for Kristin to complete the lap she was driving around the parking lot. I hopped in the van and tossed the test in its brown bag on the floor in front of me.

We had gone through this ritual so many times that neither of us was very excited. The first time Kristin used one I stood and paced outside the bathroom door waiting eagerly for the results. The indicator couldn't change fast enough for us. It was negative. The second time she used one I stood by the bathroom door, but it was taking sort of long, so I went and sat on our bed. It was negative. This was test number twenty-something.

"I guess I'll go take this test," Kristin said after we had been home for about half an hour.

"Okay," I said, "Let me know how it turns out." I went into the kitchen and started washing dishes. I could hear Dominique and Lorenzo watching TV in the living room. I was almost finished when I heard Kristin.

"Jim?" she called to me. I put the towel down on the green counter from the 1970s and shook the water from my hands. I walked past the kids who were too zombified by the afternoon cartoons to even noticed that I went through the room. I turned down the short hall that leads to our bedroom, and Kristin was standing in the doorway. Her arms were up and resting on the doorframe. She wore purple and smiled at me.

"So, do you want a boy or a girl?"

Chapter XXXV

Kristin and I had wanted a baby for about a year. This was the biggest thrill of my life, but it also made me think about money again.

Since we were barely getting by, would we have enough for a brand new person? Is it fair to bring that person into the world to join our middle class poverty? I never spoke these thoughts because my happiness far outweighed my fears. However, the monster that was the ticking clock of my credential expiring was now joined by thoughts of my child going hungry because I didn't make enough money. They both met me in my room at 2 in the morning at least once a week. Sometimes I had to take them with me out to the living room to sit in the dark and pray to God they would go away. They always attacked at night because once the sun hits the land, nothing seems as scary.

I had taken a night job during the school year teaching English and spelling/vocabulary to court-reporting candidates at a business college. It was one night a week, and it gave us $35 every two weeks. Because the pay was so low, the payroll people didn't have to take out state income tax withholdings, and we got a bill for a couple of grand that April 15.

"We don't have that kind of money laying around! What am I supposed to do now?" I asked Greg, Kristin's tax accountant. It wasn't his fault, but I was frustrated enough to kill this messenger of bad news.

"You can try to arrange payments with them," he said as he handed me my paper work. I stepped out of his door into the night with the papers in my grip. Something somewhere had to give.

The summer after my third year, I took a job teaching summer school to pay the taxes. I worked from 8 am to noon each day, and then

I went home and prepared for the next day for an hour or two. It was basically a six-hour workday.

I had a creative-writing class first thing in the morning and a math problem solving class from 10 until 12. The writing class was full of soon-to-be seventh graders, and I had a great time. The afternoon had a grade span from soon-to-be second graders all the way to soon-to-be sixth graders. It was a challenge keeping the top age level challenged without completely losing and confusing the lower end. The class period was a lot of group work, and it was a nightmare nearly every day, but the job gave us the $2,000 that we needed.

My fourth year began with the expiration of the contract they had negotiated with the district office my first year. It was time to renegotiate, which means there was a fresh reason to be angry and bitter for many of the faculty. By now, my salary was up to $34, 000. My credit card bills were still astronomical, and I hardly noticed my 1 percent pay raise.

The union was in full force, and propaganda littered the walls in the staff room. I had learned to try to listen only to the facts regarding the contract dispute. The problem was figuring out which facts were true. A popular story spreading through the school was that Mr. Smith, our superintendent, had voted himself a 12 percent raise the previous year. This meant that the district had the money, and it was our chance to get some of it.

My attitude toward the union hadn't changed too much, but I was a card-carrying member now. I joined because I heard I might be able to get a scholarship towards my master's as a member. That didn't work out, but at least if I was a member no one could call me a scab, and I wouldn't have to listen to their crap. I wanted the raise though-a good one-and I was willing to fight for it. My main concern besides the raise was making sure that our new staff members didn't feel about me the way that I felt about Bert in that first year. I kept it low key, but I did whatever the union said.

After a Wednesday staff meeting in the science room, John, our most active union representative, stood in front of us to present the ETA agenda concerning the contract. Art was one of our vice principals now and could no longer attend these shouting festivals.

"Mr. Smith has rejected our request for a 10 percent raise, and he has said he wants to lessen our health benefits."

"What?!"

"You've gotta be kiddin'!" The normal people, Bert, Rich, the PE teacher, and Craig all screamed out when the spirit moved them. I understood their anger, and let them vent for me as well.

"After we made all those phone calls for him!" This voice referred to the telemarketing we did on a couple of evenings, urging voters to vote yes on a bond measure that ended up passing and bringing the district lots of money. LeyVa finally got air conditioning out of the deal, and the quality of teaching on those hot afternoons rose considerably.

I looked around the room. Everyone looked angry like the first time I went through this three years ago, but this time I felt angry too. I had a baby on the way, and it didn't seem realistic that I would be able to provide this new child with a nice life if the district didn't pay up.

The other thing I noticed as I looked around the room was that of the four people I was hired with, Steve and I were the only two that remained. Mark was not invited for a second year for making inappropriate comments to the female teachers and for hitting a kid, albeit "playfully," during a PE class. I don't know what happened to Roland, but rumor had it he had poor class control.

"Well, if my input doesn't matter to you, you don't matter to me!" Jennifer, a newer sixth-grade teacher, stormed from the room. I had been thinking of my baby and Mark and Roland, so I didn't hear what the problem was. It was typical contract time-we turned on each other and strengthened the district office.

When things quieted, John started announcing the union's suggested strategies. "We've decided to all wear black clothing on Thursdays to show our united disapproval with the district office."

"And Wednesdays," I whispered to Mike, a sixth-grade teacher, "will be crazy hat day. We'll all wear weird hats to work-that'll show 'em."

Mike and I laughed while John went on. "We're also asking for union members to place these signs in your cars." John held up a sign that said Evergreen Teachers Deserve a Fair Contract. "Just tape them to a rear window, or keep them on your dashboard so people can see them. Also, we have these buttons for you to wear everyday." The buttons were white and in red letters said, Fair Contract Now.

"Do you think they're going to care what color we wear?!" asked someone down in the front in disbelief.

"It's not that they'll care. It'll just send the message that if we can mobilize and coordinate in our clothing, we can mobilize and coordinate in more extreme tactics if we want to...or if we have to." John answered calmly.

"Screw this wearing black! We should have a sick-out!" screamed Bert.

"Yes." I thought.

"The union does not authorize or back up members that take that specific action," said John.

"Why can't we go work to rule!?" asked Raul, the math teacher. This meant arrive at school and leave school at the specific moment stipulated in the contract-a 7:30 am starting time, and a 2:45 quitting time. All after-school activities stop. Strictly interpreted, working to rule means that you don't take work home either. In the case of an English teacher, that means that your kids never get their essays back.

"That would just make your day longer, Raul," said David.

"Hey!" said Raul as he turned around and shot David a glare followed immediately by a smile.

"Work to rule is a possibility we are considering, however, we are too early in negotiation for anything that drastic," John said.

John fielded a couple of comments and questions that ranged from anger to fury in tone. He seemed stronger and more energized with each question. After all of the finger pointing and screaming that went on for an endless 15 minutes, we adjourned and headed home.

I had traded in one of my English classes that year for an Advanced Literature elective. It worked much like a college seminar. There were only 10 kids in the class. Each night they had a reading assignment and we discussed it the next day. They needed to keep a reading journal as part of the class so that I could monitor who was and who was not doing the reading each night. As a result, I was teaching eighth graders for the first time. I had Shelene in class again, and she, Amber, and Katrina were still fixtures in my room.

The day after the staff meeting was the first of about five "Black Thursdays." Before school that morning, Katrina was the first student to come in my room. "Mr. Kohl!" She shouted her usual greeting. She looked at me. "Oh my God!" she said, taking a chair across my desk. She leaned over my desk. "Did someone die?" she asked in a quiet voice brimming with concern. She looked right at my eyes.

"No." I sort of laughed. "Everything is fine. Our contract has expired, and the district doesn't want to give us a raise, so we're wearing black to show that we're not happy with them." I reached into my desk drawer and pulled out the protest button. "We're supposed to wear this too," I said. I flopped it on the desk toward Katrina. She read it.

"So, all the teachers in the school are going to be wearing black?" she asked.

"Supposedly, all the teachers in the district are going to."

"No offense, Mr. Kohl, but that's sort of lame."

"I know. But it doesn't have anything to do with you guys. Some of the teachers might complain about the contract in class, but you really don't need to be concerned about it-it's…it's sort of an ugly situation."

Katrina took it all in. You could see her analyze and process everything just by looking at her.

"Are you guys going to go on strike?"

"I don't think so." I paused and pictured walking up and down the street holding a sign and not being allowed to teach. "I...I sure hope not."

"If you guys strike, will you strike too?"

"I'll have to. But it's the last thing in the world that I want to have happen. We won't get paid the whole time we're on strike."

The door opened and Shelene came in. She took the books she didn't need for the morning and stacked them on the shelf that still hadn't been fixed. I wondered when it would finally fall off the wall entirely. Shelene and a few of the others used my room as storage so that they didn't have to carry around their heavy backpacks all day. I didn't mind, as long as they knew that I wasn't responsible for lost or stolen items.

"Hey Shelene," I said.

"Hey Mr...What's with the black shirt? You never wear black shirts!?"

Katrina helped me explain the whole thing.

"Stupid!" Shelene said, and rolled her eyes as only she could.

"I know," I said again.

"Are you going to tell your kids about it?" asked Shelene.

"No. It really has nothing to do with you guys. You have other things to worry about."

Shelene had taken a seat next to Katrina across the desk from me. "You mean you're gonna stand there in front of the class all day in black clothes and a button..."

"I'm not going to teach with the button on," I interrupted.

"Fine. But you're just going to teach in black all day..."

"Every Thursday," Added Katrina.

"Yeah," said Shelene, acknowledging Katrina's input. "You're going to teach in all black every single Thursday and not say anything about it?"

I thought about it for a second. "If someone asks, I'll tell them I guess. It's not going to take my entire class time though. I'm not gonna focus on it."

Amber came in the room and Katrina and Shelene filled her in on my attire.

When the bell rang for school to start, my students started filing in, and it wasn't very long before I got my first clothes question.

Daniella raised her hand and I nodded to her. "Mr. Kohl, is everything okay?" she asked.

"Yeah, why?"

"You're wearing all black," said David.

"Yeah, I know," I said as I hung the roll sheet from the clip by the door.

"Why?" asked Paris.

I explained the situation to them. "It has nothing to do with you guys, so if any teacher makes you feel like you should be involved in any way, please ignore them. You don't need to take a side in this issue."

"So you guys just want a raise?" asked Jayme.

"Yeah, there are more complicated issues. I don't understand all of them to be honest with you, but the raise is a primary focus." I flipped a red dry erase marker in the air and caught it.

"How much do you get?" asked Paris.

"I'm sure!" whined Daniella.

"Well, I'm just askin'?" Paris clarified while looking toward Daniella.

"I don't want to tell you what I make." I flipped the marker in the air again, but this time I missed.

"Ah! It's bad luck when Mr. Kohl misses the pen!" said Manuel. I had often said that whenever I missed.

"My math teacher tells us how much he makes," offered Samuel.

"Who's your math teacher?" I asked.

Samuel told me.

"Well, I can tell you that I make a lot less than he does because I have not been teaching for as long."

"That's why you're not as grumpy," Paris mumbled.

"Now, now, Paris," I said with one finger in the air.

"Well, it's true, man," Paris said.

"It doesn't matter," I said, shaking my head. It was time to change the subject. "Anyway, just know that this is going on, and if your teachers seem angrier than normal, it might be because of this." Being real and being honest worked best with them. "Anyway, today we're going to do some peer editing on the essay you've been working on, so if you'll get it out now…"

I had begun the lesson. The room filled with the sound of backpacks zipping and papers shuffling. It was the sound of the beginning of work. The rest of my classes went pretty much like this the rest of the day.

I had prep during third period that year. Down at the office, all the teachers I shared prep with were in black as designated by the union. I was glad to see this. James, who taught PE and computers, and I were hanging out and talking. A substitute teacher was on the computer in the staff room.

"I love the Internet," the substitute suddenly tells us. "I'm on it all the time at home."

"That's cool," I said.

"What sites do you like?" asked James. I didn't know what he was talking about. I was way behind in the computer world. I knew about places where you could buy things that all started with three "w's," but I didn't understand the appeal or the necessity that people seemed to have for the Internet. I had no e-mail, and I was silently proud of it in the way that some extremists are proud that they don't own a TV.

"I don't go to any particular sites. I just like to check my e-mail and stuff."

"I don't know about this e-mail," I said to James. "I only have acoustic mail at my house."

"You oughta set yourself up with an e-mail account. They're free at a lot of sites." James was a huge advocate of computers and exercise, neither of which really interested me at the time. He was a kick boxer with a flat-top military haircut and 17 stitches across the top of his left eye.

"The e-mail might be free. It's the cost of the computer that gets you," I said.

"You can get a really good computer system for about $1,000 these days," The substitute said.

"That's a thousand reasons why I can't get one right now," I joked, trying to make the truth a little lighter to carry. It hurt that I couldn't get a computer. Soon, the kids would need one for school.

"A thousand dollars isn't really that much. I'm sure you could afford it," the substitute pressed on.

"No, I really can't," I said bluntly.

"I'm sure you can. I'm a sub, and I'm sure you make more money that I do."

What was with this lady? I had no way of spending a grand on anything right now except bills and food, and she's telling me that I really could go out and buy a computer! I clenched my fist under the table where I sat. "You know, you don't really know my financial situation at the moment," I softly asserted. The words growled around my throat. My head was down, but my eyes were focused on hers.

"I'm just saying that if you really want a computer, you could probably afford it."

"Listen to me! You don't know who I am! You don't know what my life is like! I'll decide for myself what I can and can't afford!" I had lost it. I couldn't attack my 2 o' clock in the morning monsters, so this woman got my rage about finances. All my hate for my money problems spewed out my mouth right at her. "Are you the expert of just me, or do you know everything in the freakin' world?! Don't tell me what I can afford, I said I can't, and that's the end of the discussion! Who…"

"You're being rude to me!" she said, and turned around to pout to her e-mail.

I felt a hand on my shoulder. "We should go outside, man." It was James. I hoped he wasn't taking me outside to kickbox me. The two of us walked to the orange door that led to the main courtyard of the school. "You need to walk," he told me.

We walked the halls of the school heading back to my classroom. "You…uh…really let that sub have it, man."

"She made me mad. Who does she think she is that she knows my financial situation?" My face was losing the flush of rage.

"I know. Think about it now, man. It really wasn't that big of a deal. She talks too much-everyone knows it. It's a big joke with the whole staff. You just have to ignore her."

"I don't know, man. It's just that's a bad subject for me right now." And it had been for the last year. And it would be forever.

James talked me down, but I didn't want to apologize.

Two hours later Annalisa and the rest of fifth period came in. I was sitting at my desk, staring at the maze of papers on top of it.

"What's the matter Mr. Kohl?" Annalisa asked.

"I got mad at a sub, and now I feel bad for losing my temper."

"Hmm," she nodded. Two seconds later, she asked, "Why are you wearing all black?"

The drive home that afternoon found nothing good on the radio, and the essays I had to grade slid off the passenger seat onto the floor at a stoplight. I would've made it through if the guy in front of me were driving at a normal speed.

I pulled into the garage and scooped the essays into a hug and rattled my keys around until the house key was in my fingers. I set the papers on the desk in our room next to another pile of essays, less than half of which were graded already. I looked in the mirror. I looked like a

Catholic priest without a collar. The drawer where we kept the bills loomed to my right. At least priests could pass the collection plate, and bill collectors that hassled them probably went to hell.

The black clothes had to go. I found a pair of faded jeans and a Grateful Dead T-shirt. I put on my black canvas Converse high tops, then I glanced back at the twin piles of essays before heading to the living room.

Kristin came home. We were three months away from our baby girl's due date, and she showed beautifully.

"Hey, honey," I said from the couch.

"Hi sweetie!" she said as cheerful as you could want. "What's the matter?"

"You know honey," I said, "sometimes I wish I wasn't a teacher. I love the kids. They brighten my day, but we're so poor all the time. We can never do anything. We can never get anything we want, and sometimes buying food is hard. I don't want to be poor forever. This..." I stopped myself because I didn't want her to know my concerns about the new baby.

"What?" she asked, moistening her hand on my cheek.

"I don't know. It's just too hard to have a family and be a teacher."

"If you had never met me, you wouldn't feel this way. If you didn't have me and the kids, you wouldn't have these worries." She nearly whispered these words. She had said them before. She sat by me on the couch and took my hand.

"I love you and the kids, but I worked hard to be a teacher, and we should be paid like professionals. You know-just like these Silicon Valley computer guys that sit in cubicles all day." I squeezed her hand.

She tilted her head to the side, "But honey, if you don't teach, what do you want to do?" she asked. "You're so smart, and you have a degree. You could make a whole lot more money out there, but what would you do?"

"I have no idea. Maybe I could be a technical writer or something." I didn't even know what that was, but Craig said his stepson got into it and was making $50,000 by his second year. All he had going in was an English degree.

"You love teaching, and you're a good teacher. Those kids love you. They need people like you in the schools." She paused and sighed. "I support you no matter what you decide."

"I want to teach. I want to get paid what we deserve though."

"Doesn't everyone?" she asked.

The following Monday morning, David and I met out in front of the school and started our ongoing discussion about education and the meaning of life and other such topics appropriate for a couple of scholars like us. It was what my friend Dan called cigarette talk. At its core was the notion that you have to be intrinsically motivated in order to be truly successful at something.

"Did Hemingway write for the money when he was poor in Paris?" David would typically ask.

"Of course not!" I would answer.

"Exactly! He wrote because he had to and because he loved to." David opened the door to the office and allowed me to enter first. "He wrote because of what was inside him. That's why he ended up as successful as he was. He cared about the sentences and putting them together nicely." We paused in the lunchroom and continued the talk.

"They were good sentences. And the beer was cold." I joked.

"Yeah, damn good sentences." David added. "It's the same with the kids. Have you noticed the difference between someone that cares about their writing assignment and someone that is after the good grade? What questions does the grade-motivated student ask?"

"What does this have to be about? How long does this have to be?"

"Exactly! Do you know what I tell them?"

"Long enough to tell the story well?" That's what I always said.

"Yes! And it drives some of them crazy! I tell them I don't grade by the pound."

We continued the discussion and headed to the teachers' boxes to pick up the roll sheets. It was still 2 days until the next Black Thursday, so the school had a bit of a lighter feel.

Rick was putting notices in the boxes. "Good morning, Rick," David called.

"Hi guys," he said as he continued slipping the papers in our boxes one at a time. He didn't look at us.

"What is this?" David asked no one as he picked up the paper Rick was handing out. I picked up mine to.

It was a two-page letter from the district office. Loribeth Primmer, an assistant superintendent, wrote it. The letter was addressed to all of the teachers in the district that didn't have a CLAD certificate. I got a letter, as did David and about 30 other LeyVa employees. It basically said that without a CLAD certificate, we would not be qualified to teach as of January 1999. The letter's tone left us feeling as if we were not good enough or qualified enough to do our job.

David was incensed and took it out on Rick. "I won't get this thing!" he yelled. Teachers were against the CLAD because it came from legislators, and it was just another way to get us to pay money for a class to keep our credential. You had to keep taking classes to keep your job as a teacher. You had to have taken the latest addition to the credential that Sacramento or Washington deemed necessary, even if it completely contradicted the addition that they legislated for you three years earlier. "I teach English! My kids speak English!"

"David, I'm just passing out the papers from the district office..." Rick tried to explain.

"Fire me! Just fire me! I won't do this." David and I walked away.

Rick would be hearing more and more about this as the day went on. David was sort of easy on him compared to many of us. I left him alone. I couldn't afford more classes; I couldn't afford the ones I needed just to

clear my credential. I headed to class with the letter in my hand con-
templating what Shelene, Katrina, and Amber would say if I told them,
that according to the district, I was not qualified to teach them. What
would Elizabeth have said? How could I not be qualified to do what I
had been doing for the past three years? David had been teaching
"unqualified" for the last 20.

"What's wrong Mr. Kohl?" someone from first period asked.

"Nothing," I told them. "I'm fine."

CHAPTER XXXVI

Two mornings later brought the second Black Thursday, and I slipped into my dirge outfit and headed back to work. It was 7:45, and I had to run from my room to the office to take care of something when I walked in on an impromptu teacher's meeting in the lunchroom. The room hummed and kicked with anger, and many of the staff were waving around their "you are unqualified" letters.

"Did you get one of these letters, Jim?" asked Jennifer, the sixth-grade teacher.

"Yeah. It seemed sort of rude to me," I said.

"I'm paying to clear my credential right now," she told me. "I don't have the money to take these classes as well. I've only been teaching for two years."

I nodded. "I know."

"I e-mailed Loribeth and told her all about it, but she didn't even get back to me!"

"I'm sure a lot of people have complained to her," I said.

"Good! She deserves all the hate in the district for writing a letter like that."

Jennifer turned to someone else, and I walked through the room and listened to other bits of the conversation.

"I'm going to call a lawyer and see if this 'law' they're talking about is even on the books!" Craig said.

Carl, the math and woodshop teacher, seemed beaten. He sipped his coffee and held his letter up next to his face. "I'm going to frame this thing, and the next time someone from the district asks me to do something, I'm going to look at it and remind myself that I'm unqualified." Carl had been teaching at least 20 years. "Then I can tell them 'no.'"

"If it comes to it, I can always retire," Monica said.

"I'm only in a couple more years anyway," bragged Raul. "And I've got enough sick days to make it through those two years without working if I want to."

"They don't even treat us as professionals."

I looked around the room and saw all the disheartened and angry faces. Their voices swirled to a blur of fury and venom. "If the administration and the legislation, who never even visit our classrooms, would let us teach, we might be able to get things done," I thought. I tried to think of another job where a law would suddenly come down and force you to make an addition to your degree-where the reward for this additional education was you got to keep your job at the same pay rate.

When I tried to explain these things to people not directly involved, they would sometimes say, "Yeah, well you get summers off. You only work nine months of the year, so you should only get nine months worth of pay." I tried to think of the last time I didn't have to work at school and then at home too. I tried to remember a weekend during the school year when I wasn't at least planning lessons. I tried to think of another job that was 24-hours, 7 days a week for nine months. I tried to remember the last time I had a summer off.

I forgot why I even went to the office that morning, and I headed back to my room when the bell pulled me from my daytime nightmare.

During the classes that day, I couldn't get the letter and the staff's response to it out of my head. I still had it sitting on the corner of my desk, so I saw it in between each period. I got angrier at the letter and its author, Loribeth. Who was she? I couldn't even picture her face. I don't think she had ever been to LeyVa, and I know she had never been to my classroom, yet she was such a genius about who was and who wasn't qualified to teach! Maryanne was the other assistant superintendent, and I at least knew her. This Loribeth seemed like she wrote letters to justify her own existence in the district. Did we really need two assistant superintendents? "Maybe I should write to Sacramento and have them decide? Maybe having two assistant superintendents is a misappropriation of funds,' I thought.

Halfway through first period as we were going over the homework, Tamika shook her head down at her paper and raised her hand. "Mr. Kohl," she said as I called on her, "I just don't understand what an adverb is."

"How am I supposed to explain it to you, kid? I'm not qualified. Didn't you read Loribeth's letter?" I thought. Somewhere from years ago I could hear Lynne's voice, *"You're here for the kids."* Lynne was right, and that fact was buried under all the money problems, all the black clothes, and all the letters from administrators who probably became administrators because they couldn't handle teaching my kids. "Okay, Tamika," I said as I flipped the green dry erase marker in the air and caught it, "Do me a favor though, and as I explain it, stop me if you get confused at any point. Okay?"

She nodded with her light brown eyes focused on the board and me. I explained, defined, and gave examples until she had that spark in her eye that told me she got it. I wondered where Loribeth was when Tamika first understood adverbs.

After school that day, I decided it was time to go over and get Craig's perspective on things. I walked into the center room where Monica had turned the ancient computer artifacts into a working Macintosh lab with three printers and 24 workstations. Craig's inner door was diagonal from mine, so I walked around the large rectangular computer table and to his door.

Craig was preparing his board for the next day of school. He had eight students after school doing the homework that they had skipped that day. I knew six of them, and they all greeted me silently. I waved and smiled. I warned them last year about doing their homework for Craig.

"Hey, Craig," I said.

"James! What do you know?" Craig was copying something onto the board and didn't turn to look at me.

"Well," I said, "according to the letter from Loribeth, not a whole lot."

Craig turned around. "Did you get one of those too? For some reason I thought only the older teachers got that because CLAD didn't even exist when we went through school." He held the paper he had been copying off in one hand and his uncapped red dry erase marker in the other.

"The year I came through school for my credential, CLAD was optional. They didn't make it mandatory at National until the year after me," I explained.

Craig cocked his head and wrinkled his brow, "How long have you been here now?" he asked.

"Four years." I took a desk in the front row of his room two seats up from the closest student.

"Man, it seems longer than that." Craig put his hand out in a stopping motion, "No, no offense, I didn't mean that in a bad way."

I nodded. "I overheard you say you were going to look into whether that law about the CLAD was really on the books. What are you talking about?"

"Oh, I called Loribeth, as many of us did, and asked what she meant by this letter. She said that Sacramento has passed a law about some set percentage of each district's teachers having the CLAD credential, and her hands were tied on the issue."

I watched Craig get more intense. His body and jaw tightened as he spoke. I could picture him marching on Washington just to do it.

"Anyway, that wasn't good enough for me because I read the paper everyday, and I didn't see how a decision that big could've got past me. I started snooping around a bit. I called a friend of mine that teaches over in Cupertino and another in Los Gatos, and wouldn't you know-they had never heard of such a thing, James! Can you believe it? I mean, I know that you can. So there's this lawyer that's supposed to work for our stinking union-I mean, I don't know how you feel about the union, but in the last few years I think they've really ignored what we want," He spoke like a machine gun, and he paused to reload. "So anyway, this lawyer-I have a call into his office to confirm whether this 'law' is really on the books. If it's not, I'll have him write a letter stating such and head down to that district office to read it to Loribeth."

I laughed.

"I'm kidding. I'm sure she can read. Probably." He shook his head. "Anyway, how long are we gonna let it go on, James? How long are we going to accept everything they say we have to do in the classroom?" Craig was nearly yelling, "They walk all over us cause we let them! If we keep saying, (he switched to a baby's voice) *Okay, is there anything else you need me to do?* they're gonna pile it higher and higher. They don't even come in the rooms to see what we are dealing with in here! When are we going to all say, 'No!' I don't think anyone has the guts to. We're like beaten, abused children-we just take it-whatever they have for us because we are in the habit of letting other people dictate what we will do and won't do professionally. I'm not getting a CLAD."

I laughed to myself at the obviousness of the last statement. "I don't know, man, I'm almost thinking about getting out. My family's hurting for money. In the industry, my wife makes as much money as I do here, and she never even graduated from college. I mean she works hard, she deserves her money, but I worked really hard my whole life in school for nothing." In Silicon Valley, when you say the industry, everyone knows you mean high-tech.

"I know it James, it makes me sick. My stepson became a technical writer with just an English degree. He's making 10 grand less than I am, and they're saying within a year he'll earn that much more. My wife started as a secretary, and the only reason we can live in Los Gatos is because of her salary. People just work their way up, and here we are. What sort of job are you thinking of?"

"I was actually thinking of technical writing…at least to start with."

"That's exactly it, James," Craig pointed at me, "People get their foot in the door doing whatever!" He shook his finger as if he were lecturing me. I got out of my desk seat and sat on top of the desk instead. The kids, one at a time, turned in their late assignments and left throughout our talk. "My stepson didn't know technical writing from anything, but he got in. He knew he didn't want to teach just from listening to me all these years."

We went round and around on this. We each complained and whined. When I left and headed back to the quiet of Room 5, I felt better. At least my feeling of poverty was validated. I drove home and was short with everyone that evening.

Because all the teachers were so angry about Loribeth's letter, the district scheduled a meeting where Loribeth would have to address all of us and "clear up" any misunderstanding that the letter may have caused. It was the following Tuesday afternoon at Chaboya, our district's newest middle school. Craig would have his homework done by then I was sure.

I talked with Lou, the special education teacher, and David, who had since calmed down on the issue. Lou had been on the negotiating team in past contract disputes, and his perspective during these times was always insightful.

"The main reason they passed out that letter right now-the middle of negotiations-is they are trying to have a documented reason not to give us a good raise, and the second reason probably is to distract us from the actual issues of the contract dispute. It's all very strategic." The three of us sat at desks in David's room after school as Lou explained this. I slumped down in mine the way I had as a seventh grader.

"You mean they're trying to make us feel worthless so they can justify not paying us more?" I asked. I couldn't believe it. I was naïve enough to believe that the district wanted to support us so that we could improve the education in their district.

Lou sensed my surprise at this. "I've seen them do things like this before." Lou nodded and smirked. David stroked his white beard and listened as Lou continued. "What's interesting this time is that with the new laws about class size in the primary grades, people are talking about switching districts and moving down to second or third grade somewhere else, and it's not going to be as hard to do as it used to be." Recently, a law had been passed stipulating that grades kindergarten through third had to have no more than 20 kids in a room with a single teacher. The reduced class sizes created a huge demand for teachers since class numbers ranged from 30 to 40 before the law. Classes were broken up mid year in some cases, and a lot of classes were forced to meet in school libraries and even cafeterias until enough portable class-rooms were built and delivered. People without credentials were given full-time jobs. Many substitutes got their own classrooms, and there was a shortage on subs now. Lou was right; teachers were in demand, but the salaries didn't go up, making teachers the only people in the world exempt from the law of supply and demand.

"I'm thinking of getting out all together," I mentioned. I was testing the water really. No one left the profession.

David was uncharacteristically quiet during this discussion.

"No you're not," said Lou, shaking his head and grinning. "You're a good teacher. The kids need people like you around."

"Thanks," I said, "but the truth of it is, I don't know if I can afford to go get this CLAD thing. I have three more classes to take to clear my credential, and I am having a hard time coming up with that money. So…" I had nothing after "so." Like the future, I knew it was there, but I couldn't begin to fathom it.

"Well, go to that meeting next Tuesday, and see what they have to say," said David. "Since so many district employees need this thing, it would behoove the district to provide it to us at a reduced cost, or maybe as a workshop or something."

Lou and I nodded. It seemed like solid advice. I had given my resume to my sister. She was working for a large software company at the time, and there were some openings for technical writers. I was pretty sure I could do it if Craig's stepson could with his English degree. I turned in that resume a week earlier, and I hadn't heard anything back. If nothing happened, I could just stay in teaching, but it didn't hurt to throw a resume out now and then. I didn't tell anyone I had taken that step.

On the drive home, my mind raced to the future. I could see myself scraping to get the CLAD and the rest of my classes paid for. I could see my family and I wondering if the food would last until more money came through. I could see myself tearing my hair out every three years to fight for a raise. I could feel the bitterness growing in me. I could see why Leon, the veteran history teacher, told me that he didn't understand why young people still got into teaching in the first place, and the fact that I understood that brought tears to my eyes. Through it all, I could see myself going to Room 5, shutting the door, and very quietly working with my kids to try to help them be the best that they could be. Because despite all the garbage that is thrown at you and in your way, the kids are all that matter.

I came home and sat on the couch. I still had my teacher clothes on. Lorenzo was outside playing with a plastic sword, and Kristin was in the room changing. The TV babbled mindlessly. Dominique was in her room doing her homework. I stared through the TV at the wall behind it. The wall in my head played and replayed the movie of all the talks with Craig and Lou about the CLAD. In between those scenes were countless ETA meetings and the shouting and unhappiness that makes them what they are. I saw scenes of my current problem students, and I searched my mind for solutions for them.

"Jim...?" It was Dominique that yanked me from my internal cinema of horror.

"Yeah?" I looked to my left. Dominique stood there with an open textbook, a piece of paper and a pencil.

"I need help on this." She walked closer to me and put the book and paper down on the brown coffee table. The pencil was barely sharpened, and she used the eraser end to point to the problem in the book that she was stuck on.

Dominique was in third grade, and the problem was telling time. There were pictures of analog clocks, and the students were supposed to list the time in written form. Dominique must have been absent the day that this concept was introduced. I started her from the beginning.

"Okay, notice that each clock has one hand longer than the other." She nodded.

"Good. Okay, when you want to write the time, the number that the shorter hand is closest to comes first. What number is the shorter hand closer to in this picture?"

She looked. "5?"

"Are you sure?" I didn't know where she got that. The clock said 7:30.

She looked again. I pointed to the one I was talking about to make sure we understood each other. She nodded.

"Dominique! Look at it," I said, beginning to lose my patience.

"I am." Tears started to well in her eyes. Her voice was small and whiny.

"Dominique, what number is this?" I pointed to the 7.

"7."

"Good. Now do you notice that the hand of the clock is also pointing to that number?"

She just cried.

"I'm not going to help you if you don't at least try!" I hollered in frustration. "Go back to your room and figure it out."

She ran away crying.

Kristin saw the scene go down and looked angry as she came down the hall from the room. "You know what?" She said in a tone that told me I was going to find out "what" even if I didn't answer her. "You're more patient with those hoodlum kids at school than you are with her!"

She had informed me of this on countless occasions, and each time I took it as a testament to the quality of my work. It never occurred to me that it was also a commentary on the sort of father I was.

On Tuesday after school, we all piled in cars and headed over to Chaboya for Loribeth's meeting. I read the letter in my classroom one last time to make sure my anger was fresh when I walked through the Chaboya's gym door for the meeting. "I hate this woman, and I don't even know what she looks like," I told Lou in LeyVa's parking lot as we headed for our cars.

"She's actually a really nice lady," he said.

Chaboya's parking lot was pretty full when I got there. It was 15 minutes until the meeting was supposed to start, and the bleachers in the gym were already filling up with unqualified teachers. There was a table near the entrance of the gym that had piles of papers with information about how to sign up to get a CLAD certification added to your credential, so you could be qualified until the next legislative trend came around. I dutifully took the papers and found a seat behind Craig. Mike, the sixth-grade teacher, sat to my right. Monica was to my left, and we were all about eight rows off the gym floor.

Cliff, who had narrated the bus tour of the district that I took on new-teacher orientation day, introduced Loribeth. It was all very Hollywood to me; I didn't see why they needed to have her introduced.

"I was afraid to come to this meeting today," Loribeth said when the minimal applause had died down. She stood at a podium in the center of the gym floor behind a microphone. The podium had the Evergreen seal on it. It was as if she were trying to look like a government official. "I know how many of you feel from your e-mails and your phone calls. I understand how you would feel, and why there is so much frustration and anger in the room. Believe me, I do." She paused and scanned the crowd looking for a reaction. "I told my husband how I dreaded coming in today, so he went into the attic and found this for me in an old trunk." She pulled an old military helmet from behind the podium and put it almost all the way on her head. She wouldn't want to mess up that hair.

There was a tittering of laughter throughout the crowd. No one from LeyVa laughed. Saying we were unqualified was not funny no matter how many hats she had back there.

Loribeth went on to explain how it was a law, and she had nothing to do with it. She told us how unfortunate it all was. "Many of you have complained about the tone of my letter, but I assure you that letter went through several drafts before it got to you, didn't it?" She turned to Mr. Smith who was sitting slightly behind the podium to the right next to Maryanne and Cliff. He nodded, and straightened the sleeves of his suit jacket. "The truth of the matter is…There was just no way to sugar coat the message that the letter brought you."

"I'm doing my best to leave this district," Mike whispered to me. "I made some calls, and no other district got a letter like this one. There's something weird here." I thought about what Lou said about the letter coming because of negotiations.

"I'm thinking of leaving the profession all together," I whispered back.

"What are you going to go do?" Monica asked.

"I'm looking into technical writing."

"How much money can you make doing that? They don't make that much money," Monica said.

"They have to make more than I make right now."

Loribeth continued to blather on about how we could sign up for classes and how the district could provide a discount so that we could get our CLAD for a little less than we could in a college. Her tone was so jovial now-hardly the attack that her letter was.

It was question time. Craig's hand went up. "You keep saying this is a law and that it's out of your control." Craig stood and held a piece of paper. "I have here a letter from a lawyer in Sacramento stating that there is no such law on the books." This got everyone's attention.

"Yes it is," Loribeth answered.

"I've called around to other districts, and they have not heard of this 'statewide law,'" Craig continued.

"It's possible that they have just not heard of it yet, Craig." Cliff interjected. Cliff prided himself on knowing everyone's name. Loribeth looked at Cliff when he spoke, and her eyes darted back to Craig. She looked like she was watching tennis, and it was clear that control of the meeting was no longer in her court.

"Cliff, I have this letter here. I can provide you with a copy. It's written pretty clearly, and there is no such law," Craig insisted.

"Yeah, please get us a copy, but I don't think that lawyer is correct." Cliff said.

"Well, I'm not getting a CLAD or even signing up for classes until you can show me documentation proving that there is such a law. I would urge everyone in this room to do the same." Craig looked around at everyone seated silently around him. "No one's willing to stand up for themselves." He muttered as he took a seat.

There were a few more questions, but no one else challenged the truth that it was a law despite Craig's written proof.

The meeting adjourned, and most people got in line to get flyers and pamphlets on how to get the CLAD. I even got some. I was angry, though, and I couldn't leave until Loribeth knew that.

Craig was showing her the letter when I walked up to talk to her. When he was done, she greeted me with a smile.

"I'm Jim Kohl from LeyVA." I stated. "I'm not the sort of guy that e-mails or calls. I'm more of a face to face sort. I want you to know that I found your letter rude, unprofessional, and condescending. And you talked about how you couldn't sugar coat the message in the letter, but you sure sugar coated it today."

Tears started to glaze her eyes. "I'm sorry," She said.

"It's okay," I told her, and I walked away. I felt better that she knew how I felt. I could forgive her, but I would never forget.

On the way out of the meeting, I ran into Bert. I laughed to myself wondering if he was going into the parking lot to slash someone's tires. He and I were walking toward the lot. Our eyes met, and we both shook our heads and sighed in disgust. "They make it more ridiculous to keep this job every year."

"I'm thinking of getting out of it all together," I told him.

"If I was younger, so would I," he said.

Chapter XXXVII

Our baby girl was due in December, and around the second week of November, Kristin left work on maternity leave. Maternity disability would pay two-thirds of Kristin's gross salary, so it would be just like her take-home pay.

The ugliness of the contract negotiations peaked, and eventually, they gave us a pretty nice raise. I was making almost $35,000 as a result of it, which I felt was some serious money.

"Hey we got 6 percent this year! Then we get 5 percent next year and four the following." Lou told me with a huge grin. "Last time we got 6 percent total for the three years."

All that was left were some feelings of bitterness. Many teachers that felt we should have gotten more. The district administrators felt we were robbing them, like always. Interestingly, the issue of the CLAD and the teachers being unqualified vanished as soon as the contract was approved. We never heard of this "state law" again.

Kristin stayed home and rested. Christmas was coming, and we already had the presents for the kids because we weren't sure if she would be up to shopping much closer to December. We paid mostly in cash for Christmas that year, but a good portion of it still landed on the cards, which I figured we would just never pay off.

One day near the end of November, I came home and found Kristin on the couch with the TV on, but she wasn't looking at the TV. She hadn't even looked my way when I opened the front door. The wall above the fireplace mantle had her full attention.

"Hey, honey," I said as I set my black briefcase down on the floor near the coffee table.

"Hey," she said. The day's mail was neatly piled on the coffee table right in front of Kristin.

"What's going on?" I asked.

"Nothing. How was your day?" She stretched up and wanted a hug. I gave her one, but I knew that there was something else going on. I tend to worry more than Kristin, so when she worries she keeps it inside. She's afraid I'll completely lose it if she doesn't hold it together for us. I could tell this was one of those times.

"It was all right, you know. I'm just glad I don't have to wear black tomorrow, and I can get rid of this stupid button." I threw the button on the floor. "What's the matter with you?"

"Nothing." She said, but her face seemed pale and her eyes were vacant. "It's just I thought that I would have gotten a disability check by now."

I had been thinking about this too. It had been a month since my last paycheck, and Kristin normally got a check in the middle of the month. We were still six days away from my next check, and we had about $50 to last us.

"Well, I'm sure it will get here," I said, telling the biggest lie possible at that moment. "We may have to grocery shop on the credit card again."

"Yeah," she said. We both knew that grocery shopping on a credit card was proof that we had reached desperate times. Normally, Kristin would say, 'At least we have a credit card to buy the food with-things could be worse.' There was no room for that sort of optimism on this cloudy afternoon. We both stared at separate walls and wondered if there was room on the credit card for one more load of groceries.

Two weeks later, I headed home with my arms full of gifts from my students to begin my Christmas break. Like every day since the beginning of her maternity leave, Kristin waited for me on the couch. "What did you get?" she asked with a smile.

"Some stuff," I said, smiling back. I showed her my pile of loot.

"Those kids spoil you. They love you," she said. She held her arms up for a hug. They had given me my December check, but most of it was for rent at the end of the month. We had hardly any room on the credit card, but in her arms I was a millionaire. "Did you get the mail?"

"No, I'll get it." I headed out the front door and headed right to the row of gold colored, locked mailboxes. I inserted my key and thought about how nice the kids I teach were. I put out candy for them to take today, but that was all. They didn't have very much money either, but many of them got me something for Christmas. I grabbed the pile of mail. I didn't even go through it. I took it in and handed it to Kristin.

"My disability check came!" she gasped. I moved closer to her on the couch like a kid trying to see another's toy. The afternoon talk shows blabbed on, and we were saved! She ripped the envelope the length along the top. She took out the check, and her eyes dropped. Her smile ran away, and she paled.

"What's wrong?" I asked.

"It's $48." She looked up so the tears wouldn't cloud her view.

I said nothing for a minute or two. "Why do you think it's so low, honey?" I finally asked. She didn't have an answer for me. No one would have except maybe the government. How could 66 percent of nearly $1,000 equal $48? The check after my next one wouldn't be until the end of January. We had $600 to use until then, a month and a half, unless another disability check that was a little more generous showed up before that.

"I feel like this is my fault." Kristin cried. I hugged her.

"No. It's no one's fault. It'll be okay." I didn't believe that for a second. I was pretty much positive that we were destroyed. We sat there scared for a good 10 minutes. For the first time ever, the 2 a.m. monsters had come to both of us in the middle of the afternoon.

"This check is worthless!" Kristin said. She threw it down on the coffee table.

"Well…we could use it to go out to dinner." I said. This was completely irresponsible, but we hadn't been out in weeks. "You're going to be induced in less than a week. We won't be going out after that. We could put the 48 in the bank, but what is that really going to do for us?" I pointed out the positives. "At least the kids gifts are all bought." I tried.

She looked at me.

"C'mon," I said. "Where do you want to go for dinner?" I gave Kristin a tissue.

"You wouldn't be in this position right now if you didn't have me and the kids." She cried.

"That's true," I agreed, "But I would already be a grouchy old teacher with no gifts from his students." I motioned to my pile of love.

Kristin laughed.

On the 23rd of December, Kristin and I drove down to the hospital to have our baby. Brighid came at about 7:38 in the evening, I think. I know for sure I was there, and I remember being up all night in the hospital waiting for Kristin's fever to break. I remember going to McDonald's across from the hospital to buy a breakfast with money that I had bummed off my brother-in-law. I remember fatigue so intense it was like I was watching myself do these things on TV.

On the 24th of December, our van died. It cost about $300 to fix, and that left half of our money to last us a month. The bills were late. Disability didn't help. I shouldn't have been a teacher in the first place. This new baby kept me stressed around the clock. What did I know about being a dad? Was I feeding her enough? Was I feeding her too much? Was that little sound she made really a burp? Is she still breathing? Before I knew it, it was time to re-open good old Room 5. Christmas break was over.

January marked the beginning of the one-year countdown to the year 2000 when the computers would crash, the world would end, and my credential would expire if I didn't take those three classes in the next 365 days. I couldn't afford those classes, and let's face it, where else could a teacher get a job? The answer my gut always gave was "Nowhere." Who would hire someone who had been teaching in some form for the past seven years? I had no knowledge of anything else. I had no experience as far as the professional world was concerned.

I had once gone to a company that specialized in helping people change careers. He looked over my resume. "You know, you could send this to every company in Silicon Valley, and I bet you wouldn't get a single call back."

"Why?" I asked from across his desk. He looked down on me.

"Well, because you have chosen either not to list your computer experience, or you just don't have any," he told me. "It's like that Peter Frost poem, the 'Road Less Traveled By'; you chose to be a teacher and that's what you are. This is a teaching resume. We can help you, but you're going to have to commit."

The way he said commit sounded expensive. Besides, in his attempt to show me that he knew about literature, he didn't even know the title of the poem or Frost's first name. I realized he was a dolt, but I left feeling helpless. I felt that way even more with the 365-day clock ticking away. Maybe teachers really weren't anything but that-underpaid people who were stuck forever barely getting by.

Kristin's next disability check was a little healthier. It was almost $600, and it came in mid-January like a letter from a guardian angel. We could breathe, but we couldn't breathe too deeply. We could only afford the essentials. We were still paying for fun we had months ago on the credit card bills that invaded our mailbox on a daily basis. I had grown accustomed to the fact that we would always be in debt and that we would never have a savings.

Kristin went back to work, and things got a little better. On paper we had an extra $800 a month now that we had her real salary back. The baby needed to be in day care though, and that was $400 a month. Our financial life was always one step forward and at least a half step back.

"You know," I said to Kristin one evening when the kids were in bed, "they did tell me that teachers don't make a lot of money when I got into this, but I thought I would at least be comfortable. I'm not comfortable."

The TV news was babbling away.

"Oh, honey. Teaching is what you love."

"Yeah," I said, staring into the gas fireplace that sat cold and broken since the day we moved in.

The news started talking about a 27-year-old who was the CEO of some dot-com company. He was resigning to go and search the world for proof of extraterrestrial life.

"What a nut!" Kristin said.

"Yeah," I said, "but he has the money, literally, to run around the world on a wild goose chase." I shook my head. "There's a lot of money in this valley. That's the crazy thing."

"Hey, have you written to the mayor yet to ask him about that housing deal he's offering?" The new mayor of San Jose got elected partially by promising that he would attract good teachers to our city by helping them buy homes. Since I was already here, I figured I might be able to benefit from this new program as well.

"No." I hadn't written to him. There was no real excuse for this, but I told myself it was because I was too busy. It would have taken me about 15 minutes to write to him, including taking out my old portable typewriter, but I hadn't done it.

"Well..." She didn't need to say anything. I knew that no one would help me until I decided to help myself. "If he gets your letter first, he might be able to help you first."

"Yeah. Okay. I'll write it this week," I promised. I didn't do it.

During the morning commute, if you pay attention to the talk news and you're a teacher, you can be driven crazy before your drive to work is finished. The news will talk about some kid who robbed a 7-Eleven, and the commentator will say something like, "Another fine product of our public schools."

On some mornings, you can't help but take it all seriously and personally. I work hard everyday to not only teach my kids English, but also to try to provide them with a positive role model. In all honesty, my morals shouldn't matter, but somehow I was now responsible to make sure that none of my students grew up to be criminals. Thieves were considered "fine products of our public schools" and people rarely asked where the bad kids' parents were. They were usually described as hard-working people who tried to provide for their family while the public schools turned their kids into thieves. It felt thankless sometimes, especially when money was at its tightest.

I parked my car, grabbed my briefcase from the trunk, and headed across the grass to Room 5 where I taught my kids to steal from 7-Eleven. Denise, who that taught next to me, was already in her room getting her notes and papers together for today's U.S. History lesson. She tested her overhead projector as I came through her door. "Hey, Denise."

"Hey, how's it goin'?" Denise came from New York, and her accent came with her.

"Pretty good. Hey, have you heard about the new mayor's program to help teachers buy houses?" I asked, trying to keep it in my mind so that I would write that letter.

"A little. I haven't heard what sort of help it offers," Denise said. She and her husband Scott, who worked in sales in the computer industry, had just bought a house in Campbell.

"Yeah, me neither," I said as I opened the yellow curtain between our rooms and headed into mine.

"Had you heard that Governor Davis is proposing that all public school teachers take competency tests?" Denise called to me.

I stopped dead on the way to my desk. My lights were still off. I turned back. "No I hadn't heard that one yet."

"Yeah, he announced it last night." We both sat in disgust for a moment. Hadn't I already proven my competence by earning my degree, completing the credential program, interviewing, and getting hired? Hadn't the fact that I had been doing it for four years and they didn't ask me to leave prove I was competent? It was insult after insult, and we had all voted for this guy because he was a "strong supporter of education."

"Well, I'll take that test right after he takes one proving he's competent to run this state," I said, "and if he and the legislators are going to write our test, we should get to write his."

Imagine the job that you have. What questions would be on the written exam that would measure your competency at your job? More than likely, you can't think of any, and you might even be wondering how competency is measured. Yet when it comes to teachers, people don't seem to feel that these sort of suggestions are ludicrous.

I headed back to Room 5 after Denise and I vowed to vote against Governor Davis the next time around.

The bell rang, and I shut the door right on the governor, competency tests for teachers, my debts, the way the disability payment system works, the CLAD, contract negotiations, Loribeth, every legislator that ever passed a piece of educational law without even going into a classroom, and every radio commentator on earth. I was Mr. Kohl, and no one could stop me from being the best teacher I could be now that my door was closed. We were talking about poetry today. We were learning about Allan Ginsberg.

The day before, I had taught about his life and we had read the early poem about seeing Walt Whitman in the supermarket. Today, I was showing them a later poem that was not as good, in my opinion, as the earlier one. My attempt was to show that once you're a famous poet, anything you scrawl out will be published-regardless of the quality. The poem was about how he had been up all night writing letters. I had read it a million times, and I saw nothing there except a paragraph posing as a poem that described the view from the speaker's city window as the sun rose. He was Ginsberg, though, so it was published and anthologized. This is how I saw it, but Precious in fifth period saw something more.

"You, see," I said after we read the poem in class and discussed it at some length. "There doesn't seem to be anything going on here." I held the single page copy of the poem in my hand and waved it around as I spoke. "We don't find the allusions to earlier work or the sense of daydreaming and wondering that we saw yesterday in the 'Supermarket' poem."

That's when Precious raised her hand. She was an African-American girl with strong opinions that she always expressed with the greatest of respect in my room. I heard horrible stories about her behavior elsewhere in my rare appearances in the staff room, but she always had something to say in my class, and she always had an intelligent way of saying it. She wasn't afraid to vocally disagree with me or with anyone else, but she didn't disagree for the sake of disagreeing. Precious never faked her opinions, and she always had a reason to back up the way that she thought.

"Yes, Precious?" I said.

"Mr. Kohl, isn't he just sort of equating himself with the pigeons that he mentions here?" She suggested, pointing to the line where he talked about the pigeons.

I had no idea where she was going with this. I scratched my chin. "What do you mean?" I asked. My face was curled with confusion.

"Well," Precious continued, "the speaker is looking out of an apartment window as the sun comes up. He had been up all night writing letters, and since he's a famous writer, that would make all the words he wrote very important."

"Okay," I prompted and nodded. I was standing a few rows away from her with my hand resting on the front desk in that row. Precious was in the third seat back in the row closest to the door, and for those few minutes, it was like we were the only two at the school.

"Well, in the poem," Precious continued fearlessly, "he looks down on a lot of things, but the only thing that is on the same level is the pigeons that he can see straight out his window across the street. Pigeons are dirty birds that just eat garbage. Most people find them to be annoying and gross. I think the speaker sees himself this way too because they are the only thing in the poem that is also four floors above the street."

I put the poem down on my cluttered table near the front of the room. "You know," I said, "I've read this thing more times than I can even remember. This is my fourth time through it today." I threw my hand into the air. "I have never seen that in this poem before in my life, and I think you're right."

Precious smiled huge.

"You're a genius." I went on, "I'm completely blown away right now." I hadn't even taught them about Ginsberg's interest in Zen because I thought it would be too complicated for them, but Precious had hit on it; Ginsberg's speaker was a dirty pigeon and a famous poet simultaneously. I looked at the clock. There were 20 minutes left in class. "Look, uh...I don't know what else to say after that. Great job, Precious. Thanks for showing me that."

"Sure."

"Anyway, uh...Why don't you guys practice your social skills for the rest of the period, and tomorrow we'll start another poet."

This was what it was all about. I had given Precious the opportunity to explore her own thoughts about literature, and she had taken that opportunity and used it to come up with an interpretation that I never would have dreamed of. With any luck, this experience would turn her on to poetry and literature for life. I swelled with pride, knowing that I had done my job well. The pride lasted all through sixth period when I taught the poem using Precious's interpretation and giving her full credit for coming up with it. I was beaming with the internal rewards that make teaching the most satisfying job in the world.

But like a drug addict who always chases a high, sooner or later you come down, and when you do, the world is still there and your bills are still piled high. The governor still wants to test your competence, and the radio still blames you for the youth gone wrong. Job satisfaction doesn't pay the bills. Could the high I got from teaching keep me alive, or would I end up in the gutter like any other junkie?

CHAPTER XXXVIII

"Man!" I said to Kristin one evening while we tried to unwind in front of the TV. "Everything is something or other dot-com these days."

She nodded.

"I feel so out of the loop." My parents had the Internet at their house, and I had used it twice to look up information on authors that we were studying in class. The kids in my class would occasionally say that they were going to meet online and chat, but I had no idea what they were talking about.

"We have that stuff at work," Kristin said, "but who has time to use it?"

"I think we might have it too." I was pretty sure we had it on the computer in the staff room. I thought about the sub I yelled at that day. I think she was using it. "I don't see how it could even be any fun. We have people on staff that spend their entire prep period messing around with it." It was rumored that a couple of us actually spent the entire teaching day on it, but every job has these people.

The commercials ended, and I forgot all about these dot-com people for the time being, but I thought I might sit a little closer to James the next time he was messing with it.

At prep period the next day, I wandered down to the staff room and found James on the computer. He had had his stitches removed, and he had been training for what would be his first amateur fight. "How's it going, man?"

"Hey, what's up, Jim?" James barely looked back at me.

"Not much." I sat at the end of the long brown table in the staff room nearest the computer. I looked over his shoulder to see what he was doing with whatever dot-com he was messing with. It looked like a newspaper page with blue headlines that were underlined. James would use the mouse to move a small white arrow around the screen and then he would click on one of the blue headlines. After a few seconds, a page worth of writing would appear with the same headline that James clicked on at the top in black.

"This is just like a newspaper, dude," I announced.

"Yeah, it is," James said. He turned to me, "You haven't used the Internet too much, have you?"

"Just a couple of times," I said.

"Do you have e-mail...oh wait, you only have acoustic mail, I forgot." James laughed.

"Yeah," I began my formal speech again, "we really can't afford a computer right now..."

"I know, man, you don't have to yell about it with me." We both laughed. "Well you know, you can get e-mail even if you don't have a computer."

"Really?"

"Yeah." James pivoted the chair around to face me. He looked up as if in thought for a couple of seconds. "There's a couple of ways you can get it. Do your parents have Internet?"

I nodded.

"Are they AOL?"

I wrinkled my forehead at him.

"America Online?" He clarified.

"Oh...yeah." I remembered seeing that name when I was researching Edgar Allan Poe.

"If they have any extra user names, they can hook you up, and all you have to do then is come in here and enter your user name and password, and you'll have e-mail. That's what I do," he said.

"So like when you check your e-mail here, you're hooked up to your parents' house?" I asked.

"Not really. I'm just hooked up to their account."

All this was new to me. I watched in silence as James clicked around and pointed things out to me on occasion. I had a lot to learn. Later that day, I went by my parents' house and I hooked myself up with an e-mail account. I was **Jr_Kohl1012@aol.com.** I started writing to my sister, my dad, and to Kristin every day at prep period. I was completely hooked.

A couple weeks later, James came into the staff room and found me perched in front of the computer. "How's it going, Mr. Acoustic mail?" he asked.

"Hey, man." I said. I barely looked back at him.

"I remember, Kohl, when you would sit as far from that thing as possible. Then, after a while, you were sort of looking over my shoulder. Now look at you...no one else can even get a chance to use the thing during prep!"

"I'm sorry. Did you need it? I can get off right now." I turned to him. Who knew how long I had been on?

"No, I'm just messing with you. Take your time." James left the staff room, and I caught a glimpse of the back of the coach's windbreaker that he always wore as I turned back to the monitor.

Kristin came to me about a week later while I was sitting on our bed reading a stack of essays. "I think we should buy a computer," she said.

I put the essay down on the unmade bed and stared at her with my eyebrows raised. "That would be cool, honey, but I have no idea how we would afford such a thing." Computers were supposedly getting cheaper, but we didn't have $1,000 sitting around in the spare change coffee cup that we kept on the dresser.

"I saw an ad for Gateway computers that said we could finance it, and it would only cost us $99 a month." She sat next to me on the bed. "Besides, pretty soon the kids will need one for school."

I thought of how cool it would be and how technologically behind we were for not having one. "Will it have Internet and all that stuff?" I asked.

"Yeah," she nodded. She could tell she had sold me on the idea. "It even comes with a full year of Internet service."

"I don't know honey, we already have so many bills that we're trying to pay off."

"This is something that we need," she said. The truth was that I really wanted a computer, but the bills were really bad. I couldn't imagine that we needed anything enough to justify adding more to them.

"Well," I said with a sigh, "I guess it couldn't hurt to go down to the store and take a look."

Two days later I found myself in the Gateway Country store on Stevens Creek playing with their computers while Kristin worked the whole deal out with them at the counter. Every once in a while she would come to me and say things like, "For $400 more, we can get a color printer to go with it."

"That's cool," I would say. We were already in serious debt, and if we were going to add an extra thousand, we may as well add a million, so I wasn't going to worry about it. We walked out of there spending nearly twice what we had intended, but we had a better computer that I ever thought I would own in my lifetime. Now I just had to learn how to use it.

One of the classes that I had to take was Tech Ed 1. The class was supposed to teach you about software that you could use to enhance what you do in the classroom. Through a catalog that was always in the school office, I found that you could take the class online. I had a whole year's worth of free Internet use, so this seemed like the perfect time to sign up. The class was $300. I squeezed it onto my credit card.

The 2 a.m. monsters were not as strong as they used to be now that I had signed up for one of the classes. I came home from work and took the class at least four days a week. I had a month and a half to complete all the work, but it was easy to get through two or three day's worth of assignments in an afternoon. I learned all about Word, PowerPoint and Excel through the interactive online tutorials. I loved learning these things, and I couldn't believe that I had waited so long. Computers were not the tool of greedy corporate scum; they were fun.

"You're still messing with that thing?" Kristin asked as she came in from work. She set her blue Mickey Mouse lunch bag and the mail down on the coffee table.

"You know honey, I think I could work on a computer all day. I like messing with the software and stuff," I said, getting up to greet her.

"You could make a lot more money doing that too," she told me. "But you shouldn't change jobs for the money."

"What other reason is there?" I asked, incredulously. I followed her back to the room.

"Well, I mean, you're a great teacher, and you do a lot of good for those kids. You also love the job."

"I do love the job, and I love working with the kids," I said as I sat on the bed.

Kristin sat on the bed next to me. "You would be making enough money as a teacher if we had never met." She told me. "I just want to be sure that you're not thinking of giving up something you love just for money."

"Who said I was thinking of leaving teaching?" I said, shaking my head, but I was thinking of leaving; I thought about it more every day. Teaching was all I ever wanted to do, and now suddenly, I had discovered computers. I also liked the idea of the possibility of more money. I was a little tired of struggling from check to check and giving all our money to the credit card companies. It was time for a change, but how is such a change possible?

The monsters came again that night. They knotted my stomach and pulled me from sleep. The end of February closed in quickly, and I had only signed up for two of the three classes that I needed to clear my credential. The last one cost $450, and I didn't know where that was coming from. We owed taxes again this year, and that wasn't a problem until April, but it still was a problem. I left our bed as quietly as possible and headed for the couch where I sat in the dark.

Could I change careers? All the letters and propaganda put out by the district during negotiations pointed to No. We were lucky they gave us jobs as teachers because we weren't even truly qualified for that. They did us a favor by letting us teach. The darkness of the room relentlessly held me against the couch like an insect pinched between two fingers.

It was no use; no one would hire a teacher except another school, and then I would be in the exact same position anyway. The first signs of the morning sun crept into the living room through the slats of the blinds before I could relax enough to think about going back to sleep. Things would seem better in the morning.

CHAPTER XXXIX

The next afternoon, Katrina, Amber and Shelene came by to visit me after school. They were graduating that year, and it was only four months away. They were starting to realize how quickly time passes, and they came to talk to me about it.

"Mr. Kohl!" Katrina announced as she threw open my door. Shelene and Amber followed her in. The three of them flopped their backpacks down and surrounded my desk with chairs before I even had a chance to say hi. Shelene sat in her chair, the one on my right side. Amber was in the middle, and Katrina sat to my left.

"How's it going, guys?" I asked. I dropped my red pen on my desk and pushed aside the pile of tests I had been grading.

"Pretty good," Shelene said. The other two nodded.

They waited, and I looked at each of them alternately to see who had something to say.

"Well, we're graduating." Shelene said. She was normally the spokesperson for the three of them.

"Yeah, you guys are," I answered. These were the greatest kids I had ever taught. They did most of their work, and they were more like friends to me by the time they were in the eighth grade. Besides David and Pam, my best friends at LeyVa were these three.

Amber looked down. "I don't want to go."

"Me neither," Shelene said.

I looked at Katrina, who just smiled.

"I don't want you guys to go either." I said, "I'm going to miss you terribly. At the same time, I'm glad you are going because it means that you are moving on and you didn't flunk." I laughed at my own attempt at lightening the mood.

"This is just like the end of a chapter for me," said Katrina. "I mean, I'll come back and see you, Mr. Kohl, but I'm looking forward to see what is next."

"Good, Katrina. I think that's a good attitude," I said. I had just told these guys that I would miss them terribly, but the truth was that there wasn't a word in any language that would capture how much I would miss them. They had been my students, my nieces, my lunch friends, and I trusted them more than I did many of the staff. They trusted me too, and as a result, I had more of a chance of helping them because they would tell me exactly what their problems were.

"Well, I don't want a new chapter!" Shelene said. Tears ran down her face, and she lowered her head into her hands. Amber put her hand on Shelene's back. Katrina watched. I silently prayed to God that I would think of the right thing to say. I had made that prayer often with these guys, but this time the words got tangled in my emotions on the way to my mouth. "Mr. Kohl," Shelene went on, "what are we going to do without you?" She cried more and Amber joined her.

The real question what was I going to do without them? I was a teacher. My students defined who I was. These students in front of me now defined me the way Steven, Jessica C, Oscar, Troy, Elizabeth and Maile had before.

"When Maile left, Mr. Kohl," Amber said through her tears, "she told me to be sure that I took care of you. I can't leave, Mr. Kohl, because I haven't found anyone to take my place."

"I'll be fine, Amber. And I'll be right here in Room 5 whenever you need me. You guys have a lot of cool things to do in this world, and I'll still be here in seventh grade waiting to hear what you're up to." It struck me how sad that was. I was never going to get so close to a group of students. It wasn't going to be the same around here. My work with them was over. I had helped to shape them, and it was time to move on.

Others needed me, but I felt a bit like Puff the Magic Dragon when the boy grows up and all Puff can do is go into his cave alone.

Amber and Shelene cried on as long as they wanted. Katrina sat with dry eyes and bit her lip. "It's not that I don't care about you and that I won't miss you, Mr. Kohl."

"I know, Katrina. You're just ready to move on, and that's okay."

The three of us met like this many more times before the end of that school year.

The Internet had not lost its novelty, and each evening I would click around it looking for things of interest to me. I looked at the sites of all my favorite bands and writers. Nearly everyone and everything had a site. Nearly everything and everyone was selling something on the Web. I was a late comer, and I had a lot of surfing to do to catch up.

"Have you written to the mayor yet about the housing program?" Kristin asked.

Guilt stunned me out of my cyberspace buzz. "No," I answered.

"Well, why don't you see if the City of San Jose has a website. Maybe you can e-mail him from there."

"What a great idea!" I said.

"I thought you'd like that."

I was getting pretty good at finding what I wanted with search engines. It was just a few minutes before I was looking at a picture of our newly elected mayor with his e-mail link in blue below the picture. I clicked on the link and started writing an e-mail that I figured would change my life. If I was able to get a house with this computer, then it more than paid for itself.

It was a quick e-mail. The more concise the better, isn't that what I had told my students about writing business letters? I told the mayor who I was and where I taught. I explained quickly about how hard money was. I told him I appreciated the program he was starting to help teachers buy homes. I asked for information about that program. I included my acoustic mail address. I clicked on the send icon.

"There we go!" I said. "I just wrote to the mayor, honey."

"Good!" she said. "Now come and pay attention to me."

I waited a month and hadn't heard anything from the mayor. "What's going on with this guy?" I asked Kristin one evening.

"He's the mayor. He probably gets hundreds of e-mails a day. You have to be patient."

"Yeah," I said.

I sent the mayor another copy of the same e-mail and waited another month.

A professional mathematician wouldn't be able to count the number of times that the mayor mentioned this program when he was trying to get elected, and now that he was in office, he won't even get his hired people to answer e-mails about it. I told Kristin this.

"He's a good mayor." She told me. "You just have to wait."

"It's been two months already," I said. I threw up my hands in disgust. "I can't believe that I trusted another politician after I've watched what they do to teachers for the past four years!"

"He's not like that," Kristin reassured me.

I sent a third e-mail.

A month later, a letter from the mayor's office came in the acoustic mailbox. I opened it eagerly. There was a pamphlet there that described the mayor's program. He really did care. He really did want to help teachers.

"See, I told you he'd come through," Kristin said with a smile.

"Yeah. I shouldn't have doubted him."

"Or me," she added.

It was about that time that I got to the fine print. The blood rushed from my face. On the back of the pamphlet was a T-chart. One side of the T-chart was the number of people a family could have, and on the other side were corresponding incomes that you could not exceed if you were to apply for the housing program. According to the chart, a family of five, which we were, could not apply to the program if their combined annual income was more than $41,000. That excluded us, and probably everyone else in our position because in 1999, in Silicon Valley, if you were a family of five making $41,000 a year, you would be homeless. I didn't memorize the other income requirements, but they increased slightly as the family member number increased

I gripped the paper until my knuckles whitened. "Thanks Gonzales!" I said, "Thanks for nothing." I had a few other things to say about him and his political lies. Here it was again: Political lip service about caring for teachers and education. The useless sheet of paper was in the trash before it had been in my house for five minutes.

"I'm sorry, honey," Kristin said. "I really thought he was different."

"I can't wait to vote against him, even if he's running against Satan." I stopped believing that the government would ever do anything for education and for teachers. They want good teachers, but they don't want to have to pay for them. In this world, you get what you pay for, but they still expect teachers to work for and live on one third the salary that they could get in the business world. "Well," I said, feeling defeated, "why should we get breaks on buying houses anyway? No one else does."

"Everybody else makes a decent living." Kristin put her hand on my shoulder. We sat on the couch together.

"I don't mind not getting the help," I said, "but I hate being lied to. This program is set up so no one can qualify. He probably had people working around the clock doing the math so he could say a program was in place even though it would never have to pay out. The government does more for welfare cases that don't even want to work. Of course, those people are just products of the public schools, I guess." I rubbed my face with my hands.

"I'm sure the program helped somebody," Kristin said.

I looked at her.

"I'm not voting for him again either though, cause he didn't do anything for us. This time though, he was the better of the choices." She put her arm around me.

"At least the other one was honest." I said pressing against her. "She came right out and said she wouldn't do anything for us. At least we knew where we stood with her."

We allowed this moment to fade into memory, but the theme of it would remain constant. At election time the politicians are all for education and teachers. Once they're elected, they pump the money into anything but education. I thought of the laughter on my first day at LeyVa when Rick mentioned the California Lottery money, and I wondered how much more of this I could take.

The school year ended like it always did. The last day of school was full of tears on the faces of eighth grade girls that suddenly realized they had no idea where they were going and what their lives would be like. Shelene and Amber stayed in my room all day, and the three of us shed many a tear. Katrina came by a lot too, but she didn't cry. She was ready to go, and she thanked me for all I had done for her.

They were all heading for high school, and I was staying here. "Why can't you come teach high school?" Amber asked me.

"It's not that easy to just get a new job." I told her. "Besides, you and Shelene are going to different schools, so where should I teach?"

They looked at each other. "Do half a day at each school," Shelene suggested, and she smiled through her tears.

"We get him for lunch," Amber claimed.

"Well, I'm cutting out of school everyday to come over and eat at your school," Shelene joked.

"Now, now, Shelene. I don't even want to hear you joke like that." I said.

They laughed and cried at the same time, and I knew they would be all right. I was the one staying behind while they went off and hopefully built high paying careers for themselves. I had done the best I could to get them ready, but I couldn't help but wonder if I could've done more. Can you ever really give enough?

I said goodbye to my best group of students yet, and headed off into the summer.

CHAPTER XL

The first morning of summer burned through my bedroom window. After working around the clock for nine months, I had nothing to do. I had to drop the kids off at the free day camp we found for them, but after that, the day was mine. I was completely free for a week, and then I had to start planning summer school lessons. After I dropped off the kids, I would head to the coffee shop and read something written by a professional writer. The spelling would be correct, and I could leave the red pen at home. I couldn't wait.

We owed taxes again, so after my free week, off to work I went to help pay the government back for all it did for me. This year for summer school, I had a seventh-grade advanced literature class. I also had a fourth-grade advanced vocabulary class. To my disappointment, the kids were not necessarily ready for advanced vocabulary, and so the last two hours of my summer workday were a glorified day care center.

David sang my praises to Lori, the principal at my summer school, so she couldn't wait to meet me. David and Lori had worked together the previous summer, and the two became friends.

"How's it going, Mr. Kohl?" Lori asked me one morning at yard duty. The big red rubber balls bounced all around us as we stood on the blacktop. They were being used for dodge balls, kick balls, and four-square balls. A kid with a short spiked haircut sprinted past us, and Lori called for him to walk. "These kids don't slow down," she told me. "Anyway, how are your classes?"

"They're fine. I really like the literature class. Those are some of the brightest kids I've ever worked with. I'm not so hot on my later class. I don't think I can do little kids anymore. I used to be good at it. I student taught young kids, but I think I'm happier in middle school now." I knew I had said too much, but it was one of those times where I just couldn't stop. Lori said nothing more to me. She pressed her lips together and shook her head as she turned away, telling me to have a good day. She probably wondered what David saw in me.

That night David called and we talked back and forth about our summer school kids. He was doing Shakespeare with kids heading into high school, and a creative-writing class. About 10 minutes into the conversation, he asked me, "So how do you like Lori?"

"She's cool," I said as I pulled out a kitchen chair and sat at the table. "Oh, she says she wants to take your college class." David had his doctorate and was scheduled to teach a class to teachers at Santa Clara University this summer.

"Yeah, she called me, thanks for giving her the number."

"Sure."

"Listen," David said. "What are you doing for lunch tomorrow?"

"Nothing. You wanna meet somewhere?"

"How about the Fault Line? You know, the same place as last year. They have good food there." He paused, "Good food there."

"Cool, about 1 or so?" We both were done teaching each day at 12:30.

"Yeah, give or take," David said. "Listen, buddy," he started, "Lori says you seem a little burned out. Is everything okay?"

I couldn't believe what I had just heard. Burned out teachers were the ones that sat and complained about kids all day in the lunchroom. I had no idea where this was coming from. Who did Lori think she was, making judgments like that about me?

David and I confirmed the lunch meeting, and hung up.

An hour later it was still with me. "Burned out?" I thought, "I'm Mr. Kohl. I never get burned out on teaching. Teaching is one of my only distractions from my money problems. It keeps me sane, and it's the most important and challenging job in the world." I knew this, and I always had-as long as I could remember.

Kristin and I wound down for the evening in front of the TV as the words seared inside me. "Burned out." I always swore that I would leave the profession before I got burned out and became a hindrance to the kids. Was I burned out? Can you even tell if you're burned out?

"Honey," I began, "the principal at my summer school told David I seem burned out. Do you think I'm burned out?"

The commercial came on and was louder than the show. Kristin hit the volume button a couple times on the remote control and turned to me. "I'm sorry. What now?" she asked.

I repeated my question.

"I don't think you really want to teach summer school," she told me. "You kind of have to because of the way our money is and the taxes, and I'm sorry for that. You're a great teacher, and I think you just hate summer school."

"So, when I get back to LeyVa, things will be fine." It was really a bit more of a question than a statement.

"I'm sure they will, honey. You're too smart and professional to be a babysitter, and from what you've said, that's what the afternoon class is like. I wouldn't worry about it. Who cares what people say?"

"Yeah. You're right." I needed to get back to LeyVa where my real life's work is. That's where the next Katrina, Shelene, Amber, Joseph, and Elizabeth were waiting for Mr. Kohl to show them all about Edgar Allan Poe and writing. That's what it was all about. Summer school was just to keep the government pacified.

The show came back on, and I walked to the kitchen and stared at the fence outside the window over the sink. There was about 15 feet between the window and the fence. The brown paint was worn in places, and I had no idea what was on the other side of the fence-a mere 16 feet from my window. I turned away and went back to the couch.

Kristin came home from work on a Friday and put her lunch bag in the kitchen. She started cooking something while I entertained the kids. Soon Dominique grew bored of me and headed into her room, and Lorenzo and I were left messing around in the living room.

After dinner, I cleaned the kitchen and Kristin got all the kids ready for bed. We let them watch TV for a while, and they went to bed. It was time for us to unwind, and the night was going just as always. During a commercial break, Kristin turned to me, "I want a new job."

"Really?!" Kristin loved her company. She had been there for four years, and most of her closest friends worked there.

"Yeah. Could you hook me up to the Internet, sweetie?"

"Sure." I had no idea why.

Kristin got on a relatively new site called Monster.com, and started filling out information about herself in the little rectangles they had there on that page. She put her resume on there as well. She started looking for jobs that were listed on the website. She applied right from the website too.

"You mean," I began, as I stared at the screen in disbelief, "that all you have to do to find a job these days is that?" I looked down at my hands and pictured them covered with the newspaper ink that had smeared itself into every crevice of my palms the last time I looked for a job outside of teaching. "Then you just e-mail your resume, and you don't even have to lick a stamp or find a fax machine?"

"Yeah. Do you remember? We saw the add for these guys during the Superbowl." Kristin said.

"Barely," I said. I suddenly had a thought. "Do you think I could stick my resume on this thing-just for the heck of it?"

"Sure, honey. What sort of job do you want to try for?"

I thought of the conversations that I had had with Craig about his stepson the English major. "I want to be a technical writer." I had said that before, but I had never said it at a time that I wasn't frustrated with the district's administration or with money. I started a quest for a career change that evening as I typed my information onto the Monster.com website.

"You love teaching," Kristin reminded me. "And you're good at it. And the kids need you. Are you sure you want to try to leave it?"

"You have to grow up sometime. We are being held back and the kids… it's hard to support the family on my salary. I need to do this for us. Yeah, I love teaching, but I love you guys more." I told her.

"You wouldn't be in this situation if you had never met me and the kids."

"Well, I did, and I wouldn't trade that for anything-even if it would bring Jerry Garcia back and the Grateful Dead could last forever. I need to do this for the family. Besides, I really like working with this computer, and I know that the more I know about it, the more money there is to be made in this valley." I typed the rest of my information, and pasted my resume in the field that they provided. I applied to about 20 writing and editing jobs. It was early July, and I began my wait for a new job and life.

Each day, I checked my e-mail when I got home from teaching summer school to see if my Monster.com search agents had found any jobs for me to apply for. My heart beat faster when I saw that there were new messages in my inbox, and I would enthusiastically logon to Monster and send my resume out into cyberspace. I would occasionally get a letter or an e-mail letting me know that my resume was being "kept on file" until a position that matched my skills became available. These letters were victories to me because it at least meant that I was trying. It had only been two weeks, and I had received four of these victory letters.

"Have you tried out this Monster.com thing?" I asked my sister one day on the phone.

"No. I've heard of it though." Diane was very happy at her job, so of course she hadn't messed around with Monster yet.

"It's really a trip." I told her. "All you do is point and click, and you can apply directly for like…20 jobs in 15 minutes if you want to. It's a totally different world from when I was last looking for a job. No more newspapers and circling adds and all of that. They've made looking for a job just like playing a video game or something."

"Yeah!" Diane laughed. "Can you hold on a second?" she asked.

"Sure." I sat and listened to her company's hold music as I dreamed of getting a new job and the freedom that more money would bring. Diane clicked back on.

"So, you're leaving teaching for sure?" She asked.

"If I get a job, I'm going to go," I boldly stated.

"You don't like teaching anymore?"

"I do." I didn't want anyone to get the wrong impression. "I love it, but the thing is, we're hating it for money right now. We're always scraping, and I'm afraid that we always will be if I don't look for something that pays more."

"And you want to be a technical writer?" I could hear in her voice lots of concern and worry. I was a teacher, in her eyes, and she knew how important my students and my job were.

"Yeah. I like writing. You know, I've always been writing." I could picture her nodding on the other side of the phone line.

"Well," she said, "as long as you're sure."

I was pretty certain I was sure.

I checked the e-mail and the phone messages constantly when I wasn't working on summer school stuff. There were never any calls for me, but one day there was a call for Kristin. She had an interview with a rather large corporation! I called her immediately. This would bring us more money for sure.

"How much do you think I should ask for?" she asked with a gasp.

"I don't know. What do other buyers and planners get?" Her excitement infected me, and I couldn't believe that she got a job interview just by using the computer in our living room!

"I'll ask Steve."

Steve was a guy that Kristin worked with that became a job finding/interviewing advice guru for the both of us. He was the "Yoda" of career searching. Kristin told him I called him that once and he said, "Cool, does that mean I get to ride on Jim's back and hit him with a stick?"

Kristin dressed up that morning, and headed out the door for work. She was going to drive over for the interview during her lunch. I piled the kids into my car, gave her a kiss for luck and headed off to drop the kids and then go teach summer school. If she got this, she might be able to save us financially. This could be the break we were looking for. I could only hope, as I turned into the parking lot, that we would catch a break. Maybe I would never have to teach summer school again.

Kristin interviews well. She's really good at selling herself and letting people know that she can take charge and make things happen. This interview was no exception. About 1 that afternoon, she called me from the cell phone. "Hey!" I greeted her, "How did it go?"

"They really seemed to like me!" She said through the static of the worst cell phone in the Silicon Valley. "I liked them too. Fran, the Human Resources lady, is really nice. I just sat there and answered all his questions, and I was able to tell him what I would do in certain situations. Like he asked me..." I tuned out. I had no idea what she meant when she got into the specifics of her job, but I knew that she did it well. "...and I told him I would..." She tittered on like a 6-year-old talking about an amusement park. It was great to hear! "Oh, honey, I just really hope I get this job. I asked for $14,000 more than I'm getting now, and they didn't even flinch!" Kristin already had an offer pending through a recruiter, but the company lagged on getting the paperwork together.

"That would be great!" I said. "That's more than $1,000 a month for the year!" I was so excited I stood up and started pacing the living room.

"But I don't have it yet, but...Oh, my God, I want this job, honey!"

"I'm sure you did fine, honey. And even if you don't get this job, you'll get something. Plus, now you know the sort of money that you can make."

When we hung up, I got back on the Internet to see how my own job search was going. I had yielded nothing so far except for those letters saying that my resume was being kept on file. Those letters were starting to feel less like a victory and more like a strong recommendation that I don't call them, they'll call me. I pretty much knew that holding my breath while waiting for them to call would be fatal. The novelty of a computer driven job search had worn off, and I could almost picture the newsprint on my hand as I typed in the names of a couple more job databases, CareerBuilder.com and HotJobs.com. It had been three weeks, and I was nowhere.

Within the next week, Kristin had two offers on the table. I heard her on the phone with her recruiter. "Well, are they serious? Because you said the papers would be signed by Friday, and here it is," she looked at her watch, "almost 6 o'clock on Thursday, and they haven't prepared the paperwork."

Kristin was losing her patience. She had gone to the company twice, having been told they had an offer letter for her to sign, and twice the paperwork was not completed. I sat on the couch while she paced the living room and talked the recruiter into a corner. "Look, I got a call today from another company, and if they have the paperwork ready for me tomorrow, I'm signing, and by the way, they're offering more money. They're offering almost what I'm worth." She shot me a smile as I watched her listen to the recruiter. "That's right," she said, "I interviewed with them yesterday, and I'm going to look at the offer letter tomorrow." She pressed the Talk button, slid the phone onto the coffee table and sat by me on the couch. "They need to know they lost me because they couldn't get themselves organized."

"It's probably best that you found this out now, rather than finding out when you work there that they can't get their junk together," I said.

I had a college degree, and she had two job offers to my none. Experience is vital.

"You don't feel bad that I'll be making almost twice your salary, do you?"

Ouch! Right to the core! I thought carefully about my answer. "I don't have some macho hang up about needing to make more money than you because I'm the man, if that's what you mean. I certainly don't begrudge you the money; I think they're paying you what you deserve...or almost what you deserve, like you said. I just wish I could find a job that pays me what I think I deserve."

Kristin hugged me, "You realize, that my raises are our raises, right? I only want to work hard and do well because of you and the kids. I had no motivation for responsibility until I met you, you know?"

I just looked at her. Her words curled around me and held me safer than her arms could alone.

"I want a new job too," I said. "I want to feel like I'm contributing to making us better too."

"Something will come along for you." She assured me. "It'll work out."

I didn't believe it, but it was nice of her to say.

The 2 o'clock in the morning monsters didn't take summer off. They met me that night reminding me again that I had two more classes to clear my credential, five months to do it, and no money to pay for it.

"I'm getting a different job anyway." I told them.

They explained to me that that was impossible. They reminded me that I was a teacher, which was a career that people with no practical skills went into. The monsters explained to me that no one would hire a teacher to do anything but teach, and they replayed the scene between me and the career change counselor, which I had so carefully thrown to the dustiest corner of my memory. They reminded me that the counselor had said that my resume wasn't good enough to get any callbacks.

I lay in bed and listened to Kristin breathe beside me while the red numbers on the digital clock progressed tirelessly towards morning.

I finished off the last couple of weeks of summer school by coasting as much as I could. My fourth graders weren't listening, and I just had to stop them from hurting each other. Most of them were there because their parents made them, while most of the kids in my seventh-grade literature course were there to get a jump on middle school. None of this mattered anymore, really-summer school never really does.

The last morning I drove to that job was the best morning I ever spent going there simply because I would not have to go back again. I had found a coffee shop in an outdoor mall directly across the street from DeAnza Junior College. I was a half-hour early, so I walked in to the soft jazz and loving smell of espresso to enjoy a moment of potential. The espresso gave me the boost I needed to believe that I could solve my money problems while I sat and read *The Metro*, a local free tabloid sized events magazine with a liberal twist to it.

I occasionally glanced out the glass wall of the café and watched people rush by like fish in an aquarium. One guy at a table on the other side of the glass wall typed madly away on a laptop computer. That's what I wanted-I wanted to write on a laptop at a coffeehouse and get paid to do it, but I had to go and babysit.

I couldn't say goodbye to those little fourth graders fast enough that afternoon. When the last one left my room, I followed them and locked the door. I turned in my key at the office and said my goodbye to Lori. "It was great to meet you." Smile, smile-yeah, yeah. All I wanted was to be on the freeway heading into the future. I had the kids at LeyVa to think of, and I had resumes shooting through cyberspace to desktops all over the Silicon Valley. I had three weeks to make something happen before school would start at LeyVa again.

"What are you going to do if you get offered a job after school starts?" My mom had asked me about a week earlier.

"Well," I told her, "I hope that doesn't happen. I hope I get an offer before the first day of school. But if the offer comes after school starts, and it's more money than what I'm making…"

I shook the memory from my mind as I bulleted my car down highway 85 back toward San Jose. I had to check my e-mail and see if anything was happening. I had a pile of student work that I collected today on the seat next to me. I would be tossing it all as soon as I parked this car. I drove into my apartment complex, and grabbed the pile of papers. I thought better of it, and I stacked the papers in a box with a bunch of stuff for my regular classroom that I was storing in my garage. You never know when you might need an example of student work.

I headed into my house and I couldn't get the computer booted up fast enough. I logged onto the Internet and checked my incoming messages. There was one from MSN.com, one from Lifeminders, a couple of jokes from friends, and one from a name I didn't recognize with the words, "Your resume" in the subject line. My heart thudded in my chest as I moved the mouse cursor to the message and clicked twice.

Greetings Jim:

We (Leetech Software) have received your resume and are interested in speaking with you further about a possible match we have for you in our documentation department. I would like to arrange a time when we can have a phone interview to discuss your skills. Please let me know a good time to call you. Thank you, and I hope to hear from you soon.

Regards,

Pete

I couldn't believe it!! I had an interview! Even though it was only over the phone, it was start. I wrote back to Pete and told him a time he could call me. He wrote back within a few minutes and said he would call at that time. I forwarded the messages to Kristin, to my dad, and to my sister. They all wrote back within minutes to congratulate me.

I told you you'd get something!! Wrote my sister.

Ask for big money. My dad joked.

Kristin told me how wonderful I am, and called with some advice about interviewing. "Remember to sell yourself. Remember how great you are, and be sure you make it clear to them how great you are." Just as it came out of her mouth, I started questioning how great I was. I was a teacher. I had no experience in technology or in the business place. Who would want to hire me?

CHAPTER XLI

The phone interview with Pete was scheduled for two days after I got his first e-mail. That morning, I dropped off the kids and headed for the corner booth of the Boulangerie for coffee and some reading. I stared at the same page in my book for five minutes before I finally gave up. I sipped at my coffee and looked at the people who filtered in and out of the shop. I saw men with laptops in black leather cases grab a quick coffee and head back out the door, and I hoped that I would be among them soon.

At quarter after 9, I scooped my things into my arms and headed for the door, leaving a half-empty cup of coffee on the table. I got home and slouched onto the couch with 35 minutes until Pete called. I flipped around the TV channels. Now, to wait.

I picked up my book again, but I never read a word, so I stared at the wall, and fantasized what it would be like to walk into the district office and resign to work in the computer industry. Those district office people would have to drop the façade that teachers were lucky we even had jobs that we weren't really qualified for. If I left, maybe more teachers would be able to see that there were other opportunities, and that no one was ever really stuck anywhere. I dreamed a little ahead of myself.

I headed to the kitchen to get a glass of water. I passed the computer desk and was halfway past the refrigerator when the phone rang. The phone was in its second ring when I fumbled it and got it to my ear. "Hello?" I said, trying to control my breathing.

"Hello, Jim?"

"Yes." This was it. The next step to my rebirth as a professional.

"This is Pete from Leetech Software. How're you doing today?" The voice was friendly-he didn't sound like a corporate scum at all. What does a corporate scum sound like anyway? I could've sworn I had that all figured out at one point or another.

"I'm doing well, thank you. How're you?" I always made a point to use 'well' in these conversations because I was trying to get a job as a writer, and 'well,' though underused, was grammatically correct.

"I'm great." We made some small talk before we got down to business. "Well, this morning," Pete told me, "what I'd like to do is tell you a bit about the company and hear a little about you, and from there we can decide what to do next. Okay?"

"Great!" I said. I could tell that Pete was a good guy just by talking to him on the phone. He went on to tell me about LeeTech's history-when they were founded and all of that-as I started trying to picture working in a company like this. I tried to picture a cubicle with my stuff in it. I could hear Pete's voice, and I figured I better tune back in. "So that's a bit about the company. Why don't you run through your resume for me really quick."

I was on! "All right, well, I graduated from San Jose State in 1992 with an English degree. I started substitute teaching at that time. I liked it, so I got my teaching credential, and I got a job as a seventh-grade English teacher. I've always like writing, and I've done quite a bit of it for fun. I've even written some things for Microbar Corporation. My wife worked there, and I wrote some letters and things for them on a volunteer basis."

"Would you be willing to write for us on a volunteer basis?" Pete broke in.

I sat for a second with my heart sinking, and then I laughed. "No. Thanks though." I answered. It was an interview, and this guy is messing with me. This guy was cool.

"Well, it couldn't hurt to ask, you know." He laughed.

"Sure," I said. We paused here, and I looked around my rented apartment dreaming of home ownership. David was just working on buying his first place ever, and he was in his late 40s and single with no kids. I didn't want to have to wait that long, and he shouldn't have had to-not with his doctorate and work ethic.

"Well let me ask you the big one..." Pete said, melting my dream house out of my brain. "Why do you want to leave teaching?"

Did I want to leave teaching? I never heard it out loud in such a permanent context before. I loved teaching. I was good at teaching. I was a teacher, and you're born that way. I couldn't say money because you never say money, but I had to say something, and I didn't have a prepared response for this one. "Well," I said, "I just bought a computer recently. I took a class online dealing with all the Microsoft Office Software, and since then, I have been interested in learning more about technology. As well, I really like writing, and I want to use it more in my career." There was my answer.

We spoke for a few more minutes, and then Pete said, "Well, I know enough about you to the point where I know I'd like to bring you in and meet with you face to face-assuming you'd be interested in that."

"Absolutely."

We settled on the following Monday.

I pressed the talk button on the cordless phone and enjoyed my success alone for a second. I held the phone and pictured what it would be like to swap a classroom for a cubicle. I rushed into the corporate fantasy and laughed at the administrators in the district office and their negotiation year tactics. I had an interview that could lead to more money than those administrators would ever make. Wait! Is that all I cared about-money? I let the question fade unanswered as I glanced at a picture of my three kids on the wall above the brick fireplace. I dialed Kristin's number.

Her voice mail came on. "Hey, honey. Give me a call when you get a chance." I called my mom.

"Hello?"

"Hey mom!"

"Hi!" We paused for a second.

"Well, I had my phone interview." I announced for the first time.

"Oh yeah! How did that go?" she asked.

"He's having me come in for a real interview next Monday at 1 o'clock!"

My other line beeped, so I hung up, and clicked over to Kristin. We talked about how great it was. Then I called my sister, dad, and everyone else I knew who didn't teach at LeyVa.

"I knew something would happen for you!" my sister, Diane, said. "I'll be sending good thoughts to you next Monday at 1!"

"You're not going to teach anymore!?" my friend Martin asked.

"I'm going to keep teaching unless I get hired somewhere," I said. I realized, for the first time while talking to Martin, that this news seemed out of the blue unless you were in my family. "I love teaching, man, it's just that we're hating it for money. The only way I have a prayer of making more is to get out of teaching and…get a real job."

Martin laughed and said, "Right on, man." but I wasn't sure how funny that was. Teaching was a real job after all, but it was definitely in a different world than the one I was interviewing to enter. I was going to be a writer, and the biggest challenges I would have to face were probably deadlines and learning more about technology. I wouldn't have to deal with the inflated problems of adolescence. I would never have to adapt to a student's needs again. But I loved solving those problems, and I loved helping those kids. And those kids were real. And those kids were my job. I went out and browsed through Tower Records until I didn't feel torn anymore.

All I thought about for the next few days was the interview. I sent my sport jacket and a couple of shirts to the dry cleaners. I polished up my black Doc Martins. I even had a tie ready to go a good three days before the interview.

I took the baby over to visit my parents the weekend before, and the interview was all I could talk about.

"Where is the company?" my dad asked.

"Over there in Cupertino." I told him. "Right near DeAnza and the school I just finished teaching summer school at."

"What are they called again?" asked my mom. She held the baby who was very content nestling in Grandma's lap and drinking a bottle.

"LeeTech Software." I told her. The three of us sat in the family room of the house I grew up in.

"Are they public?" My mom was in an investment group, and was always very concerned about public companies and the like, but I had no idea what she was talking about.

"I don't know, what does that mean?"

"Can you buy their stock in the stock market?" she clarified.

"I have no idea."

"That's something that you should ask in the interview," my dad advised. "And if they're not public, do they have plans to go public and what's the timeframe on that. You could be a millionaire overnight if you're lucky."

"A millionaire…that would sure solve a lot of problems." I thought. I leaned back in the green chair and let that all sink in. "That would be cool," I said. "But for now, I'd like to get hired. I'd like a cubicle with my name on it and a computer hooked up to the Internet. I'd like some business cards with my name on them. I want an e-mail address that is jkohl at something-or-other dot com."

We all laughed.

"Those are all the things you used to hate, Jim," my mom reminded me with a smile.

"I know."

"Yeah," my dad said, "those things were all for corporate scum."

"I know." I smiled and lounged the green chair back even further. I linked my fingers behind my head. "I know."

I suited up once again on that Monday afternoon in July. The heat beat down and back up again at me as I walked the walkway to my garage.

I thought of the videotaped interview that I shot one day five years ago in Cupertino. I wondered if that tape was still around somewhere. I would like to see it now. Pete didn't mention any cameras, and he sounded like a cool guy on the phone, but the monsters made a rare appearance in the middle of the afternoon that day. "You're just a teacher," they taunted. "You're not qualified for this." I turned up my Buddy Holly CD to make the monsters fade away, but they would not.

I thought of Kristin. That morning she had assured me that I was a talented writer and a hard, dedicated worker. If this company didn't see that, it was their loss. "Someone is going to pick you up, and they're going to be glad they did. Don't sell yourself short." I rubbed my cheek where she had kissed me goodbye, and the monsters bailed out my car window somewhere between San Jose and Cupertino on Highway 85.

I turned off at my exit and turned down the car radio to help me find where I had never been. The directions I got off of Yahoo.com were plain enough, and I saw the business park street that I needed to turn off on. With a gut in chaos, I aimed my car to the building that Pete had described to me on the phone as "diagonally across from Wells Fargo." I found a parking spot right next to the building and turned off the car with 20 minutes to spare before the interview started.

On the passenger seat, I had a leather folder that Kristin had given me. I had two writing samples-things I had done for classes toward my credential-and a copy of my resume in the folder. It looked much more professional than my manila folder of interviews gone by. I approached the door of enemy territory. I was heading into the heart of corporate scum land, and this time, I wanted them to set up a cubicle for me.

I opened the tinted glass door and walked inside. There was a square courtyard there with a tree growing in the middle. Offices formed the perimeter of the square, and the courtyard opened to the sky the way they did in the homes of wealthy citizens in Ancient Rome. Pete had said that LeeTech was on the second floor. I found the stairs.

The LeeTech office doors were to the right of the stairs about halfway down the hall. I opened the door and found a small lobby area with a receptionist desk on the right hand side. The desk was strewn with papers, and the computer was on, but no one was there. Within a minute, a small Asian girl came. "Could I help you with something?" She asked, pleasantly.

"Yes. I'm Jim Kohl, and I'm here to interview." I said. I moved my hand to a dry spot on my leather folder.

"Do you know who you're supposed to interview with?" She asked.

"Um…Pete." I said.

"I'll go find him. If you'd like, you can go right into that room over there and have a seat." She suggested, pointing to what looked like a boardroom. "Can I get you something to drink?" She asked as I headed to the boardroom.

"No thanks, I'm fine."

The room was off the left-hand side of the small lobby and had large wooden double doors that were wide open. The boardroom was the den of corporate scum in Silicon Valley. It's where lies were told so money could be made. It's where millions of dollars were made at the expense of millions of people. I was a little boy in the lion's den, and I had forgotten my slingshot.

I wanted this though. I was a writer. I could write in iambic pentameter, albeit poorly, and I could certainly produce anything these guys may want to read. I took a seat in one of the cushy leather chairs in the boardroom, put my leather folder on the table and waited for Pete. I could picture him now-a full suit on this hot day in July and a pair of wingtips or some other expensive shoe from Italy. I was about to meet a corporate scum and ask him to make me a clone of him.

"James?" a voice asked. I turned and stood. There was a young looking guy with a white pullover shirt on. He had black jeans and tennis shoes on. A well-trimmed moustache centered his face, and his hair was a bit long in the back. 'Oh my God, I'm way overdressed!' I thought, but I could hear my mom's voice reminding me that you're supposed to be overdressed at an interview.

"Yes," I said.

"I'm Pete, thanks for coming down." We shook hands.

Pete took a chair directly across from me. "Well James, I want to spend our time today telling you a little more about the company, and I want to hear a little more about you. We've been doing business under the name LeeTech Software since 1987. We made a lot of middleware software to hook the legacy databases such as the HP e3000 to newer databases and operating systems."

I nodded, having no idea what he was talking about. He went on like this and I still kept nodding. He may as well have spoken to me in Greek, and there were times when I was pretty sure that he was.

"More recently," he continued, "we are going through a name change, and we're going to be called Abovehealth. You can see the flow chart for our new website on that paper flip chart right there." He pointed to his left. In black letters on the paper, it said Abovehealth.Web, and there were branches in all directions leading to boxes that were all labeled. It was drawn freehand, and it looked like a cave drawing to me. I did notice that a dry erase marker, the sort that I used in my classroom, was on the tray at the bottom of the paper flip chart. I couldn't believe they would use dry erase markers on paper. Nothing dries them out faster.

"We're working to make web-based software that will run in medical offices. Patients and doctors will be able to access the same database via the Internet." Again with the database stuff! I nodded like a bobble head in the back window of a car. How was I going to impress this guy without being able to even attempt to speak the same language?

"Do you understand what I mean?" he asked.

"A little. Some of that I saw on your website." Always look at the website of the company you're going to interview with.

"Oh!" Pete made a pained expression, "That thing is so badly written!"

"Yeah, I saw some things." I responded honestly with a laugh.

"You see, we need someone like you around here to tell us where to put the commas. We practically have to have a company meeting around here to vote on punctuation, and it still doesn't come out right. A lot of our engineers have English as their second language, so we make a lot of mistakes."

'Where do I sign?' I thought, but the conversation didn't take that turn. My confidence rose though, maybe he didn't expect me to know all that database lingo.

"In the past," Pete continued, "we would hire contract technical writers, but we don't want to do that anymore. They would come in and stay for as long as was necessary to get the job done, and then they would leave. The problem was, if something changed in the product, we wouldn't have anyone here to make an update in the documentation. We've reached a point now where we are ready to bring on a permanent writer or two to own all our documents and make sure they are as current as possible, as well as create new ones. Does this interest you?"

"Absolutely!" I said. I kept as much eye contact with Pete as was comfortable.

"Super! Well, let's take a quick tour of your resume, and then I'll answer any questions you might have."

I took him through my degree and substitute teaching. I told him about my writing and editing for the school on different grants and proposals. I told him about the career change I was attempting, and my blossoming interest in technology.

"Super." Pete had been nodding and listening the whole time. "Besides the grants and proposals, what other writing experience do you have?"

I thought for a second, "Well, as an English major, of course, you write constantly. I've written songs and poems. I published a poem once in a small East Coast magazine."

"I need to know that," Pete said, and he jotted it down on the yellow legal pad that he kept in front of him during the interview.

"I really enjoy writing, and I think it would be fun to get paid to do it." I couldn't emphasize my technical skills because they were next to nothing, but I was a writer.

"Great. Do you have any questions for me?"

"What sort of benefits do you guys offer?" I asked. I always asked this, but I hardly ever listened to the answer.

"We have a PPO or an HMO. We have dental coverage, but I can't remember the name of the provider…I think it may be Delta."

I nodded as if I had any clue what he meant. I had Kaiser, and that was all I really understood.

"Anyway," Pete went on, "we're not a public company, but we do have plans to go public within the next few months. We're also in the process of shopping for a 401K plan."

"That's cool, I nodded."

"You know, I'd like you to meet some folks around here. Why don't we take a quick walk around and see if anyone's back from lunch." This was a good sign. They don't show people that they are not interested in around–that was my feeling anyway. As we walked through the office, Pete pointed out things to me. "Here's our servers and our firewall. Here's our engineering section." He introduced me to the few people that were hanging around, but most of the cubicles were empty, and the people were gone to lunch. "Here's the kitchen. You missed it…this morning the whole thing was full of food. Different people just randomly bring things in to share, and for some reason, today nearly everyone did."

"That's cool."

"I'd like you to meet Dana, our COO. He's a good guy. He rides a Harley and stuff."

"Right on."

"He works over on the other side." Pete led me back into the lobby and out the door. We walked the outside hallway to a door that was directly across from the door we had just entered."

"This is all you guys over here too?" I asked.

"Yeah, we're growing fast, and as a matter of fact we're planning to move within a month or two to San Jose. Isn't that where you're from?"

"Yeah," I said as Pete held the door for me.

"Are you familiar with the corner of Hamilton and Bascom?"

My eyes bugged in surprise. "I live like two seconds from that intersection!"

"Cool!" Pete said, "We're going to be in one of the eBay buildings over there. That would be a great commute for you if you come aboard, huh?"

"Yeah." I said, "If the alarm ever went off in the middle of the night, I could be the first one there."

I met a few more people, but Dana was not around. Pete asked if I had anymore questions for him. "When can I expect to hear from you?" I asked.

"You can hear from me right now. I'm right here," he said.

I laughed.

"We're in the first round of interviews, and I'm not sure when a decision will be made...within a month for sure," Pete said. "Feel free to e-mail me as often as you want to check in. You can't piss me off, it's impossible."

Pete walked me out and down the stairs. "Did you like what you heard?" he asked.

"Yeah." I said, "I'm really excited about it. I'm much more excited than I let on up there." I answered.

"All right, great, well, thanks for coming in James, and it was a pleasure meeting you."

"You too. Thanks a lot."

I walked to my car amped with adrenaline. 'This seemed like a good possibility.' I thought. I got back in my car, fired up the air conditioning, and headed back home.

CHAPTER XLII

When I got back, I home changed into my shorts and T-shirt, the uniform of summer, and relived the interview in my head. The analysis quickly went overboard. I picked apart my every mistake and started listing all the things I wished I had said. Worse yet, I started listing all the things I wished I hadn't said. By the time I headed out to the living room again, I figured I had better get back on the Internet and start applying for more jobs. The phone rang.

"Hello?"

"Hey, sweetie." Kristin said. "How was your interview?"

"I think it was okay." I said.

"Did you like the look of the company?"

"Yeah. It was all right. They're going to move soon anyway. Check this out, they're moving right down the street!" I said with excitement. "If I get in there, I'll have like a 20-second commute or something."

"Wow! That would be great."

"I don't know though, honey." I figured I better tell her about my doubts. "I'm a teacher, and it's not going to be hard for them to find someone with more technical experience. Plus, I keep replaying the interview in my head and I don't like what I see. There's a lot of things I would've said differently if I had it to do over."

"Oh, honey," she said, in the reassuring tone that only love can bring, "you can't sit there and second-guess yourself. You're going to drive yourself crazy."

"I'm already there," I said. "And like my dad always said, 'That's not a drive for me, it's just a short walk.'"

"I'm sure you did fine. You have to just let it go now. Everything happens for a reason, and if you were meant to get this job, then you'll get it."

"Yeah, okay. I just hope I can make a move before school starts so I don't have to leave a bunch of kids." School started in less than a month. I knew it would be bad for them to lose a teacher in the middle of the year. I knew how strong they were, but I hated the thought of betraying them when they knew they could count on me.

"Well…I'm sure your interview went fine. Did you send that guy a thank you e-mail?"

"Not yet. I figured I'd do that as soon as we get off the phone."

We hung up.

I hooked up to the Internet and wrote Pete a quick e-mail thanking him for the interview and telling him how interested I was in the position. I sent it off and I hoped a reply would come soon. He told me nothing would happen for about a month, which would get me hired and in right before school started.

For the rest of that month, I continued to send out resumes over the Internet. Most of the time, there was no response, but occasionally I would get a call back. During that August, I first learned about recruiters-headhunters they're called. They surf the Internet like cyber-space pirates and find your resume wherever it is posted. Then they call you and ask permission to send your resume on to a company on your behalf. In my case the conversation went like this:

"I saw your resume on Monster.com. I have some technical writing positions open that I think you would be a fit for. If you send me your resume, we can talk further." I would usually come home and find messages like that on my answering machine. I had myself listed as a technical writer even though I had never done any technical writing. After I heard the message, I would send them the resume and call them.

"Hi, this is Jim Kohl. I sent you my resume."

"Oh yes, Jim Kohl. Let me find your resume." Depending on the nature of the recruiting office or the individual recruiter, I would hear a series of mouse clicks or piles of shuffling paper. "Oh yeah, here you are...Have you actually ever done any technical writing?"

"No. I wrote letters for a corporations accounts payable department, and I helped edit and write some grants and proposals at the school where I teach, but that's about as close as I've come."

"Hmmm." That's when I knew I was dead. "Well, it can't hurt to send your resume to them. I get the feeling from the hiring manager that they are looking for someone with more experience." Someone with more experience would be pretty easy to find. The real challenge would be to find someone with less experience.

"Okay, well, great. Send it in, and let me know how it goes." I would never hear from them again. I tried following up with them, but it seems that recruiters can only place people who are ready to hit the ground running.

Then again, Kristin didn't take the job a recruiter got her because they never had the papers ready for her to sign, and she found a company that got the papers together faster on her own. I started to think that recruiters might be an unnecessary step that just prolongs the end goal of new employment. To me, they are an added complication and one more person that might take a day off when you really need to get ahold of them.

In the middle of August, two weeks before I went back to school, I had another interview with a start up company-one of the dot-com places. The interview was grueling. I spoke with four people in two hours and left with a fuzzy brain. They were different. One of the women I spoke with told me that start-ups are pretty wild and that people could be running up and down the isles barefoot. The next guy started out by asking me to tell him a story.

"A story?" I asked. Here I sat in my usual suit with my leather folder full of resumes and writing samples in front of me on the table. The man sat across from me in a black turtleneck and a goatee, and he wanted to hear a story.

"Yeah, just about anything."

"You're a psych major, aren't you?" I asked.

"It was my minor."

I told him a story about these two guys I sat near in the coffee shop that morning. They sat for about an hour and congratulated each other on how they were sensitive men and how they were different from most men. Then they started talking about this one girl that was dating the older of the two men and was a few years younger than the younger of the two. From what I could gather, there was a 20-year difference.

The older guy talked about how he wanted to take the girl dancing but that he wasn't satisfied there. It was clear what his intentions were, and it was clear that this guy was different from most men simply because he didn't use the 'F' word when he spoke of these intentions. What a sensitive guy!

The goatee guy seemed to like my story, but nodded indifferently at the end and asked me how I came up with it. Then he played a word association game with me. When my psychiatric evaluation was over, a regular guy came in.

"Why do you want to leave teaching?"

I gave him the speech about a new interest in technology.

"When can you start?"

"School starts in two weeks." I told him. "If you were to hire me today, I could start tomorrow. But if I get hired any later, I would have to give the school at least two weeks notice."

This last guy gave me a tour of the company. All the cubicles were gray and the walls were directed with the company's red logo. I thought of Elizabeth.

"Check back with us in a few days," The HR representative told me. "Generally, positive responses are contacted by phone and negative ones are sent a letter."

"Well then, call me," I thought. I thanked him and headed into the street.

By the time I was back in my shorts and T-shirt, I knew I had to call David. I had listed his name as a reference, and I didn't want him to be surprised should they contact him.

David and I were intellectual partners at LeyVa. He was the only person I could talk to about Hemingway. He was in teaching for life and had expected and wanted the same for me. I held the phone in my hands for several minutes before dialing, playing out the whole conversation in my head.

I stared at the empty wallet that I had tossed on the bed and dialed the number. It rang twice; maybe I could just leave a message. He picked up on the fourth ring.

"Hey David! It's Jim."

"Hey buddy. What's going on?"

"Not much."

"How did summer school end up for you?"

"It was all right. How about you?"

"Great. I had some brilliant writers…brilliant writers. I had this one girl whose poetry rivaled Teresa's."

"Hey that's awesome, man." I lay on the bed while I talked. David quoted a couple lines of the girl's poetry to me. She was good. I spoke a little about the honors kids that I had a chance to work with.

"I'm writing a letter to Rick," David told me. "Lou and I were talking and we think there should be an honors eighth-grade English at LeyVa. I'm going to write to Rick and make that recommendation along with the recommendation that you teach it. All my honors kids read Shakespeare in seventh grade only to be thrown in the heterogeneous population for eighth. They're bored at best, and they act out at worst. They need someone like you to keep them on track."

"Thanks, man." Could he have made it any harder to say what I had to say? "Dude," I couldn't believe I started that way, "it's not easy for me to tell you this, but I've been interviewing."

Silence. "With which districts?"

"Oh," I said, "I'm not interviewing with any other districts. I wouldn't want to teach at any school except LeyVa-that's where they need me. I'm looking to get out of teaching all together."

"Would it make a difference if I could get you the eighth-grade honors English?"

"I'm afraid not, man. What it comes down to, I'm afraid, is money. We're barely getting by. Things are tough in this area with three kids and rent being the way it is. I just need to find something that pays more."

"I'm sorry to hear that…sorry to hear that," he said.

"Me too." I assured him. "Anyway, I hope it's okay…I listed your name as a reference at an interview I had this afternoon. If they contact you, could you tell them what a great guy I am? You know…you can lie if you need to."

He gave me a courtesy laugh. "I'd be happy to give you a good recommendation. But I sure wish this wasn't going on. I wish you luck in your job search at the same time. What sort of jobs are you looking into?"

"I'm looking at technical writing jobs. Today's interview was for a web content editing position," I said.

"Do you think that's going to provide an outlet for your creativity?" He didn't want to see me stifled in a cubicle.

"There's always an outlet for that. It doesn't have to be at your job. I'm sure I'll find some project or another." I paused. "Maybe I'll write a book, or I can concentrate on my music some more." David and I played in a rock band with a few other teachers at LeyVa. We named ourselves the Referrals after the slips of paper that kids got when they were thrown out of class.

"Well, best of luck to you, but I sure wish this wasn't happening," he said.

"I know. You're the hardest to tell. You're also the first person from the school that I've told. Do me a favor and please don't mention it to anyone."

"No problem, buddy," he said, "No problem."

A week later, I still had not heard from Pete or the other company. I called the hiring manager of that start up dot-com and explained to her who I was and asked her if a decision had been made.

"Oh, you need to call Phil in Human Resources."

I dialed his number and left him a voice mail. Just to be sure, I got on the Internet and e-mailed him the same message. Then I got on Monster and CareerBuilder and HotJobs and any other job website I could think of. I applied for 20 jobs or so. I stopped caring if the job description called for more experience than I had. I sent my resume everywhere for any job that had anything to do with writing or editing or words at all.

I thought of how Pete had told me that it was impossible to piss him off, so I e-mailed him as well. "Pete will probably at least get back to me one way or another," I thought. "He seemed like a good guy."

The month went on, and before I knew it, I was headed back to LeyVa to begin setting up my room. School was going to start a week later, and if I didn't get hired before that, then I would have failed.

The next day, I received a letter in the mailbox from the dot-com company. I knew what it would say; their HR guy made it clear enough, but I opened it anyway. It was in the trash as fast as the mayor's housing assistance plan was.

My e-mail inbox wasn't much better. Pete wrote me and explained that he was sorry, but that the position had been filled. My heart sank, but I typed back to him that I understood and should anything open up, please let me know.

I applied for another virtual pile of jobs that day. "At least I have a job." I thought. "And I like my job."

The monsters reminded me that my credential was expiring in four months. They also reminded me of my debt. I shook my head and stared at the computer monitor for many minutes.

Chapter XLIII

I still had some coffee in my "to go" cup when I pulled into LeyVa's parking lot that day in late August. There were four other cars. I only recognized two, so some of the new teachers had arrived. One of the sixth-grade teachers was back, which didn't surprise me because their decorating was a lot more detailed than my 20 posters. Pat, the secretary was here, and that meant I would be able to get my key.

I pulled my coffee from the cup holder and stepped out of my car into the heat. I was thankful that the rooms were air-conditioned now. Moving and banging the desks around was a lot easier when you didn't break a sweat in the first five minutes. It had been almost three months since I used the air-conditioner, and I hoped it still worked.

I sipped at my coffee through the plastic sip hole in the lid and found that my coffee, of all things on this blistering day, was no longer warm. I gagged it down and carried the cup with me into the front office.

"Hi! Welcome back!" Pat greeted, as I walked through the orange door.

"Hi!" I smiled. Pat and I had run into each other over the summer at a swim meet between the team I used to coach and the team that her daughter coached now. "How did your daughter's team end up doing?"

"Oh…They had a good time."

"Yeah, same with my old team." I smiled.

"Let me get your key for you, just a second."

"Did you keep your file cabinet key?" She asked.

"Yes." I said, patting the keys in the pocket of my shorts.

"Okay. As long as it's not lost. I need you to sign here please."

I stepped around the counter to Pat's desk and signed the check out form.

I left the office through the faculty room and threw away my coffee cup in the trash can by the door, then I headed across the cement quad to the pod of English rooms. This would be my fifth year walking these halls, and I would probably be walking them for the rest of my life.

I turned the corner and passed Room 6. My first year it had been empty. Then Julie had been there, but she had a hard time adjusting to the culture of the school. Then there was Eric who took off to Singapore to teach on the American Army base. Now Denise had the room, and she was the first one who would be on the other side of the curtain from me for more than one year in a row.

I stood in front of Room 5 for a second. It was like coming home after a vacation. The door and even the stucco wall around the door were so familiar to me that the imperfections in each were like decorations that I had chosen.

I turned the room key the full circle and entered, turned on the lights and opened the curtains. All was exactly as I had left it except it was glazed with three months worth of dust. The desks were scattered from the last time someone vacuumed. My desk sat where it belonged, but the top was completely cleared. The walls were bare. "This is the room where the learning happens." I thought. "Here is a room full of potential."

I walked around the room to get a feel for it, and more importantly, to fire up the air-conditioner. In the back corner of the room, I could see the black ink stain in the dark orange carpet where Elizabeth's pen broke open one day. I smiled. I could hear her voice in my mind's ear, "I didn' do nothin'!"

I crossed the room and was relieved to hear the air-conditioner roar to life after I turned it on. I headed back to the front of the room and saw a couple of white stains in the carpet where Erica's cake mix had exploded during a "How-To" speech on making a cake. She had dropped three eggs, and tried to open the cake mix bag without scissors, covering herself and a good portion of the front of the room with white powder. People laughed, and she burst into tears as class ended.

I kept her in the room after class until she calmed down a little. It took her about 20 minutes. I took her to the office, and had Irene, one of the vice principals, call her math teacher for permission to take her test the next day.

I shook the memory from my head and started setting up my desk, opened the drawer and returned the coffee cups that held my pens to their homes. I sat at my desk and arranged it just like it was supposed to be, and pictured Shelene, Amber and Katrina surrounding me. They didn't want to go, but they were gone. I knew they were fine. If by any chance they weren't, they knew where they could find me. "Justin would be back this year." I assured myself, and I started hanging posters.

A half-hour later, my walls were covered with the old posters and the two new ones I had picked up for this year. I went out of my room, and saw that David's car was in the lot. I went back in and dialed his extension.

"Hey, man!" I said when he answered.

"Hey you're back!" he said. "But for how long?"

"Well, for now, I'm here. I don't have any offers yet, and it seems like all the possibilities I had are on hold for now. So here I am. I'm glad to be here." This room held so many memories for me that it was really nice to be back and have it set up in a way that felt like home. "You know what?" I asked him rhetorically, "I'm teaching social studies this year. My second-period English is going to be my third-period social studies. I hope they're good kids."

"I had heard that John was doing that, but I didn't know you were."

"I guess I better learn something about Ancient Rome by next week," I joked.

"Stay a page ahead of them." David said, knowing that you needed more than that to be on top of your game in any class. "Well, this is silly to talk on the phone. Let me swing by there in a couple of seconds."

"Cool."

David came over and took a seat in a green plastic chair across from my desk. We talked about summer school, Hemingway, and the teaching philosophy we shared: treat the children as humans. For a good hour we talked of all the things we knew to be true. It was good to be back.

I spent the next week getting a feel for what I needed to cover in social studies. And then, two days before the first day of school, I received an e-mail from Pete:

Jim:

Greetings. I am writing to inform you of the strong possibility of an entry-level technical writing position here at Abovehealth. If you are still interested, I would love to have you come in and talk with a couple people about the position soon. Please let me know as soon as possible, and I will contact you soon as far as when we'd like you to come in.

Regards,

Pete

I wrote him back and told him I was thrilled. I clicked on the send button in my e-mail, and celebrated that I was in the running again. I called Kristin immediately.

"That's great news, honey! Will you leave if they hire you after the year has started?"

"I have to. You have to move when the opportunity is there."

Next, I called my mom, dad and sister.

I went out to the record store and browsed the CDs. Soon, and it seemed more real this time than the last time, I may be working for a software company. I clicked through the CDs on the rack and looked for nothing in particular. The store was cool with air-conditioning, and I just wanted top use my two last days of summer vacation doing lazy things. "These could be my last two days of summer vacation ever," I thought.

I held on to summer longer than most adults get to. Even though I had to work away most of it, a week or two of it was mine the way it was when I was 16.

Before I even knew I left the CD store I was pulling into LeyVa's parking lot with a coffee from Starbucks in my car's drink holder. We went through our day of meetings and wisdom and then headed home to sleep before the real teaching began. I made a sign for my door before I went home: Mr. Kohl; 7th Grade English and Social Studies.

I had the roll sheets on my uncluttered desk, and my seating charts with the new names on them were ready to be displayed with the overhead. My dry erase markers were new and waited dutifully in the tray by the white board. The room was stocked with grammar, literature anthologies and social studies books. My course descriptions were still warm from the copy machine and sat on the small table that Eric left me when he went to Singapore. The desks were lined up in six rows of six. I was even more ready than the room.

I looked to the desk where Elizabeth used to sit. Then I pictured Maile in her old desk. Then I looked where Shelene, Katrina, and Amber sat. I thought of Jessica C. and Steven and realized they would be starting seventh grade somewhere this year even though I had left them as toothless second graders. "I hope they're great friends." I thought.

My door opened. "What's up Mr. Kohl! Geez man! Don't you shave in the summer!" It was Justin. He was going to be my student aid this year and the link to my past.

"No I don't. But don't worry, it'll be gone by the next time you see me." I motioned to my shorts and black T-shirt. "My teacher costume will be back on as well."

"Hey, I picked this up for you in Cancun." He gave me a shot glass with Cancun written on it in colorful letters.

"Thanks, man." I said.

"Well," he said, "I gotta go. I saw your car and I just wanted to see if I could see you."

"Right on, man. I'm glad you did. I'll see you tomorrow."

I didn't sleep that night.

I pulled into the parking lot early, but there were already kids hanging around. "Hey Mr. Kohl!" some shouted. I waved and smiled in different directions. I opened up my room, and it wasn't long before a few came to see me. Justin, Justine, Michael and Annalisa (my favorite middle school couple) and Jasmine came by.

"How's it going guys?" I asked from behind my desk. "How was summer?"

"It was all right."

"Boring."

"Well you know," I said, "you're responsible for making your own fun. So if summer was boring, you have no one to blame but you." A few seventh graders that knew the eighth graders checked me out. They watched my every move and listened to my every word so they could assess my personality with unquestionable precision within 10 seconds of hearing me speak for the first time.

We chatted away about whatever. I had missed them all more than I had let myself know.

The bell rang, and we all knew that summer was over. "Have fun, guys," I called as they told me goodbye and headed for first period.

My seventh-grade kids sat shy outside my door. I shined the seating chart on the white board and helped them find their seats. When they were all seated, I began. "I'm Mr. Kohl and this is seventh-grade English. I've been teaching here at LeyVa for five years now, and before that I worked in the Santa Clara district."

I went through the same old rules and expectations, and they all sat looking scared and wondering what was to become of them. Had they always looked so scared? Maybe I finally noticed because I wasn't nervous anymore at all. Some of my last year's students walked by my window and waved, already late for class. I waved back as I showed my new students the main points in the room.

"I'm going to call your name. Please tell me if I pronounce your name incorrectly. If you don't tell me today, I will probably say your name wrong for the rest of the year, and I don't want to do that. I did that to Fabiana from a couple years back, and she never corrected me until the last week of school." A couple kids snickered. I shrugged and shook my head. "There's no reason for that."

I gave them each a grammar book and a literature anthology. "Keep these at home. You don't need to bring them back until the end of the year. By the way, does anyone have any questions?" I looked around the room. There were the blank stares and eyes avoiding mine that I knew and loathed. "So I explained everything perfectly, and I deserve a huge raise because I am such a great teacher?"

Nothing.

It was a typical response, especially for the first day. Yesterday at this time, they were all sleeping.

Before I knew it, second period came in. I went through my routine and got pretty much the same reaction. A couple of them told me how to pronounce their names. A girl named Krystle wrinkled her nose and shook her head when I asked her if she was related to Angelica, a girl I had taught the year before who had the same last name.

I was in cruise control. I spoke and thought of other things, wondered if I would hear from Pete today or not. I wondered if he would have scheduled an interview for me. I wondered if I would be here next week or the week after that. My brain stayed on Pete and my future while I heard my voice describing my homework policy.

I focused on what I was saying again. In no time they had refused to ask me any questions, I had given them their books, and they were filling out my first day of school survey.

I sat at my desk and thought about my possible career change. My dad had spoken to me a couple days earlier. "Don't you get short-timers disease at that school and start slacking off," he had warned.

"Don't worry, Dad. I have the most important job in the world. If this is my last year teaching, then I'm not going to have the end of a very fulfilling period in my life go down in flames."

"Mr. Kohl." I shook my head out of my thoughts and looked at the boy in the front row. I checked the seating chart.

"Yeah...Tim, is it?"

He nodded, and his spiky hair stood stiff with mousse.

"What if we don't know where our parents work?" He pointed to a blank line on his survey sheet with the eraser end of his pencil.

"Oh, don't worry about anything you don't know. Just fill in as much as you do know for now," I said.

Two minutes before the bell rang, I stood in front of the quiet group. "You are some of the most unlucky kids in the school. You will soon see that I am the meanest teacher that LeyVa has, and unfortunately for you, you have to come back and have me again next period. You will keep the same seats next period as well. We have a 10-minute break that begins at the bell. At the end of the break, we will come back here and have social studies. Does anyone have any questions?"

Of course not.

"Okay, I will see you after the break."

The bell whined through the air again, and off they went. Justin, Michael and Annalisa, and Jasmine dropped in to complain about their first two periods.

"You guys will do fine," I said. "And if you need any help with anything, just let me know."

"Do you miss us?" Annalisa asked with a big smile.

"Of course I do. It always feels weird on the first few days because I see all the kids from last year go by my door and I think, 'I know those guys. I want to be with those guys.' These new kids seem nice, but you know, everyone seems nice on the first day of school."

"Not my English teacher!" Justin chimed in. "Dang! She already yelled at us!"

"See, she's got you figured out already."

Justin let that sink in for a second. "Shut up!"

We all laughed.

The bell rang, and it was time to go back to being formal. They all took their same seats, and I stared at them in a business-like manner. "Before I describe the social studies class, does anyone have any questions about the English class?"

They all stared-some at me, some at the wall, some at the top of their desk.

"Does anyone have any questions about anything at all?" I sometimes throw this out, but I knew what a can of worms it could be. I looked at each pair of eyes, and finally, Tim raised his hand.

"Do you have a girlfriend?"

"No, my wife doesn't let me date." I held up my left hand to show the ring.

A girl in the back row put up her hand.

"Tell me your name, please."

"Melissa."

"Melissa," I repeated, "Okay, yes?"

"Do you have any kids?"

"I have a step-daughter, a step-son and a baby girl."

"How pretty!" one girl said.

Hands went up everywhere. I answered anything that they wanted to know, except my salary, for the next five minutes. They wanted to know who I was, and I felt they had a right to, considering they would be in my class for two hours a day. The more we knew about each other, the more we could work together. I became closer to that second and third period class in a shorter amount of time than almost any other class I had ever taught.

That year fourth period was my prep period. My fifth-period class had a high population of troubled kids and wannabe gangsters. The days of the red clothing were gone, but many of the kids in my fifth period still had the attitude. Justin was my student aid in there, which helped. Although they were apathetic at best and confrontational at worst, between Justin being there and my knowing that fifth period was only 50 minutes, I got by.

My sixth-period class was a lot of fun. I had Melissa R. and Amanda in that class. Both were bright, and they hated each other. Melissa R. was street smart and Amanda was a model student, and both achieved high grades. The clashing of opinions during discussion was a great way to end the day.

Sixth period wanted to know all about me.

"What kind of music do you listen to?" Melissa R. asked when I threw out my "ask anything you want question."

"Classic rock and alternative."

"So you listen to Live 105?" Melissa R. continued the interrogation.

"Yes." I answered, ready for the next question. Amanda sat in the front row and shook her head.

"He probably listens to country!" Someone volunteered. The class erupted in laughter, and I tried to figure out why my classes always assumed I listened to country. Further, why would it be funny if I did?

"You got any kids?" Melissa R. was not finished cross-examining.

I gave them then rundown of my family.

"Where do they go to school?"

"My stepdaughter is at Holly Oak, and my stepson is as Laurelwood."

"Why don't they go to the same school?"

"Geez, man that's personal!" objected Joseph, who sat near Melissa R.

"He can answer if he wants!" She glared at him. He looked down at his desk.

I did answer. Then I got their books to them and started them on the student survey.

The bell to end the first day rang sooner that I could believe, and as they walked out the door, I noticed I was smiling. My smile stuck until the room had emptied, and I realized that I had a great group of kids. I was going to make it without Katrina, Shelene, and Amber the way that I had without Elizabeth and Maile. I had Justin, Michael and Annalisa, and the rest of them. "Yeah, there will always be the kids that you never forget," I said out loud to myself.

At home that afternoon, I fired up the computer and logged on to the Internet. There were 5 e-mail messages, and I grabbed a soda. I looked down the bold print list of new messages-Lifeminders, South Bay Ticket Alert, Dad, Diane, Pete.

My heart thumped as I clicked Pete's message open. He wanted me to come in one day next week to meet with the hiring manager for the technical writing position. I sent him a wide variety of options, and a few minutes later, he sent me back the time he wanted me to come in. I wrote back and told him I would see him then.

"This could be it!" I thought. "The beginning of the end of my financial problems." All I needed was my foot in the door, and I could prove myself through hard work and dedication.

It was a good feeling to know that my attempt at a career switch wasn't dead after all, but my smile left and my stomach knotted when I thought of Melissa R, Amanda, Justin, and the rest of them. Their hope filled eyes haunted me. I called Kristin to tell her about the interview and tried to shake the kids from my mind.

CHAPTER XLIV

I began to be confident that I would be hired before the end of the school year, so I taught some of my favorite units at the beginning of the year. If I did leave, I wanted to teach about Edgar Allan Poe and Ernest Hemingway at least one more time. I taught about Poe in October and Hemingway soon after that and gave my students a lot of what I knew they wouldn't get from the next teacher-a literature emphasis where they learned about an author's life, read some of the author's work, and discussed the two together. It wasn't the current buzzword, Reciprocal Teaching, but they responded and had fun. More importantly, so did I because if I wasn't passionate about what I taught, how should I expect them to care at all? That was one of the points that David and I preached to each other tirelessly.

Kristin and I decided to take our credit problems by the reins. We enrolled in credit counseling and got rid of all our credit cards. A set amount was to be taken out of our checking automatically each month for the next five years until the debt was clear. Should we come upon more money at any time, we had the option of increasing the payment and clearing the debt faster. From now on, everything we bought would be in cash.

I was scheduled to go and interview for the second time with Abovehealth. The day I was supposed to go, my pager went off in the middle of sixth period. In mid-sentence, I checked the page.

"Mr. Kohl, you're not supposed to have pagers at school," Joseph told me.

"You know, Joseph," I said, "there are rules that are different for me because I am an adult-it's just the way life is even if it doesn't seem fair. For example, I'm allowed to drive a car to school, and you're not supposed to."

While they thought about that, I went to the phone and accessed my pager's voicemail. It was Pete telling me that the people I needed to meet with were in LA at an industry show. We were going to need to reschedule. I was disappointed, but there was no time for that now. The show had to go on.

I apologized for answering the page in class, but that it may have been an emergency concerning my kids. "Everything is fine, though." I assured them. I finished the lecture, explained the homework, and sent them packing as the bell signaled the day's end.

I got out my calling card and dialed Kristin at work. "Pete cancelled on me," I said as she answered.

"What?"

"Yeah, he left me a voicemail about how the people I needed to meet with were out of town or something." I threw a dry erase marker from my desk, trying to make it land on the white board tray. It skittered off the board and onto the floor, losing its yellow cap.

"Oh, honey, I'm sorry," Kristin consoled me.

"That's cool. You know this is just their way of getting rid of me because they don't want to hire a teacher. I don't have any real experience or skill."

"Pete's not going to do that to you, because if he does, I'll call my cousins and they'll show him how rude that is in no uncertain terms." Her voice let the threat go in a sing song manner. She joked; her close cousins weren't that way. Her gangster talk made me laugh and lightened the load in my head.

True to his word, Pete contacted me a week later and rescheduled. He apologized and explained that things were sort of crazy during the move to the new office, and that the company wasn't originally scheduled to attend that industry show. He gave me a new day and time to come in, so one day in October, I left work right as the bell rang. I went home, suited up, and slid a fresh printed version of my resume into my leather folder.

Abovehealth's new office was two minutes from my house, just like Pete had told me it would be.

The elevator doors opened into a hallway about the size of a living room with brown carpeting. Suite 200 was to my right, and the door had a teal nameplate that said: LeeTech Software Inc, Abovehealth Corporation, Abovelearning Corporation in white letters. I swallowed to put my heart back where it belonged and opened the door.

A reception desk was there, but no one sat at it. To my right was a long line of cubicles. Almost everything, except the green carpet, was gray. I stood there with my folder in my hand and looked around, waiting to be noticed like a new kid would at the middle school. From a windowed meeting room, a man called out, "Are you looking for Pete?" His voice turned my head, and I saw his tie and glasses. He leaned back in a chair and was talking with another man whose back was to me.

"Yes," I said, taking three steps toward the room.

"He's got the first office to your left." The man pointed the direction.

I found Pete in his office, staring at a monitor. I stood in the doorway and knocked lightly a couple of times.

"Oh, hey dude, you're here!" he said.

"How's it going?" I asked. "You guys are all moved in."

"Yeah, it's been about a week, I guess. It's been a mess. There's a couple of folks I'd like you to meet with today; how are you for time?"

"I have plenty."

"Good. Well, let me see who I can get you with first."

I spoke first with a young woman named Evelyn, who had a small Mickey Mouse stuffed animal on her desk. I thought of Kristin and took the Mickey Mouse as a message not to be so nervous. Evelyn told me that she used to do most of the writing for the company. "I hate doing it.

I'm moving into marketing now, which still has a lot of writing, but it's not as tedious…I'm sorry," she said looking at me.

"That's okay. I like writing, or I wouldn't be here."

She told me all of the things Pete had told me about the company. "Do you have any questions for me?" she finally asked.

"What would a day at work be like for a technical writer?" I asked.

"I'm not really sure what your day would be like because when I did the writing, I squeezed it in whenever I could around the other fifty billion things that I was trying to do."

We talked a little while longer, and then she walked me back to Pete. "What's a day as a teacher like?" she asked me as we walked.

"I get to the school about 7. I get last-minute things ready for the day's lesson plan-most of it I would've put together the day before. Usually some kids come in around 7:30 to ask for help on something or just to hang out. Class starts at 8. Each class is about 50 minutes. I get one period off a day to plan and grade stuff."

"Do you take a lot of work home?"

"Not as much as I should." I admitted. 'If I really worked the way I should have, I would never talk to my family until June.' I thought.

Pete took me over to meet with Tuan, the hiring manager. He and I spoke briefly about teaching and why I was leaving. I gave him my canned, less than honest answer about a new interest in technology because leaving for a decent wage sounds so greedy.

"What the job entails," Tuan told me, "is playing with the software and describing how to use it in simple terms. My wife is not a technical person, but the idea is to make it so that someone like her can read the document and use the software-that sort of thing."

"It's like teaching," I said. "You take something that is complicated and present it in such a way that people can understand it."

Tuan nodded. There was a long pause.

"Some of the guys we have working out there, English is their second language. Do you feel comfortable communicating with people that speak mainly Mandarin Chinese?"

"The school I work in has a diverse population, so I've dealt with second-language issues the whole time I've been teaching." I was relieved that he wasn't asking me if I had a CLAD credential.

We paused again.

"We're on a flex time here, so as long as you get your job done, I don't care what time you come and go. I treat my guys like professionals, and as long as the job gets done it doesn't matter. No one's watching to see what time you come and go."

I was in a world with no bells. Tuan and I finished talking, and he mentioned something about hoping that I joined. Could this be it? I went back to Pete's office to wrap things up, and he told me they would be in touch and walked me to the door.

"How was the interview?" Kristin asked as I walked in.

"I feel really good about it, honey." I said, motioning for her to follow me to the room so I could change. I told her all about it and how nice the people were. I told her about the Mickey Mouse on Evelyn's desk. "I felt great there. I really hope I get in!"

I hadn't heard anything the next day. They didn't call the day after that either. I was still waiting to hear the day after that. "It takes a long time." Kristin told me.

I called my mom during my prep period about four days after the interview. "You need to be patient," she told me. "By the way, I was talking with Jan about this. She says if the offer comes through, you need to go. Don't let anyone down there in the district office make you feel bad or make you feel undedicated. You need to do what is best for your family."

"Oh yeah, I know. I'm not going to hesitate at all. We need the money." I flipped the phone cord around and accidentally knocked a small statue of Steve Young off the shelf that was behind my desk and beneath the phone.

"And isn't it a shame that we don't pay our teachers enough. We hand them our children, and we don't want to pay them well to make sure our children are educated."

"I know."

Lilah, from my last year's fifth period, was picking up attendance. She poked her head in my door and smiled and waved. I smiled and mouthed "Hi" to her.

I kept teaching and kept waiting each day. Each night, I would apply for as many jobs as I could on Monster and the other job databases, but nothing seemed to be breaking. I really thought that all of this would be over before Halloween.

I taught right through Halloween, when I always had the kids share "true" ghost stories that they had heard. It was one of my favorite days to teach because everyone always had a cousin who had a friend that had lived in a haunted house. It's amazing how they can fill a period sharing stories with each other. Even kids that never did homework and were failing the class had a story to tell. Even kids with major behavior problems would raise their hand and wait to be called on to talk about a ghost they had seen. They all listened and were interested in what everyone else had to say. The day was always a victory, and with the kids hyped up on candy like they were, it could have been a disaster had I tried to teach a lesson.

My own monsters came back a few nights later. November was about three days old when I woke in the night realizing that I had two months to find a job or renew the credential. Renewing was impossible. I stared into the darkness at the ceiling and listened to Kristin's even and relaxed breathing beside me. I crept out of bed and went to sit in the living room in the dark. Uncertainty swirled around me and twisted up my common sense. I was reduced to silently sniveling away like a child. Why didn't they just hire me? I'm a good guy. I'll work hard for them if they just give me a chance. Why didn't anyone else call me in for an interview?

"Why didn't you renew your credential when you had a chance?" the Monsters asked. "Why do you put control of your life in the hands of others? The credit cards, credit counseling, the teachers union, the people that you want to work for, us. You have a pattern of letting other people have your self-control. If you had renewed the credential like we have been warning you to for the past year, the new job wouldn't be so crucial. When are you going to stop letting people push you around? How much are you going to take?"

I sat on the couch in the dark beating myself up. An hour and a half later, I was finally able to go to sleep.

The next morning, I stood in front of the mirror and shaved. Kristin walked into the bathroom on her way to the shower. "Good morning, honey."

"Good morning!" She reached up and kissed me on the shaved side of my face while the other side still hid in thick white foam. She backed away from the kiss and then stared at me. She wrinkled her eyes and reached up to my cheek right below my eye. With her thumb, she rubbed the area. "What is this?" she asked.

"I don't know," I said, "I look like some sort of leper-it's a rash or something." There was a red blotchy rash that had been getting worse by the day lately right below my left eye. It started as a small red patch just below my eye, but it was halfway down my cheek and visible from across a room now.

"Did something bite you?" Kristin asked as she turned on the shower.

"I don't know, did you?" I asked. I tried to make a joke, but silently I was thankful that it wasn't on my face for my last interview. When I walked into a room, this blotch was all anyone could see. A few days earlier, a student asked me if my baby had scratched me by my eye, and I didn't know why she asked that until now. The blotch was bigger now. "Great," I thought, "I'm no good inside or out."

On the drive to work that morning, I had barely noticed Dominique and Lorenzo bickering in the backseat. Two blocks away from the house, I couldn't turn right at the light because the car in front of me stopped on the right side of the lane. Each traffic light turned red 20 feet before I got there. Pete hadn't gotten back to me yet. The radio played jabbering commercials with repetitive boinging sound effects on station after station until I finally turned it off in disgust.

"What's the matter, Jim?" asked Dominique.

"Nothin'."

They weren't going to hire a teacher. Anyone could walk into that company and have more experience than I. I reached for the plastic commuter cup of coffee. A bump in the road jostled it enough to scald my fingers and stain my pants. Can it get worse than going to teach middle school with a liquid stain on your crotch? I shook my fingers and dried them on the car seat.

"How come you're not talking?"

"I don't know-I just don't have anything to say. I'm tired."

I was a good worker. If they gave me a shot, I know I would work really hard to make myself of value.

"Are you sure you're okay?"

"Yes!"

The guy in front of me didn't think it was necessary to enter the freeway at freeway speeds, so the two of us attempted to merge onto highway 280 at 40 miles per hour. "Maybe I taught Ernest Hemingway and Edgar Allan Poe a little early," I thought for a second. "If I waited until after January like I normally did, the kids wouldn't have been so eager to please me, and they might not have tried as hard to learn about them. I'll teach Poe and Hemingway early in the year next year too," I decided right there on the highway.

"There won't be a next year. Your credential expires in January," the monsters reminded me. "Two more months-the clock is ticking."

"How come you turned the radio off?"

"There's nothing good on it."

I dropped off the kids at day care and reminded them to be good and to learn something at school. I drove the last two blocks to LeyVa in silence, pulled into the second to last parking place, and wished for the end of the workday.

CHAPTER XLV

Pam, the school psychologist, had a small office just outside of the main office door. It was an 8-foot by 6-foot box with her desk, a two-person table with two small plastic chairs, and a couch. The couch and the small table were one step apart, and her desk was one step away from each. Teachers who felt Pam was too easy on the kids called it Romper Room.

Now and then, I went to Pam's office for some free psychological help and to hang out because I thought she did a great job with the kids, and I considered her a good friend.

I knocked on her orange door one day during my prep and was told to come in. Pam was in the room with Sylvia, an eighth-grade girl whom I had in class last year. "Hi, Mr. Kohl," Pam greeted me. "Do you know Sylvia?"

"Yeah, hi Sylvia."

"Hello."

"I was just telling Sylvia here that she needs to go back to class, and do you want to tell Mr. Kohl what you told me Sylvia?"

"I don't want to go."

"And tell Mr. Kohl what you said you would do if I made you leave my office." Pam turned in her chair, grabbed her glasses off her desk and slid them on.

"I would go home." Sylvia stood pursing her lips and shaking her head. Her lips were carefully outlined in black, and her eyes were well surrounded by make up as well.

"How come you don't want to go to class, Sylvia?" I asked.

"Because I hate that guy. He makes me feel stupid. He tells me I'm stupid!" Her tone raised in desperation.

Pam and I convinced her that it didn't matter what people said. We told her that she wasn't stupid, but that she needed to do her work so that people would be able to see how smart she was. She finally agreed to go to class if Pam would walk her down there. Pam agreed, and I sat in her office and waited until she came back.

Pam had two of the same posters-one in Spanish and one in English. They were for the teen hotline number. The Spanish one showed a Mexican kid who looked like a gang member, and the English one showed a white girl with the torn up look of a runaway. Both of them had the same toll free number at the bottom in red. These were Pam's clients, and she got to know them much better than any of their teachers did. These kids needed to talk, have someone listen, and know that someone cared. Pam was that person. She listened to and she cared for what a selected few of LeyVa's teachers had discarded-unsuccessful students.

Pam came back. "That Sylvia!" she said. "She thinks she is so stupid. She thinks she is the dumbest kid that ever set foot on the LeyVa campus. She thinks she's hopeless, so when that teacher tells her she's a stupid loser, it is no news to her. But can you blame her for not wanting to go to class?!" Pam's voice became shrill. "Who wants to go somewhere and hear how stupid they are, especially when they already know?"

I shrugged and shook my head.

"I'm stupid too you know, they told me that all through high school." Pam had a master's in psychology. She sat back down in her desk chair and exhaled long. "So what can I do for you, Mr. Kohl?"

I took a deep breath. "You know, Pam, do you remember when the CLAD thing was going on during negotiations last year?"

She nodded.

I fidgeted my hands. "I told you that I was thinking of leaving teaching all together. A lot of teachers said that, but…"

"No!" she said.

"Well, I haven't been hired anywhere yet, but I wanted to let you know that I was looking. I've been interviewing actually."

"No!" she repeated. She took her glasses back off and sighed as she set them on her desk. She dabbed at her eye.

"Yeah. Please don't mention it to anyone. I've only told you and David." I swallowed hard.

She shook her head and looked out the tiny window at LeyVa's front parking lot.

"I don't even know that I'll get anything," I said.

"Oh, Jim, you'll get something all right. As smart as you are? Please! What a tremendous loss for LeyVa and its kids-especially the kids." She kept shaking her head. "And me. You're one of the only people here that likes me."

"That's not true, Pam."

"It is true. You're the only one that modifies programs. At least Elizabeth is gone."

I thought about her and her red clothes and deep brown eyes that would kill one minute and need a hug the next. "I couldn't have left if she were here."

"Tell me about it!! She'd kick your butt!"

We laughed.

"Is it just because of the CLAD?" Pam asked. "Don't you like teaching anymore?"

"I love teaching. My family and I are not making it. We need more money, and I'll never get that here. Sadly." I itched my eye.

"What are you going to do?" she asked.

I explained about technical writing, and I told her about all the interviews I had had. I told her how I came to the decision, and how my credential was going to expire. I felt self conscious about the rash beneath my eye, and I tried to keep that side of my face away from view as much as possible throughout the conversation. Finally, we started talking of other things.

"Well," Pam said, as the bell rang for lunch. "Thank you for telling me, and keep me posted on things as they happen."

"I might not even get anything."

"You will."

We said goodbye, and I headed to my room to meet the kids for lunch.

A few days later, my pager buzzed in my pocket after school let out. I checked it, and it was an unfamiliar number. "Probably a wrong number." I thought as I dialed the number. Ever since I got this pager, various convenience and liquor stores had paged me when they needed a janitor.

"Pete speaking?" said a voice after a ring and a half.

My heart quickened. "Hey, Pete! It's Jim Kohl."

"Jim! How's it going, bud?"

"Pretty good, man, how are you doing?"

"Great! Listen, I'd like you to come in and meet with a couple of folks as soon as possible. What are you doing tomorrow?"

"Well, I could come after 2:30," I said.

"Is there any way we could get you in earlier in the day? The reason is, the sooner I can get you in here, the sooner I can get an offer letter out to you."

My eyebrows raised. "I have a prep at around 11, but I would need to be back to school by 12:30 at the latest."

"That won't be a problem. I'll tell these people that you're on a limited time frame. We'll get you back to the kids on time." Pete laughed.

Here I went again to another interview with them. This would be a total of four interviews including the phone interview. As I headed home that afternoon, I couldn't help but think that they were jerking me around. "They know me already," I thought. "Why do they need to talk to me again?" I turned up the radio and watched the East Side disappear into my rear view mirror.

The next morning, I broke the news to Denise, the U.S. history teacher who taught across the curtain from me. She, like everyone, was shocked, but she understood. She could afford being a teacher because her husband was the V. P. of marketing at a software company.

"I don't know though," I told her, "they've interviewed me three times already. I think they should know me enough by now to make a decision."

"Not necessarily," she told me. "It took my husband a long time to find a job. These companies take their time in hiring."

I felt a little better about it.

That day, as my prep began, I headed out to my car and drove toward home. Denise said she would open the curtain and watch my fifth period if I was a little late coming back. I didn't think that would happen. Pete guaranteed me I would be back on time.

I ran into the house and started changing into the interview suit that I had laid out on the bed that morning before I went to work. I grabbed the leather folder after I tied my tie. On the way back out, I slid a couple copies of my resume that I printed out the night before into my brown leather folder. I bounded to the front door and locked it behind me as I walked on the verge of a run to my car.

Three minutes later, I pulled into Abovehealth's driveway. I stood at the silver first floor elevator door and breathed deeply to slow down.

I found Pete in his office. "Hey!" he greeted.

"How's it going?"

"Great. Well, I know you're on a limited time, so let me set you up in the conference room, and I'll go get our C.O.O." I learned this stood for chief operating officer.

The C.O.O. came into the conference room and sat across from me. He wore a blue and white Hawaiian shirt, and I knew this would be a cool company. He was the man who had directed me to Pete's office at the beginning of my last interview.

"I know you're pressed for time, James, so I'll be brief." We talked about the company and its plan to go public. That meant that if they gave me stock, I could be a millionaire overnight the way many of Silicon Valley's Dot-Com employees were. He asked me a couple questions about research and how I would go about finding the answer to a problem.

"I guess I would find someone to ask around here," I answered.

"Suppose no one here knew, or the people that knew didn't have time to talk to you for one reason or another?"

I thought for a second. It must be more complicated than it sounds, but I was going to go with my gut instinct. "I guess I would go to the library and look it up."

"Yeah, or you could use the Internet. We had another guy come through for the job that had far superior technical skills, but he floundered on questions about simple research techniques."

This was very encouraging.

The C.O.O. and I broke up our meeting, and Pete ushered me down to the chief executive and owner's office. His office had a waiting area with a lush leather couch the color of a triple espresso latte.

"This guy is the owner." I thought. "There is no way I'll be interviewing with anyone after him." I still carried my resumes in the brown folder. No one wanted to see one today. I sat across from him at his hardwood desk. Pictures of his family were around. He had an oversized black chair.

"Besides doing writing for us," he said at one point, "maybe you could use your teaching skills to train new clients on the product?"

"Yeah, absolutely!!" I said.

The owner laughed and told me it was nice to meet me.

Pete told me he would be in touch, and walked me to the door. I thanked him again and headed back to the house to change into my teacher costume. I got back to LeyVa five minutes before the end of lunch.

I don't remember fifth period that day at all. My head swam in adrenaline and excitement clouded by absolute emotional exhaustion. I was running off to interview in the middle of the school day like a married man having a lunchtime affair with some chick he met at a bar. I had been grilled four times by this company, and I hoped that they would be nice enough to hire me after that sort of ordeal. I only had two months until the credential expired, and they were my most realistic hope at this point.

Sixth period came in and took their seats. They did their opener while I took the roll. I went from desk to desk checking their homework, and half of them hadn't done it.

"You know," I told them when I returned to the front of the room, "15 of you didn't do your homework, the beginning of the autobiographical incident essay, last night. This essay is going to be built slowly over time, and 15 of you…that's half…decided not to do it. That means that half of you have started behind, and it's not going to be easy to catch up." I shook my head in disappointment.

They all stared at me.

I went on with the lesson on how to write dialogue, which they needed to be able to do in the autobiographical incident essay. I shined the overhead transparency on the board that had Dialogue Rules at the top. The rest of the transparency was covered with a paper, forcing the students to not jump ahead in copying the notes. Experience told me that if they moved ahead in the notes, they don't listen to what you're saying, and when they finish copying the notes, they don't think they should have to listen anymore at all.

I was in the middle of explaining the first rule when Melissa raised her hand. "Isn't dialog spelled d-i-a-l-o-g?"

"Actually, either spelling is accepted in English." I answered. "It's just one of those weird things."

"So if this was a spelling test, you could spell it either way?" she pushed.

"Yes, in this class." I thought of the eighth-grade English teachers, and I didn't want to speak for them. "But if you're in an English class in eighth grade and you have it on a spelling test and the teacher wants it spelled a certain way, you need to spell it the way they say."

"But my spelling was correct?" She asked, and I saw clearly what this was about.

"Yes, Melissa, your spelling was correct."

"Thank you."

I nodded. "Anyway, the first rule of dialogue writing is everything your character...the person that you are making talk...says out loud needs to be in double quotes." I moved the paper down and exposed the first rule on the white board. The kids copied the blue writing from the board into their notebooks.

Joseph turned and whispered something to Melissa with an adolescent smile filling his face. She shot him a scowl. I went on.

When I had reached the third rule, "Use a comma or another form of punctuation to separate what is being said from the person that said it," Melissa had her hand up again.

"Yes, Melissa?" I flipped the dry erase marker in my hand.

"My teacher last year told me that it always has to be a comma."

"I expect that she did. When you're in the lower grades, they tell you that just so you can have a precise rule. What I'm telling you is that you have the freedom to write something like this:"

I wrote: "I have a question." asked Melissa.

"You see," I explained, "It is really unnecessary to have a comma after the period in that example." She looked at me with a wrinkled forehead. "Of course, if you're more comfortable doing it the elementary school way for now, go ahead. But I encourage you to experiment with this so you can get used to it."

Amanda, the girl in the front, nodded and smiled at me.

Joseph turned and muttered something to Melissa again.

"Shut up!" She commanded. He turned and faced forward and attempted to stifle his laughter.

"What's the problem over there, you guys?" I asked, staring at them.

"I don't have a problem," Melissa announced. "Joseph?" She turned to him and raised her eyebrows, anticipating his response.

"I don't...have a ...problem," Joseph said, pausing so that he wouldn't burst out laughing.

Just then, Jose thought I wasn't looking and threw a paper wod at a girl three seats in front of him in what I can only assume was some form of primitive courtship. Since my attention was with Joseph and Melissa, he figured he had a free shot.

I stared at him. His face reddened. "My patience is going, guys," I announced sternly. "You're going to end up here past the bell."

"What if we need to catch the bus?" someone asked.

Amanda clicked her tongue and sighed; she looked over her shoulder to see who would've asked a question like that.

"That sounds like a personal problem," I said. I paced back and forth in front of them. I saw another girl pass a note to one of her friends. I walked to the recipient and held out my hand for the note.

She hesitated. "I'll need to write you up if you don't give me the note." She handed it to me.

"Mr. Kohl," whined the author of the note, "please don't read it."

"It's mine now, and I'll decide what I'll do with it." I put it in my shirt pocket. Later that evening, I would read it with Kristin while we sat on the couch. It was usually good for a laugh or two.

"But Mr. Kohl!"

Finally I had had it. "You know what," I said, "I've had it with you guys today! It's really sad because I look forward to this class all day, and then you come in here, and you won't focus on this lesson! You need to know about this essay for the writing proficiency test, and that is only four months from now!" I paused and looked around.

Most of them were looking down. "You're one of my favorite groups. I have a lot of fun while you're in the room, and you make me happy, but today...this is ridiculous!" I paced in front of them. I let my words hang down on them. "You know, we don't have a lot of time to, work together." I said pleadingly. "It's going to go by faster than you think. I don't want to waste a day with you guys." I uncovered the rest of the dialogue notes. "Copy down the rest of these rules. Add dialogue to your rough draft tonight for homework. I'll be sitting over here if you have any questions."

Too much of the period was gone for me to continue the lesson formally. I would have them take the notes and do the assignment, and then I would fill in any gaps tomorrow when we talked about the homework. My pulse raced in frustration and my throat was clogged with sadness.

The announcements blabbed on, and the final bell rang. "See you tomorrow." I called out.

"I'm sorry, Mr. Kohl." Melissa said, as she passed my desk.

"That's okay, Melissa. It wasn't just you, and I'm not mad at you at all."

She smiled. "See you later, Mr. Kohl."

"Bye."

I sat in comfortable silence and tried to let the day peel off of me. I turned off half the lights in the classroom and sat at my desk, waving to kids as they walked by the room and either waved or called my name. I put my head in my hands. Sometimes, the lesson just doesn't happen for one reason or another, but it's a terrible feeling. It feels like you didn't do your job.

My pager went off. I grabbed it from my pocket and checked the number. It was Pete. I fumbled to my feet and nearly dropped the phone as I tore it off the receiver. I dialed the number, and changed my life.

"This is Pete."

"Hey Pete, it's Jim Kohl."

"Hey, dude. I am happy to tell you that I just e-mailed an offer letter to your house."

"Great! Oh, man, this makes my whole day. You would not believe the terrible sixth period that I just had."

"The beasts are getting to you, huh?" he asked.

"Oh yeah, it was really bad. They're good kids, but today was really bad." I had waited for this phone call for four months. I sat at my desk and took in the news. "All right man, so what's the next step?" I asked.

"I can take a verbal approval for now, and then as soon as you can, if you could just reply to the e-mail and that will be written approval. You can sign on your first day of work. When will that be by the way?" His voice's enthusiasm matched my own.

"I have to give two weeks notice to the school…" I looked at my large desk calendar, which was covered with pen markings and doodles. "The 19th could be my first day."

"Let's see…" I could picture Pete checking his calendar. "Okay, I'll write you down for that date, and we'll see you then."

"Great, thanks!"

"Thank you. And welcome aboard."

"Thanks." We hung up and I had my room to myself again. I looked at the pile of papers on my desk-they had instantly lost their meaning. I sat back in my chair and breathed. I put my hands behind my head and smiled. I sat and looked at the wall and thought about what it would mean to be a technical writer.

I called Kristin, but she was not at her desk. I left her a message simply telling her to page me.

I called my mom, and told her all about it.

"Oh, Jim, that's wonderful! I'm so happy for you!" We both knew that this was the beginning of the end of my financial problems. I wouldn't have to worry as much about taking care of my kids now. "So when do you start?"

I told her.

"Have you told the school yet?"

My stomach wrenched. Teachers didn't quit in the middle of the year! I had told myself that I would do this without a problem. I wasn't going to think twice. I was going to tell them, and I was going to drive away listening to the Dead Kennedy's version of "Take This Job and Shove It." Now that the day actually had arrived, I thought twice and I was on my millionth thought by the time I caught myself. I didn't even have the Dead Kennedy's CD in the car.

"I'm going to tell them tomorrow, and my last day is two weeks from tomorrow." I finally answered. I looked at a line of student photographs that I used to decorate the drawers of my desk. "You know mom," I said softly, "when I look into the eyes of these kids here at the school, it makes it really hard to leave."

"I know, Jim," she answered. "and I knew you would feel this way. But when you look into the eyes of your own children, doesn't it make it impossible not to?"

CHAPTER XLVI

The next morning, I turned on the light in the bathroom and looked in the mirror. As I rubbed my eyes and the light no longer blinded me, I saw that the rash beneath my eye had gotten worse overnight. I had come home to congratulatory hugs and kisses from Kristin. We had a celebration dinner. I had been awake for quite a while during the night. I dared the monsters to come and harass me about money and my credential, but the best that they could come up with was a half-hearted, "You're going to have to tell Rick."

I dreaded telling Rick, and as I examined the rash under my eye, I feared he may take it personally. I didn't want that because it had nothing to do with him, the students, or the school. I had to do this to support my family. I was not a corporate scum chasing the dollar at all costs. I was a father.

"Geez, that thing by your eye is getting worse," Kristin said sympathetically.

"I think I need to dust this room or something. I think there's too much dust in here," I said rubbing the rash.

"Stop touching it!" Kristin said. "Here, put some of this lotion on it." It was some sort of prescription lotion that she had for severely dry skin. She handed me the blue and white tube.

I took a shower and got ready to go. "Are you going to tell Rick?"

"Yeah, at some point today."

She laughed an evil giggle. "Call me when you tell him, and tell me what he says."

"Okay." Kristin had a tabloid story sort of interest in this.

I didn't hit any red lights that morning. As I parked the car and stepped onto the campus, I felt evil. I loved LeyVa and all the kids. I thought of Rick as a friend and a mentor. I was really fond of Dolores, and I didn't want them to hate me. I had two copies of a resignation letter sitting in white unsealed envelopes on the passenger seat on the way to school. It had taken me an hour to write the letter, and I went over it and over it in my head on the drive into work that day:

November 5, 1999

To the Evergreen School District Human Resources Department and Rick:

It is with a heavy heart that I write this letter. I know that what I announce here will be unpopular and will probably cause much distress (and stress), but I hope that when the smoke clears, those I have grown close to here at LeyVa Middle School will understand and share my joy.

My personal situation has caused me stress and discomfort for the past year. Financially, my family and I struggle on a month to month basis, and I am often depressed and stressed over money. My students have sometimes suffered because of my inability to always conceal my emotions. This weakness of mine has reached a climax recently. I don't want this anymore.

My credential is expiring in January of 2000, and I don't have the money to buy an extension. This cold fact, frustration over money, and a budding enthusiasm for technology inspired me to search Silicon Valley for a company that may want an English major with a love for words and writing. I have found one, and I have been offered a position as a technical writer with an up and coming software firm. I want this career change very badly. Therefore, I need to ask to be excused from my teaching position at LeyVa Middle School as of November 18, 1999.

I have loved all my time here. I have grown as a person. I love the kids most of all. When I look into their eyes, this is especially hard for me, but when I look into the eyes of my own children and into the core of my soul, I know that this is the correct road for me to take. I cannot allow this to be the road not taken and always wonder what would have happened. Thank you for four great years.

Sincerely,

James R. Kohl

Now all I had to do was muster the guts to give it to Rick. I took the letter to my room and locked it in my desk drawer. I would do this during my prep. I had to do it today.

My stomach crawled, and the rash on my face itched. The kids would be in my room soon, and I would have to be Mr. Kohl. I would have to seem normal and happy. I would miss them a lot, and I already felt sad for them and for me. I was supposed to be here for them. I was the one they could rely on.

Those first two classes flew by. I taught them something. Then we had the 10-minute break. I went to the office and passed through the staff room where everyone sat around the donuts that someone brought and argued the same old issues.

"You know, in the real world, if these kids keep going through stop signs, sooner or later they're going to get nailed. It should be the same with their homework and their attendance-at least it should be."

"We're not really a bilingual school. We're a multi-lingual school."

"I'm just glad I can retire in two more years and not have to worry…"

"This last contract was no good anyway…"

Soon, I would be leaving all this. I was being given $40,000 a year, a 22 percent increase just for leaving teaching. I was entering the industry really low, but I was a gamble for them. I was not a proven entity, and once I was, I could make a lot more. I already had friends at big companies telling me to get a resume to them in a year. I pushed open the staff room door and let it close behind me.

Third period came and went. As the last kid left the room, I looked around at all the desks and could see all the faces that had ever been in them. "I'm sorry, guys," I whispered to them. I took out my key and unlocked the drawer. It took me two tries to get the key in correctly. Both of the letters were just where I had left them.

I thought I had better make a copy of the letter so I went to the front office door and was going to go in, but I checked Pam's office instead. She wasn't there, so I had no means of stalling this. "That's just as well," I thought.

"Hi Jim!" called out Carmen.

"Hi. How's it going?"

"Fine, how about you?"

"I'm okay." I said, heading for the copy machine.

"And how's the baby?"

"Oh she's great."

"You have to bring her in one day so we can see her."

"Yeah, I know, I really should." Carmen's phone rang, so I had my chance to make my copy. Rick's office was just to the right of the copy machine, and it was empty. Just looking at the office made my stomach and throat tighten up. I had to do this now, and I wasn't so confident that I could. "I could do it after school," I thought. That would mean I would have to wait through two more classes, and I didn't want that. I headed to the Student Center to see if I could find Dolores. Her office was empty too. Art was in his, but he was with a student and a parent.

"Who are you looking for, Jim?" asked Maria, the Student Center clerk.

"Dolores," I said turning towards Maria.

"She's over in the gym watching the sixth grade basketball game."

I walked toward the gym. Rick was standing right outside his office door about 20 feet from where I came out. I held the envelopes in my hand and elected to look for Dolores.

The gym roared with cheers from parents as their children ran up and down the court. That hollow, continuous thud of the basketball and the shriek of sneakers sprinting and skidding on the gym floor brought the room alive and gave me the feeling, in my heightened emotional state, that none of this was real. Teachers don't resign.

Dolores stood with her arms folded and her keys in one hand at the close end of the court and zoned on the game. I walked up to her.

"Dolores," I said.

"Hi, Jim." She glanced over at me and then returned her attention to the game.

"Um…Listen…I need to talk to you. Can we go outside for a second?"

"Oh, I can't really leave the game," she said. "I'm the only LeyVa person in…" She looked over at me. My eyes clouded over as tears and fell.

Dolores's mouth and eyes widened in concern. "Let's go," she said, and I followed her out the door opposite the one I came in.

We were out behind the gym. The closest people were the seventh and eighth-grade students who were in PE about 50 feet away. "Hi, Mr. Kohl!" someone called to me. I turned and waved and smiled, not sure whom I was saying hi to or even where they were.

I turned back to Dolores. I wrung my hands and breathed the thick air as much as I could. My heart beat against the inside of my chest, and my mouth dried. I had to be direct. Dolores looked at me, and I could see she was starting to worry. "I have to resign," I told her.

Her face dropped, and she just stared at me.

"I don't make enough money here, and my family is really struggling to get by. I just can't make it as a teacher anymore, and I haven't really been able to for the past year. The new baby came, and we had to get a bigger car for the car seat, and I'm not saying we didn't want the baby…"

"Of course not," Dolores interjected.

"It's just that with a family of five we're really not doing too well. We weren't doing that great as a family of four either. My credential is expiring in January, and I don't have the money to buy the classes to make it a clear one."

"You only had a preliminary," she said.

"Yeah," I said, and started to panic. My words poured out like freed prisoners. "Oh, my God, and this is not how I wanted it to turn out when I got in this career. I always thought this was it, you know? And I love LeyVa and I love the kids. You guys have always been very nice to me-my leaving has nothing to do with anyone here." My face was moist, and I rubbed my cheek dry. I felt sweat drip down my forehead.

"As an administrator, and on a personal level, I'm really sad to see you go. You do have a job to go to, right?"

"Yeah, I've been hired as a technical writer at a software company. It'll be different for sure. It's more money-not a lot more at first, but the potential…"

"Is much more than you'll ever see here."

I nodded. I kept looking from Dolores to the wall behind her all the while we talked. In the distance, I could still hear the basketball game and the kids at PE.

"Have you told Rick yet?"

I shook my head. "I've been sort of a wuss about that. I don't want to hurt his feelings, and I don't want him to take it personally." I wiped my cheek again.

"Rick has always believed that he only wants people to stay here if they want to stay here." Dolores put her hand out toward me. "Not…not that you don't want to stay here…but…I think he'll understand. Would you like me to prepare him for you?"

This was more than I had hoped for. I rubbed my eye. "Yes. That would be great."

"I'd be happy to. Where do you want to be, and I'll come and get you after I have talked with Rick."

"I'll be in my room," I said like a child who was in trouble.

I took the walk back to my room and sat in the newness of the direction of my life. I was going to be paid to write. I was going to be a professional writer-not in the way Hemingway was, but he didn't begin as a novelist. I looked at the posters on the wall that I had been collecting over the past five years. Meaning started to leave all the things I had been accumulating, and I decided right then that I wouldn't take anything with me except my personal novels and poetry books. I sat and shook my head. I wished I had kept that letter about the CLAD so I could rip it into a million pieces and include it like confetti in the resignation letter the district office would receive. What was the point? I didn't feel any way at all about that letter anymore.

I still had to tell Rick. I thought of Dolores sitting in his office and preparing him for me. What would Rick say? Teachers don't quit. I figured my phone would ring, and I would be called to the office at any minute.

I looked at the empty student desks in my room and shook my head again. "It's all right," I told myself, "they'll be all right." Even as I said it out loud, I could hear the mantra in Lynne's voice ringing in my soul - *You're here for the kids.*

Dolores opened up my door just then. She stood in the doorway in her brown leather jacket and told me, "He's ready for you."

My body tightened. I stepped away from my desk and headed out the door with Dolores. It clicked shut behind us. I could hear Denise's New York accent as we passed her door. I listened to her until I was too far away to hear anymore.

"How was he with it?" I asked when we were halfway to the office.

"He was okay. It's going to be okay."

I felt the sweat forming on my brow as we walked through the orange office door. I wiped it away with two fingers. I passed the copy machine. Dolores was a little behind me. My body felt too light to touch the ground and too cramped to ever loosen up. I walked into Rick's office, and I could hear Dolores shut the door behind us. Rick looked at me with his mouth shut in a straight line across his face. "Congratulations," he said and shook my hand.

I breathed again. I sat in the black padded chair directly across from Rick, and Dolores sat next to me. "I mean that, truly, Jim. Congratulations. You're making a decision based on the most impor-tant thing in the world-your family. It's, I believe, a huge loss for us and our kids. You're a teacher-a born teacher-and I've always been impressed with your work ethic. And the kids love you. They just love you."

"That's proven every day at lunch if you just walk by his room," added Dolores.

"Thanks Rick." It was very warm in his office that day, and the sweat continued to form on my forehead. "I hate to leave. I love LeyVa, and I love teaching…"

"And I know that, Jim," Rick interjected. "And as I say, you're a born teacher. And we will truly miss you…truly. And I don't have to say that." Rick smiled. "There are plenty of people that work here that I would not miss!" We laughed. "I'm kidding. But seriously, I know from looking at you now and from what Dolores told me that this was not an easy deci-sion for you, but you have done the right thing. You did this for your family, and I can't emphasize that enough-family has got to come first. In this job, it's not always easy to have them come first…"

Rick paused and read over my letter quickly. "We definitely wish you the best of luck. And please let me know if there is anything we can do to make your last two weeks with us more comfortable. Would you like the rest of the day off?"

"No. I have to be with my kids." Dolores handed me a tissue. "I'm going forward like always. I'm going to teach right until the end. This is my last chance to make a big difference for middle school kids. I'm not even planning on telling the kids until a couple days before I leave. Night time conferences on the 18th will be my last act as a teacher." We had parent teacher conferences all day on the 17th and in the evening from 7 until 9 on the 18th to accommodate parents who can't get off work.

"Okay," Rick nodded. "Are you sure you're okay to finish today?"

"Yes."

I shook Rick's hand again and headed to my room where my kids would be meeting me for lunch. I washed off my face in the bathroom before heading back to Room 5.

Chapter XLVII

I kept working and never mentioned my leaving to anyone else except for David, Denise, and Pam. Pam seemed devastated, David didn't seem to want to talk about it, and Denise was really happy for me, but she was afraid of what might move in next door.

"Oh, my God, I wonder who they'll end up hiring?" She wondered out loud. "I hope it's not that one sub!"

"Oh, it couldn't possibly be. I don't think they want that sub full time, or they would have hired her by now," I reassured her.

My kids came in each day, and I was tempted to tell them a couple of times, but I didn't. I didn't want a big fuss, and I knew there would be one. Anything out of the ordinary, including a rainy day, can knock these kids right off the track. It's the nature of middle school. I wanted a quick and clean break. I figured I would announce it on the Tuesday before I would leave. The next day would be daytime conferences, and the kids wouldn't be at school. They could prepare for a day, and then we could say goodbye.

"You have to give them more time than that, Mr. Kohl!" Pam told me with narrowed eyes when I visited her office during my prep one day. "They need more time than that to get used to it and to say goodbye."

"I can't tell them too early because then they won't listen to me anymore," I argued. "I need to keep them on track for the proficiency test."

"Mr. Kohl…" Pam shook her head. "What are you doing to me?"

"I'm sorry," I told her. "I have to do this."

"I know," she said.

I kept teaching. There was a lecture or some other activity each day. Each night, there was homework.

About five days before I was scheduled to leave, Rick put a note in my box and asked me to see him in his office at my earliest convenience. I twisted and rolled the small green paper in my fingers and wondered what he wanted. I went to see him right then, about 35 minutes before school was going to start. I approached his door with much more confidence than the last time I went to his office.

The door was open, and Rick sat at his desk studying a pile of papers. I knocked twice softly on the open door to let him know I was there. He looked up, "Oh come in, Jim, and shut the door please." I sat in the black padded chair across from him.

Rick sat with his hands folded on the top of his desk. "We've found a new teacher," he informed me, looking straight into my eyes, "and I just wanted to let you know. She has worked in middle schools in the Campbell district, and she's really big into Reciprocal Teaching." Rick smiled and shook the palm of his right hand back and forth at shoulder height. "I know you're not!"

I smiled and shook my head no in agreement. RT, as it was called, was the latest in the line of magic cure-alls to teach kids to read without phonics. Two teachers from Monterey were pedaling it up and down California.

"Anyway, I just wanted to tell you. She'll be on campus tomorrow and you'll have a chance to meet her."

"Great, I'm glad you guys were able to find someone so soon. It takes away a little guilt, you know."

Rick reiterated how I was doing the right thing for me and that I shouldn't feel bad. "Although we'll miss you, we'll survive."

"I have no doubt," I said. "So is the new teacher going to be in my...in the room all day?" I hoped not.

"I don't know. That's really for you and her to work out."

"I think she should at least observe and see what the kids are like."

Rick pressed his lips together and nodded. "So how are you feeling?"

"I'm okay."

"All right, well, as I say, if there's anything we can do for you, let us know."

"Okay. Thanks."

The sky was still clouded on that November morning. I cut across the grass in front of the office on the way back to my room. She would be there tomorrow, and I had a sudden sense of insignificance. I was just biding my time all of a sudden. I wondered if I already stopped being a teacher.

Room 5 still opened with the key I carried in my pocket. My posters, all 20 of them or so, were still on the wall. This room and all that went on here was still mine. Tomorrow, she would be here, but she's not here yet. My kids were heading in to see me and learn from me. I was still a teacher-just as I always had been.

Why did I even care? I chose to leave. I needed to for my family. We would have no future otherwise. Justin, Annalisa, Michael, and Justine all came in one at a time. We talked and joked like we did every day before school. I had something to tell them, but it could wait. For now, we could keep things the way they always had been. I taught well that day.

Joelle met me at the door to the room the following morning. She was young and had professional short brown hair. She had an English degree, had taught at Price Middle School in Campbell, and had moved to Reno for this school year. Things didn't work out up there, so she was back, subbing until this came along. "So…thanks." She told me.

"No problem."

I made coffee in the room and borrowed Denise's cup for Joelle to use. I told her all about the standardized tests and how the school needs to do well on them. I showed her the binder of information and practice exercises that she could use to get the kids ready for the writing proficiency test. I told her about Craig, and how intense he is on the subject of test scores. She took it all in. I was pleased; I knew my kids would be fine.

"So I figured I would watch you teach for the next couple of days," she said to me from across my desk.

"That's cool," I said. "Whatever you want is fine with me."

It occurred to me that if she were in my room for the next two days, lame explanations wouldn't fly with the kids after a while. I had nearly a week before I left, and she would be on campus. I owed it to the kids to tell them why she was here. I had never lied to them before, and I wasn't going to have a lie be part of my last action as a teacher.

Joelle went to the office to make copies of her class rules.

I called Rick. "Just so you know," I told him when he picked up the phone, "I'm going public with this today."

"Okay." he laughed.

All the kids who hung out in my room came in like they normally did. Christina was first that morning, but I wanted to tell them when most of them were there. I didn't want to explain this too many times. Justine came in, and the three of us talked like we always did. They told me about junk that was going on with their families and the fun things they do with their friends-teenage stuff.

Annalisa and Michael came in next. I got out of my seat and I stood by the two of them right near the center of the group.

"Who is she?" asked Annalisa as Joelle came back in.

I breathed deeply, and Annalisa looked at my face. "You're leaving!" she said

I was shocked into silence. I couldn't get my mouth around any words.

"You're leaving!" she repeated. She stared right through my eyes.

When I finally got control of my tongue I said, "My family and I have had a really hard time with money lately." Michael just stared at me with wide-open eyes and a matching mouth. "Because of this problem, I have been forced to get a different job that pays more money. I've taken a job with a software company, and I'm going to write stuff for them. Next, Thursday will be my last day here at LeyVa." I took a deep breath in and stuttered it out.

Christina sat at my desk and cried.

Justine stared at the floor with her arms crossed.

Annalisa looked up in my face with her endless brown eyes. "Would you stay if you had a million dollars?" she asked.

I laughed. "Sure," I said, nodding and smiling.

"Well, you should've said something to us sooner, because we would need more time to get a million dollars for you." She stared into my eyes in all seriousness.

"Oh, Annalisa..." I said shaking my head and laughing. "Thanks."

Justin walked in just then. Justine muttered something to him. "You're leaving!" He said to me his mouth hung open and his face was thrust forward from his shoulders. His black backpack slipped off his shoulder and thudded on the floor.

I nodded and went through the whole speech again.

"That sucks!" He shook his head. "You're serious?" It was a question, but he phrased it like a statement.

"Yeah, and I know it does, man."

The bell rang. "Look guys, come by at lunch today and I'll talk to you more about it. I'm sorry." I called to them as they headed out the door toward their first period classes.

"See ya later, Mr. Kohl," one of them said. They weren't mad, and that was the important thing.

My phone rang as my students started coming in. It was Judy, one of the special education teachers. She was a lot of fun, and very funny. "All right, Jim, tell me what's going on."

"What do you mean?"

"Don't mess around. Tell me what's going on because I just met your replacement in the office a few minutes ago."

I recited the story again.

At the end of first period, I made the announcement again. They sat silently when I talked about money and the problems I had. Many of them knew of these problems too. "Anyway, you're bound to hear rumors about me...People might make stuff up about why I'm leaving. But what I've just told you is the truth, so please keep what I've said in mind if you hear anything different. And please, above all, remember that this has nothing to do with any of you or with any other kid in this school. I like you all very much, and I'm going to miss you quite a bit-everyday. I have to do this for my family."

"When's your last day?" Stacey asked.

"Thursday."

"Where are you going?" asked Grant.

I told them.

"Will you come visit?" asked Natasha.

"I hope so. I'll try my hardest. I don't know when, but I'll get back at least a couple of times before the end of the school year."

I stood in front of them and took all the questions they could come up with for the last five minutes of class. I introduced Joelle by the name they would be calling her, and she waved from her table by my desk.

The bell rang. Some kids walked by with tears in their eyes. I did my best to keep mine dry.

Natasha came up and hugged me on the way to the door. "Don't worry Mr. Kohl. We understand. No one will be mad at you."

"Thanks Natasha," I said. She was one of my biggest Edgar Allan Poe fans. I looked on my bookshelf and found one of my copies of Poe's stories. "Here," I said, "this is yours now."

"For reals! Thanks!"

"Sure. Thank you," I said.

Natasha slipped the book into her backpack and headed out of the room.

"That's the hardest part. It was easier to tell the district office than it is my kids because the kids...some of them feel like I'm betraying them," I said to Joelle as I sat at my desk for the few minutes between classes. "And I guess I am, actually."

The other classes were pretty much the same with the news. For some reason, it didn't travel as fast as the news of my engagement had those years ago. I made the announcement and the speech about rumors and how it wasn't because of them. They asked their questions, and I gave my answers. It was just another part of that day's lesson by the end of fifth period.

Fifth period, easily the one I was hardest on because of their confrontational nature, took the news the best. I'm sure they welcomed the chance for a fresh start. I felt okay because most kids seemed to understand, but then came sixth period.

As I stooped over my desktop to mark the roll sheet, Melissa's hand went up.

"Melissa?" I said, nodding toward her.

"Is it true you're leaving?" I didn't want it to work this way, but what I always enjoyed about Melissa came back to haunt me that day-she had a way of bringing unpredictability to a discussion.

I straightened up and walked slowly to the middle of the silent classroom. The room was half darkened so they could see the opener shining on the board from the overhead projector. I stood in the center and looked at them all. They had stopped working and held their pens and pencils parallel to their papers as if poised for a spelling test. "Yes," I said.

Several started crying. I explained the circumstances and used the same speech that had worked so well all day.

They sat quietly.

When I was done, I invited the inevitable questions.

They still sat quietly. Tears showed on many of their cheeks.

"C'mon, doesn't anybody have a question?" I begged.

Nothing. This is the class that asked me every detail of my life on the first day of school, and they had nothing to say.

"Melissa? C'mon. Ask me anything you want."

She shook her head no, and looked down at the ground.

"Are you guys mad?" I asked.

No words, but Tina picked up her head from the desk and shook her head no for me to see. I saw her tears too, and they nearly killed me.

"If someone wants to yell at me, that would be fine. I'd like that a lot more than this silence."

Nothing.

They were supposed to take a quiz that day, but I let them wait until Monday. I had hurt them, and Mr. Kohl wasn't supposed to do that. I was here for the kids. We just sat with each other the entire period. I told them they could use the period to study for anything they wanted but that I recommended they study for Monday's quiz.

Amanda sat in the front row and just looked at me. "I'm sorry, guys," I said as I sat at my desk. Amanda nodded.

The bell rang, and they left. On her way to the door, Melissa came to me and handed me a note that said, "I understand that you have to do this for your family. I'm not mad at you, but I'm sad about this."

I sat at my desk for 45 minutes and felt like garbage.

The last week of teaching went faster than the last week of summer. They all wanted to know if we were going to have a party on my last day.

"You guys can have a party after I'm gone," I said. "I don't give parties, and I hate to clean up after parties."

"We'll clean up!" they insisted.

"I've heard that one before," I told them, smiling.

I had told the kids instead of telling most of the staff because I figured word would get around faster that way. The kids joked about how their other teachers didn't believe them when they were told I was leaving.

"No he's not," insisted one Science teacher. "That is just a rumor."

"You're not leaving, are you?" Monica asked me outside our doors one day during break.

"Yeah," I said nodding and not really knowing what to do.

"That's a shame," she said as the two of us headed to the office. "The kids are losing a good teacher."

"Thanks," I said. I wanted to believe that was true, but I couldn't help but ask myself if a good teacher would really leave.

The staff room hummed and buzzed, and I finally saw Craig. It was time to tell him. He was standing by the teacher's boxes just outside the staff room.

"Hey, Craig."

"Hey, James," he said, looking at the stack of papers he had just pulled out of his box. "What do you know?"

"Hey, man, I got a new job. I'm joining the industry."

He dropped his papers to waist level and checked my face to see if I was joking.

"I got a job as a tech writer for a software company. I start this coming Friday." I continued.

Craig smiled big, "I gotta tell you James, if this were 20 years ago, I would do the same thing. Congratulations, mate!" He shifted his papers to his left hand and shook my hand. "So is it a big pay increase?"

"Not so much at first, although I am getting a big raise compared to here. Within a year, I may be able to double my salary though. There's a lot of money to be made out there."

"Man, I tell you, my stepson did the same thing. This year, his salary passed mine and he's been doing it for…" Craig looked up at the ceiling and calculated, "Three years now? Four years? Anyway, I've been busting my butt in the schools for 20 years, and this kid already makes more than me! C'mon," Craig motioned toward the door, "walk with me and tell me all about it."

We went through the staff room and out into the courtyard. I explained to him as much as I knew about the job. Craig pulled his blue jacket tighter around himself as we walked. Joelle walked from Room 5 into the courtyard. I called her over.

"Craig, this is Joelle, my replacement," I said. The two shook hands.

"What school were you at last year?" Craig asked. "I want to look up your test scores."

"Yeah, like those matter at all!" Joelle said and leaned backward and laughed.

I laughed too, knowing what was coming.

"No, I'm serious. I want to see what your test scores were."

I walked away and let the two of them have this discussion.

"Mr. Kohl, you're leaving!" Daniella from my last year's first period called to me.

"Yes," I said and did the stupid nod that was becoming a trademark of mine.

"Oh, man!" she said. We went our separate ways.

That day at lunch, Krystle from my second and third period core class came and took a chair across my desk from me.

"Hi Krystle. How's it going?" I said.

"I don't like the new teacher."

"Now, now. You don't even know her. You have to do me a favor and please give her a chance. You're the only person that could end up hurt by not liking her," I explained.

"But you can just look at her and tell she is not like you," Krystle said.

"Thanks. But she is a very nice woman."

"Whatever!" Krystle said. "You know, Mr. Kohl, you're going to have to talk to adults now, and they are so boring! Have you ever talked to adults all day?"

"A couple times," I said, trying not to laugh.

"They have nothing cool to say at all!" Krystle rolled her eyes and shook her head to emphasize this point. "Who are you going to kick it with at lunch?"

"I don't know," I answered. I would miss this job-there was no doubt in my mind.

On Tuesday after school, the newspaper club that I helped run threw me a surprise party. They got me a cake and soda and every sort of chip that the Safeway sold. There was music and a huge poster that said, "Goodbye Mr. Kohl." They all signed it and wrote me a note. I went home with my arms full of the poster and their hugs and my eyes full of tears. This was getting harder all the time.

The Wednesday conference day came and Joelle started taking my things off the wall while I sat and talked with the parents. She began putting up posters and decorations of her own. The room looked less like mine with every staple she drove into the wall. At the end of each conference I said, "And as you may have heard, I'm leaving, and this is my replacement." I would motion to Joelle who would walk over and shake hands with the parent.

The night before my last day was like any other in my house. I came home and helped the kids with their homework. Kristin made dinner, and I cleaned up the kitchen. We put the kids to bed and watched some TV. I looked more inside my head than I did at the TV, and I watched seven years of dedication to children and their education play over and over. I saw myself coaching the swim team and substitute teaching-I even saw those two horrible weeks in Shepherd Middle School and thought how much better I could have handled that situation now. I saw myself working with Lynne and learning to be there for the kids. I saw myself teaching Sammy to read. I saw my first year of LeyVa with Troy and Elizabeth. I watched all my kids' faces react to the story of Edgar Allan Poe's life. I saw Maile and Shelene, Katrina and Amber. I saw Justin, Annalisa and Michael, and I watched my room fill with kids at lunch each day. I saw all my current students' faces when I told them I was leaving. I saw sixth period completely silenced. I saw Joelle taking down my things and putting up hers.

"What's the matter, honey?" Kristin called to me from the other side of the couch.

"Nothing," I said. I squeezed my eyes shut and rubbed them.

"Come here," she said. I went over for a hug. "It's going to be okay."

"Those kids need me. I'm being so selfish."

"They're not paying you what you're worth. They don't pay any good teacher what they're worth."

We held each other for the rest for the evening.

That night when we headed to bed, I felt light-headed and my throat dried up. I knew I could teach, but what about this technical writing thing? It was the unknown.

For seven years I had headed to a school for work. I was used to the baggy pants and the baseball hats of the boys. I was used to the girls wearing a lot of makeup as they experimented to find the face they wanted. I was going to have to talk to adults now. I lay in bed for quite a while. "You monsters have anything to say!" I called out in my head. They were silenced now, but I lay awake all night waiting for them.

The next morning, I showered and dressed and headed in for my last day of school. I wanted to be with the kids today, there would be no schoolwork. We would just hang out. I pulled into the parking lot at the same time as Dolores.

"Hey!" she called to me, "How are you feeling?"

"I'm okay," I said, heading over to her. "I didn't sleep much last night."

"But I'm sure it's a much different type of stress…a good stress."

"Yeah," I said, smiling. "That it is."

My kids threw surprise parties in three out of four of my classes that day. In some cases, their parents helped organize it, and in some cases they did it all alone.

When my second and third period core class came in, they were silent. Joelle was not there yet.

"Well guys, I had a great time with you and…"

"Stop, you're going to make us cry!" said Christina.

"Okay."

Krystle looked angry. "What's the matter Krystle?" I asked.

"She took down your stuff." Krystle motioned to the walls. The other kids looked around, and some of them noticed the changes in the room for the first time.

"I know she did, and that's okay."

"No it's not! You're still here! She could at least wait until you were gone."

I paced in front of the room as I always did when I wasn't sure what to say. "She didn't do this as any sort of disrespect for me," I tried. "I told her she could do it. She's going to start teaching you tomorrow, so she has to have the room set up. It's hers now."

"Not yet it's not," Krystle shook her head. A few of the kids agreed that it was out of line to redecorate in front of me.

"You guys…" I didn't know what to say, but I felt very warm. "As a favor to me, please give her a chance. She's a nice woman. She's going to be different than me, that's true, because everyone has their own teaching style. You're used to me, and now you need to get used to her. Please be nice to her. This is not her fault."

"We were used to you the first day." Tim called out.

"I know. I had a great time with you…"

"Stop!" Christina reminded me. She had her hand up.

We all laughed. I hoped I would laugh at my new job.

As each bell rang that day, the kids came to me for a hug or a handshake. Some just called a "Good luck" as they headed out the door. During prep, I filled my car trunk with all of my things worth packing. My books, pictures, and desktop toys were put in boxes and ready to go. I was ready to go. I had two more hours and night time conferences to get through. The two final classes were filled with cake and talking and music. It was a nice and happy farewell, and the kids really did clean up at the end of each party.

Art came down to my room at the beginning of sixth period. "Rick would like to see you very quickly." I headed down to the office. In the Student Center where I had first met and interviewed with Rick, he and

Dolores and Irene gave me a blue leather notepad that said, California Distinguished School on it. My name was also on the cover in gold letters just above the name of the school. There was a blue pen in the leather notepad that had the same words on it.

"It doesn't really equal our appreciation for what you have done for LeyVa's kids for the past five years, Jim," Rick said. "You are and you always will be a great teacher. No matter what your job title is, you have the gift and the ability, and I'm sure you'll succeed at whatever you end up doing. Just think of this as the close of one chapter in your life." They all stood around me as I sat at a table in the middle of the Student Center.

I smiled up at them. "Thanks guys. I'll never forget you, and if I ever see my company throwing away anything the school can use, I'll grab it for you."

We all laughed the nervous, awkward laugh that comes at the end of a relationship.

"Well, we'll let you get back to your kids. I'm sure they're missing you," Rick said.

I thanked them again and headed back to the room.

We finished off the rest of the day and the rest of the cake. When the final bell whined, I stood there not being anything. I wasn't a teacher anymore, and I wasn't a technical writer yet-I didn't even know what it meant to be one. All the kids came to say goodbye to me, and I was surrounded by a group of them that waited for a handshake or a hug, or just to be acknowledged one more time. There was steady flow of kids around me, and when my sixth period was gone, my other periods were there. When they thinned out, the kids that I taught last year were there. That was starting to thin out, and Maile came in from the high school. A few minutes later Katrina came in. They hugged me and I cried like a child because I realized then, possibly for the first time, that it was over.

Katrina and Maile stayed with me as long as they could and we talked about the good times they had had in my room and they told me what a difference I had made for them.

"Shoot, Mr. Kohl was the only teacher you could trust," Maile said.

Katrina agreed.

"I wouldn't have done any of this if it wasn't for people like you," I told them. I had been here for the kids.

I handled the evening conferences that night with Joelle right next to me. I talked less and less with each parent and Joelle talked more. At the end of the conferences, it was time to say goodbye to the staff. They all gave me well wishes, and told me to keep in touch. A drunk and belligerent parent was occupying Dolores, so I just waved to her. I walked out of the gym and into the dark.

I walked across the LeyVa campus at night like I had after many dances where I had seen kids break and fix and fill each other's hearts. They would get by. They would be okay. They would recover from this faster than I would.

"Goodbye, Mr. Kohl!" some kids called to me.

"See ya later," I said, as I walked diagonally across the parking lot. I paused and looked at the office and saw Pam's darkened room. I was about 20 feet from my car. I looked over and saw the walkway that led to Room 5. I saw a pencil on the ground. I reached down and picked it up. It had been run over and was rough and a bit chewed up. I broke it in two with my fingers and dropped it on the ground. I smiled, walked to my car, and tried not to look back.

AFTERWORD

A friend of mine used to tell me that teaching was a noble profession when I would tell him I was going into it. I loved to hear that at the time because I love the connotation carried with the word "noble." That meant I was selfless and giving. That meant I was better than your average greedy person. I was willing, like a saint or a martyr, to give of myself for the benefit of others. The Romance that filled that notion ran over the top of me and obscured my vision.

Why is it that teachers have to settle for that? As a society, it's just accepted that teachers don't make a lot of money, and that's all there is to it. Most people agree it's not right, but no one really wants to do much about it. Most people become angry when teachers strike to try for more money, and I've even had one man tell me that "some professions shouldn't be allowed to strike" when we were talking about teachers. When did it become a fact that teachers should have to struggle for the equivalent of a master's degree, settle for $30,000 to start, only have the potential of doubling that after 20 years, and like it?

"Well, they didn't have to become teachers," people might say. Rick told me recently that they were having a hard time filling four positions for the 2000-2001 school year. I wasn't the only one from my school who left teaching and joined the technology industry. I ran into another teacher from my school who told me she was leaving in June to join a dot-com. Few young people are becoming teachers, and young teachers are leaving to find decent wages. Who's going to teach the kids? What's the solution? Come on, do I really have to tell you?

In a single anecdote, I can illustrate the sad state of affairs that our schools are in. On my first day at work as a technical writer, my manager was giving me a tour of the office. At one point, we approached a large beige cabinet. "This is the supply cabinet," he told me. "Whenever you need something, take it."

He opened the cabinet to reveal many boxes of writing pens in a multitude of colors, boxes of dry erase markers, reams of writing paper, high-liters, tape, staples, post it notes, and paper clips. There were tissue boxes that you could take whenever you needed one. You could take two if you wanted. There was a pile of mouse pads. Now I knew why my classroom never had any supplies-they were all here in this cabinet!

"I don't have to sign out these things, I can just take them?" I clarified.

"Yeah," he said. He looked at me like I was nuts. "We try to make things available so that our people can perform their job to the best of their ability."

I felt like I had just come from a Third World country and was being shown a grocery store for the first time. "What a concept," I thought. "Give your workers the supplies they need to do a good job." I thought of the pathetic way that teachers have to scrimp and grab supplies from wherever they are left lying around. I thought of how they have to buy their own staplers and many of the other supplies they use in the classroom, and then guard them so they don't disappear. If education is as important as the politicians all claim during an election year, then why can't we do something simple like give the schools the supplies they need to run well?

It is August 2000 as I write this, and I recently saw a speech at one of the presidential conventions where the main candidate said (I'm paraphrasing) that this country needed to treat teachers like the professionals they are. He said that we need to give teachers the extra training they deserve, and that we need to provide them with this training to raise test scores. He went on to say that it wasn't about money. Well, Mr.

Presidential-Hopeful, what extra training have you had to do the job of running the country? And I'm sorry, but until prices go down and we can all eat and live for free, everything is about money! The notion of the noble profession has been replaced by the realism of noble poverty.

If our kids are worth it, we should pay the teachers to educate them and pay them well. To treat teachers like professionals means to pay them like professionals. I have increased my salary 66 percent in less than a year by leaving the teaching profession. Don't get me wrong. The money is great, and my family is much more comfortable, but compare the importance of writing manuals to the importance of teaching. Everyone believes we should get what we pay for as a society. Why should we pay educators nothing and expect everything?

Printed in the United States
3419

9 780595 167913